New Era – New Urgency

New Era – New Urgency

The Case for Repurposing Education

F. Joseph Merlino and Deborah Pomeroy

LEXINGTON BOOKS

Lanham • Boulder • New York • London

Lexington Books
Bloomsbury Publishing Inc, 1359 Broadway, New York, NY 10018, USA
Bloomsbury Publishing Plc, 50 Bedford Square, London, WC1B 3DP, UK
Bloomsbury Publishing Ireland, 29 Earlsfort Terrace, Dublin 2, D02 AY28, Ireland
www.bloomsbury.com

First published in the United States of America 2024
Paperback edition published 2026

British Library Cataloguing in Publication Information available

Library of Congress Cataloging-in-Publication Data

Names: Merlino, F. Joseph, 1951- author. | Pomeroy, Deborah, 1943- author.
Title: New era – new urgency : the case for repurposing education / F. Joseph Merlino
    and Deborah Pomeroy.
Description: Lanham, Maryland : Lexington Books, [2024] | Includes bibliographical
    references and index. | Summary: "Despite a new era, we are stuck with a
    40-year-old education system whose purpose is obsolete. New Era – New Urgency
    presents a historical case for the need to repurpose education given the challenges
    of the new century. Merlino and Pomeroy describe their work repurposing education
    in Egypt and elsewhere"—Provided by publisher.
Identifiers: LCCN 2023058909 (print) | LCCN 2023058910 (ebook) |
    ISBN 9781666949766 (hardback) | ISBN 9781666949773 (ebook) |
    9798216380375 (paperback)
Subjects: LCSH: Education—Aims and objectives. | Education—Forecasting. |
    Educational change.
Classification: LCC LB41 .M56 2024 (print) | LCC LB41 (ebook) |
    DDC 370.1—dc23/ eng/20240207
LC record available at https://lccn.loc.gov/2023058909
LC ebook record available at https://lccn.loc.gov/2023058910

For product safety related questions contact productsafety@bloomsbury.com.

∞™ The paper used in this publication meets the minimum requirements of
American National Standard for Information Sciences—Permanence of Paper for
Printed Library Materials, ANSI/NISO Z39.48-1992.

For our families

Contents

PART III: THE PROMISES AND ILLUSIONS OF EDUCATIONAL REFORM

Acknowledgments

We want to acknowledge and thank the many dedicated people we have worked with who regarded teaching more as a calling than a job, who cared deeply about their students' learning, and who persisted in honing their craft despite daily frustrations with trying to manage up to thirty or more students in a classroom. We have worked with thousands of such people, too numerous to name here, but without them this book would not have been possible.

We want to give special thanks to the thought leaders who paved the way for us. The late Dr. Joseph Bordogna, former deputy director of the National Science Foundation (NSF) and later one of 21PSTEM's board members, believed in and supported our work in education reform. Dr. James Hamos, our program officer at NSF for nine years, thoughtfully guided our work and encouraged us to write this book. And scholars in cognitive development, such as Professors Eleanor Duckworth of the Harvard University Graduate School of Education and Preston Feden from LaSalle University, stimulated critical explorations of our ideas about teaching, learning, and cognitive change.

Our colleagues in the United States, Dr. Dave Smith, Dr. Victor Donnay, Dr. Steve Kramer, Dr. Edward "Ned" Wolff, and Dr. John Baker, have played major roles in several large-scale NSF projects with us spanning almost two decades. We have drawn on their experience, insights, and energy along with dozens of other staff members and consultants who deserve our special thanks for their tireless efforts at school reform. Thanks also to Dr. R. Lorraine Bernotsky, president of West Chester University, and Dr. Jill Feldman, who provided much early editorial feedback. We are grateful for Dr. Charles Coble, former dean of education at the East Carolina University, who provided meticulous reviews of the near-final draft of the book, as did Dr. Nancy Songer, dean of education at the University of Utah.

Our colleagues in Egypt, Dr. Reda Abou Serie, former first deputy minister of education Egypt, and Hala El Serafy, former senior program officer at the U.S. Agency for International Development-Egypt, have led two extraordinary efforts at establishing new high school and teacher preparation models over the past decade. They have been joined by Dr. Zeinab Nagger, Amany Mostafa, and Dr. Amany Abd El Aziz.

We gratefully acknowledge Dr. Antonia Felix's provision of three years of constant expert editorial support. We want to thank Sara Noakes, our editor at Lexington Books, for her enthusiasm and editorial guidance in bringing this work to published form. Finally, we want to thank Hadriane Hatfield, a recent college graduate and family member, who urged us to speak to her generation. They will be the ones who will be living through and contending with most of the challenges of this new era. We have learned much from our students and the teachers with whom we have worked. Like Hadriane, their struggles and perseverance as learners and their hope for the future are what inspired us to write this book.

Introduction

New Era–New Purpose

> Education is the key to personal development and the future of societies. It unlocks opportunities and narrows inequalities. It is the bedrock of informed, tolerant societies, and a primary driver of sustainable development. The COVID-19 pandemic has led to the largest disruption of education ever. The future of education is here. We have a generational opportunity to reimagine education.
>
> —António Guterres, Secretary-General of the United Nations[1]

Guterres wrote these words in 2020, and in the immediately ensuing years, we see even more disruptions, not only to education but also to global stability and the world order. These disruptions are separate in nature, but together they signal that a new era is surely upon us. Several of the more dramatic signs of this new era include the January 6, 2021, attack on the U.S. Capitol; the February 24, 2022, Russian invasion of Ukraine, the first land war in Europe in more than seventy years; worldwide megadroughts and floods; and the COVID-19 pandemic (2019–2023). These seemingly disconnected events all point to deeper changes that represent this new era. Disparate as they are, they are bound by several important themes: they raise questions of truth and justice; their implications span national boundaries; they are emblematic of a surge in violent anti-democratic forces and organized science denialism; and they feed on and are fed by the Fourth Industrial Revolution, which includes stunning advances in artificial intelligence and communications technology. Most importantly, they all have implications for how we raise and educate our children.

This new era has already motivated people to demonstrate brave activism and idealism to counteract its malevolent aspects. Energetic young people around the world are responding. These youth are our hope. But we must better equip them to deal with both the dangers and opportunities this new era presents. As Guterres implored, the future of education is here: "We have a generational opportunity to reimagine education."

Success in fundamentally reimagining and recreating education *is* possible; we have played a part in doing so—in Egypt and elsewhere from 2012 to the present. What we helped develop and implement for the Egyptian Ministry of Education was a collaborative *process* of repurposing high school education around the country's Grand Challenges, backward designing an integrated, student-centered curriculum that serves this purpose, along with developing a custom suite of multi-assessment measures. Twenty-one national model STEM schools were established with support from the United States Agency for International Development (USAID) along with U.S. partners. Based on the early success of this project, we were invited to do similar work in Bosnia and Herzegovina in 2017 and later work in Turkey for UNESCO's International Bureau of Education. At the invitation of nonprofit cultural organizations and with support from a local foundation, we initiated an education repurposing process for high schools in the Philadelphia area.

In what follows, we make the case for the urgency of repurposing education in the United States for its 75 million school-aged children for this new era and how to do it. The purposes arrived at may be different for each local context, but the process of curricular and instructional redesign is similar.

CHANGES IN THE UNITED STATES

The United States is undergoing profound changes in its racial/ethnic and social identity. According to U.S. Census data in 2020, 40 percent of the U.S. population is comprised of Asian, Black, Hispanic,[2] Native American, and Pacific Islander people. Already, a *majority* of school-aged children in the United States are people of color. By 2065, immigrants to the United States who come from more than 156 countries and their first-generation U.S.-born children are projected to represent more than one-third (36 percent) of the 441 million U.S. population.[3]

Who we *were* and *are* as a people and a nation is being reexamined as never before. Pressures for greater inclusivity and equity in all sectors of political, social, and economic life will only continue to mount. The voices of the dispossessed, assaulted, and marginalized shout "I Matter" through Black Lives Matter, #MeToo, March for Our Lives, and other movements supporting the LGBTQ community, women, people of color, sexual victims, people living in poverty, and the health impaired and vulnerable.[4] These pressures also derive from an internal moral force, our conscience, calling us to use our strengths to build a more just and inclusive society. Amid this heightened sense of our plurality are the countervailing voices of White Christian nationalists who reject others' equal standing and strive to go back to an era of naked White Supremacy and misogynism. Into the third decade of the twenty-first century, we once again find ourselves confronting the questions of who we are, who we want to be, and the kind of society we want to live in.

Amid changes in the U.S. population and its identity, children born in this century are facing many threats to their futures from worldwide changes. One such threat is the far-reaching impact of global climate change. One impact is the projected one-foot rise in sea levels by 2050, as much as an eight-foot rise within a child's lifetime. This projected rise potentially threatens the 30 percent of the U.S. population that lives along the coastline.[5] The expected rise in sea levels also threatens global population stability and, with it, U.S. security. An October 2021 report submitted to the U.S. National Security Council by the U.S. Department of Defense warned:

> Climate change is reshaping the geostrategic, operational, and tactical environments with significant implications for U.S. national security and defense. Increasing temperatures; changing precipitation patterns; and more frequent, intense, and unpredictable extreme weather conditions caused by climate change are exacerbating existing risks and creating new security challenges for U.S. interests.[6]

The security risks of climate change are global. Famine can lead to mass migration across international borders due to more frequent "megadroughts."[7] Seventy-five percent of the Earth's landmass is estimated to be degraded already, with degradation projected to rise to 90 percent by 2050. By then, scarce land resources are estimated to displace 700 million people, resulting in a huge number of climate-induced refugees.[8] Current migration at the U.S. southern border is already reflecting such pressure, while at the same time, the southwest United States has experienced persistent drought conditions for two decades, making it the worst drought in 500 years. Central Chile is also experiencing a thirteen-year "megadrought"—the longest drought in that region in more than a thousand years.[9] The world's food chain is also at risk from a loss of biodiversity. For example, more than 40 percent of amphibian species are threatened with extinction.[10] The oceans have seen a 30 percent increase in their acid content, which threatens marine ecosystems and, in turn, the three billion people around the globe who depend on it for food and their livelihoods.

The COVID-19 pandemic has affected billions worldwide, resulting in 1.2 million deaths in the United States alone. Researchers estimate there is a 38 percent probability of similar pandemics in this century.[11] Moreover, other researchers have also found that more than half of infectious diseases worldwide have been aggravated by climate change.[12] At the same time, medical advances are pushing the boundaries of ethics and law.

These threats to the global environment and public health are worsened by vast global economic inequalities where the top 10 percent of the world's population holds 75 percent of its wealth while the bottom 50 percent possesses only 2 percent.[13] This disparity in wealth leads to failed states as well as transnational crime syndicates trafficking in drugs, guns, and humans.

At the same time, the twenty-first century has brought a new era of previously unimaginable innovations in worldwide information and communications technologies (ICT). Consider how recently the largest social media companies were born. On September 4, 1998, Google was founded, followed in February 2004 by the launch of Facebook. YouTube was introduced on February 14, 2005, and Twitter a year later, in March 2006. Four years later, on October 6, 2010, Instagram was made public. In August 2018, TikTok invaded the U.S. digital landscape. The number of social media users has grown rapidly. As of 2022, over five billion people use social media,[14] providing them with instantaneous real-time audio and video streaming capabilities from anywhere in the world—including remote places in developing countries with little access to distributed electricity or water. The communications and cable outlets are too numerous to list, and along with them have come astounding changes in digital storage capacity, processing power, and cloud-based technologies that have led to the generation of "big data" and artificial intelligence (AI). By 2025, the worldwide production of data is projected to reach 175 zettabytes (equivalent to a trillion gigabytes).[15] By comparison, a two-hour movie uses about six gigabytes of data. The connectivity of devices, dubbed the Internet of Things (IOT), is leading to the Fourth Industrial Revolution (Industry 4.0).[16]

There is, however, a steep price to pay for the wonders of this new digital era: the threat posed by bad actors both domestically and internationally who want to overthrow democracies through the spread of disinformation and algorithms that amplify disunity and discord. In the United States and elsewhere, people are losing the ability to engage in civil discourse. We hear of radical theologies, extremist rhetoric, and propaganda from every conceivable source and direction. The sheer volume of messages bombarding the public blurs the distinction between fact and fiction, truth and lies. In its most pernicious form, this new era can mobilize millions with Big Lies to stage insurrections against democratic institutions and invasions of other countries where the aggressor is portrayed as the victim. This social vulnerability is exacerbated by insufficient critical thinking skills. For example, in the largest study of its kind on critical thinking as applied to online content, 3,446 high school students were given six online tasks where they were asked to tell the difference between authentic and fake information. Nearly all struggled.[17]

SHIFTING THE PARADIGM

The thesis of this book is a simple one. Historically, large-scale social, demographic, and technological changes have ushered in new eras, creating both new realities and new challenges that have given rise to new fundamental purposes of education. By the same token, new eras depend on changes in the purposes of education. The two are joined at the hip, inseparable. Schooling is both the product of profound social change and the process by which society evolves, solves its problems, and moves forward.

To this end, we find relegating education as an institution apart from its larger social context to be self-defeating, especially when a new era arrives. Unfortunately, this bifurcation of education and society into separate domains is the current paradigm, so prevalent that it is as unnoticed as water is to fish. It is a paradigm, we would argue, that needs to shift. Based on our thirty years of working on educational reform, we felt compelled to write this book after concluding, time and again, that no program or reform can be successful without a clear purpose for education. This purpose must be meaningful and compelling enough to arbitrate the choice of curricular content from a universe of possibilities. It should provide the foundation and impetus for all educational decisions.

New purposes of education are urgently needed to equip young people to address the realities and challenges of the new era they and we are experiencing in the twenty-first century. This new purpose should inform the content of the curriculum and provide coherence to its many subjects, how they are taught, and how learning is assessed. Our definition of *curriculum* is how discrete content topics are selected, sequenced, and contextualized for the learner so that it is meaningful. When content is sterilized, stripped of context and purpose, it is of little value. It is equivalent to memorizing random phone numbers. This is why defining purpose and fitting a curriculum to that purpose is essential for deep and durable learning.

Identifying a new purpose of education should reflect the aspirations of the wider community within which public schools sit. The subject of education demands public engagement and discourse if the dreams for our collective future are to be realized. The difficult discussions about the purposes of education in this broader sense of community have implications for how we should relate to each other and what we should strive for collectively. For this reason, discussions about the purpose of education are about values and morals in the context of the times in which we live. Yet the current playing fields for such community conversations seem mired in divisive attitudes. How do we communicate about something as broad as the purpose of education when our media, social or otherwise, hampers our ability to weed out fact from fiction about issues ranging from coronaviruses to effective policing to honest political candidates—let alone education?

Improving education and providing equitable opportunities for all students is vital. Diversity, equity, and inclusion (DEI) are important education goals, but they are unanswerable in the final analysis without first defining a high-level purpose of education that is relevant to students as they are experiencing their world. What are the dreams we share for the future, and how should we shape education to achieve these aspirations? How do we agree about what needs improving, expanding, or eliminating in the first place? Who should have the power to ultimately define the purpose of education? Considering the size of the U.S. education system and those of other countries, is creating and implementing a new relevant purpose of education even possible? We say, *yes*. We base our optimism on our experience working on educational reform in the United States and our transformative work in Egypt and Bosnia and Herzegovina, as well as our work with the International Bureau of Education at UNESCO for schools in Turkey. We have seen and helped develop new, more relevant, school-level purposes of education.

FINDING A RELEVANT PURPOSE

In part IV, we present three case studies that collectively illustrate how to make this transition to more purposeful education. In our work in Egypt, for example, building on conversations with many Egyptian educators and leaders, and with support from the USAID, we helped the Egyptian Ministry of Education design and implement a new model of high school education. Instead of starting with a list of traditional high school classes, we asked the Egyptian teachers in the inaugural model school to define their dreams for their country's future and the kinds of personal qualities, abilities, and knowledge they wanted for their graduates. The result was a purpose-driven high school designed to "equip students to address Egypt's eleven grand challenges," such as climate change, alternative energy, and the use of arid land. We were key members of a large project team that developed an integrated, project-based curriculum and created a suite of completely new, non-traditional assessments. By January 2024, Egypt had established twenty-one of these highly successful model "Grand Challenges" public residential high schools throughout Egypt that are beginning to influence the rest of Egyptian education. The rapid and widespread public support for these schools bore evidence of the alignment of the new purpose of the schools with broad public aspirations. This ongoing effort is being joined by another project we are leading to help establish new teacher preparation programs in five Egyptian universities involving the development of 180 new courses. These new programs are being developed with the active participation of fifteen Egyptian deans, three from each university.

When we worked on another USAID project to help the war-torn country of Bosnia and Herzegovina to develop another new model of schools relevant to their particular context and aspirations, their education leaders came up with a very different purpose for education. Their answer went something like this: "We have so many divisions in the country that we need something to unify us. We want peace. We want a unified curriculum that points to the knowledge-based economy to provide a way for the country's political interests to talk to each other." We worked together with their university professors to backward design a core science, technology, engineering, and mathematics (STEM) curriculum to serve the goal of empowering a new generation of students to value unity and humanity along with the cognitive skills to build their lives and prosper in their country. The teachers became vested in a new sense of hope that the new curriculum they helped create would move their country into a peaceful era. In yet another project, this time in Turkey, we were part of an international team supported by the International Bureau of Education (IBE-UNESCO) to design a future competency-based curriculum for thirty-one private schools.

Based on our groundbreaking work in Egypt and Bosnia, in 2017 we were asked to convene a group of 130 Philadelphia regional educators, businesspeople, and cultural leaders to articulate their aspirations for the future and reimagine high school education as a result. The biggest issue for them was how to live together in a large and diverse regional urban community. In summary, they stated, "We want to be able to live in harmony with each other. We do not want to be a place where one group is assimilated into a dominant culture." From this collective aspiration, we then asked the group to articulate a new purpose of education that would embody that aspiration.

These brief examples, both at home and abroad, offer a glimpse of how public education can be redesigned to serve *all* students and fulfill the aspirations of local communities and the country. What we learned from the success in helping to design new curricula in Egypt, Bosnia, and elsewhere holds the key, we believe, to repurposing not only American education as an institution but *America itself* in this new era. It took us decades of teaching and working on educational reforms in the United States and abroad to appreciate the magnitude of the importance of purpose in schooling and how different purposes emerged from one era to another. In chapter 5, we describe the circumstances that led to the current dominant purpose of public education, which emerged some forty years ago.

We have organized this book in such a way as to help policymakers, university faculty, researchers, educators, school administrators, and the public understand these critical lessons and apply them to the task of repurposing education for the new era.

In part I, "Change and the Purposes of Education," we provide a historical and contemporary perspective on how profound demographic, technological, and socio-political changes since the early English settlements in North America in the 1600s led to the successive emergence of different purposes of education as the United States evolved. The overriding message of part I is that changes in the purposes of education have always been in a reciprocal, co-dependent relationship within a wider historical context of profound change. As a relatable way to describe these large-scale changes, we organized them into five eighty-year lifetimes laid end-to-end. We describe how these massive changes over these five hypothetical lifetimes since the early English settlements resulted in the emergence of new aims or purposes of education.

In part II, "The Corruption of Purpose," we borrow Swiss psychoanalyst Carl Jung's concept of the "shadow" to describe the dark side of the American dream, and the hidden influences that have worked to corrupt education across the centuries. These shadows have coursed through every era. In our experience, we have witnessed how they undermine and twist the educational ideal. We devote a chapter to each of four shadows: extreme wealth inequality, White Protestant nativism, legalized White supremacy, and fundamentalists' anti-science claims. We describe these shadows, their origins, and their impacts on education, and show how they have cast a pall over modern reform efforts.

In part III, "The Promises and Illusions of Education Reform," we describe the many illusions within modern schooling and the intractable problems of educational improvement we have encountered. These chapters derive from the authors' hard-won lessons from our educational reform efforts, where we have worked with over 400 schools and administrators and 6,000 teachers and heard from countless more students.

The last of the illusions we discuss drives to the very heart of beliefs about effective teaching and learning. We relate stories of how experienced teachers and professors, who were expert lecturers, had epiphanies that led them to completely transform their teaching using a *student-centered* approach involving a markedly different classroom environment. This is the ground-level beginning of another type of paradigm shift. Here, we discuss the role of misconceptions in the learning process and how teachers and mentors can help students confront their misconceptions and develop deeper understanding. These strategies are not only important in the classroom but also in other aspects of our society, where misconceptions often confound meaningful discussion.

In part IV, "Repurposing Education for a New Era," we tell the amazing story of how the Egyptian Ministry of Education was able to define and implement a new purpose of education with the help of USAID grants, in which the authors played major roles. We recount how our U.S. project team, together with hundreds of Egyptian educators, collaborated to develop a totally new purpose-driven, integrated curriculum and assessment system for new model high schools throughout Egypt. After twelve years, these model schools are now influencing the rest of Egypt's education system. We also describe a second, large USAID follow-on project in which our Egyptian-based project team, together with U.S. faculty members, is assisting five large Egyptian universities and fifteen deans in designing an entirely new STEM undergraduate and graduate programs that will break their cycle of traditional teacher preparation.

We conclude this part with a discussion of other educational repurposing projects in Bosnia and Herzegovina and greater Philadelphia. We use these experiences to provide a realistic look at what it will take to redesign education for a new era, while *at the same time* recognizing that there is much value in preserving and building upon the current system. We address the practicalities and strategies needed to begin repurposing education while addressing the many questions and issues that are likely to arise.

NOTES

1. António Guterres, "The Future of Education Is Here," United Nations online policy brief, August 4, 2020, https://www.un.org/en/coronavirus/future-education -here.

2. The authors note that while "Latinx" is sometimes preferable, "Hispanic" is used in the U.S. Census.

3. Pew Research Center, "Modern Immigration Wave Brings 59 Million to U.S., Driving Population Growth and Change Through 2065," September 28, 2015, https:// www.pewresearch.org/hispanic/2015/09/28/chapter-2-immigrations-impact-on-past -and-future-u-s-population-change/.

4. It is noted that while there is a long history of marginalized groups calling for equity and justice, their voices are now being heard to a much greater degree with the advent of the global reach of social media.

5. William V. Sweet et al., "Global and Regional Sea Level Rise Scenarios for the United States: Updated Mean Projections and Extreme Water Level Probabilities Along U.S. Coastlines," February 2022, National Oceanic and Atmospheric Administration, https://oceanservice.noaa.gov/hazards/sealevelrise/sealevelrise-tech-report -sections.html.

6. Department of Defense, Office of the Undersecretary for Policy (Strategy, Plans, and Capabilities), "Department of Defense Climate Risk Analysis: Report Submitted to National Security Council," 2021, https://media.defense.gov/2021/Oct /21/2002877353/-1/-1/0/dod-climate-risk-analysis-final.pdf.

7. Benjamin I. Cook et al., "Megadroughts in the Common Era and the Anthropocene," *Nature Revisions Earth & Environment* 3 (2022): 741–757, https://doi.org /10.1038/s43017-022-00329-1.

8. Michael Cherlet et al. (Eds.), "World Atlas of Desertification," Publication Office of the European Union, 2018, http://wad.jrc.ec.europa.eu.

9. World Meteorological Organization, "State of the Climate in Latin America and the Caribbean 2020," WMO-No. 1272, 2021, https://library.wmo.int/doc_num .php?explnum_id=10876.

10. United Nations, "UN Report: Nature's Dangerous Decline 'Unprecedented'; Species Extinction Rates 'Accelerating'," 2019, https://www.un.org/sustainabledeve lopment/blog/2019/05/nature-decline-unprecedented-report/.

11. Marco Marani et al., "Intensity and Frequency of Extreme Novel Epidemics," *Proceedings of the National Academy of Sciences* 118, no. 35 (August 23, 2021), https://doi.org/10.1073/pnas.2105482118.

12. Camila Mora et al., "Over Half of Known Human Pathogenic Diseases Can Be Aggravated by Climate Change," *Nature Climate Change* 12 (2022): 869–875, https://doi.org/10.1038/s41558-022-01426-1.

13. Lucas Chancel et al., "World Inequality Report 2022," World Inequality Lab in partnership with United Nations Development Programme, https://wir2022.wid .world/.

14. "Global Social Media Statistics," Datareportal, October 2022, https://datare-portal.com/social-media-users.

15. David Reinsel, John Gantz, and John Rydning, "The Digitization of the World from Edge to Core," International Data Corporation White Paper #US44413318, November 2018, https://www.seagate.com/files/www-content/our-story/trends/files/ idc-seagate-dataage-whitepaper.pdf.

16. Grischa Beier, Silke Niehoff, and Mandy Hoffmann, "Industry 4.0: A Step Towards achieving the SDGs? A Critical Literature Review," *Discover Sustainability* 2, no. 22 (2021), https://doi.org/10.1007/s43621-021-00030-1.

17. Joel Breakstone et al., "Students' Civic Online Reasoning: A National Portrait," *Education Researcher* 50, no. 8 (2019): 505–515.

Part I

CHANGE AND THE PURPOSES OF EDUCATION

The existing practice [of education] is perplexing; no one knows what principle we should proceed—should the useful in life; or should virtue; or should the higher knowledge be the aim of our training; all three opinions have been entertained.

—Aristotle[1]

Nothing quite stirs the blood like the topic of schooling. Nearly everyone has experienced it, and nearly everyone has feelings and opinions about it, in many cases quite strongly held ones. While philosophers of education may offer us a deeper analysis of and more cogently written advocacy for what education should be, ordinary folk also have passionate views about education that must be engaged if change is to be enacted on the ground. This condition of multiple diverse opinions, as Aristotle observed, is a major reason why reaching a consensus about public education can be so vexing.

This book is not a survey of educational thought, nor is it a book about what is wrong with education. It is about how we move forward into a new era, a future for children we can only imagine based on what we know now. To do so, it helps to have a perspective as to where we have been—how different eras of the past with their profound changes, challenges, and struggles have forged different purposes of education. In this part of the book, we chronicle 13 different purposes of education that have emerged over 400 years since the first English settlements in Massachusetts in the early 1600s. Each of these different purposes over the years has left their distinct imprint on today's schooling; each purpose layered upon the other, somewhat hidden, jostling for attention.

Throughout our years of working in educational reform, we have informally asked a wide sample of people, including students, about their thoughts on schools and schooling, and we received a variety of responses. Our interviewees expressed a prevailing sense that schools are not meeting the current and future needs of students and society. Probing further, we asked what the purpose of schools should be. Again, we got a wide variety of responses, a cacophony of competing ideas. Even among teachers, we found a surprising lack of clarity and depth about why they were teaching what they were teaching.

We define the purpose of education as having three elements: (1) developing a cognitive capacity, ability, or aesthetic within students; (2) cultivating their moral and social sensibility; and (3) providing a compelling rationale for selecting content for students to learn from all that is possible to teach in school. Such a purpose, as understood by students and adults, would answer the question, "Why are we learning and teaching this?" We wondered if the dissatisfaction with schooling was due to a lack of a compelling purpose, too many competing purposes, or even contradictory ones.

Today's purpose of education may seem obvious until we distance ourselves from our current time and place to see that there are many possible aims of education. Analogously, one does not fully realize the culture in which one lives until experiencing another. The same is true regarding one's life, which is set in an ongoing historical context that may be difficult to fully appreciate. In the next five chapters, we describe thirteen archetypical aims, or purposes of education, each of which grew out of a unique historical context involving profound changes. The birth of each archetypical aim was always accompanied by an extended period of struggle, not unlike the struggle we are experiencing today. In each case, the weight of historical circumstances made a compelling argument for each aim's emergence, and to a large extent, it is the same rationale for its enduring appeal, notwithstanding its diminished relevance.

In the arc of a long life, a person would likely witness several profound and even unsettling changes. In this part, we sketch out the broad outlines of such social, economic, demographic, and technological changes as people might have experienced them over five consecutive lifetimes and relate these changes to the emergence of new purposes of education.[2] In using these storylines, we hope to illuminate how particular aims of education emerged and why they have persisted in one form or another. We represent each kind of educational aim through the use of an archetype—an iconic school or movement that we believe captures the essence of the aim.

Each archetype had a compelling reason for its emergence based on its historical context. However, with each new educational purpose, there was also a photo negative of it, influenced by four shadows that act to corrupt the new purpose. In Part II, we illuminate these shadows and their impact on education. For example, the mega-changes in daily life wrought by the second industrial revolution gave rise to the urgent need for industrial education, a welcome means to supply skilled labor to a growing industrial economy and provide employment to millions of people. But industrial education was also misused as a means to subjugate Black and Indian children, as we will later discuss.

Suffice it to say that there has scarcely been a time when education has not been a contentious topic, with many calling for its reform. Given the enormous changes that have occurred over the span of even a single generation, let alone a lifetime, education policymakers never quite reach the goals they have set for students before disruptive economic, social, and technological changes occur yet again. As a result, education seems to be in a constant state of crisis because it is always, to some degree, playing catch up with what had been planned in the past while trying to address the new realities children will face. Avoiding this lag time requires an active imagination to think about the future in a discerning way. To do this, we need to understand the trajectory of history. We describe these thirteen aims of education in chapters of this part. When parts I and II are taken together, we hope to provide the reader with a perspective about how different purposes of education come about in response to large-scale change and why our current times require a new purpose for education.

We begin with the educational archetype that defined the original purpose of education in the New World—those of the Puritans of the Massachusetts Bay Colony—to establish a New Israel. We conclude this part with the thirteenth purpose that has been the dominant one for the past forty years, but one, as we will explain in part III, that is now largely obsolete. Defining and implementing a more relevant purpose for new generations is what constitutes the hope of education. This we will do in part IV. But first, permit us to introduce you to the Reverend Governor John Winthrop.

NOTES

1. Aristotle, *Politics, Book VIII, Part II*, 350 B.C., http://classics.mit.edu/Aristotle/politics.8.eight.html.

2. For simplicity, we are not counting Walter Raleigh's Roanoke Colony, whose residents vanished within three years of its founding in 1587.

Chapter 1

The Landing—Early Colonial America
Change in the First Lifetime (1620–1700)

Wee shall finde that the God of Israel is among us, when tenn of us shall be able to resist a thousand of our enemies; when hee shall make us a prayse and glory, that men shall say of succeeding plantacions: the lord make it like that of New England: for wee must Consider that wee shall be as a city upon a hill. The eyes of all people are uppon us.

—Governor John Winthrop, 1630[1]

THE BEGINNING OF AMERICAN EDUCATIONAL ARCHETYPES

The birth of America in the early seventeenth century was ushered in by an epic political and religious movement that had swept across Europe a century before—the Reformation. Inspired by Martin Luther in Germany, Jacques Faber and John Calvin in France, Zwingli in Switzerland, and John Knox in Scotland, the Old World order began to crack. And when it cracked, the blood of Europe poured out. The 1,200-year-old marriage of the Holy Roman Catholic Church to earthly kings, each supporting the other in an often unholy alliance, ended. In England, by a 1534 act of Parliament, King Henry VIII, not the pope, was deemed the "supreme head of the Church of England." Henry VIII quickly proceeded to close 856 Catholic monasteries, tortured and beheaded monks, and those who sympathized with them were hung, drawn, and quartered.

King Henry VIII's brutal tactics created strong elements of internal opposition within the Church of England so that by the end of his reign in 1547, an underground English Reformation movement began within the larger continental Reformation movement. The goal of the English reformists was

15

to "purify" the corruption and errors within the Church of England and, by implication, its governing monarchy. A splinter group within this English Puritan "non-conformist" movement was comprised of separatists who considered reform hopeless. In 1620, a small band of 102 of these Puritan separatists, known as Pilgrims, embarked on a treacherous two-month journey across 3,100 miles of the North Atlantic Ocean. They hoped to establish a "New Israel." Where other wayfarers before them had failed to establish a sustainable colony, and despite half of them dying within the first year, these pilgrims succeeded in establishing a small settlement over 600 miles north of Jamestown, Virginia—the site of the first American settlement. As the Episcopal Church historian, William Manross, describes,

> The Plymouth settlers had come to America, not to found a haven of religious freedom but to establish a spiritual commonwealth, or a new Israel, in which the state should act in close collaboration with a Church restored to what they considered its original purity. The laws of the colony were to agree as nearly as possible with the legal codes of the Old Testament.[2]

A few years later in 1629, the Pilgrims' more aristocratic Puritan brethren were granted a charter from King Charles I to form another settlement, the Massachusetts Bay Colony, which was close to Plymouth. A year later, its wealthy patron, John Winthrop, was appointed governor of the Bay Colony. Based in Boston, Winthrop's arrival was accompanied by 1,500 more settlers, "many of whom were distinguished for their quality, as well as their intelligence and piety."[3] In Winthrop's vision, the Bay Colony was to be a religiously pure community—a "City on a Hill."[4] It was to be a communal place where all would

> commerce together in all meekness, gentleness, patience and liberality . . . delight in each other, make others conditions our own rejoice together, mourn together, labor, and suffer together . . . our community as members of the same body . . . the Lord will be our God and delight to dwell among us.

Alone in the New World, surrounded by strange natives, the Puritan hope had a mystical, apocalyptic dimension to it. Early America historian Avihu Zakai has argued that the Puritan sacred imagination involved their belief that they lived in a special dimension of time—the biblical millennium—that would culminate in the Second Coming of Christ. According to Zakia,

> Puritans left England both because they had given up all hope of achieving genuine reformation there and because they were deeply convinced that the Old World would be destroyed by the eschatological and apocalyptic violence that would precede the millennium. Consequently, they believed themselves sent by

God's divine providence into exile in America to establish Christ's Kingdom upon the stage of the world . . . and to the establish in New England of the utopian New Jerusalem described in the Book of Revelation.[5]

It was from the brutal schisms and political persecution of the Old World that renewed hope emerged in New World and with that, the first purpose of education emerged: education for salvation of the elect.

THE PURITAN EDUCATION ARCHETYPE— EDUCATION FOR SALVATION OF THE ELECT

To ensure the sustainability of their theological-based settlement in the New World, the Puritans needed to raise clergy who were not wedded to the Church of England. Thus, in 1636, the Puritans established the first college in America, New College. The reason for its establishment was expressed by its principal benefactor, the Reverend John Harvard:

After God had carried us safe to New England and we had built our houses, provided necessaries for our livelihood, reared convenient places for God's worship, and settled the civil government: One of the next things we longed for and looked after was to advance learning and perpetuate it to posterity; dreading to leave an illiterate ministry to the churches, when our present ministers shall lie in the dust.[6]

For the Puritans, the Bible was the final scriptural authority—not the Church hierarchy. It was therefore necessary that every member of the colony have the ability to read the Bible for themselves in *English*—not Latin. The mass distribution of English Bibles was made technically possible by two developments: John Wycliffe's first translation of the Latin Bible into English in 1380 (followed by another ten translations culminating with the officially blessed King James Version in 1610) and Gutenberg's printing machine. The colonists' children, however, still needed to be able to read. This goal became the basis of The General School Law of 1647, otherwise known as the "Old Deluder Satan Law" requiring every town in the Massachusetts Bay Colony having more than fifty families to establish a grammar school. Merely being indoctrinated to believe in God was insufficient. Education for the discernment of satanic-inspired deceptions was seen as crucial for the colony's survival.

It being one chief project of that old deluder, Satan, to keep men from the knowledge of the Scriptures, as in former times by keeping them in an unknown tongue, so in these latter times by persuading from the use of tongues, that so that at least the true sense and meaning of the original might be clouded and corrupted with love and false glosses of saint-seeming deceivers; and to the end that learning may not be buried in the grave of our forefathers, in church and commonwealth, the Lord assisting our endeavors. It is therefore ordered that every township in this jurisdiction, after the Lord hath increased them to fifty households shall forthwith appoint one within their town to teach all such children as shall resort to him to write and read.[7]

The Puritans' aim of education, whose influence dominated the early colonial period throughout New England, represents America's first educational archetype. Its educational aim was salvation. The object of Puritan teaching was to know the Christian Bible and their reading primers were the psalms. Their goal was to develop children's ability to critically examine religious claims so that they would not be deceived and seduced into heresy. The socializing element of Puritan education was to maintain a special type of religious, social, and political community: those who belonged, and those who didn't. Calvinistic theology reserved God's salvation to the predestined—the elect—and the colonists believed they were it.[8]

Modern Manifestations of the Puritan Education Archetype

The Puritan archetype of education for the salvation of the elect is alive and well in the United States today, with nearly 23,000 private religious schools that enroll over four million students.[9] Not all of these schools resemble the Puritan archetypical aim of education in all its essential features, but many do. The Puritan archetype is not merely about schools with a religious focus; recall that one of the features of the Puritan archetype was well-defined boundaries as to who belongs and who does not. These schools required an unquestioning adherence to doctrinal purity to produce a homogeneous Christian community of like-minded people. And, while the original Puritan archetype pertained to Christian schools, its archetypal features can also be found in other religious-based schools that insist on the same kind of doctrinal purity and membership exclusivity. The American Association of Christian Schools (AACS), for example, advertises itself as "one of the leading organizations of Christian schools in the country, serving over 100,000 students in member schools throughout the United States." But, AACS warns, "membership will not be afforded to those associated with, members of, or in accord with the World Council of Churches, the National Council of Churches, the Modern Charismatic Movement, or the Ecumenical Movement."[10] Additionally, one can find examples of such schools in the United States and elsewhere that have similar doctrinal membership restriction but are not Christian, for example, Orthodox Jewish yeshivas and Islamic madrasas.

While the Puritan religious culture dominated early New England life, there were also strong Congregationalist currents that resisted autocratic rule by either secular kings or ecclesiastical bishops. For early New England Congregationalists, small-town local self-government was the defining forms of political and economic interactions. It was out of this sense of individual self-awareness sufficient for self-governance that a second education archetype emerged.

BOSTON LATIN SCHOOL ARCHETYPE— WESTERN CLASSICAL EDUCATION

At the same time New College was being established, the first "Free schoole" in the United States was also being launched in 1635 in Boston.[11] By "free," they meant the school was not restricted to certain classes of children and was supported in part by the payment of tuition from parents. It was not funded from taxes but from money pledged as endowments by its wealthier inhabitants, sufficient to fund a teacher for one year. For nearly fifty years, the Free School was the only public school in Boston. Its program of study consisted of learning Latin and Greek and the literature of classical antiquity. Their model resembled the Latin schools in England[12] and, in turn, became the model of the many Latin grammar schools throughout early colonial New England.

The educational aim of these schools was to develop a particular character and quality of intellect that its proponents argued could only be achieved, in its highest degree, through a classical education. As the Rev. David Cole, principal of Trenton Academy, wrote 230 years later about the aims of classical education,

We know our business is to discover to our pupil his intellectual resources, to excite his powers to profitable exertion, to get him upon a track of thought, and draw out the dormant energies of his soul by stimulating him to inquire, to think and to carry on process of thought for himself. . . . To train up a community of independent thinkers, then, is the main object of school instruction. These are the only men who produce important results.[13]

A modern reader might ask if the study of mathematics or science does the same. Cole's answer was that there is nothing more practical than to study language. It is "the most potent and primary of all agents in effecting the changes that take place in the moral, intellectual and material world."[14] The study of language is the study of the mind. And the most powerful way to study both language and mind, according to Latin advocates, is through the classical languages, literature, and philosophies of Greco-Roman antiquity. L.F. Cady, principal of the Public High School in Rhode Island, wrote in 1862,

> The power to think readily and clearly, and to express thought with force and precision, is the most valuable man can possess; and it is our conviction that the discipline of no branch of study is so perfectly adapted to develop this power as that of the classics.[15]

It is noteworthy that many of the early New England grammar schools were run by town councils, or "selectmen." The New England town was a unique form of governance not found in England. A state without a king, far removed from the arm of English rule and surrounded by strange and hostile Natives, the early colonial settlers organized themselves in small self-governing clusters for their common good, transacting their common business in town meetings. As historian Francis Baylis writes, "The whole of New England divided into a vast number of little democratic republics, which have full power to do all those things which most essentially concern the comforts, happiness, and morals of the people."[16] It was through the seeds of these many little democratic republics that local public school districts sprung up. Boston Latin was the first, and it remains part of the Boston Public School system to this day, nearly 400 years later.

Modern Manifestations of the Boston Latin School Archetype

Schools that focus on the Latin and Western classics are still alive in the twenty-first century. According to a 2007–2008 national survey of foreign language high school students, over 205,000 U.S. students took courses in Latin, ranking it fourth in popularity behind German. Many U.S. schools are reporting a surge in Latin course enrollments. In 2010, 138,000 students from 2,743 schools took the National Latin Exam in their own schools. Latin language courses, however, are only one feature of the Boston Latin archetype. Most important is the emphasis on the Western classics. An example is The Classical Academy in Colorado Springs, founded in 1997 as a public charter school. It is now the largest K-12 charter school in Colorado, with an enrollment of 3,500 students across three campuses. The Academy strives to "instill traditional values through the study of quality, time-tested history and classical literature." Its instructional philosophy is based on the following classical ideas: the Trivium (grammar, logic, and rhetoric); lifelong pursuit of truth, beauty, and goodness; literature and ideas that have survived the test of time.

As of 2013, there were 123 public and private schools in the United States with either the word "Latin" or "Classic" in the school's name, many of which were established in the early twenty-first century, for example, the Brooklyn Latin School (2006), the Washington Latin Public Charter School (2006), and the Boys' Latin of Philadelphia Charter School (2007).

CHANGE IN THE FIRST LIFETIME (1620–1700)

To appreciate the evolution of educational archetypes emerging from the profound changes in the United States over each lifetime, think about the dramatic changes a girl born in the first Plymouth settlement might have witnessed. In her Plymouth neighborhood alone, she would have seen "The Great Migration" (1630–1643), during which about 200 ships docked in Boston, unloading 21,000 new arrivals to New England. She would have seen the larger colonial population grow to 100 times its original size, from a few thousand settlers in 1620 to 251,000 by 1700.[17] She would have heard about nearly all of the eastern coast organized into twelve English colonies from New Hampshire to South Carolina.[18] And she would have witnessed a dramatic displacement and decline in Indigenous populations.

But perhaps the most profound change she would have experienced was the slow evaporation of the Puritan utopian dream of a "New Israel"—the Kingdom of God being established in the wilderness. Troubling discord grew within the Puritan community, as exemplified by Roger Williams' banishment from the Puritan colony in 1636, to where he established another community, Rhode Island. As other reformation sects from England, Sweden, Holland, Germany, and Francesettled into the New World, sectarian feuding and intolerance also settled in. More perniciously, the New Israel ideal was being degraded by the spread of African slavery, first in Virginia and the Bay Colony itself, and then throughout the colonies. Worse still, many churchmen, such as Puritan preacher Cotton Mather, justified slavery on the grounds that Blacks were the "miserable children of Adam and of Noah" for whom slavery had been ordained as a punishment.[19] The New Israel ideal would be contradicted by the repeated violent conflicts with local American Indian tribes, first in the Pequot Indian War of 1637[20] and then in King Philip's War, where more than half of New England's ninety towns battled Indian warriors. It would be compromised by a devil's bargain where the defeated were traded south for African slaves shipped to the north.

Finally, the first of what would be four French and Indian Wars, King William's War (1689–1697), crushed whatever hope was left of a Puritan utopia by the geopolitical realities of Europe's rapacious claims over North America. Despite large gains in population, the colonies were a mere one-twentieth the size of England.

The colonists would still need Mother England's protection against the big dogs—the French, Spanish, and Dutch—biting off vast amounts of territory to the north, south, and west. It was in the midst of these enormous changes that our young girl, now approaching the age of seventy, would have witnessed the emergence of a new American educational archetype.

THE FRIENDS (QUAKER) EDUCATIONAL ARCHETYPE—CONSCIENCE, TOLERANCE, SERVICE, PACIFISM

In a bucolic section of northwest Philadelphia sits one of the oldest schools in the United States, founded in 1689. Its founder was a follower of George Fox, a dissenting preacher in England who was frequently imprisoned, and his followers were repeatedly tortured, imprisoned, and killed. Their crime: advancing the ancient Christian notion that a person's relation with God is mediated by neither the church nor the state, only by the Word made flesh, most eloquently expressed in the Gospel of John. For Fox and his followers, God was a matter of individual conscience, of an "inner light" whose authenticity was not a matter of state-sponsored church worship. Fox called his group the "Religious Society of Friends" or "Quakers." The Friends were among the group, also known as "Plain people," who renounced religious bigotry and the values and lifestyles of the wealthy English aristocrats. The Society of Friends not only called for leaving the Church of England, as did the Pilgrims, but the separation of *all* churches from the civil government as well. For their prophetic criticism of the Church of England and its practices, the Quakers were labeled as seditious.[21,22]

Fox and his followers would probably have remained in jail to die were it not for the sympathies of one young, wealthy English lawyer/sailor/ soldier, William Penn, Jr. Penn became so enamored with the Society of Friends' theology and their Christian gentility that he defended Fox and his followers numerous times in English court and suffered as well with them in prison. Penn's father, Sir William Penn, a well-respected admiral in the King Charles II fleet, embarrassed by the radical consorts of his son, almost renounced him. When the elder Penn died in 1670, King Charles II owed him 16,000 pounds. The younger William Penn persuaded the king to fulfill his debt by granting Penn Jr. 45,000 square miles of land along the eastern coast of the New World that stretched between the Duke of York's territory to the north and Lord Baltimore's territory to the south. In honor of his late father, this densely wooded territory was given the Latin name *Sylvania*, meaning "woodlands." Penn's 45,000 square miles of woods thus became *Pennsylvania*.

With money and land in hand, Penn conceived of a "Holy Experiment" in the New World where the Quaker principles of religious freedom and individual liberty could thrive, especially for his Society of Friends' brethren. To ensure the survival of the new colony, Penn recruited fellow Englishmen of every trade and skill to join him. When he landed in Philadelphia in 1682, Penn had written the *Frame of Government of Pennsylvania*, a new colonial government document that reflected the influence of his friend John Locke.[23] Locke, and other seventeenth-century Enlightenment political thinkers, advocated religious tolerance, individual liberty, and a social contract political theory. Penn wrote in the Preface to his 1682 Frame of Government:

> Governments, like clocks, go from the motion men give them; and as governments are made and moved by men, so by them they are ruined too. Wherefore governments rather depend upon men, than men upon governments. Let men be good, and the government cannot be bad; if it be ill, they will cure it. But, if men be bad, let the government be never so good, they will endeavor to warp and spoil it to their turn. . . . That, therefore, which makes a good constitution, must keep it; viz., men of wisdom and virtue, qualities, that because they descend not with worldly inheritances, must be carefully propagated by a virtuous education of youth.[24]

To preserve the vision of his Holy Experiment for future generations, Penn established a Philadelphia Friends Public School in 1689. In sharp contrast to the Puritan aim of education to maintain a theocratic-based community of the "elect," the private William Penn Charter School was and still is open to Quakers and non-Quakers, rich and poor, male and female. Its aim is to instill the Quaker ethos: to provide the rudiments of literacy and morality for all Philadelphians and to cultivate wise and virtuous citizens. As the Friends schools express their aim of education:

> The central concept that 'there is that of God in every person' colors what we do throughout the school. That tenet leads us to value each child for his or her accomplishments, to believe in encouraging students from diverse ethnic, racial and religious backgrounds to attend the school, to discuss peaceful resolution of difficulties whether those difficulties occur on the kindergarten playground . . . or in the world beyond Penn Charter, and to foster a commitment of service to others.[25]

In sum, the Friends Quaker educational archetype was a perfect adaptive response to the profound changes that occurred over seventy years in early colonial America, in terms of its explosive population growth, the diffusion of diverse religious sects, the vacillating periods of tolerance and repression by Mother England toward non-conforming church members, and the savage battles between East Coast Indian tribes and European settlers.

Modern Manifestations of the Friends School Archetype

The Friends' ethos of tolerance, service, and the Inner Light of Conscience represents those morally nurturing and social-justice-engaging private schools that are open to all races, creeds, and nationalities. Its progenitor school, the William Penn Charter School in Philadelphia, is the fifth oldest school in the country and the oldest Quaker school in the world. Since its founding in 1689, Penn's Charter School[26,27] has spawned ninety-three other Friends-related schools, such as Sidwell Friends in Washington, D.C., attended by the children of several U.S. presidents. The Friends schools with high academic standards also include nationally renowned Philadelphia area Bryn Mawr College, Haverford College, and Swarthmore College. Nonetheless, more radical changes lay just ahead in the second lifetime that would spawn very different and new aims of education.

NOTES

1. John Winthrop, "A Modell of Christian Charity (1630)," in *A History of the U.S. Political System: Ideas, Interests and Institutions*, Richard A. Harris and Daniel Tichenor, eds. (Santa Barbara, CA: ABC-CLIO, 2009).

2. William W. Manross, *A History of the American Episcopal Church* (Milwaukee: Morehouse Publishing, 1935), 20.

3. Charles A. Goodrich, A History of the United States (1852), as quoted in "Massachusetts Bay Colony: A Brief History," Celebrate Boston, http://www.celebrateboston.com/history/massachusetts.htm.

4. John Winthrop, "A Modell of Christian Charity (1630)." From the Collections of the MA Historical Society (Boston, 1838), 3rd series 7:31–48. Accessed Feb. 13, 2023. http://history.hanover.edu/texts/winthmod.html (All quotes from this source).

5. Avihu Zahai, "Theocracy in Massachusetts: The Puritan Universe of Sacred Imagination," *Studies in the Literary Imagination* 27, no. 1 (March 1, 1994): 23.

6. "History and Mission," Harvard Divinity School, https://hds.harvard.edu/about/history-and-mission.

7. Old Deluder Satan Act of 1647, https://www.mass.gov/doc/old-deluder-satan-law/download.

8. David Hall, *The Legacy of John Calvin: His Influence in the Modern World* (Phillipsburg, NJ: P&R Publishing, 2008).

9. U.S. Department of Education, National Center for Education Statistics, "Characteristics of Private Schools in the United States: Results From the 2007–08 Private School Universe Survey," March 2009, http://nces.ed.gov/pubs2009/2009313.pdf.

10. "About Us," American Association of Christian Schools, https://www.aacs.org/about-us/.

11. Robert Francis Seybolt, *The Public Schools of Colonial Boston* (Cambridge, MA: Harvard University Press, 1935).

12. Henry Barnard, "Biography of Ezekiel Cheever with Notes on the Early Free of Grammar Schools of New England," *The American Journal of Education* 1 (1856).

13. David Cole, "Classical Education," *The American Journal of Education* 1 (1856): 71–72.

14. Cole, "Classical Education," 77.

15. L. F. Cady, "Elementary Classical Instruction," *The American Journal of Education* 12 (1862): 563.

16. Francis Baylies and Samuel Gardner Drake, *An Historical Memoir of the Colony of New Plymouth: From the Flight of the Pilgrims into Holland in the Year 1608, to the Union of that Colony with Massachusetts in 1692* (Boston, MA: Wiggin & Lunt, 1866), 240.

17. U.S. Census, *A Century of Population Growth: From the First Census of the United States to the Twelfth, 1790–1900* (Baltimore, MD: Genealogical Publishing Company, 1969), 9.

The figures for the period 1610–1780 given in series B 12 antedate the first census of the United States in 1790. They represent the considered judgment of a number of eminent scholars and are based on materials ranging from relatively complete enumerations for some of the colonies to fragmentary data such as contemporary local population estimates, militia registrations, tax records, church records, and official vital statistics.

18. Georgia, the thirteenth colony, was colonized in 1732, after our imaginary girl's death.

19. Cotton Mather, *Diary of Cotton Mather, 1681–1724* (Boston, MA: Massachusetts Historical Society), 176.

20. The Pequot War of 1637 between English and Dutch settlers of Massachusetts and Connecticut and the Mashantucket Pequot Tribal Nation led to the death of 50 percent of the tribal population.

21. George Fox, Some Principles of the Elect People of God Who in Scorn Are Called Quakers (London, 1661), http://www.qhpress.org/texts/gfprinc.html#s19.

22. George Fox, *Journal*, Vol. 2, 8th and Bicentenary Edition (London: Friends' Tract Association, 1891), http://www.qhpress.org/quakerpages/qwhp/dec1660.htm.

23. John Locke, "Two Treatises of Government," in *The Works of John Locke*, Vol. V. (London, 1823), https://www.yorku.ca/comninel/courses/3025pdf/Locke.pdf. Much was developed prior to the publication date.

24. William Penn, "Preface to the Frame of Government," May 5, 1682, https://avalon.law.yale.edu/17th_century/pa04.asp.

25. "About Us," William Penn Charter School, accessed April 15, 2023, https://www.penncharter.com/about-us/quaker-education.

26. William C. Kashatus, *A Virtuous Education: Penn's Vision for Philadelphia Schools* (Wallingford, PA: Pendle Hill Publications, 1997).

27. William Penn's unique concept was to create a school of "arts and sciences" open not only to the wealthy but also to students of limited means. Penn Charter was among the first to offer education to different religions (1689), financial aid (1701), education for girls (1754) and education for all races (1770). Betsy Ross; African American abolitionist and businessman James Forten; and Roberts Vaux, the man who led the movement for a public school law in Pennsylvania, were all students of the original Penn Charter.

Chapter 2

The Colonies Become a Nation

Change in the Second Lifetime (1700–1790)

The most effectual means of preventing this [the perversion of power into tyranny] would be to illuminate, as far as practicable, the minds of the people at large, and more especially to give them knowledge of those facts which history exhibiteth.[1]

—Thomas Jefferson

A boy born in Boston in the early 1700s would have witnessed enormous social, political, and intellectual upheavals in colonial America during his lifetime. Out of these upheavals, a set of three new aims of education would emerge.

THE BEN FRANKLIN EDUCATIONAL ARCHETYPE—EDUCATION FOR VIRTUE, SERVICE, AND USEFUL LEARNING

The first of these new educational aims would be drawn from the experiences of a ten-year-old Boston school dropout, one of seventeen children and the youngest of ten boys, fathered by Josiah Franklin, a candle and soap maker. Benjamin Franklin was born in Boston in 1706 and enrolled in the Boston Latin School at age eight.[2] Two years later, he left due to his father's limited means to pay the tuition. The young Franklin, however, was a voracious reader—and dreamer. He longed for the sea, but his father disapproved of such adventures as his second oldest son took sail, never to be heard from again. So, at his father's urging, when he was twelve years old, Benjamin signed papers to become an indentured servant to his older brother James, with whom he could apprentice as a printer. As might be expected in those times when one sibling is set as "master" over another, Benjamin suffered repeated beatings at the hands of his older brother. The saving grace, however, was that as a printer's apprentice, Benjamin gained access to books and customers who had private libraries. At age seventeen, Benjamin became a fugitive, running away from his older brother in Boston and making his way down the coast by boat to Philadelphia. Poor and dirty, the young Franklin would spend his first night, as fate would have it, sleeping in a Quaker meeting house.[3] The Quaker influence of Philadelphia would have a lasting impact on Franklin.

Philadelphia's population in 1720 was the size of a small town—about 10,000 people. It ranked second behind America's most populous city, Boston (pop. 12,000), and ahead of New York's. (pop. 7,000). All three towns were seaports bustling with commerce and trade. In his remarkable autobiography, young Franklin details his intellectual, romantic, and commercial adventures as he established his printing business in Philadelphia and published its first newspaper, *The Pennsylvania Gazette,* in 1728. He was a noted vegetarian who advised his fellow printers to drink water with their bread rather than the usual six pints of "strong beer" for strength for the day's labors. His voracious appetite, however, was not for food but for "useful knowledge." In his autobiography, Franklin recounts his wide-ranging and relentless inquisitiveness about poetry, morals, metaphysics, natural philosophy, and politics. But for our purposes, what is most relevant to Franklin's story is his establishment of a new aim of education in late colonial America.

In the intellectual zone of early Quaker Philadelphia, free from the threat of inquisitions from the Church or imprisonment from the state, a young mind could freely immerse itself in a new Age of Reason that was revolutionizing thought throughout Europe. As the Reformation wrought massive theological and political changes in the early 1500s, advances in astronomy, physics, chemistry, and mathematics were leading a new assault against popular superstitions and intellectual arrogance about new insights into natural phenomena. From Ulugh Beg's astronomical mathematics and observatory in the early 15th century, to Nicolaus Copernicus' Earth-shattering heliocentric hypothesis in 1543, to Tycho Bache's voluminous collection of precise astronomical data in 1600, his student Johannes Kepler's elegant mathematical equations of planetary orbits in 1619, and Galileo Galilei's telescope and experiments in physics in 1630 to Isaac Newton's formulation of calculus and classical physics in 1687,[4] a capacious intellect could relish in the recent revelations of the natural world. As Kepler wrote when he discovered the elegant geometric secret of planetary motion, "I have attested it as true in my innermost soul and I contemplate its beauty with incredible and ravishing delight."[5]

There was much to delight Franklin's wide-ranging curiosity, provided he could get books, which were scarce and expensive. His fledging Philadelphia printing and newspaper business provided him with both a means of making a living and making new friends within his growing social and political network. Frugal and industrious, young Franklin organized a small informal reading group called the Junto that soon evolved into a subscription library he chartered when he was twenty-five years old with fifty founding shareholders. From that small group of shared books eventually came the Library Company of Philadelphia, with over half a million documents.[6] Also springing out of the Junto was the American Philosophical Society that Franklin organized in 1743, whose members would include several of America's Founding Fathers, such as George Washington, John Adams, Thomas Jefferson, Alexander Hamilton, Thomas Paine, Benjamin Rush, James Madison, and John Marshall. Although Franklin, like many in his circle, extolled the "excellency of the Christian faith," he was a Deist who, while believing in a higher power, was agnostic as to the divinity of Christ.[7]

It was out of this tolerant Philadelphia Quaker ethos situated in an era where reason and science were challenging Old-World paradigms that Franklin in 1749 wrote his *Proposals Relating to the Education of Youth in Pensilvania*.[8] Franklin drew on the thinking of six other influential educational thought leaders[9] to set forth the organizing principles of the Public Academy of Philadelphia. As to the aims of his academy, Franklin acknowledged his dilemma:

> As to their studies, it would be well if they could be taught everything that is useful and everything that is ornamental, but art is long and time is short. It is therefore proposed that they learn those things that are likely to be most useful and most ornamental; regard being had to the several professions for which they are intended.[10]

Franklin cited important things to learn: "swift writing in a fair hand, drawing, arithmetic, accounting, some first principles of geometry and astronomy, grammar in one's own tongue, writing style for the purposes of being clear and concise, reading, pronunciation, oratory, geography, such as reading maps, and mechanical philosophy." All these subjects, Franklin argued, were useful to the "gentleman" in everyday life. He advocated that students study merchant accounting not so that gentlemen might use it to *obtain* an estate, but to *preserve* it. Franklin saw the teaching of morality and history foremost for their practical value so a gentleman could learn the advantages that flowed from a virtuous life as well as how to avoid life's pitfalls and loss of position.

> Morality by descanting and making continual observations on the causes of the rise and fall of any Man's character, fortune, power, etc., mentioned in History; the advantages of temperance, order, frugality, industry, perseverance etc.

> Indeed, the general natural tendency of reading good history must be to fix in
> the minds of youth deep impressions of the beauty and usefulness of virtue of
> all kinds, public spirit, fortitude, etc.[11]

Franklin concluded his proposal with what he considered to be "the great
aim and end of all learning"—which was not personal gain, but rather public
service:

> The idea of what is true merit, should also be often presented to youth, explained
> and impressed on their minds, as consisting in an inclination joined with an abil-
> ity to serve mankind, one's country, friends, and family which ability is (with
> the blessing of God) to be acquired or greatly increased by true learning; and
> should indeed be the great aim and end of all learning.[12]

The public academy that Franklin and his small group of associates would
establish two years later was renamed the University of Pennsylvania. As
of 1751, it was only the fifth college in the American colonies and the first
founded with an orientation toward business and public service rather than
the preparation of clergy.[13] As such, Franklin's emphasis on *useful learning,
the cultivation of personal virtue,* and *public service* constituted a new educational archetype in America. With educational aims that were not expressly
Christian but sympathetic to them, this archetype was well aligned with
Quaker sensibilities. Indeed, atop Philadelphia's City Hall stands the statue
of William Penn Jr., the Quaker, overlooking the University of Pennsylvania
campus.

Modern Manifestations of the Ben Franklin Archetype

In 1757, the University of Pennsylvania graduated its first class of twelve
students. Today, the University of Pennsylvania is a sprawling network of
165 research centers and institutes, twelve graduate and professional schools,
and a regional health system including a network of hospitals and related
medical centers. It is the largest employer in Philadelphia, with 31,650
employees and six billion dollars in revenue.[14] Franklin's aim of public service has endured. During the 2009–2010 academic year, for example, 1,575
Penn students enrolled in sixty-one Academically Based Community Service
(ABCS) courses taught by forty-eight faculty members organized through
its Netter Center for Community Partnerships.[15] The Franklin archetype of
practical knowledge gained through service learning has been incorporated in
most colleges and universities to become a mainstay of twenty-first-century
higher education.[16]

THE JEFFERSONIAN ARCHETYPE—FREE, UNIVERSAL EDUCATION FOR DEMOCRACY

During Benjamin Franklin's life of eighty-four years, he witnessed many profound changes. To an ordinary person, the sheer volume of change in colonial America between 1700 and 1790 must have been disorienting. The colonial population grew exponentially at a compound rate of 3 percent per year, or 35 percent every decade, due in large part to British and Northern European immigrants. Not only did Philadelphia's population multiply by a factor of ten,[17] but the total colonial population increased to *thirteen times* its size, from 275,000 in 1700 to nearly four million by 1790—roughly half the population of Mother England.[18]

Perhaps even more disorienting than the exponential colonial population growth was how the colonists were caught up in the geopolitical battles waged by the European superpowers against each other: Great Britain, France, and Spain, among others. Through four French and Indian wars, the colonial militia joined British forces in savage battles against French forces and American Indian tribes as part of an eight-nation[19] world war spanning two continents.[20] The fourth and final French and Indian War in America ending in 1763 coincided with the end of the Seven Years War between eight European belligerents. As part of the Treaty of 1763, France relinquished all its territory *east* of the Mississippi to Great Britain, except for New Orleans. At the same time, Spain agreed to give up Florida in return for Cuba. But within a mere twelve years, this new world order would unravel.

Great Britain, deeply in debt from war, faced more expense in running and defending its newly acquired territories east of the Mississippi from Indian attacks. To finance its colonial garrisons and limit provocations toward the Indians, the English parliament imposed a series of draconian taxes, tariffs, settlements, and trading limitations on their colonists.[21] The American colonists did not receive these impositions well. Feeling themselves more muscular in numbers and possessing greater verve, the colonialists engaged in a series of mass protests. British repression followed, creating an escalating cycle of violence and intimidation on both sides. Finally, in April 1775, American colonists openly rebelled. They began their rebellion in Lexington and Concord, Massachusetts. By the summer, the colonists were waging a full-scale war of independence.

After three years, in 1778, France switched sides to back the colonists against their mortal enemy, Great Britain, turning a civil war into an international conflict. Spain, seizing the opportunity, also declared war on Great Britain the next year, in June 1779, bringing them into the war. Meanwhile, George Washington's Continental Army spent eight years slogging up and down the American east coast in a war of attrition for independence. Finally, the British surrendered at Yorktown in October 1781, and by January 1784, the Treaty of Paris was signed. The American Revolutionary War was officially over. In an instant, the territory under the control of the Continental Congress *doubled,* leaping westward from the Allegheny Mountains to the Mississippi River and stretching north to British Canada. Six years later, by 1790, all thirteen colonies had ratified a new constitution binding them together in a new nation, The United States of America.

From a European viewpoint, the American Constitution was unprecedented. There was no provision for a king. No state sponsorship of any church. Few limits on free speech. No cruel or unusual punishments. No public displays of disemboweled dissenters. No imprisonments without a trial. No limits on states having their militias. No way to raise taxes without the consent of those being taxed. In short, all the traditional instruments of power wielded by European monarchs and Roman tyrants to intimidate and control the masses were missing in the American system.

Thirteen separate states joined in a union. But where was the center? How could these many diverse states be held together as one? Half free, half slave. Would this new experiment eventually disintegrate from the centrifugal forces of slavery, ethnic and religious sectarianism, huge war debts, and competing state interests? Would the resulting chaos and disorder between these thirteen states give former British Loyalists an opening to reunite with the British crown? Would there be a military coup? Perhaps a counter-revolution financed by wealthy English aristocrats to foment the dissolution of the United States Constitution, paving the way for an American monarch . . . or tyrant? After 170 years of allegiance to England since the settlements of Jamestown and Plymouth, this new concept of governance was exceedingly fragile.

Thomas Jefferson, the principal author of the Declaration of Independence, expressed his worry about the sustainability of the new nation. For Jefferson, also a Deist, the United States Constitution was the new sacred text. He considered the knowledge of it by the common man to be essential for its preservation. Jefferson's high-stakes wager was that the center *could* be held together by the "natural power" of the citizenry itself—but only if they were kept broadly informed of the truth of current political and historical affairs. To reiterate and expand upon Jefferson's words quoted in the epigraph to this chapter:

The most effectual means of preventing this [the perversion of power into tyranny are] would be to illuminate, as far as practicable, the minds of the people at large, and more especially to give them knowledge of those facts, which history exhibiteth, that, possessed thereby of the experience of other ages and countries, they may be enabled to know ambition under all its shapes, and prompt to exert their natural powers to defeat its purposes.[22]

Within this new and radically different social and political environment of post-colonial America, Jefferson regarded education as indispensable to its survival. The fundamental aim of education, therefore, was the preservation of democracy, a government of, by, and for the people. Without this aim, no other educational goals would be possible. Expressing this in a letter to James Madison, Jefferson wrote, "Above all things I hope the education of the common people will be attended to, convinced that on their good sense we may rely with the most security for the preservation of a due degree of liberty."[23]

In 1780, Jefferson proposed "A Bill for the More General Diffusion of Knowledge" in the Virginia House of Delegates, which argued that "without regard to wealth, birth or other accidental condition or circumstance . . . it is better that such should be sought for and educated at the common expense of all."[24] As to the objectives of elementary school, Jefferson proposed:

> Reading in the first stage, where [the people] will receive their education to be chiefly historical. History by apprising them of the past will enable them to judge the future; it will avail them of the experience of other times and other nations; it will qualify them as judges of the actions and designs of men; it will enable them to know ambition under every guise it may assume; and knowing it to defeat its views.[25]

With the help of James Madison, the bill was finally passed in 1796. In 1819, Jefferson founded the University of Virginia. Like Franklin, Jefferson envisioned that his university would educate leaders in public service and practical matters; unlike Franklin's University of Pennsylvania, the University of Virginia was publicly supported.

Modern Manifestation of the Jeffersonian Archetype

It is safe to say that most public schools in the United States teach some courses in American history, civics, and/or social studies that recount the history of the country, its democratic foundations, and the role of government. But truly understanding the meaning of self-government requires some experience in collective decision-making guided by ethical values within proscribed boundaries. Knowledge alone is insufficient. A sense of responsibility and duty toward others is essential. A citizenry cannot hope to govern themselves without participating in the act and art of self-government. It is the mutuality of self-possessed virtues and the reciprocity between oneself and others that make collective self-government possible. Without these virtues and reciprocal affections, the whole process dissolves into factionalism and, in the extreme case, civil war. Education for democracy, therefore, is more than academics.

If a school's aim is to instill democratic values, it must also develop within the child a tolerant temperament, a democratic disposition, and an ethical character. The Noah Webster Micro Society Magnet School in the Hartford, Connecticut, school district is such a school. Noah Webster, a pre-K-8 school of 600 students, embodies the Jeffersonian archetype of education for democracy by creating a time and place for its students to actively participate in a "miniature society" complete with a student-run government, legislature, court, police department, bank, and entrepreneurial businesses.

> In the Micro Society program, students collaborate with parents, community members, and teachers to build a miniature community in the school and establish a center of commerce and governance in which every child and adult participates. Children create and manage business ventures that produce goods and services. They also run agencies that handle governmental functions and lay the groundwork for organized accountability.[26]

About 120 Micro Society school sites exist throughout the United States and Canada and abroad.[27]

THE BENJAMIN RUSH ARCHETYPE—CHRISTIAN
EDUCATION FOR DOMESTIC TRANQUILITY

Jefferson's optimism in the "good sense" of the common man was not shared by all, however. In contrast to Jefferson, Dr. Benjamin Rush, a Philadelphian physician and signer of the Declaration of Independence, had a more pessimistic view of human nature. Not all had gone well in the land of William Penn's Holy Experiment, his "Peaceable Kingdom," where Indians and White settlers were supposed to coexist. A particularly gruesome example of Penn's Paradise Lost was the infamous massacre in December 1763 of twenty innocent Christian Conestoga Indian men, women, and children in nearby Lancaster, Pennsylvania. The crime was committed by a mob of fifty Scots-Irish Presbyterian frontier settlers from Paxton Township, a mountainous area about a hundred miles west of Philadelphia along the Susquehanna River. In revenge for the Indians joining the French against them, the Paxton boys, as they were called, wanted to rid the Susquehanna Valley of the Indians. After the 1763 treaty, the French pulled their forces out of the valley, leaving the Indians to fend for themselves. William Henry, a resident of nearby Lancaster City, recounted the atrocities that he witnessed committed by the Paxton Boys against the Indians hiding in a building in town. "The man's hands and feet had also been chopped off with a tomahawk. In this manner lay the whole of them—men, women, and children—spread about the prison yard; shot, scalped, hacked, and cut to pieces."[28]

The Paxton Boys swelled into a mob of more than 200 men and marched to Philadelphia the following month, in January 1764. It was the first physical confrontation between what was becoming a Pennsylvania divided between unprotected frontier mountain men and the genteel Philadelphia Quakers. The savagery of these murders shocked the Pennsylvania citizenry, provoking a paper war of over 300 pamphlets written by those either condemning or defending the Paxton Boys.

In contrast to Jefferson's regard for the common man's "good sense," Rush instead regarded men as "ungovernable animals." While both Jefferson and Rush advocated for universal education, Rush's aim of education was to create homogeneity within a growing population whose origins were becoming increasingly divergent from immigrants who had English roots. Rush saw these diverse origins as the seeds of disloyalty to the new republic. The education of the young, therefore, was critical as a means of developing loyal citizens.

> I conceive the education of our youth in this country to be peculiarly necessary in Pennsylvania, while our citizens are composed of the natives of so many different kingdoms in Europe. Our schools of learning, by producing one general and uniform system of education will render the mass of people more homogeneous, and thereby fit them more easily for uniform and peaceable government. . . . From the observations that have been made it is plain, that I consider it is possible to convert men into republican machines. This must be done, if we expect them to perform their parts properly, in the great machine of the government of the state. That republic is sophisticated with monarchy or aristocracy that does not revolve upon the wills of the people, and these must be fitted to each other by means of education before they can be made to produce regularity and unison in government.[29]

How Rush would "convert men into republican machines" differed sharply from that of Jefferson. Rush advocated publicly funded *Christian religious* education as a means of producing virtuous citizens. He outlined a deductive argument for the primacy of the Christian religion, in state-supported schools—a vociferous point of contention among the constitutional framers. As Rush argued:

> I proceed, in the next place, to inquire what mode of education we shall adopt so as to secure to the state all the advantages that are to be derived from the proper instruction of youth; and here I beg leave to remark that the only foundation for a useful education in a republic is to be laid in Religion. Without this, there can

be no virtue, and without virtue there can be no liberty, and liberty is the object
and life of all republican governments. Such is my veneration for every religion
that reveals the attributes of the Deity, or a future state of rewards and punishments, that I had rather see the opinions of Confucius or Mohammed inculcated
upon our youth than see them grow up wholly devoid of a system of religious
principles. But the religion I mean to recommend in this place is the religion of
Jesus Christ.[30]

But unlike the Puritans, for Rush, the purpose of studying Christianity was
not so much for salvation as it was for the promotion of public order and
virtue against a mob of otherwise "ungovernable animals":

In order more effectually to secure to our youth the advantages of a religious
education, it is necessary to impose upon them the doctrines and discipline of a
particular church. Man is naturally an ungovernable animal, and observations on
particular societies and countries will teach us that when we add the restraints
of ecclesiastical to those of domestic and civil government, we produce in him
the highest degrees of order and virtue.[31]

Modern Manifestations of the Benjamin Rush Education Archetype

The Benjamin Rush archetype of using Christian values and practices to bri-
dle the behavior of unruly children is evident still today in Protestant Christian and Catholic parochial schools and Christian Military Academies.[32] For
example, in 2017, the Association of Christian Schools International (ACSI)
commissioned a research study that asked parents of current and prospective
Christian school students to choose the top five purposes of education. For
both current and prospective groups of parents, the most selected goal of
education was "to instill strong principles and values" (current: 69 percent,
prospective: 53 percent)."[33] While the stated aim of these schools is the for-
mation of Christian faith, many parents also value the safety and discipline
within these institutions. According to the ACSI study, when parents were
asked about their specific priorities when it came to choosing a school, safety
came in first. If parents value a school because they perceive their child to
be safe within it, then by implication one must conclude that the school is
either selecting only children who are already well-behaved and/or the school
disciplines *other people's* children to ensure their child's safety. In a study
of the disciplinary policies of Catholic secondary schools from two dioceses
within a major U.S. metropolitan area, researchers found that "expulsion
was more commonly offered as a response to a wide range of behaviors
compared to suspension . . . For mild behaviors, expulsion was offered about
as frequently as suspension. However, expulsion was mandated more often

than suspension for moderate and severe behaviors."[34] In more Fundamentalist Christian schools, perhaps the threat of eternal punishment awaiting the unrepentant sinner scares kids straight. Whatever the reason, there is little doubt that Christian schools are perceived to demand and enforce a higher degree of uniformity and order from their students than public schools, with school uniforms being the most visible but by no means the only manifestation of such order.

The urgency of Jefferson's and Rush's call for free universal education to preserve the union would prove to be prescient. Traumatic changes lay ahead for the new republic, which would tear it in two, North versus South. Despite Jefferson's hope of education being the guarantor of democracy and Rush's hope that a universal, uniform Christian education would tame ungovernable animals, the Civil War involved three million Federal and Confederate soldiers who would fight and kill 600,000 of their fellow Americans. What had become of the hope of education? In the next chapter, we trace new and enduring aims of education that emerged from a crucible of change over the third lifetime.

NOTES

1. Thomas Jefferson, "A Bill for the More General Diffusion of Knowledge," June 18, 1779, https://founders.archives.gov/documents/Jefferson/01-02-02-0132 -0004-0079.

2. The Boston Latin School, founded in 1636, is both the first public school and oldest existing school in the United States, http://www.bls.org.

3. Benjamin Franklin, *Autobiography of Benjamin Franklin* (New York: Henry Holt & Company, 1916; originally published in 1791), https://www.gutenberg.org/ files/20203/20203-h/20203-h.htm#III.

4. Isaac Newton, *Mathematical Principles of Natural Philosophy* (usually called the *Principia*), 1687.

5. Edwin Arthur Burtt, *The Metaphysical Foundations of Modern Physical Science* (New York: Taylor & Francis, 2014), 47.

6. The Library Company of Philadelphia is an independent research library that includes over half a million rare books, pamphlets, manuscripts, and graphics documenting every aspect of American history and culture through the end of the 19th century, http://www.librarycompany.org/.

7. James Breig, http://www.history.org/foundation/journal/spring09/deism.cfm.

8. Benjamin Franklin, *Proposals Relating to the Education of Youth in Pensilvania* (1749), https://archives.upenn.edu/digitized-resources/docs-pubs/franklin -proposals/.

9. John Milton, John Locke, Hutcheson, Obadiah Walker, Mons. Rollin, and Dr. George Turnbull.

10. Benjamin Franklin, *Proposals*, para. 14.

11. Benjamin Franklin, *Proposals*, para. 24.

12. Benjamin Franklin, *Proposals*, para. 35.

13. Franklin and the first Trustees purchased Penn's first campus in 1750 and also assumed responsibility for the Charity School (though it had never opened, the Trust was still alive and well). Both the Academy and the Charity School opened in 1751, https://www.upenn.edu/about/history.

14. This includes 16,300 faculty and staff plus its Health System, which includes a hospital with a regular workforce of 15,553 employees.

15. The Barbara and Edward Netter Center for Community Partnerships, University of Pennsylvania, http://www.nettercenter.upenn.edu/about-center/our-mission.

16. Campus Compact, "Deepening the Roots of Civic Engagement: 2011 Annual Membership Survey," https://compact.org/sites/default/files/2022-04/2011-Annual-Survey-Executive-Summary-1.pdf.

17. Susan E. Klepp, *The Swift Progress of Population: A Documentary and Bibliographic Study of Philadelphia Growth 1642–1859* (Philadelphia: American Philosophical Society, 1991).

18. Campbell Gibson, "Population of the 100 Largest Cities and other Urban Places in the United States: 1790 to 1990," U.S. Bureau of the Census, Population Division Working Paper No. 27.

19. Austria, France, Great Britain, Hanover, Prussia, Russia, Saxony, and Sweden.

20. For a lucid description of the geopolitics of the American colonies, see Amaury de Riencourt's, *The American Empire* (Dial Press, 1968).

21. The Proclamation of 1763 limiting settlement west of the Appalachian Mountains; the 1764 Sugar and Currency Acts; the 1765 Stamp and Quartering Acts; the 1766 Declaratory Act; the 1767 Townsend Revenue Acts; the 1774 Coercive Acts, and the 1775 New England Restraining Act.

22. Thomas Jefferson, "A Bill."

23. "To James Madison from Thomas Jefferson, 20 December 1787," *Founders Online,* National Archives, https://founders.archives.gov/documents/Madison/01-10-02-0210.

24. Thomas Jefferson, "A Bill."

25. Thomas Jefferson, "Notes on the State of Virginia, Queries 14 and 19," (1784), para. 1, https://press-pubs.uchicago.edu/founders/documents/v1ch18s16.html.

26. Noah Webster MicroSociety Magnet School, Hartford Public Schools, Hartford, CT, https://sites.google.com/hartfordschools.org/nwmms/about-us/what-is-a-microsociety.

27. "About Us," MicroSociety, accessed May 7, 2023, https://www.microsociety.org/about-us/.

28. Lykens Valley, "Massacre of the Conestoga Indians, 1763 (2)," https://www.lykensvalley.org/massacre-of-the-connestoga-indians-1763-2/.

29. Benjamin Rush, "A Plan for the Establishment of Public Schools and the Diffusion of Knowledge in Pennsylvania; to Which Are Added, Thoughts upon the Mode of Education, Proper in a Republic" (1786), 14, 27, https://quod.lib.umich.edu/e/evans/N15652.0001.001?rgn=main;view=fulltext.

30. Benjamin Rush, "A Plan," 15.

31. Benjamin Rush, "A Plan," 17.

32. See, for example, Gateway Academy in Florida, https://christianmilitaryschool .org/.

33. Barna Group. "What Parents Look for in Christian Schools," Aug. 22, 2017, accessed Nov. 30, 2023, https://www.barna.com/research/parents-look-christian -schools/.

34. Daniel L. Philippe, Claudia M. Hernandez-Melis, Pamela Fenning, Katie N. B. Sears, Emily M. McDonough, E. Lawrence, and M. Boyle, "A Content Analysis of Catholic School Written Discipline Policies," *Journal of Catholic Education*, 21, no. 1 (2017), http://dx.doi.org/10.15365/ joce.2101022017.

Chapter 3

The First Agro-Industrial Revolution

Change in the Third Lifetime (1790–1870)

> Gentlemen: I take the liberty to address you upon a subject in which I feel great interest, as it is one with which I know the welfare and happiness of our country to be intimately connected. It relates to the blessings of education.
>
> —General Andrew Jackson[1]

Let us consider that in 1790, the year the last former British colony of the original thirteen colonies ratified the United States Constitution, a girl was born into slavery in Virginia. In Virginia, as in all the slave states, it was a crime, under penalty of twenty lashings, for anyone to confer the blessings of education upon her or her brother, father, or mother. In her lifetime, however, she would experience astounding, disorienting, and emancipating changes. The American population would explode to ten times its size, from four million people in 1790 to forty million by 1870—greater than the population of Great Britain (31.4 million).[2] This predominately rural, agrarian American population would grow at an astonishing rate of 35 percent increase per decade. Immigration accounted for one in four of the increase, nearly all from Europe. In fulfillment of President James Madison's prophecy of Manifest Destiny, the United States' western boundary would thrust another 2,100 miles to the Pacific Ocean. During this same period, the land size of the United States more than tripled to three million square miles. Twenty-four more states were added to the original thirteen. Throughout this period of unprecedented expansion, half the population remained under twenty years of age. If ever a situation called for the establishment of a free, universal education to preserve the republic, surely this period of astounding transformation in America in the early to mid-nineteenth century would be it. Yet it took decades for states to act. By the time they all did, young Americans would fight, maim, kill, and die in a total of five foreign wars, forty domestic wars against American Indian tribes, and one cataclysmic civil war between the Northern and Southern states.

Notwithstanding the purported necessity of education for the survival of democracy, as articulated by Jefferson and Rush, the U.S. Constitution made no mention of education, thereby leaving such matters to the states under the Tenth Amendment.[3] President Andrew Jackson held the popular anti-Federalist position that the federal government should be small and frugal. Federal funds should not be used for "internal improvements" that are not national in character. Even then, he stated,

> if the money can be collected and applied by those more simple and economical political machines, the State governments, it will unquestionably be safer and better for the people than to add to the splendor, the patronage, and the power of the General Government.[4]

Yet, of the original thirteen states' constitutions, only five contained education clauses. Moreover, while provisions for education may have been written into a state's constitution, enacting legislation to organize and fund it was an entirely different matter. Instead, in the early 1800s, it was left up to charities, sectarian churches, or local towns to establish and operate schools, or to parents to provide private tutors or pay for "subscription schools." From a state politician's point of view, a private market, laissez-faire approach to education made an enormous amount of logistical and political sense. In 1790, the country was 95 percent rural, with a population density of only 4.5 people per square mile. Even New York City, the largest urban center, had only 33,131 people.[5] Although explosive U.S. population growth followed, the territory available for settlement *also* expanded, thus keeping the population density low and predominantly rural. Under these conditions, the efficient management of many dispersed one-room schoolhouses from a central authority was difficult, if not impossible.

The other obstacle to state involvement involved different lines of partisan attacks against public schools. Many taxpayers objected to paying for the education of someone else's children. Moreover, having just waged a war of independence from a remote and oppressive governing regime in Great Britain, the prevailing mood, as articulated by Jackson, was to be distrustful of a too-powerful central government that could lead to a loss of their liberty. Yet another force of opposition to state-funded education came from some religious sects whose members looked upon education as a form of "worldliness." To acquire knowledge was to "turn worldly"—an evil to be avoided.[6] Other, more aristocratic-minded opponents warned against education for everyone, fearing it would incite discontent and even foment revolution. The landed gentry worried that education for the masses would give ordinary workers exalted images of themselves, raising their expectations for life to the extent that they would not want to do manual farm labor.

Considering the conditions of some of these schools and the unruly behavior of many of the older students, such objections to public education could be considered overblown. The preponderance of schools were one-room schoolhouses taught by a single teacher who had to teach children of different ages and ability levels at the same time. Essayist and revolutionary soldier Robert Coram wrote in 1791 about the condition of country schools:

> The country schools through most of the United States, whether we consider the buildings, the teachers, or the regulations, are in every respect completely despicable, wretched, and contemptible. The buildings are in general sorry hovels, neither wind tight nor watertight, a few stools serving in the double capacity of bench and desk and the old leaves of copy books making a miserable substitute for glass windows. . . . The teachers are generally foreigners, shamefully deficient in every qualification necessary to convey instruction to youth and not seldom addicted to gross vices.[7]

And yet, despite these objections, a palpable sense existed that education, however poor its current condition might be, was of value to the individual, a "blessing" in its own right that all should have. The blessings here refer to basic education: the ability to read, write, count, and calculate.

If the American mood was strongly opposed to centralized control, it was also strongly anti-aristocratic with powerful egalitarian sentiments. It favored giving people an equal chance to make their way in life, free to pursue their ambitions and happiness. This sense of fairness, to provide every American child an equal opportunity, the princes as well as the paupers, was the heart of the Common Free School Movement. (It must be noted, however, that in practice, "every" American child did not include Black or American Indian children.)

THE FREE COMMON SCHOOL ARCHETYPE— EQUALIZING THE "BLESSINGS" OF EDUCATION FOR ALL

Pennsylvania was an early leader in the Common School Movement. In 1790, it was the most populous northern state, with some 424,000 citizens. At its second Constitutional Convention that same year, Pennsylvania delegates adopted language that theoretically provided the legal basis to provide state-funded education to the poor: "Section 1: The legislature shall as soon as convenient may be, provide by law for the establishment of schools through-out the state, in such a manner, that the poor may be taught gratis."[8]

Subsequent legislation enacted by the Pennsylvania legislature, known as the Pauper Education Acts of 1802, 1804, and 1809, was intended to implement this constitutional provision. To receive aid, a teacher had to document the income levels of their students' parents. For reasons that would soon become apparent, this scheme proved to be unworkable. Record-keeping was abysmal. But the biggest impediment was the very idea itself. To receive aid, a family had to prove their poverty and, in so doing, suffer public humiliation. And there were many poor people.

Continued attempts to broaden Pennsylvania's support of education gave rise to the Act of 1824, which provided three years of free public education to *all*. This Act's passage caused a forceful backlash against state taxation and state intrusion into local control of schools. By 1826, the Act providing free education to all was repealed, and, with it, the reversion to the Pauper Acts. According to the nineteenth-century historian James Pyle Wickersham,

> There was not a governor's message from 1790 to 1834 in which the question was not brought forward—not a session of the Legislature in which opposing forces did not appear in battle array if not actually come to blows—not a year in which people did not agitate the subject in public meeting, or by means of articles in newspapers or petitions to the Legislature.[9,10]

The 1830 U.S. census indicated that nearly half of Pennsylvania's 400,000 children attended no school. Yet another attempt was made by Pennsylvania State Senator Samuel Breck and Governor George Wolf to pass the Free Public School Act of 1834, which provided matching state funds to townships for education, only to again be threatened with repeal in the House. Thirty-eight counties out of fifty-one sent petitions asking for an outright repeal of the law. In what many consider to be one of the greatest speeches ever given in the Pennsylvania legislature, State Representative Thaddeus Stevens rose to the bill's defense and concluded his speech with these stirring words:

> Sir, I trust that when we come to act on this question, we shall take lofty ground—look beyond the narrow space which now circumscribes our vision—beyond the passing, fleeting point of time on which we stand—and so cast our votes that the blessing of education shall be conferred on every son of Pennsylvania—shall be carried home to the poorest child of the poorest inhabitants in the meanest hut of your mountains, so that even he may be prepared to act well his part in this land of free men, and lay on earth a broad and solid foundation for the enduring knowledge which goes on increasing through eternity.[11]

The Free Public School Act of 1834 was upheld, but many bitterly opposed it.[12] Out of 987 school districts in Pennsylvania, 485 refused to enforce it, and those districts that refused contained the largest number of people and wealth. The struggle in Pennsylvania to ensure local schools were provided with the resources, organization, and personnel to educate all children continued for the next four decades with new and improved legislation and better administrative organization and implementation. In 1874, the Pennsylvania Constitution was again amended to declare unequivocally that education for all was a state responsibility:

> The General Assembly shall provide for the maintenance and support of a thorough and efficient system of public schools, wherein all the children of the Commonwealth above the age of six may be educated, and shall appropriate at least one million dollars each year for that purpose.[13]

Finally, the "blessings" of education became available to all children as well as compulsory.

Pennsylvania was only one of many states that were a part of the Common School Movement. The story of the Common School Movement and its opposition played out in all northern and midwestern states, each with their respective champions such as Horace Mann and James Carter in Massachusetts, John Pierce in Michigan, Calvin Stowe and Samuel Lewis in Ohio, Victor M. Rice in New York, and Henry Barnard in Connecticut.[14] But despite all this effort, by 1860, 40 percent of White children were still not enrolled in school.[15] Those who were enrolled attended on average only seventy-eight days per year.[16] Only 2 percent graduated high school.[17] Meanwhile, the national influx of some 7.6 million immigrants during the thirty years from 1820 to 1850, and the sheer mass of uneducated youth under twenty years of age, overpowered the opposition to universal and free schools.

By 1850, the different but convergent arguments of Jefferson and Rush were too compelling to ignore. Jeffersonian democracy presumed a certain level of literacy to be able to read the press. Rush's fear of mobs of ungovernable animals loomed as new generations of youth born in the United States and emigrating from other countries needed to be "homogenized."

We consider the Common School Movement a separate education archetype, not merely a fulfillment of the archetypical aims of Jefferson or Rush, because the purpose of education was to confer a *personal* blessing, a tangible individual right inherent in the promise of America. It was based on the belief that there can be no freedom if a person is bound by the chain of ignorance and no pursuit of happiness if a person is illiterate. Unfortunately, as we will discuss in more detail in chapter 8, the blessings of education would not be conferred to Black and American Indian children who had yet to be recognized as having human status equal to those Whites.

Modern Manifestations of the Blessings for All Archetype

While the Common School Movement was largely concerned with state funding to support equalized educational opportunities for students, the spirit of the Blessings for All archetype goes beyond equitable funding issues or schemes to ensure equal "opportunity to learn." Such things would have no real effect on children if adults in schools did not display the same blessings for all *values* in dealing with their students. One can find the embodiment of this archetype in the Coalition for Essential Schools (CES), founded in 1984 by the late Ted Sizer of Brown University. The CES core values state that a school's goals should apply to *all* students and its practices should be "tailor-made to meet the needs of every group or class of students." Teaching and learning should be personalized to the greatest extent possible. The tenth CES value principle goes to the heart of the Blessings for All archetype:

> The school should demonstrate non-discriminatory and inclusive policies, practices, and pedagogies. It should model democratic practices that involve all who are directly affected by the school. The school should honor diversity and build on the strength of its communities, deliberately and explicitly challenging all forms of inequity.[18]

In the twenty-first century, there are some 600 Coalition of Essential Schools in forty-one states and five countries, with an enrollment of about 250,000 students.

The blessings for all archetype would be followed by yet another new purpose of education that would emerge from the cataclysmic changes caused by the Civil War.

THE HAMPTON ARCHETYPE—EDUCATION
FOR VICTIMS OF SLAVERY AND CRUELTY

On September 17, 1861, under a large oak tree near the little town of Hampton, Virginia, near the end of the Chesapeake Bay, a remarkable event occurred. Mary Peake, a "free Negro," was teaching a group of twenty slaves. This scene was remarkable because teaching slaves in Virginia was against the law, as it was in many other southern states. According to the Virginia Code of 1831, all meetings of free negroes or mulattoes, at any schoolhouse, church, meeting house or other place for teaching them reading or writing, either in the day or night, under whatsoever pretext, shall be deemed and considered as an unlawful assembly; and any justice of the county . . . [may] inflict corporal punishment on the offender or offenders . . . not exceeding twenty lashes.[19]

But there, under that big old tree in broad daylight, Mary Peake was teaching slaves. In 1861, Virginia had 491,000 slaves, the most of any state, or about one slave for every two Whites. After the outbreak of the Civil War, the Union Army, under the command of Major General Benjamin Butler, seized control of Fort Monroe in Hampton, Virginia, at the tip of a peninsula about seventy-seven miles southeast of Richmond. Upon seizing control, General Butler declared that any escaping slaves would be considered "contraband of war" and not returned to their slaveholders. This declaration prompted slaves from Virginia and Maryland to rush to Fort Monroe and freedom. The "Grand Contraband Camp" was built several miles outside of Fort Monroe, and it was there that Mary Peake began to teach these newly freed slaves.[20]

If our young slave girl born in 1790 in Virginia had lived into her seventies, she might have witnessed her grandchild or perhaps her great-grandchild among Mary Peake's students. Peake died a year later, but General Butler, who would later serve in the U.S. Congress along with Pennsylvania's Thaddeus Stevens as one of the Radical Republicans, continued Peake's work by establishing The Butler School for Negro Children. The next year, on January 1, 1863, President Lincoln issued an Executive Order, The Emancipation Proclamation, and in so doing, released more than 3.6 million African American slaves in a single stroke. At the time, nearly 90 percent of all people with African linkage living in America were slaves—a linkage that stretched back 250 years to the earliest settlements in Virginia and Massachusetts. Ninety percent of those slaves were in ten southern states, and nearly all were uneducated due to state-sponsored "compulsory ignorance laws."[21] In 1860, less than 2 percent of all American Blacks were enrolled in school compared to 60 percent of Whites.[22]

In 1868, Brigadier General Samuel Armstrong opened the Hampton Normal and Agricultural Institute adjacent to the Butler School for teacher training. The educational aim of this new institute was,

> to train selected Negro youth who should go out and teach and lead their people first by example, by getting land and homes; to give them not a dollar that they could earn for themselves; to teach respect for labor, to replace stupid drudgery with skilled hands, and in this way to build up an industrial system for the sake not only of self-support and intelligent labor, but also for the sake of character.[23]

The Hampton Institute was designed to promote self-reliance by having students work in various jobs throughout the growing campus to pay for their education. Emphasizing practical skills in trades, the Institute required students to devote eight hours per day to the study of a trade for three years followed by a fourth year of academic courses. By training "selected Negro youth" to teach, Hampton also ensured institutional sustainability while creating seeds for the establishment of other educational establishments for former slaves. Booker T. Washington, for example, one of Hampton's most famous graduates, would later help establish the Tuskegee Institute in Alabama in 1881.

Modern Manifestations of the Hampton Archetype

The courage of Mary Peake to teach groups of fugitive slaves in the middle of the Civil War in Hampton, Virginia, sees its modern manifestation in Hampton University, which evolved from the Butler School for Negro Children to become a modern university with an enrollment of 5,400 students, 91 percent of whom are African American. The Hampton archetype represents an aim of education devoted to the personal, social, and economic amelioration of historically excluded and neglected populations through practical, wage-enhancing skills. It is manifested in the network of 105 Historically Black Colleges and Universities (HBCUs) and Tribal Colleges and Universities (TCUs). Within the Hampton Archetype are also the many modern institutions dedicated to serving students with special needs, that is, those children who are migrant, homeless, or in foster care; children with disabilities, mental health conditions, learning disabilities, and substance use disorders; and children impacted by the justice system and cast to the margins.

MORE CHANGES IN THE THIRD LIFETIME

As if a ten-fold increase in population, a tripling of the land size of the United States, the near genocide of American Indians, a catastrophic Civil War, and the emancipation of 3.6 million slaves were not enough change, our Virginia slave girl born in 1790 would have also seen the rise in America of the first great agriculture and industrial revolution. In the context of this agro-industrial revolution, we see the emergence of yet another new educational archetype—education aimed at state economic development through studies of new agricultural, mechanical, and military technologies.

In the first eighty years after the ratification of its Constitution in 1790, the United States underwent profound technological transformations. A rapid-fire series of inventions and innovations in cotton fiber cultivation, clothing manufacturing, food production, building construction, transportation, power and energy, metallurgy, and weaponry had wide-ranging impacts on everyday life. For example, Eli Whitney's invention of the cotton engine or "cotton gin" in 1793 revolutionized southern agriculture. By automating the separation of cotton seed from its fibers, the cotton gin made it feasible to grow cotton as far west as Texas. More cotton to harvest meant more demand for slave labor. In Mississippi and Alabama, the states with the largest production of cotton, the number of slaves in those states skyrocketed from 80,263 in 1820 to 871,711 by 1860. Within a lifetime, cotton production soared from 3,135 bales in 1790 to 4.5 *million* bales in 1861.[24]

In the early 1800s, New England's Samuel Slater and later Francis Cabot Lowell imported English textile technologies such as the spinning jenny, spinning mule, and power loom to build textile mills in New England. By the start of the Civil War, the U.S. textile industry had grown to 1,091 mills, with more than half located in New England. With over 5 *million* spindles, the textile industry was processing a quarter of all U.S. cotton production.[25]

Advances in agricultural technology, such as McCormick's reaping machine in 1831 and John Deere's steel plow invented in 1837, greatly increased farm productivity. Wheat yield per man hour more than doubled, for example. With food surpluses, American heavy industry could develop and spread. Beginning with Thomas Newcomen's Atmospheric Steam Engine in 1712, which pumped water from mines, advances in steam power led to the development of the steam locomotive. The first engines to pull cargo loads were built and successfully tested in the early 1800s. Chartered in 1827, the Virginia-based Baltimore and Ohio Railroad became the first westward-bound railroad company in America. By the 1830s, the railroad industry had exploded from a mere twenty-three miles of track operated to nearly 53,000 miles by 1870.[26] Almost half of the railroad miles were *west* of the Mississippi. In 1869, after seven years of work, the first American transcontinental railroad was completed, making it possible to move people and heavy freight from California to Chicago and New York in a matter of days, not months.

American patents for agricultural and industrial innovations grew exponentially. In the first decade of the United States' existence (1790–1800), only 268 patents were issued, about twenty-six per year. But by 1870, nearly 72,000 had been issued—more than a thousand per year! Driven by agricultural, rail, and trade expansions,[27] seven Midwestern states experienced phenomenal population growth as settlers and immigrants rushed westward. These seven states—Illinois, Indiana, Iowa, Michigan, Missouri, Ohio, and Wisconsin—accounted for 31 percent of the United States population in 1870, up from just 4 percent in 1810. To put it in perspective, these seven states grew *ten times* faster than the rest of the country, which was already experiencing quadrupling growth.

THE LAND GRANT ARCHETYPE: EDUCATION FOR STATE ECONOMIC DEVELOPMENT VIA STUDIES IN AGRICULTURE, MECHANICAL, AND OTHER TECHNOLOGIES

The great changes wrought by the agricultural and industrial revolution and the strong surge of the U.S. population westward applied tremendous pressure on states to develop and spread technical skills among the masses of workers to promote economic development. The mechanical, agricultural, and applied scientific fields suffered a desperate lack of trained workers. The Iowa state legislature was typical of many states. In 1856, it enacted legislation to establish the State Agricultural College and Model Farm, purchasing 648 acres at a cost of just over $5,379. The Illinois legislature went further. At the urging of the Illinois Industrial League, ironically led by a Yale-educated classics professor and botanist, Jonathan Baldwin Turner, also a devoted Christian missionary and abolitionist, the Illinois legislature adopted a resolution urging its congressional delegation to fund a national system of industrial colleges in every state. This bold initiative had broad support among farmers, who employed nearly half of the U.S. workforce. At the 1852 Farmers Convention, the delegates adopted three declarations for a "common man education bill of rights," which were introduced by Turner:

> *Resolved,* that as representatives of the industrial classes, including *all cultivators of the soil, artisans, mechanics, and merchants,* we desire the same privileges and advantages for ourselves and our posterity in each of our several pursuits and callings, as our professional brethren enjoy in theirs; and we admit that it is our own fault that we did not also enjoy them.

> *Resolved,* that, in our opinion, the institutions originally and primarily designed to meet the wants of the professional classes as such, cannot, in the nature of things, meet ours, any more than the institutions we desire to establish for ourselves meet theirs. Therefore, *Resolved,* that we take immediate measures for the establishment of a university, in the State of Illinois, expressly to meet those felt wants of each and all of the industrial classes of our state.[28]

After ten years of political agitation, a compromise was reached with the representatives of the eastern states. In 1861, U.S. Senator Justin Morrill from Vermont introduced and President Lincoln signed legislation that was, at the time, a revolution in American education: The Morrill Land Grant College Act of 1862. The Morrill Act authorized the federal government to donate 30,000 acres for each U.S. Senator and congressional representative of each state for the endowment, support, and maintenance of at least one college where the leading object shall be, without excluding other scientific and classical studies, and including military tactics, to teach such branches of learning as are related to agriculture and the mechanic arts, in such manner as the legislatures of the States may respectively prescribe, in order to promote the liberal and practical education of the industrial classes in the several pursuits and professions in life.[29]

The rather dry language of the Morrill Act and follow-on legislation does not convey the spirit and almost missionary zeal that its proponents pursued to establish land-grant colleges. Their passion was akin to the earlier Common School Movement. As William Kerr, President of Oregon State Agricultural College, described in his 1910 address,

There is general agreement among the land-grant colleges as to their mission and place in education. . . . (1) They were established as a revolt from the old–type college. The purpose was to provide a new type of institution, occupying a distinctive field as schools of applied science. (2) They were to be colleges and not trade schools. (3) Their work should not be confined to an agricultural one, but should cover the broad field of technical education. (4) They should provide an education that should be liberal as well as practical, training not only for industrial efficiency, but for the truest type of manhood and womanhood, the highest standard of citizenship.[30]

Modern Manifestations of the Land Grant Archetype

The legacy of the college land-grant system has been spectacular. These institutions continue to power both state and national economic strength. Consider Iowa State Agriculture College, the first school to be designated as a land-grant college. In 1872, it had an enrollment of only 100 students, graduating its first class of just twenty-four students. By 2010, the now-named Iowa State University (ISU) had an enrollment of 28,682 students and nearly 218,000 alumni. True to the Land Grant archetype, a major mission of ISU continues to be the economic development of Iowa and the general well-being of its residents. For example, between 1950 and 2023, Iowa was hit by 3,180 tornadoes that resulted in ninety-four fatalities and 2,280 people injured causing close to $3 billion in damages.[31] In keeping with the aim of the land-grant colleges, ISU is home to the world's largest tornado simulator for wind energy research and the highest-resolution immersive virtual reality lab.[32] Joining Iowa State are 111 other land-grant colleges and universities, including eight statewide university systems, located throughout all fifty states and five territories and enrolling about 1.5 million students.[33] A point to note here is that while these are universities and not K-12 schools, they represent an archetype of American education in that they are focused on supporting the growth of a state's economy.

In the next chapter, we begin the story of the fourth lifetime in America and the astounding changes made possible by the tectonic forces unleashed by the Second Industrial Revolution. From these massive changes, two new purposes of education would emerge.

NOTES

1. James Parton, *Life of Andrew Jackson* (New York: Mason Bros., 1860), 826.

2. United Kingdom, Office for National Statistics, "UK Population Estimates 1851 to 2014," (July 6, 2015), https://www.ons.gov.uk/peoplepopulationandcommunity/populationandmigration/populationestimates/adhocs/004356ukpopulationestimates1851to2014.

3. U.S. Constitution, amend. 10. The powers not delegated to the United States by the Constitution, nor prohibited by it to the states, are reserved to the states respectively, or to the people.

4. Andrew Jackson, "Fourth Annual Message," December 4, 1832, http://www.presidency.ucsb.edu/ws/index.php?pid=29474#ixzz1KxreOKkS.

5. Campbell Gibson and Kay Jung, "Historical Census Statistics on Population Totals by Race, 1790 to 1990, and By Hispanic Origin, 1970 to 1990, for Large Cities and Other Urban Places in the United States," Working Paper No. 76 (February 2005): 81, https://www.census.gov/content/dam/Census/library/working-papers/2005/demo/POP-twps0076.pdf.

6. Edmund Cocks, *Early History of the Public School System in Bucks County*, "Doylestown Meeting, May 7, 1938," The Bucks County Historical Society Papers Reads Before the Society and Other Historical Papers, Volume VIII, 21, https://archive.org/stream/buckscountyhisto08buck/buckscountyhisto08buck_djvu.txt.

7. Robert Coram, *Political Inquiries, to Which Is Added a Plan for the Establishment of Schools Throughout the United States* (Wilmington: Andrews and Brynberg, 1791), 94.

8. James Pyle Wickersham, *A History of Education in Pennsylvania* (Lancaster: Inquirer Publishing, 1886), 262.

9. James Pyle Wickersham, "The Fight for Free Schools in Pennsylvania," *The School Journal* 39, no. 12 (June 1891): 499.

10. Another advocate for public education was the Society for the Promotion of Public Schools, formed in Philadelphia in 1827.

11. Lewis R. Harley, "The School System of Pennsylvania: An Historical Review," Education 20, no. 7 (March 1990): 393.

12. James Pyle Wickersham, "The Fight for Free Schools," 502.

13. Pennsylvania Constitution, art. 10, sec. 1.

14. Carl F. Kaestle, *Pillars of the Republic: Common Schools and American Society 1780–1860* (New York: Hill and Wang, 1983).

15. U.S. Census Bureau, "Series H 433-441: School Enrollment Rates Per 100 Population, by Sex and Race: 1850 to 1970," *Historical Statistics of the United States: Colonial Times to 1970* (Census Bureau, 2003), 369–370.

16. U.S. Census Bureau, "Series H 520-530: Public Elementary and Secondary Day Schools—Attendance and Instructional Staff: 1870 to 1970," *Historical Statistics of the United States: Colonial Times to 1970* (Census Bureau, 2003), 375.

17. U.S. Census Bureau, "Series H 598-601: High School Graduates, by Sex: 1870 to 1970," *Historical Statistics of the United States: Colonial Times to 1970* (Census Bureau, 2003), 379.

18. Coalition of Essential Schools, "Common Principles: From 9 to 10," http://essentialschools.org/common-principles-from-9-to-10.

19. "An Act to Amend the Act of Concerning Slaves, Free Negroes and Mulattoes" (April 7, 1831), *Encyclopedia Virginia*, https://encyclopediavirginia.org/entries/an-act-to-amend-the-act-concerning-slaves-free-negroes-and-mulattoes-april-7-1831/.

20. Lewis C. Lockwood, *Mary S. Peake: The Colored Teacher at Fortress Monroe* (Boston, MA: American Tract Society, 1862).

21. Meyer Weinberg, *A Chance to Learn: A History of Race and Education in the United States* (Cambridge: Cambridge University Press, 1977).

22. U.S. Census Bureau, Series H 433-441, 370.

23. "History," Hampton University, accessed April 29, 2023, https://home.hamptonu.edu/about/history/.

24. U.S. Census Bureau, "Series K 550-563: Hay, Cotton, Cottonseed, Shorn Wool, and Tobacco—Acreage, Production, and Price: 1790 to 1970," *Historical Statistics of the United States: Colonial Times to 1970* (Census Bureau, 2003), 518. Production is measured in equivalent 500-pound bales, gross weight.

25. "Textile Industry Meets Demand of Booming US Population," Textile World, October 1, 2005, https://www.textileworld.com/textile-world/textile-news/2005/10/textile-industry-meets-demand-of-booming-us-population/.

26. U.S. Census Bureau, "Series Q 321-328: Railroad Mileage and Equipment: 1830 to 1890," *Historical Statistics of the United States: Colonial Times to 1970* (Census Bureau, 2003), 731.

27. Guy Stevens Callender, *Selections from the Economic History of the United States 1765–1860* (Ginn and Co., 1909; See Chapter 7: *The Rise of Internal Commerce*, 271–344).

28. William Jasper Kerr, *The Spirit of the Land-Grant Institutions* (Association of Land-Grant Colleges and Universities, 1931), 10.

29. Morrill Act (1862), National Archives, https://www.archives.gov/milestone-documents/morrill-act.

30. William Jasper Kerr, "Some Land Grant Problems: Proceedings of the Twenty-Four Annual Convention of the Association of American Agricultural Colleges and Experiment Stations, Washington, D.C. November 16–18," (1910): 51.

31. "Tornado Archive: A History of Twisters: Tornadoes in Iowa since 1950 as of 2023," Des Moines Register, accessed May 8, 2023, https://datacentral.desmoinesregister.com/tornado-archive.

32. Iowa State University, "Fact Book 2010–2011," http://www.iastate.edu/about/fact/fact2011.pdf.

33. "National Education Association Research Land Grant University Brief No. 1: Land Grant Institutions: An Overview" (2022), https://www.nea.org/sites/default/files/2022-03/Land%20Grant%20Institutions%20-%20An%20Overview.pdf.

The Second Industrial Revolution

Change in the Fourth Lifetime (1870–1945)

To invite labor leaders affiliated with the American Federation of Labor to become members of the Society [for the Promotion of Industrial Education] would be tantamount to inviting the devil and all his imps to participate in a movement for the promotion of the Christian Religion!

—H. E. Miles, Chairman, at the Twenty-First
Annual Convention of the National Association of
Manufacturers, New York City, May 15, 1916

A young boy born in Nebraska after the end of the Civil War would experience tectonic changes over the course of his life, the fourth consecutive lifetime in the American saga. The term "tectonic," referring to the deep underground forces that move continents and oceans, seems an apt term for the magnitude of the social, economic, scientific, technological, and geopolitical changes experienced by this post-Civil War generation. This boy's peers would be the great-grandparents of today's baby boomers. This generation becomes more personal for us as old family stories often include their adventures, misadventures, struggles, and achievements. They lived in tumultuous times through wrenching, disorienting changes in the American landscape and cityscape.

We present here only the barest outlines of this momentous period, but perhaps sufficient to provide some context for the emergence of two new and different aims of education. In this chapter, we focus primarily on the arduous emergence of industrial education as a new purpose of education. We end the chapter with a short story on the emergence of another purpose, as exemplified in the Modern School Movement.

During our country's fourth lifetime, the U.S. population tripled from nearly forty million in 1870 to 123 million by 1930,[1] surpassing any

European country, including the USSR. The U.S. population grew to be greater than the combined populations of Great Britain, France, and Spain, the once great powers of the colonial era.[2] Geographically, the United States rapidly consolidated its hold on North America. Purchasing Alaskan territory from Russia in 1867 suddenly added more land to the United States than the next three largest states, Texas, California, and Montana *combined*.[3] By 1912, all the remaining contiguous continental territories were granted statehood, adding another eleven states to the union.[4] After 300 years of warfare and disease, the last of the American Indians were dispersed to remote areas west of the Mississippi. These reservations represented about 2.4 percent of the total U.S. landmass and were controlled by the U.S. Bureau of Indian Affairs. The country now laid uncontested claim to a vast expanse of North American land. Protected by two oceans on its eastern and western borders and buffered by its economically and militarily weaker Canadian and Mexican neighbors on its northern and southern borders, this surging American population was able to exploit its immense resources without fear of external or internal threats to its existence. Despite a devastating Civil War, by the end of the Spanish-American War in 1898, the United States had become the dominant hemispheric power. And by the end of World War II, the United States had

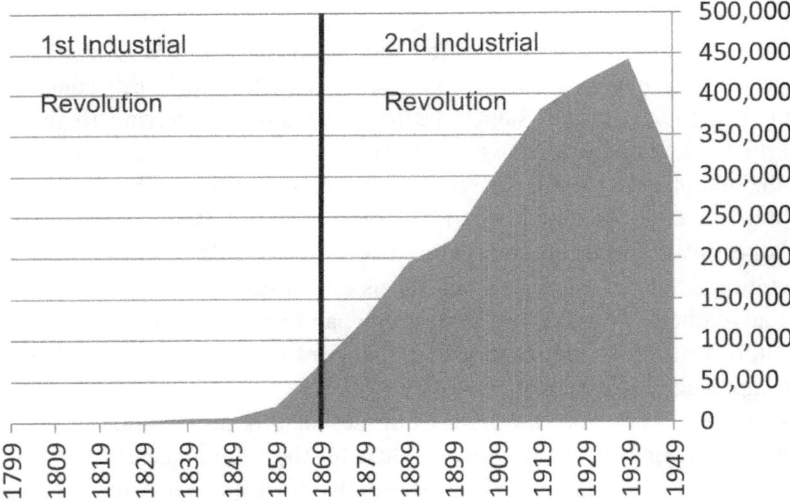

Figure 4.1   Number of U.S. Patents Issued by Decade, 1799–1949. *Source*: From U.S. Census Bureau, "Series W 96-108: Patent Applications Filed and Patents Issued, by type and by Patentee: 1790 to 1970," Historical Statistics of the United States: Colonial Times to 1970 (Census Bureau, 2003), 958-959).

become the only truly global superpower capable of projecting its military and economic power from Asia to Western Europe to the Middle East.

As significant and substantial as these demographic, geographic, and geopolitical changes were, what made them possible were the forces resulting from the unprecedented advances in science, technology, engineering, mathematics (STEM), and capitalism—The Second Industrial Revolution.[5] Whereas the First Industrial Revolution produced technologies in steam power, textile manufacturing, and iron production, the Second Revolution was far more extensive in the sheer number and diversity of stunningly new and powerful, life-changing technologies. One indication of the difference between the two revolutions is revealed in the number of U.S. patents granted, as shown in figure 4.1. In the eighty years from 1790 to 1869, the United States granted 108,485 utility patents (inventions). During the next eighty years, from 1870 to 1949, nearly 2.4 *million* patents were granted by the United States.[6]

By 1915, the United States had become the undisputed leader in innovation and industry. Worldwide, from 1883 to 1915, the number of patents granted was over three million, with the U.S. accounting for almost one-third.[7]

Four features were striking about this explosion in innovations. First, basic science and mathematics led to many new inventions. In turn, these new technologies had a reciprocal effect on expanding basic scientific inquiry. For example, Nobel laureate Wilhelm Roentgen's discovery of X-rays in 1895 led to new imaging technologies, which in turn allowed visualizations of such things as tumors, fractures, and bullet wounds.[8]

A second feature of this era of innovation was the collaborative research culture facilitated by national and transatlantic communications and conventions, which increased the speed at which new scientific discoveries and technologies became known. Contrary to the popular myth of the lonely genius inventor, inventors built upon the past work of others and had many contemporary collaborators. Thomas Edison, the iconic wizard of Menlo Park and the third most prolific inventor in obtaining patents, for example, had a research laboratory the size of two city blocks filled with a large research staff.[9]

A third feature is how innovations in one field enabled innovations in a *different* field. For example, it took nearly all of the nineteenth century to develop a commercially viable, petrol-based internal combustion engine, an effort undertaken by many inventors from different countries.[10] This progress, in turn, enabled the Wright brothers to commission their machinists to custom-build an engine that could fit onto their new airplane design. In 1903, their airplane made its first successful test flight on the Outer Banks of North Carolina at Kitty Hawk.[11] Historian Vaclav Smil called this period the "Age of Synergy,"[12] using a term from the Greek meaning "working together."

A fourth feature is how quickly new scientific advances and technologies were converted into burgeoning new industries, often by the innovators themselves. Many companies bear their names to this day: Friedrich Bayer, George Westinghouse, Nikola Tesla, Alexander Bell, Gottlieb Daimler, Karl Benz, Rudolf Diesel, and Henry Ford.

AGRO-INDUSTRIALISM

The frenetic pace of Western-led scientific, technological, and engineering advances powered by a capitalist economy led to massive and dislocating changes at every level of society. The scale of the unfathomable horrors of World Wars I and II would not have been possible without these new technologies. Nonetheless, Smil makes the case that much good was derived from these scientific advances that benefited billions of people. He argues that perhaps the single biggest benefit was the industrial-scale synthesis of ammonia.[13] The reason is nitrogen. Without nitrogen, plants cannot grow, and grazing livestock cannot eat. Nitrogen is an abundant gas, comprising 78 percent of the Earth's atmosphere, but unlike oxygen and carbon dioxide, plants cannot use nitrogen in its gaseous form. They must get it from the soil, where it is chemically bonded with other elements, hence the search for both naturally occurring nitrogen in the ground and synthesized nitrogen to use as fertilizer. The world's first commercial nitrogen fertilizer, sodium nitrate, was mined in Chile and imported to the United States and Europe starting in 1830. Then, in 1909, Fritz Haber and Carl Bosch from Germany developed a breakthrough method of converting nitrogen gas to synthesized ammonia, a compound containing reactive nitrogen, and commercializing it on an industrial scale. During the Second Industrial Revolution, the use of commercial fertilizers on U.S. farmland rose dramatically. By one estimate, the Haber-Bosch process had enabled 48 percent of the world's population to be fed by 2008.[14]

Another boon for farmers was mechanization. Our Nebraska boy grew up on a farm that used horses and mules to pull an array of farm machinery: gang and sully plows, disks, harrows, planters, cultivators, mowing machines, combines, and reapers. In 1910, there were more than twenty-four million horses and mules providing animal power. But what made farm productivity soar was the replacement of animal power with *mechanized p*ower. Beginning in the first decade of the twentieth century, the use of farm tractors, trucks, grain combines, corn pickers, and milk machines skyrocketed.[15] As our Nebraskan lad was reaching his mid-forties, he and his fellow farmers would have seen the sales of farm tractors climb from one thousand in 1910 to nearly *one million* by 1930 and *3.4 million* by 1950.[16] The rise of agricultural science and mechanized farming resulted in far more food being produced with far less labor.[17] Whereas in 1800, it took 373 worker-hours to produce 100 bushels of wheat, by 1945, it took only 67 hours.[18] With greater farm productivity, the number of people living on a farm fell sharply, so that by 1950, only one in seven people lived on farms[19] (in 2022, less than 1 percent of the workforce was devoted to farming).

THE URBANIZATION OF WORK

While this Second Agro-Industrial Revolution[20] may have resulted in a loss of farm jobs, a host of new jobs were being created in the burgeoning industrial sectors of manufacturing, transportation, energy, and communications. Consider the innovations in steel production. George Bessemer, an Englishman, patented a process in 1855 for making better steel at less cost. His innovation was soon followed by Carl Wilhelm Siemens, a German-born engineer, who teamed up with the French engineer Pierre-Émile Martin in 1865 to design a process to rapidly produce large quantities of steel. In the United States with vast tracts of open land and a growing population, there was a nation to build. Steel was the way to do it. Steel production grew exponentially from a mere 15,000 short tons per year in 1865 to nearly eighty *million* short tons per year by 1945.[21] (A short ton equals 2,000 pounds). Cheap steel enabled more railroad tracks to be laid, so more locomotives and freight cars could ship cargo. In just thirty-five years, the amount of rail tracks laid and operating across the United States climbed from just under 53,000 miles in 1870 to nearly six times that number by 1915.

At the same time, another new invention appeared—the truck. In a mere twenty years, truck registrations soared from just 700 in 1900 to over *1.1 million* by 1920. Another innovation, refrigerated rail and truck freight, made it possible to ship large amounts of meat, produce, and grains to growing urban markets.[22]

Although masses of people moved from farms to cities (as shown in figure 4.2), more factory workers were needed. Millions of Europeans migrated to the United States to work.[23] Chicago, for example, increased its population from just under 300,000 people in 1870 to more than 3.6 million by 1950—a twelve-fold increase. Detroit, home of automobile production, grew at a rate *twice* that of Chicago, from about 80,000 in 1870 to 1.8 million people.[24] By 1950, Chicago and Detroit ranked second and fifth among all U.S. cities, respectively.

From these ground-shifting changes in social and economic life, two new aims of U.S. education emerged.

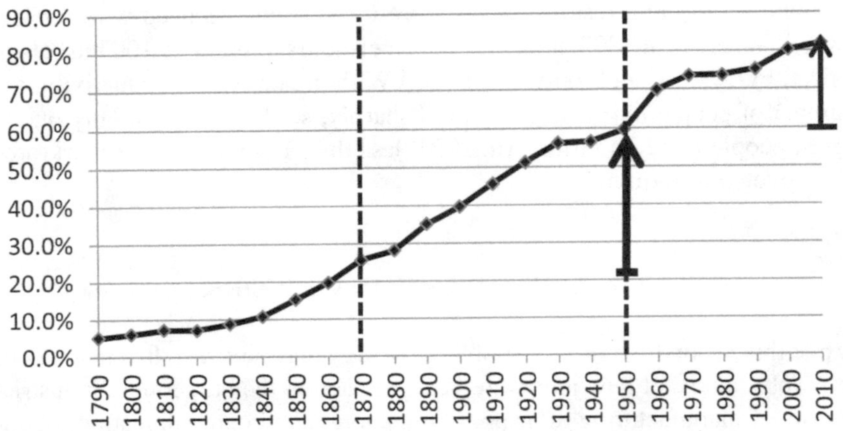

Figure 4.2 Percent of Urban Population in the United States. *Source*: From U.S. Census Bureau.

THE NEW YORK TRADE SCHOOL ARCHETYPE: INDUSTRIAL EDUCATION (VOCATIONAL TRAINING)

While there had always been skilled artisans in colonial America, for example, soap makers, tanners, potters, and bricklayers, the advent of the Industrial Revolution greatly expanded the diversity and magnitude of manufacturing.[25] Shortly before he died in 1872, Horace Greeley, a famed New York City journalist, editorialist, and U.S. presidential candidate, published a mammoth 1,300-page historical summary of the origin and growth of 155 of the chief "industrial arts" of the United States, everything from shipbuilding to curtain fixtures and railroad cars to ladies boots.[26] The 1870 U.S. Census recorded statistics on 274 mechanical and manufacturing industries.[27] More than two million workers were employed in some type of industrial production. There was just one problem—where to find skilled labor, particularly in the aftermath of an estimated loss of as much as 851,000 deaths from the U.S. Civil War.[28]

The colonial apprenticeship system was modeled after the old English apprenticeship system, which had been in place for hundreds of years. The *Statute of Artificers of 1563* consolidated prior English labor laws that compelled youth by *force of law* to be bound to a master. Justices of the peace were given power to apprentice not only the children of paupers and vagrants but also the children of large families, who it was thought would eventually become a burden to the state.[29] From the viewpoint of the English monarchy, mandatory apprenticeship ensured a quantity of workers for goods and services that otherwise would have been absent. The guild members of a particular craft also had a self-interest in these apprenticeship regulations because it had the effect of limiting the labor pool, thereby providing a wage floor for themselves. More importantly, trade guilds were a guard against fraud and shoddy workmanship practiced by the more irresponsible artisans. The guilds were originally formed to protect their members against unskilled and dishonest labor.[30]

In the pre-revolutionary American colonies, apprenticeship laws likewise bound youth to a four-to-seven-year period of servitude under a master with no escape clause and minimal pay, if any. In return, a master was to assume responsibility for the instruction, care, and feeding of their youthful charges, including housing and even religious instruction.[31] However, the revolutionary spirit of the United States, with its emphasis on freedom and equality of opportunity, along with the later adoption of the Thirteenth Amendment to the Constitution barring involuntary servitude, provided a countervailing force to the use of the Old-World apprenticeship model.

The apprenticeship model also proved impractical for an industrial era.[32] New inventions and processes required workers to have the know-how to operate the factories. Like the craft guilds, skilled industrial workers sought to protect their status by organizing into trade unions, which ensured quality workmanship. In addition, through collective bargaining, unions could negotiate better terms for their employment, e.g., reducing their workday from twelve to ten hours (New York City printers were the first to go on strike in 1794).[33] Thus, paralleling the spectacular rise of nineteenth-century U.S. industrialism was the rise of organized labor—industrial sector by industrial sector, city by city, state by state. By the mid-1800s, many trades had organized at the state and national levels, for example, typographers,[34] stone cutters,[35] and cigar makers.[36] But it was not until the advent of the Second Industrial Revolution that attempts were made to organize different trade groups under a single national labor union.

Membership in the first national union group, the Knights of Labor founded in 1869, grew to nearly one million by 1886.[37] In 1881, the Federation of Organized Trades and Labor Unions of the United States and Canada, a rival to the Knights, was founded in Pittsburgh, where it adopted fourteen organizing resolutions. One resolution advocated forbidding the employment of children under the age of fourteen in any capacity under the penalty of a fine and imprisonment. Another resolution stated that if an employer were to use apprentices for any mechanical trade, then those apprentices had to be employed for at least three years and be provided training to become a fully skilled workman.[38] This latter demand was a nonstarter among business owners. In an 1886 article, Colonel Richard T. Auchmuty, a New York City philanthropist, architect, and civil war veteran, summed up the dilemma for business in the use of apprentices.

This theory [of apprenticeship] fixes a certain amount of responsibility upon
the employer, which he is not always willing to incur. Businesses may increase
or diminish. At one time many workers may be wanted: and other times few
or none. If lads are employed with the understanding that at the expiration of
a certain time they are to be converted to skilled workmen, there may be time
during the customary four years of service when there will be nothing to do. If
retained, they will be a burden on the employer; if discharged the lad will not
unreasonably feel that an agreement has been broken.[39]

What was an unskilled youth to do? At the time (1880), 99 percent of students were enrolled in grades 1–8. High school enrollment was minuscule.
Out of 1 million seventeen-year-olds, only about 2 percent of them graduated
from high school, public or private. Auchmuty's plan was to fill the needs of
industry by establishing independent trade schools. In 1881, he bought land in
New York City to establish the *New York Trade School*. The New York Trade
School was not the first of its kind in the world. European countries, including Russia, had long-established technical or industrial schools. In 1830, for
example, the Moscow School of Trades and Industries was established, and
trade schools had been established in France even earlier.[40] Even so, in the
United States, the New York Trade School stood out by claiming to be the
first of its kind in America.[41]

Auchmuty's private trade school was a successful model, but alone it
could not fill the need for trained workers. By 1905, only about 7 percent of
all seventeen-year-olds had graduated high school. Despite the addition of
more than 15.5 million immigrants during this period (1870–1905), the vast
majority came to the United States of America as unskilled laborers, domestic
workers, or listed no occupation. In the year 1905, for example, more than
one million immigrants came to the United States, but only about 1 percent
were professional or technical workers, and only 16 percent were craftsmen
or foremen who had been trained in Europe's industrial trade schools.[42] Thus,
immigration alone could not fill the need for technical industrial skills. Public schools were of little help. President Theodore Roosevelt described the
urgent need for a new aim of public education:

For at least a generation we have been waking to the knowledge that there
must be additional education beyond that provided in the public school as
it is managed today. Our school system has hitherto been well-nigh wholly
lacking on the side of industrial training, of the training which fits a man for
the shop and the farm. This is a most serious lack, for no one can look at the
peoples of mankind as they stand at present without realizing that industrial
training is one of the most potent factors in national development. We of the
United States must develop a system under which each individual citizen shall
be trained so as to be effective individually as an economic unit and fit to be

organized with his fellows so that he and they can work in efficient fashion together. This question is vital to our future progress, and public attention should be focused upon it.[43]

The time for Auchmuty's vision of trade schools had arrived; the tipping point had been reached. In 1905, Massachusetts Governor William Douglass appointed a Commission on Industrial and Technical Education to "investigate the needs for education in different grades of skills and responsibility in the various industries of the Commonwealth."[44] The ensuing 680-page report, released a year later, became highly influential. The breadth of the hearings, the statistical data it collected on students', parents', and employers' needs, and its careful analyses were impressive even by today's standards. Here is one of the key findings from the report.

> The Commission was told at almost every hearing that in many industries the processes of manufacture and construction are made more difficult and more expensive by a lack of skilled workmen. . . . Manufacturers confidently believe that a system of industrial education wisely planned would tend to develop such intelligence, while it increased technical skill.[45]

The Massachusetts Commission meticulously documented the need for skilled workers sought by the state's employers. It also documented the absence of industrial education in its public schools and the problems that arose from such an absence. The Commission noted another problem. A great many students were dropping out of school after seventh grade (age 14), the last year of Massachusetts' compulsory schooling, because they were "dissatisfied with school."[46] Yet dropping out of school did not afford the young adolescent a better option. The work these young people could get was typically at the low end of the wage scale due to their lack of training. And the relationship between training levels, age, and weekly wages was dramatic. A fourteen-year-old with only some shop training averaged less than $4 per week, whereas an eighteen-year-old with technical training could command $10 per week. Moreover, this age-wage gap based on training levels continued to widen so that by age twenty-five a young man with technical training could earn *triple* that of another man of the same age without such training.[47] The Commission reported that parents, "bewailed the lack of opportunity for their children to learn a trade"[48] while expressing sympathy that "the parent does not know where to find an occupation for his child."[49] Nor was this problem confined just to the working classes. The Massachusetts Commission found that the middle and upper classes were affected as well. Their children were being raised out of touch with what it meant to work to earn a living.

There is a one-sided sense of values, a one-sided view of life, and a wrong
attitude toward labor. Not having any share in productive labor, and being out
of touch with it, the youth have no standards by which to measure time or pos-
sessions or pleasures in terms of cost. Many persons believe that about this point
centre some of the gravest of present-day social problems.[50]

Here we have stated, in rather stark terms, the twentieth century's first educational crisis. This crisis had seven sides. On one side was the United States
quickly becoming the world's largest economic power, fueled by constant
technological innovation and large-scale public and private capitalization
but increasingly stymied for skilled workers. A second side was the unprecedented increase in agricultural productivity and with it the tectonic shift
away from farm life to big-city urban factories. A third side was the collapse
of the colonial apprenticeship system under the weight of a highly dynamic
national industrial complex. On the fourth side was an insufficient quantity
and quality of skilled workers supplied by either private trade schools or
by the large numbers of new immigrants. On the fifth side were the public
schools that could not keep their dissatisfied and disenchanted students from
dropping out as soon as they turned fourteen years of age.[51] On the sixth side
was a generation of young people who had left school with minimal market-
able skills and few ways to develop them, consigned to performing low-level
work with minimal prospects for future earnings. On the seventh side were
parents, flustered and desperate as they saw their children face a Hobson's
choice of either the factory mill or pauperism.

The aspects of this problem were not unique to Massachusetts. The next
ten years would see a wave of state and national commission reports, studies,
and advocacy papers focusing on the need for industrial education as a critically important aim of twentieth-century education. State commissions on
industrial education were established in Vermont, New Jersey, and Maryland
in 1908; Michigan in 1909; and Maine and Wisconsin in 1910. As Henry C.
Morrison, Connecticut state superintendent, exclaimed in 1908,

> There have been few, if any, of the many movements in the history of American
> education which has taken such a sudden and powerful hold on the mind of the
> progressive element among American businessmen as has the current move-
> ment toward [industrial education]. . . . We are besieged with public documents,
> monographs, magazine articles, reports of investigations too numerous to men-
> tion . . . and the public is urged forthwith to establish new schools, a different
> kind of schools, additional school and so on.[52]

While a consensus was mounting across many states that publicly funded
industrial education had to be undertaken, how to do it was another matter. Soon after the Douglass Commission report was issued, a second

commission was appointed to design and establish an industrial school system for Massachusetts parallel to the existing public school system.[53] In 1909, a New York state report written by Charles R. Richards, professor of Manual Education at Teachers College, Columbia University, concluded, based on carefully gathered statistics, that "there is not *a* problem of industrial education, but a hundred different problems, varying according to the nature of different industries and . . . varying also according to the differing mental, physical and will capacities of boys and girls."[54] In 1912, the City Club of Chicago's Committee on Public Education issued a 314-page report on vocational training in Chicago and elsewhere. This report and others like it shifted the debate from whether industrial (vocational) education should be publicly funded, but what it should be, how it should be organized, and for whom.

At the same time, there was a nationally organized push for the federal government to become involved. In the summer of 1906, Richards and James P. Haney, director of art and manual training for the New York City public schools, led a series of planning meetings to assemble a meeting of some 250 people representing more than twenty states. On November 16, 1906, *The National Society for the Promotion of Industrial Education (NSPIE)* was formed to advocate for federal incentives to dramatically increase vocational education in all states. This organization was a textbook example of careful coalition building and an astute choice of leaders.[55] NSPIE's high-level officers included, Henry S. Pritchett, president of the Massachusetts Institute of Technology (MIT) and later the president of the Carnegie Foundation; M.W. Alexander, superintendent of apprentices at General Electric; and V. Everit Macy, a well-connected New York City industrialist and philanthropist and chair of Columbia University's Board of Trustees. On NSPIE's twenty-seven-member board was a mix of key leaders from business, manufacturing, organized labor, social work, and education.[56] The central idea that animated those who organized the Society for the Promotion of Industrial Education was to "unite the many forces making toward industrial education the country over."[57]

Implementing NSPIE's agenda would be no small feat. Throughout much of the late nineteenth century, capital and labor had been locked in fierce and often violent battles. President Theodore Roosevelt, in his 1906 State of the Union address before Congress, stated as much, explaining:

Records show that during the twenty years from January 1, 1881, to December 31, 1900, there were strikes affecting 117,509 establishments, and 6,105,694 employees were thrown out of employment. During the same period there were 1,005 lockouts, involving nearly 10,000 establishments, throwing over one million people out of employment.[58]

The two heavyweights of industry and labor, the National Association of Manufacturers (NAM) and the 1.7-million-member American Federation of Labor (AFL), had no love for each other. This was NAM's reaction to having the AFL involved:

> To invite labor leaders affiliated with the American Federation of Labor to become members of the Society [for the Promotion of Industrial Education] would be tantamount to inviting the devil and all his imps to participate in a movement for the promotion of the Christian Religion![59]

To build a working coalition to achieve its agenda, NSPIE's leadership used a two-pronged approach. First, they built public awareness of the need for industrial education. This was done through national conferences, symposiums, and a series of bulletins distributed nationally and by state chapters. The second approach was to quietly build coalitions behind the scenes among bitter adversaries by finding common ground. Both NAM and the AFL studied the problem, saw the need for industrial education, and wanted it paid out of public funds.[60 61] The rub was who would control it and define the curriculum. NSPIE hammered out a compromise. Other movements also joined forces with NSPIE, in particular the Progressive Movement, which advocated against the use of child labor.[62] Whatever would keep children in school and out of the factory, the Progressives were for it. As a result, Progressives developed a close relationship with the industrial education movement despite their disdain for the farmers and factory owners who used child labor.[63]

Federal action was slow to come despite the movement's bipartisan support. Of the dozens of bills introduced in Congress from 1906–1914 promoting industrial education, none passed. What finally did the trick was a Congressional resolution passed in January 1914 to authorize the president to appoint a *Commission on National Aid to Vocational Education*. The Commission was chaired by U.S. Senator Hoke Smith from Georgia and his Georgian counterpart in the House, Representative D.M. Hughes. Within six months, the Commission issued its 500-page report, outlining twelve "crying needs" for vocational education and why federal support to states was urgently needed. According to the U.S. Census of 1910, out of a total labor force of about 36 million, two out of every three workers were either engaged in agriculture (12.6 million) or manufacturing (14.3 million). Yet the Commission estimated that only 1 percent of these workers "had or are having at the present time any adequate chance to secure training."[64]

The Commission projected that to simply maintain the number of existing agricultural and industrial workers due to retirements and deaths would require a vocational training enrollment pipeline of upward of three million students. It concluded, "For this great task the facilities and resources of our public schools are entirely inadequate without the help of the larger resources of the National Government."[65] The Commission's report also included specific legislative recommendations and language. By 1917, after World War I made evident the decisive role of mechanized warfare and the indispensable role of a nation's industrial war-making capacity, President Wilson had signed the Smith-Hughes Vocational Education Act of 1917 into law.

Along with the Morrill Land Grant Act of 1862, the Smith-Hughes Vocational Act of 1917 was the second landmark piece of federal legislation that reflected the profound changes due to the Second Industrial Revolution; a new purpose of education was to be established: industrial (vocational) training. Bringing about this new purpose dominated the educational and economic agenda for nearly fifty years from 1870 to 1920. It continues to be a compelling aim of education in the twenty-*first* century.

Modern Manifestations of the New York Trade School Archetype

More than one-hundred years after the Smith-Hughes Act of 1917 was signed into law, vocational education in the United States is pervasive. Vocational education, since renamed "Career and Technical Education,"[66] or CTE, is offered at 88 percent of the approximately 18,000 public high schools in the United States.[67] The National Center for Education Statistics divides courses into three broad categories: academic, CTE, and Enrichment. Ninety-six percent of all public high school graduates enrolled in at least one CTE course. Forty-five percent are enrolled in three or more of any type of CTE course.[68] Twenty-one percent of high school graduates took three or more CTE courses[69] in a single occupational area, making them "occupational concentrators." The average CTE credits earned by high school graduates were slightly over 4.0 credits—more than math (3.67 credits), science (3.34 credits), or social studies (3.98 credits).[70] There are about 1,200 high schools in the United States where the aim is predominantly career and technical education. These CTE schools enroll about 8.6 percent of all public school tenth graders.[71] Moreover, students from all demographic groups are equally represented in CTE course enrollments.[72]

Career and technical education is not limited to K-12 public schools. Career-oriented college degrees are offered at 5,730 two- and four-year postsecondary institutions.[73] Approximately 10.6 million, or two-thirds of all college students, major in some type of career and technical field.[74] More than half major in either business or health care. And what has become of Colonel Auchmuty's New York Trade School? It would later become the world-famous *Voorhees Technical Institute*. Its curriculum was continually updated as technology advanced. In the 1920s, it introduced courses in automotive technology, and in the 1940s, courses in air conditioning and environmental controls. By 1971, Voorhees Technical Institute had trained over 500,000 technicians in its 90-year history. That year, its programs, physical plant, and faculty were merged with the New York City Community College to become the New York City Technical College of the City University of New York.

THE MODERN SCHOOLS ARCHETYPE: ACADEMIC FREEDOM, EDUCATION FOR SOCIAL CHANGE

The exploitative excesses of the industrial era, with its extreme concentration of wealth against masses of the poor, its monopolistic drives, and its anti-democratic tactics, helped spawn the Progressive movement in the areas of politics, law, economics, and education.[75] In education, John Dewey was and perhaps still is the most influential early twentieth-century advocate of a kind of pedagogy that empowers the students as learners. Dewey and other Progressive Era educationalists maintained that curriculum should be grounded in students' experiences and that instruction should value students' voices, thinking, and learning interests. The ultimate goal is to further a more democratic, equitable society. In contrast to the ideology of the traditionalists, with the teacher as authority imparting knowledge as if it were doctrine, progressive educators do not regard students as empty vessels into which teachers pour knowledge, nor are children's minds a tabula rasa, to use John Locke's phrase, a blank slate onto which the teacher inscribes content and how students should think.

A lesser known figure in the progressive education movement than Dewey was Francisco Ferrer, a modern-day martyr from Spain who, in the 1920s, inspired the Modern School Movement. The core educational aims of the Modern Schools archetype were that a school's purpose was not only to educate students about the ideas of social justice, democracy, and freedom, but for the schools and its students to be active agents for their promotion. This meant teachers would be free to teach the truth and for students to seek it. These freedoms require mutual respect and a shared sense of social responsibility. For all to pursue the truth, there can be no gender, racial, ethnic, or socioeconomic class barriers within or outside school. The pedagogy of the Modern Schools aimed to raise awareness of social myths to uncover the structure of power in a capitalist political economy. We use the Modern Schools as an archetype because these schools went further than Dewey's lab school to situate schools as *agents* of external social change. The Modern School movement sought to upend the oppressive social structures within which children lived, not just enable them to better cope with it. As one author explained:

> These Modern Schools, as they were called, differed from other educational experiments of the same period in being schools for children of workers and directed by the workers themselves. Their founders, moreover, were anarchists, whose prophets were Bakunin, Kropotkin, and Tolstoy as well as Rousseau, Pestalozzi, and Froebel, and who sought to abolish all forms of authority, political and economic as well as educational, and to usher in a new society based on the voluntary cooperation of free individuals.[76]

The anarchist influences in the Modern School archetype sit at the extreme end of the progressive education continuum. As such, we choose the Modern Schools as an archetype because it can alert us to when education takes the form of indoctrination that serves the political-corporate power structure at the expense of truth seeking, truth telling, and creativity. The Modern School archetype explicitly values social justice activism in the community. It is not enough to have the freedom to pursue the truth *inside* of school. It is also necessary to learn about and champion these freedoms *outside* of school, to correct social injustices and ameliorate conditions that impinge on the general well-being of society. Thus, the Modern School's archetypical aim involves preparing and inspiring students to be agents of change in promoting the larger public good, informed by critical social, economic, and scientific analyses. Call it service learning with an edge. Developing students' consciousness of social justice is also central to Gloria Ladson-Billings' concept of culturally relevant pedagogy, in which "students must develop a critical consciousness through which they challenge the status quo of the current social order." This aspect of culturally relevant pedagogy is dedicated to empowering communities, not just individuals.

While the last of the Modern Schools closed their doors in 1958,[77] the archetype of academic freedom, self-responsibility, and social justice activism is firmly entrenched in modern collegiate life. To freely pursue the truth by both faculty members and students lies at the very heart of the academy.[78] The 1940 Statement of Principles on Academic Freedom and Tenure remains foundational. Added to this 1940 statement is a more recent Joint Statement on Rights and Freedoms of Students, first formulated in 1967 and later updated in 1992. It has been endorsed by five national sponsors. An excerpt from the preamble to this joint statement is instructive:

> Academic institutions exist for the transmission of knowledge, the pursuit of truth, the development of students, and the general well-being of society. Free inquiry and free expression are indispensable to the attainment of these goals. As members of the academic community, students should be encouraged to

develop the capacity for critical judgment and to engage in a sustained and independent search for truth.[79]

The social justice ethos of the Modern School Movement is manifested in the form of various college-led initiatives that address issues related to health access, legal needs, housing, education, and other community concerns.[80] One example is the Arcus Center for Social Justice Leadership (ACSJL) at Kalamazoo College, established in 2009. The mission of the center is,

> to support the pursuit of human rights and social justice by developing emerging leaders and sustaining existing leaders in the field of human rights and social justice, creating a pivotal role for liberal arts education in engendering a more just world. The ACSJL provides programs and activities that teach and promote social change practices that will enable you to imagine a socially just world and be a part of creating it.

Another example is Arizona State University's Master's Program in Social Justice and Human Rights (SJHR) in its New College of Interdisciplinary Arts and Sciences. The SJHR program invites students to focus on "specific issues in international or domestic contexts, including refugee resettlement, immigration and citizenship, human trafficking, racialized violence, and international human rights law and organizations."[81]

The Modern School archetype can also appear in K-12 schools when social initiatives are led by individual teachers as well as students. An example is Amy Lindahl, a veteran high school biology teacher in Portland, Oregon, who transformed her biology course into an extended investigation of the causes of cancer in the local community and what can be done about it.[82] Yet another example is four middle school girls from Bellport, New York, who started a charitable organization to bring plastic water filtration buckets to Cambodia, where 75 percent of deaths are caused by polluted drinking water.[83]

As the Baby Boom generation came onto the scene circa 1945, inaugurating the fifth lifetime in America, more stunning and unimaginable changes would await. Two new and different aims of education would emerge, the subject of our final chapter in part I.

NOTES

1. U.S. Census Bureau, "Series A 6-8: Annual Population Estimates for the United States: 1790-1970," Historical Statistics of the United States: Colonial Times to 1970 (Census Bureau, 2003), 8.

2. Josef Haliczer, "The Population of Europe, 1720, 1820, 1930. A Paper Read at the International Congress of Geography at Warsaw, August 193," *Geography* 19, no. 4 (1934): 261–273.

3. U.S. Census Bureau, "Series A 210-263: Land Area of the United States, by States and Territories: 1790 to 1970," Historical Statistics of the United States: Colonial Times to 1970 (Census Bureau, 2003), 38.

4. U.S. Census Bureau, "Series A 210-263," 38.

5. Joel Mokyr, "The Second Industrial Revolution 1870-1914" (August 1998), https://faculty.wcas.northwestern.edu/jmokyr/castronovo.pdf.

6. U.S. Patent and Trademark Office (USPTO), "U.S. Patent Activity Calendar Years 1790 to the Present," https://www.uspto.gov/web/offices/ac/ido/oeip/taf/h_counts.htm.

7. World Intellectual Property Organization, "Historical Data Sets Prior to 1980," https://www.wipo.int/ipstats/en/#resources.

8. Timothy J. Jorgensen, *Strange Glow: The Story of Radiation* (Princeton: Princeton University Press, 2016).

9. Thomas Edison Center at Menlo Park, https://www.menloparkmuseum.org/history.

10. Yuliia Berdnychenko and Olha Petrykovets, "Evolution of World and Domestic Production of Internal Combustion Engines," *History of Science and Technology* 9, no. 2 (2019): 139–146, https://doi.org/10.32703/2415-7422-2019-9-2(15)-139-146.

11. Wright Brothers National Memorial, https://www.nps.gov/wrbr/index.htm.

12. Vaclav Smil, *Creating the 20th Century: Technical Innovations of 1867–1914 and their Lasting Impact* (Oxford: Oxford University Press, 2005).

13. Vaclav Smil, *Enriching the Earth: Fritz Haber, Carl Bosch and the Transformation of World Food Production* (Cambridge: MIT Press, 2001).

14. Jan Willem Erisman et al., "How a Century of Ammonia Synthesis Changed the World," *Nature Geoscience* 1 (September 28, 2008): 636–639, https://doi.org/10.1038/ngeo325.

15. William White, "Economic History of Tractors in the United States," https://eh.net/?s=Economic+History+of+Tractors+in+the+United+States.

16. U. S. Census Bureau, "Series K 184-191: Farm Machinery and Equipment: 1910 to 1970," *Historical Statistics of the United States: Colonial Times to 1970* (Census Bureau, 2003), 469.

17. Vanessa Duarte and Soumodip Sarkar, "A Cinderella Story: The Early Evolution of the American Tractor Industry," CEFAGE-UE Working Papers 2009/16, https://ideas.repec.org/p/cfe/wpcefa/2009_16.html.

18. U. S. Census Bureau, "Series K 445-485: Manhours Per Unit and Yield Per Unit of Production of Selected Crops and Livestock to Produce Specific -1970," *Historical Statistics of the United States: Colonial Times to 1970* (Census Bureau, 2003), 500.

19. Leon E. Truesdell, *Farm Population: 1880 to 1950*, U.S. Census Technical Paper #3 (1960).

20. Brian Page and Richard Walker, "From Settlement to Fordism: The Agro-Industrial Revolution in the American Midwest," *Economic Geography* 67, no. 4 (October 1991): 281–315, https://doi.org/10.2307/143975.

21. U. S. Census Bureau, "Series P 231-300: Physical Output of Selected Manufactured Commodities: 1860 to 1970," *Historical Statistics of the United States: Colonial Times to 1970* (Census Bureau, 2003), 690.

22. Mary Yeager Kujovich, "The Refrigerator Car and the Growth of the American Dressed Beef Industry," *Business History Review* 44, no. 4 (1970): 460–482, https://doi:10.2307/3112669.

23. Charles Hirschman and Elizabeth Mogford, "Immigration and the American Industrial Revolution from 1880 to 1920," *Social Science Research* 38, no. 4 (December 2009): 897–920, https://doi.org/10.1016/j.ssresearch.2009.04.001.

24. Campbell Gibson, "Population of the 100 Largest Cities and Other Urban Places in the United States: 1790 to 1990," June 1998. U.S. Census Working Paper Number POP-WP027 (June 1998), https://www.census.gov/library/working-papers/1998/demo/POP-twps0027.html.

25. Virginia Company of London, "A Declaration of the State of the Colonie and Affaires in Virginia, July 22, 1620," https://encyclopediavirginia.org/entries/a-declaration-of-the-state-of-the-colonie-and-affaires-in-virginia-july-22-1620/.

26. For a ground view of the magnitude of the Industrial Revolution's impact on commerce work life, see Horace Greeley et al., *The Great Industries of the United States*, 1872 (1,300 pages).

27. U.S. Census 1870 Table VII B.

28. J. David Hacker, "A Census-based Count of the Civil War Dead," *Civil War History* 57, no. 4 (December 2011): 307–348.

29. Paul H. Douglass, *American Apprenticeship and Industrial Education* (New York: Columbia University, 1921), 26.

30. Olive Jocelyn Dunlop and Richard Douglas Denham, *English Apprenticeship and Child Labor* (New York: Macmillan, 1912), https://quod.lib.umich.edu/g/genpub/AGC2692.0001.001?rgn=main;view=fulltext.

31. Paul H. Douglass, *American Apprenticeship*, 20–21.

32. Daniel Jacoby, "The Transformation of Industrial Apprenticeship in the United States," *The Journal of Economic History* 51, no. 4 (December 1991): 887–910.

33. "A Short History of American Labor," *American Federationist* 88, no. 3 (March 1981), https://oac.cdlib.org/ark:/28722/bk0003z4v2t/?brand=oac4.

34. The International Typographical Union formed in 1850. See "International Typographical Union, Local 2 (Philadelphia, Pa.) Records 1850-1967," Historical Society of Pennsylvania, https://www.portal.hsp.org/finding-aids/international-typographical-union%2C-local-2-%28philadelphia%2C-pa.%29.-record%2C-1850-1967-%28collection-2076%29.

35. The Journeyman Stonecutters Association of North America was formed in 1853.

36. The Cigar Makers National Union of the United States was formed in 1864. See the Cigar Makers' International Union, University of Maryland Archival Collections, https://archives.lib.umd.edu/repositories/2/resources/1659.

37. In 1869, the Noble Order of Knights of Labor was formed by seven Philadelphia garment cutters to be an intensely secret society along the lines of the Masons and Odd Fellows. It initially had no written principles as its code was expressed by

word of mouth. As a result, its membership grew slowly. In 1882, its name and principles were made public, and its membership soared to nearly one million by 1887. Its constitution claimed the Knights to be more than a collection of trade unions as its purpose was loftier: "Any action that will advance the cause of humanity, lighten the burden of toil, or elevate the moral and social condition of mankind, whether incorporated or not, is the proper scope and field of operation of a Local Assembly." See Carroll D. Wright, "An Historical Sketch of the Knights of Labor," The Quarterly Journal of Economics 1, no. 2 (January 1887): 137–168.

38. Stuart Bruce Kaufman, "Birth of a Federation: Mr. Gompers Endeavors Not to Build a Bubble," *Monthly Labor Review* (November 1981), 25, https://www.bls.gov/opub/mlr/1981/11/art4full.pdf.

39. Richard T. Auchmuty, "The Need of Trade Schools," *The Century* (November 1886): 83–92, https://www.unz.com/print/Century-1886nov-00083.

40. Charles A. Bennett, *History of Manual and Industrial Education 1870–1917* (Peoria: The Manual Arts Press, 1937), https://ia800206.us.archive.org/31/items/historyofmanuali00bennrich/historyofmanuali00bennrich.pdf.

41. City University of New York Archives and Special Collections, https://academicworks.cuny.edu/ny_arch/.

42. U. S. Census Bureau, "Series C 120-137: Immigrants, by Major Occupation Group: 1820 to 1970," *Historical Statistics of the United States: Colonial Times to 1970* (Census Bureau, 2003), 110.

43. Theodore Roosevelt, "The Man Who Works with His Hands," address at the Semi-Centennial Celebration of Michigan State Agricultural College (May 31, 1907), 239–240, https://archive.lib.msu.edu/DMC/Sesqui/pdf/sesqui.pdf.

44. Massachusetts Commission on Industrial and Technical Education, *Report of the Commission on Industrial and Technical Education submitted to the Senate and House of Representatives, Massachusetts* (London: Forgotten Books, 2019; New York: Teachers College Press, April 1906), 1, https://babel.hathitrust.org/cgi/pt?id=cool.ark:/13960/t8w95r05k&view=1up&seq=7.

45. Massachusetts Commission on Industrial and Technical Education, *Report*, 4, 5.

46. Massachusetts Commission on Industrial and Technical Education, *Report*, 44.

47. Massachusetts Commission on Industrial and Technical Education, *Report*, 67.

48. Massachusetts Commission on Industrial and Technical Education, *Report*, 37.

49. Massachusetts Commission on Industrial and Technical Education, *Report*, 44.

50. United States Commission on National Aid to Vocational Education, *Report of the Commission on National Aid to Vocational Education Together with the Hearings Held on the Subject, Made Pursuant to the Provisions of Public Resolution No. 16, Sixty-third Congress* (Washington: Government Printing Office, 1914).

51. United States Commission on National Aid to Vocational Education, *Report*.

52. Henry C. Morrison, "Vocational Training and Industrial Education," *Educational Review* 36 (October 1908): 242.

53. Charles A. Bennett, *History,* 515.

54. Charles A. Bennett, *History,* 522.

55. Neville B. Smith, "A Tribute to the Visionaries Prime Movers and Pioneers of Vocational Education, 1892–1917," *Journal of Vocation and Technical Education* (Fall 1999).

56. Carroll D. Wright, "The Work of the National Society for the Promotion of Industrial Education," *Annals of American Academy of Political and Social Science* 33, no. 1 (1909): 12.

57. National Society for the Promotion of Industrial Education, "Bulletin 1: Proceedings of the Organization Meetings" (1907): 7, https://www.google.com/books/edition/_/5I44AQAAMAAJ?hl=en&gbpv=0.

58. President Theodore Roosevelt, State of the Union Address Before the U.S. Congress, 1906, p. 12.

59. Paul H. Douglass, *American Apprenticeship,* 323.

60. American Federation of Labor, Industrial Education: Consisting of an Investigation and Report by a Competent Special Committee; Reports of Officers and Committees; Action of A. F. of L. Convention; the Attitude of Organized Labor and Others Toward the Problem (Washington: American Federation of Labor, 1910).

61. National Association of Manufacturers, Industrial education. Report of the Committee on Industrial Education, H. E. Miles, Chairman, at the Twenty-First Annual Convention of the National Association of Manufacturers, New York City, May 15, 1916 (National Association of Manufacturers, 1916).

62. On the historical relationship between child labor and early industrialization, see Jane Humphries, "Child Labor: Lessons from the Historical Experience of Today's Industrial Economies," *The World Bank Economic Review* 17, no. 2 (2003): 175–196.

63. Sol Cohen, "The Industrial Education Movement 1906–1917," *American Quarterly* 20, no. 1 (Spring 1968): 95–110.

64. United States Commission on National Aid to Vocational Education, "Report," 17.

65. United States Commission on National Aid to Vocational Education, "Report," 17.

66. The 2006 Carl D. Perkins Career and Technical Improvement Act renamed what had been called Vocational Education and henceforth refers to it as Career and Technical Education. Several of the national associations involved with vocational education also renamed their organizations.

67. Karen Levesque et al., "Career and Technical Education in the United States: 1990 to 2005," (NCES 2008-035) National Center for Education Statistics, Institute of Education Sciences, U.S. Department of Education, https://nces.ed.gov/pubs2008/2008035.pdf.

68. Marsha Silverberg et al., "National Assessment of Vocational Education: Final Report to Congress" (June 2004), U.S. Department of Education, https://files.eric.ed.gov/fulltext/ED483149.pdf.

69. Secondary CTE courses include family and consumer sciences education, general labor market preparation, occupational education, agriculture, business management and services, marketing, communications technology, computer and other technology, construction, mechanics and repair, transportation, materials production,

print production, other precision production, health care childcare and education, protective services, food service and hospitality, personal and other services.

70. Karen Levesque et al., "Career," 28.

71. Karen Levesque et al., "Career," 12.

72. Karen Levesque et al., "Career," 31.

73. Karen Levesque et al., "Career," 77.

74. Postsecondary career-related studies include agricultural and natural resources, business and marketing, communications, computer sciences, education, engineering and architectural sciences, health care, legal services, personal and consumer services, protective services, public/social/human, services, and trade and industry.

75. John Whiteclay Chambers, *The Tyranny of Change: America in the Progressive Era, 1890-1920*, 3rd ed. (Newark: Rutgers University Press, 2000).

76. Paul Avrich, *The Modern School Movement Anarchism and Education in the United States* (Princeton University Press, 1980), Preface excerpt.

77. Paul Avrich, "The Modern School Movement: Anarchism and Education in the United States," The Modern School Movement, http://themodernschools.wordpress.com/the-schools/.

78. U.S. Department of Education, National Center for Education Statistics, (2011) "Digest of Education Statistics, 2010: Table 5," (NCES 2011-015), 2011, https://nces.ed.gov/programs/digest/d10/tables/dt10_005.asp.

79. American Association of University Professors, "Joint Statement on Rights and Freedoms of Students," accessed May 2, 2023, https://www.aaup.org/report/joint-statement-rights-and-freedoms-students.

80. Mitch Smith, "Social Justice Revival," Inside Higher Education, Jan. 31, 2012, http://www.insidehighered.com/news/2012/01/31/colleges-embrace-social-justice-curriculum.

81. Arizona State University, "Social Justice and Human Rights, MA," accessed May 2, 2023, https://newcollege.asu.edu/social-justice-and-human-rights-ma.

82. Amy Lindahl, "Facing Cancer: Social Justice in Biology Class," *Rethinking Schools* (Summer 2012), https://rethinkingschools.org/articles/facing-cancer-social-justice-in-biology-class/.

83. Four Girls for Families, "Who We Are," accessed May 2, 2023, https://www.fourgirlsforfamilies.org/blank.

Chapter 5

The Rise of the American Empire
The Fifth Lifetime (1945–Present)

If the radiance of a thousand suns
Were to burst at once into the sky,
That would be like the splendor of the Mighty One
I am mighty Time, the source of destruction
that comes forth to annihilate the worlds.
Even without your participation,
the warriors arrayed in the opposing army shall cease to exist.

—The Bhagavad-Gita[1]

To start the story of the fifth lifetime, we need to flashback to November 1917 at a dock in New York City harbor. The dock was a major embarkation point for sending troops, supplies, and munitions to France and England to fight in World War I. An old French cargo ship, the 325-foot SS *Mont-Blanc*, was moored in the harbor. According to the freight manifest, in her hull were 3,000 tons of high explosives: 12,000 kegs of dry picric acid and 9,830 barrels of the wet variety; 5,000 kegs and cases of trinitrotoluene (TNT); and 682 cases of gun cotton. Also piled high on her deck were 494 barrels of benzol, a high-octane fuel. She was literally a floating bomb. Once loaded, the *Mont-Blanc* headed northeast toward Halifax, Nova Scotia, a small Canadian seaport of about 60,000 people.

Powered by a single propeller and lumbering along at only about eight knots per hour, the ship would be an inviting torpedo target for prowling German *Untersee boots* (U-boats) on its 600-mile journey. In the month prior, German U-boats had sunk 151 ships and damaged twenty-two others.[2] Halifax was the last relatively safe seaport in North America and the closest to the French coast, a place where the *Mont-Blanc* could join with other ships to form a safer shipping convoy bound for Europe.[3]

On December 6, 1917, the *Mont-Blanc* entered the narrow Halifax harbor. The weather was fair and mild. The seas were calm. Entering the harbor at the same time was the 430-foot Norwegian-registered SS *Imo*, a food relief ship bound for Belgium. By an accidental set of circumstances, the *Mont-Blanc* and SS *Imo* collided. The force of the impact dislodged several barrels of benzol fuel piled high on the deck of the *Mont-Blanc*. When the barrels fell onto the deck, they broke open. As the two ships continued to collide, the metal-on-metal scraping between them spewed a shower of sparks that ignited the fuel from the barrels seeping into *Mont-Blanc's* cargo hull. A spectacular fire quickly erupted, drawing hundreds of astonished spectators to the water's edge. The *Mont-Blanc's* crew abandoned the ship. By now, she had drifted ashore, setting ablaze the pier's wooden structures. As her crew members swam ashore, they raced past the bewildered onlookers, shouting warnings to escape what they knew was imminent.

At 9:04 a.m., the *Mont-Blanc* exploded. The blast instantaneously killed 1,900 people,injured 9,000 more,[4] and leveled half of Halifax. A massive fireball incinerated everyone and everything in the vicinity. (See figure 5.1.)

At the same time, the heat of the explosion vaporized the water surrounding the *Mont-Blanc* down to the sea floor, creating a 30-foot wall of water dragging people to their deaths. One survivor recalled seeing dead bodies

Figure 5.1 Halifax—Damage from the Halifax Explosion Looking East toward Dartmouth. *Source*: William James, City of Toronto Archives: Fonds 1244; Item 2435.

hanging out of windows, "some with their heads off and some [bodies] thrown over the overhead telegraph wires."[5]

THE GADGET

Twenty-eight years later, on July 16, 1945, a thirteen-pound ball of radioactive plutonium sat atop a 100-foot platform at the northern end of what is now the White Sands Missile Range in a desolate section of New Mexico. Surrounding this plutonium "softball" was a round metal encasement containing less than one-tenth of one percent of the TNT stored in the hull of the *Mont-Blanc*. The scene was called the Trinity test, the culmination of a secret national effort run by the U.S. Army Corp of Engineers of the Manhattan district, otherwise known as the Manhattan Project. At 5:45 a.m., the TNT in this device, nicknamed the "Gadget," was detonated, causing the plutonium ball to compress and then explode, resulting in destructive power seven times greater than the *Mont-Blanc* explosion. But unlike the 325-foot *Mont-Blanc*, the Gadget could fit inside the belly of a Boeing B-29 Superfortress bomber.

Twenty days later, on August 6, 1945, another device, similar to the Gadget and code-named Little Boy, was dropped on the Japanese city of Hiroshima—an atom bomb equivalent to *five* times the destructive power of the *Mont-Blanc* explosion. The estimated number of men, women, and children civilians killed ranges from 70,000 to 140,000.[6]

On August 9, 1945, a second atom bomb, code name Fat Man, *seven* times more powerful than the *Mont-Blanc* explosion, was dropped on the city of Nagasaki. The estimated men, women and children killed by civilians: 40,000–70,000. Total estimated burned and maimed: 160,000. The next day, on August 10, 1945, Japan surrendered. Within the span of twenty-five days, the world had dramatically changed—forever. If there were any doubt about the role of science and technology being essential to prevailing in World War II, the atomic bomb was the end and exclamation point to any argument. From 1945 to 1949, the United States produced 170 more atom bombs, some with a yield eighteen times greater than the *Mont-Blanc* explosion. Then, on August 29, 1949, the Soviet Union conducted its own atomic bomb test in modern-day Kazakhstan with a yield similar to the Gadget. The arms race was on. To counter the Soviets, the United States dramatically increased its production of nuclear weapons. By 1957, the United States had 5,543 nuclear weapons compared to the Soviets' 660.[7] But we were not done.

On November 1, 1952, the United States detonated the world's first thermonuclear device, a hydrogen bomb, code name Ivy Mike, on a small Pacific Island in the Marshall Islands. A hydrogen bomb uses the same energy processes as the sun. An atomic bomb is placed *inside* a hydrogen bomb. When the atomic bomb is detonated, it generates heat equivalent to the interior of the sun, causing hydrogen atoms to fuse into helium, thereby releasing enormous quantities of energy. The Ivy Mike explosion yielded an energy equivalent to ten million tons of TNT (ten megatons)—3,333 more powerful than the *Mont-Blanc* explosion and 660 times more powerful than Little Boy.

On August 12, 1953, the Soviets responded with their first test of a thermonuclear device. Although its yield of 400 kilotons of TNT was much smaller than the American's Ivy Mike explosion a year earlier, it was nonetheless twenty-five times more powerful than the bomb dropped on Hiroshima. In a massively documented volume of the emergence of the nuclear age, historian Robert Watson summarized the Cold War reality facing defense planners:

> In the months following the war, the Soviet Union had violated its wartime agreements by seizing control of almost all the countries of Eastern Europe, imposing rigid dictatorships on them and ruthlessly excluding or liquidating advocates of democracy. In China, the Soviets had assisted with massive aid the Communist insurgents led by Mao Tse-Tung in overthrowing the established government and bringing the country under a "people's democracy." A huge Communist empire, apparently under monolithic control from Moscow, stretched from the Oder River in Europe to the shores of the Pacific, its rulers publicly committed to the Marxist doctrine of conflict between themselves and the capitalist world.[8]

But that was only half the terrifying change ushered in by the nuclear age. On August 20, 1957, the Soviets successfully launched an R-7 Semyorka rocket.[9] At a speed *twenty times* faster than a jet bomber and with a range of 3,700 miles, the R-7 could carry a hydrogen bomb in its nose cone, thus making it the first intercontinental ballistic missile (ICBM). The prospect of a Soviet ICBM with a fifteen-megaton payload posed an existential threat to Europe and the United States. There was, and still is, no defense against it. The only defense was to convince the Soviets that if they ever launched a nuclear attack, we still had the means to retaliate and destroy them. Thus, the Eisenhower doctrine of "massive retaliation" was and still is the fundamental operative principle of U.S.-Soviet nuclear relations. As Secretary of State John Foster Dulles stated in an address before the Council on Foreign Relations on January 12, 1954,

> What the Eisenhower administration seeks is a similar international security system. We want, for ourselves and the other free nations, a maximum deterrent at a bearable cost. . . . Local defense will always be important. But there is no local defense which alone will contain the mighty land power of the Communist world. Local defenses must be reinforced by the further deterrent of massive retaliatory power.[10]

Operation Paperclip

In the Nuclear Age, advanced scientific, technological, engineering, and mathematical (STEM) talent is essential. Weapons of mass destruction—nuclear, biological, chemical, and the various systems to deliver them—must be developed, tested, and deployed. Many of the key scientists and mathematicians in the Manhattan Project (launched in 1939) had escaped from the Axis powers of Germany (Albert Einstein), Hungary (Edward Teller), and Italy (Enrico Fermi). More than 100 foreign scientists were involved. After the war, in 1945, the Joint Intelligence Objectives Agency (JIOA) was established to bring over 1,500 German and other foreign scientists, technicians, and engineers, including former Nazis, to work on nuclear and rocket technology as part of Operation Paperclip.[11] The Soviets did likewise. Thus, in addition to the nuclear arms race and space race, the United States and USSR underwent a scientist and mathematician *talent* race. Could the United States produce sufficient scientific talent domestically to keep pace with the Soviets in weapons and rocketry?

THE COLD WAR OF THE CLASSROOM ARCHETYPE

> New frontiers of the mind are before us, and if they are pioneered with the same vision, boldness, and drive with which we have waged this war we can create a fuller and more fruitful employment and a fuller and more fruitful life.—Franklin D. Roosevelt, 1944[12]

On November 17, 1944, President Roosevelt wrote a letter to Vannevar Bush, head of the U.S. Office of Scientific Research and Development (OSRD), which oversaw the Manhattan Project. The president asked four questions, ending with:

> Can an effective program be proposed for discovering and developing scientific talent in American youth so that the continuing future of scientific research in this country may be assured on a level comparable to what has been done during the war?[13]

Why American *youth*? As it turned out, the average age of scientists working on the Manhattan Project was 29.4 years.[14] Many groundbreaking discoveries are made by such youth. For example, Albert Einstein was only twenty-six years old when he published his papers on special relativity and the equivalence of mass and energy. Enrico Fermi, who created the world's first nuclear reactor, won the 1938 Nobel Prize for Physics at the age of thirty-seven. It was clear that the United States could not forever rely exclusively on foreign talent for national security.

In April 1945, FDR died. In July 1945, Vannevar Bush answered FDR's question in a report to President Truman entitled "Science—The Endless Frontier." Among other things, the report called for the establishment of a National Research Foundation. Five years later, in 1950, under President Eisenhower, Congress established the National Science Foundation (NSF), largely along the lines Bush had recommended. NSF's mission was "to promote the progress of science; to advance the national health, prosperity, and welfare; to secure the national defense; and for other purposes . . . to strengthen basic research and education in the sciences."[15]

The NSF's early effort in science, technology, engineering, and mathematics was to support universities in basic research and college students pursuing science through "scholarships and graduate fellowships in the mathematical, physical, medical, biological, engineering, and other sciences." The foundation announced its first awards in 1952.

This national agenda, however, was *not* geared toward promoting *general* science literacy, or to engage, stimulate, or develop STEM talent through pedagogical or curriculum interventions per se. Rather, the agenda was to support an elite few who were already deemed highly capable and willing to pursue science research, or those extremely capable who could be enticed to pursue science rather than law or other professions. As James B. Conant, president of Harvard University and the first chairman of the NSF Science Board, remarked (in the gender-biased language of his time):

By and large the United States has not yet produced its share of such scientific pioneers as compared with Europe. One of the purposes of the National Science Foundation is surely to right this balance and provide in every section of the country educational and research facilities which will assist the development of such men. In the advance of science and its application to many practical problems, there is no substitute for first-class men. Ten second-rate scientists or engineers cannot do the work of one who is in the first rank.[16]

The United States faced several major workforce problems related to national defense. In 1950, the number of youths between the ages of fourteen and twenty-four was about 24.5 million, two million *less* than in 1940. The outbreak of hostilities on the Korean peninsula in June 1950 and subsequent U.S. engagement resulted in a rapid doubling of the number of active-duty servicemen with a year (1.46 million to 3.25 million).[17] Over the next three years, a total of 133,000 U.S. servicemen were killed, wounded, or missing in action. Although college enrollment had increased to 14.3 percent of youth between the ages of eighteen and twenty four in 1950, up from 9.1 percent in 1940, due to continued college deferments and the Servicemen's Readjustment Act of 1944, President Roosevelt's question remained. Could the United States produce sufficient *domestic* advanced scientific talent for national security, notwithstanding the generally high academic marks in college received by returning veterans?[18]

In September 1950, the Ford Foundation established the Fund for the Advancement of Education (FAE) over concerns about the "difficulties encountered by the U.S. school system as a result of the mobilization of manpower," including problems at the college level.[19] One of the Fund's Board members was the U.S. Secretary of the Air Force, underscoring the nexus between higher education and national security. The FAE supported a 1951 survey of Harvard, Yale, and Princeton college students who had graduated from three prestigious preparatory high schools: Andover, Exeter, and Lawrenceville. The ensuing report detailed the lack of challenging college courses for the ablest graduates, stating, "we have been particularly concerned about the superior student." To illustrate, the General Education report quoted one student's experiences:

> The college work was too easy. So, I drank, wasted time, and ran down to New York. I didn't have to work so I didn't. My grades were excellent and if I had bothered to work, they would have been better. . . . I disliked all the courses, knew none of the professors, and didn't care to. It was a game. I was seeing how little work I could do and still keep good grades, and how much I could drink in the weeks before exam period. . . . In the second half of my sophomore year, I got an inspiring tutor and took four fine courses. I started working for the first time in 18 months. I also stopped drinking. Even now with the objectivity of two more years I am seriously convinced that I was magnificently prepared at school and that my first 3 terms at college were a total loss.[20]

This report and others funded by the FAE would eventually lead to the establishment of the Advanced Placement Exams.[21] Nonetheless, the prospect of insufficient "gray matter" worried defense planners at the highest levels. In 1946, Congress passed the Atomic Energy Act to, among other things, "effectuate the policies . . . for conducting, assisting, and fostering research and development in order to encourage maximum scientific and industrial progress."[22] The law set up the Atomic Energy Commission (AEC), whose members would assume complete control of the plants, laboratories, equipment, and personnel assembled during the war to produce the atomic bomb. One of the original members and later chairman of the AEC was Lewis L. Strauss, a politically connected investment banker.[23] In testimony before Congress, Strauss warned about the coming shortage of trained manpower in atomic energy and weaponry:

> Between 1950 and 1960, which may be the most critical decade of our national existence, Russia is expected to produce 1,200,000 trained engineers and

scientists, against our 900,000. . . . The fact is that the sciences have an overriding priority in Russian education.

This is the cold war of the classrooms. In 5 years, our lead in the training of scientists and engineers may be wiped out, and in 10 years we could be hopelessly outstripped. Unless immediate steps are taken to correct it, a situation already dangerous, within less than a decade could become disastrous.[24]

Meanwhile, the nuclear race was accelerating. On October 4, 1957, the same class of Soviet R-7 Semyorka rocket that had launched the Soviet's first nuclear-capable IBCM launched *Sputnik I*, the world's first artificial satellite. The launch put the public and politicians into a gripping panic. *Sputnik I* demonstrated what American nuclear scientists and missile engineers had always feared: the Soviet's capacity to deliver thermonuclear payloads that could annihilate American cities.

A month after the launch of *Sputnik I*, beginning on November 25, 1957, the U.S. Senate Armed Services Preparedness Investigating Subcommittee held fifteen days of hearings over three months on the status of United States and Soviet satellite and nuclear missile programs. Topics included futuristic Soviet threats, such as weather control, that could threaten American farming.[25] Why not weather control? Who could have dreamt of the destructive power of an atom bomb, which was now the ultimate linchpin of all foreign policy? Thirty-two high ranking scientists and military officers testified. Dr. Edward Teller was the first, providing riveting detail of the Soviet threat, real and imagined. What was still perplexing to many was the question of how the Soviets could catch up to and even surpass the United States in certain advanced weapons systems after suffering tens of millions of military and civilian losses and a ruined economy from the Second World War. According to Teller:

[I]n a way the explanation is quite simple and straight forward. The philosophy that the Russians profess puts a very great weight on scientific and technical accomplishments. . . . This has led in Russia to the situation where I think the scientist is in a quite unique position. Most people in Russia starve. If you do not want to starve in Russia, there are two ways to get an agreeable life. One is to get a lot of responsibility, for instance, become a more or less prominent member of their one party. The other is to become a scientist.[26] (See figure 5.2.)

Within this Cold War context, Teller stressed that America was vulnerable from an insufficient supply of "first class" scientists and technicians to keep pace with Soviet science education, stating that "the Russian scientist is very greatly honored. Scientific books in Russia have a sale which outstrips the sale of scientific books in the rest of the world by something like a factor of

Figure 5.2   Dr. Teller at Senate Hearing. Dr. Edward Teller, University of California scientist, gestures as he testifies as the first witness at the Senate Armed Services preparedness subcommittee opening hearings on missile development in Washington, D.C., Nov. 25, 1957. *Source*: Associated Press.

10. It is an amazing phenomenon."[27] Teller also repeated Dr. Lewis Strauss's warning about "the Cold War of the classrooms," explaining:

> I feel that it is most necessary that we change the situation in the schools, I mean the high schools and I mean also the elementary schools, because by the time a kid is 12 years old, he probably has adopted the mental attitudes which will make him a good scientist or else which will definitely get him interested in some field other than science.[28]

Congress responded. In the span of a year after the Senate hearings, the NSF's budget tripled to $134 million. Beginning in 1957, NSF began collecting data on science and engineering indicators, including educational attainment. Then, in 1958, the U.S. Congress enacted the National Defense Education Act (NDEA), declaring that

> the security of the Nation requires the fullest development of the mental resources and technical skills of its young men and women. The present emergency demands that additional and more mastery of modern techniques developed from complex scientific principles. It depends as well upon the discovery and development of new principles, new techniques, and new knowledge.[29]

The NDEA financial support to students, schools, and colleges was initially limited only to those students who demonstrated "a superior capacity or preparation in science, mathematics, engineering, or a modern foreign language." Title V of the NDEA provided funds for aptitude tests to "identify students with outstanding aptitudes and ability." Funds were also provided for educational and career counseling to public secondary school students and for the establishment of guidance counselor training institutes. Title VIII of the act focused on vocational education "designed to fit [youths, adults, and older persons] for useful employment as technicians or skilled workers in scientific or technical fields." As for the rest of the non-scientists and non-technicians, Teller recommended they instead receive "science appreciation courses" so they could provide the political support needed for continued investments in science. They would be an "audience" to whom scientists would play and, it was hoped, be admired more than football players.[30]

What makes the science, technology, engineering, and mathematic talent race unlike any other is the lack of a finish line. The spectacular advances in technical knowledge that produced the hydrogen bomb continue unabated to this day, with implications for all types of weaponry. Consider, for example, the tremendous advances in computing science from the days of the ENIAC, the Electronic Numerical Integrator and Computer.[31] Completed in November 1945 at the University of Pennsylvania's College of Engineering, the ENIAC was the world's first large-scale, general-purpose electronic digital computer. ENIAC's original purpose[32] was for the U.S. Army's Ballistics Research Laboratory (BRL) to calculate firing tables for various ordnances (artillery, mortars, rockets, etc.,)[33], but since the war had ended, ENIAC's first use was to perform calculations for the Los Alamos Laboratory to help determine the feasibility of developing Teller's hydrogen bomb.

The ENIAC was also immense, weighing 30 tons and occupying 1,500 square feet of space. It was constructed using nearly 18,000 vacuum tubes and about 500,000 soldered joints. As huge as it was, ENIAC's computing power was limited for the task at hand. Its limitations underscored how advances in weaponry were tied to advances in computing power. Anne C. Fitzpatrick from George Washington University, an expert on the relations between the history of computing and nuclear weapons, described the role of the ENIAC in solving the "Super" problem: whether a hydrogen fusion bomb could be ignited that would create an explosion on the order of millions of tons of TNT.

> Los Alamos's employment of the ENIAC for a hydrogen weapon calculation was not only novel in 1945, but it signaled the beginning of a crucial relationship between the nuclear weapons complex and computers. . . . The difficulty of the problem exceeded the technology of the time. . . . Even Teller realized this and acknowledged ENIAC's limitations. Teller recommended that attention be paid to developments in high-speed electronic calculators; thermonuclear

calculations so far indicated that the complexity of the problems required at least an instrument like the ENIAC. In 1946, however, there simply were no other large machines available to Los Alamos besides the ENIAC. The Super problem would have to wait . . . computing was the bottleneck.[34]

In 1995, in commemoration of ENIAC's fiftieth anniversary, a group of students at the University of Pennsylvania's Department of Electrical Engineering reconstructed the original ENIAC on a silicon chip the size of a dime.[35] The tremendous advances in information, communications, and computing technologies in all its many facets since the days of the ENIAC, from the iPhone and the internet to supercomputers and robotics, have been variously characterized as the Third Industrial Revolution.[36] With this technological revolution have come new threats to national security that include potential cyberattacks on critical infrastructure,[37] hostile social media disinformation campaigns,[38] and crypto currencies to fund terrorists,[39] to name a few. Thus, we see the ongoing nexus between accelerating scientific advances, new national security threats, and the need for a corps of highly technically competent but also morally grounded youth to deal with both.

Today, the Cold War of the Classroom archetype can be seen most clearly in high schools for advanced students who take demanding STEM courses of study. For example, in 2011, 30,000 New York City students took the Specialized High Schools Admissions Test (SHSAT) to gain entrance into one of nine specialized high schools. Stuyvesant High School was one of them. Founded in 1904 and located in Lower Manhattan, Stuyvesant High School is a public school with 3,200 students and arguably one of the most elite schools in the nation, both in terms of admissions selectivity and prestige.[40] Stuyvesant's acceptance rate is only 3.8 percent, compared to Harvard's rate of 5.9 percent.[41] Four Nobel Laureates are Stuyvesant High School alumni,[42] as are many others of note in the sciences. Its curriculum includes second-year college-level courses in mathematics and science, such as differential calculus, organic chemistry, and astronomy.

Another example is the North Carolina School for Science and Mathematics, NCSSM, a special admission residential public high school for rising eleventh and twelfth graders. It was established in 1980 by Governor James Hunt as part of the University of North Carolina system for "academically talented students to become state, national, and global leaders in science, technology, engineering, and mathematics."[43] Newer elite schools for math and science have been established since NCSSM. Thomas Jefferson High School for Science and Technology (TJHSST), established in 1985, has an enrollment of 1,800 students. This school is ranked sixth in STEM and first in high schools overall, according to *U.S. News and World Report*.[44] Thomas Jefferson has a sixteen percent acceptance rate,[45] drawing its students from Fairfax

County, home to over one million residents. Fairfax has the second highest household income in the nation, and six out of every ten adults have either a bachelor's or graduate degree—more than twice the national average.[46]

In 1988, Stuyvesant and Thomas Jefferson, along with thirteen other selective admissions high schools, formed the National Consortium for Specialized Secondary Schools in Mathematics, Science, and Technology (now the National Consortium of Secondary STEM Schools [NCSSS]) to "foster, support, and advance the efforts of those specialized schools whose primary purpose is to attract and academically prepare students for leadership in mathematics, science, and technology."[47]

As of 2022, NCSSS has grown to nearly 100 high schools[48] and the *U.S. News and World Report* identifies 250 top STEM public high schools.[49] However, changing global economy and military circumstances beginning in the 1960s and extending into the present era led to the emergence of yet another new purpose of education that is complementary to but distinct from the Cold War of the Classroom archetype.

THE NATION AT RISK ARCHETYPE—
POSTWAR CHANGES IN THE U.S.
GLOBAL POSITION (1945–PRESENT)

The baby boomers, children born in the United States after World War II, roughly the period from 1945 to 1973, grew up having to contend with two opposite and extreme realities unprecedented in human history. At one extreme was the unlikely but very real possibility of nuclear annihilation by the Soviet Union, whether on purpose or by accident. Two U.S. atom bombs had already wiped out two cities in Japan. The frightening specter of nuclear war was routinely on the nightly news from 1945 to 1963 as the United States and the Soviet Union exploded 538 nuclear devices in the atmosphere.[50] The largest, the Soviet's 50-megaton Tsar hydrogen bomb, exploded on October 30, 1961.[51]

A year later, on October 14, 1962, a U.S. aircraft flying over Cuba captured pictures clearly showing sites under construction for nuclear payload capable medium-range and intermediate-range ballistic nuclear missiles (MRBMs and IRBMs) in Cuba, taking both countries to the brink of nuclear war.[52] At the time, the United States had nearly ten times the number of nuclear weapons as the Soviets (22,229 to 2,922), but by 1964, the Soviets had more than doubled their nuclear weapons stockpile (5,242), and by 1970, they had amassed 19,055 nuclear bombs.

At the other extreme, the United States enjoyed unprecedented postwar prosperity, social freedom, and mobility. The United States had survived

World War II intact, while Europe and Japan were devastated. Russia is esti-mated to have lost twenty-six to twenty-seven million people from the war,[53] including upward of three million dead from starvation.[54] Approximately seventy-two percent of the world's two-and-a-half billion people in 1950 lived in poverty, and more than half lived in extreme poverty.[55] Asia, includ-ing China and India, accounted for three-quarters of the world's bottom sixty percent in poverty.[56]

In stark contrast to the rest of the world, from 1945 to 1973, the United States enjoyed rapid increases in median family income. In 2019 dollars, real median income nearly doubled from 1950 to 1973.[57]

Consumers had access to new inventions and labor-saving devices. For example, in 1946, few households had a television set, but by 1955, nearly two out of three households had a set and by 1970, more than nine out of ten households owned one.[58] Americans also became much more mobile. In 1950, roughly half (fifty-four percent) of all households had an automobile. But by 1970, eighty-two percent had at least one automobile and twenty-eight percent had two, leading to a near quadrupling of miles driven by automobiles and trucks since 1945.[59]

Another indicator of domestic prosperity was the surge in college enroll-ments, from about 2.4 million in 1947 to 9.6 million by 1973. Part of this increase in college enrollment can be explained by the Baby Boom surge in births from 1946 to 1964. Indeed, while the U.S. population increased by sixty-five million from 1945 to 1970, thirty-six million, or *fifty-five percent*, was due to an increase in those below the age of twenty-five years. Another factor in increased enrollment was the surge of veterans who took advantage of the tuition-free policy granted them in the G.I. Bill. More than a million veterans crowded onto college and university campuses in 1947–1948, and by the end of the program, 2.23 million veterans had used the tuition benefit.[60] The other component of greater college enrollments was due to the greater portion of young people enrolling in college versus entering the workforce or military service. Whereas in the fall of 1946, about 12 in 100 young persons between the ages of eighteen and twenty-four were enrolled in college, by 1975 that number had swelled to 40 in 100 young persons.[61]

This existential contradiction between living in a country full of material abundance and educational opportunity on the one hand and the threat of nuclear annihilation on the other hand was perfectly captured in the 1964 Cold War classic, *Dr. Strangelove or: How I Learned to Stop Worrying and Love the Bomb*. As director Stanley Kubrick described his concept,

I started work on the screenplay with every intention of making the film a serious treatment of the problem of accidental nuclear war. As I kept trying to imagine the way in which things would really happen, ideas kept coming to me which I would discard because they were so ludicrous. I kept saying to myself: "I can't do this. People will laugh." But after a month or so I began to realize that all the things I was throwing out were the things which were most truthful.[62]

A Loss of Confidence

In 1945, the United States stood at the pinnacle of world supremacy and prestige. But in the subsequent thirty-five years, the public's confidence that U.S. military power alone could prevail over any foe seriously eroded. The loss of confidence began in 1953, when North Korea, with the help of China, fought South Korea and the United States to an uneasy armistice that is still in place to this day. Then, on April 15, 1961, the Bay of Pigs invasion of Cuba to overthrow Fidel Castro with 1,400 Cuban exiles recruited by the CIA ended in a humiliating defeat.[63] But perhaps the greatest loss of national confidence was due to the Vietnam War, which dragged on for nearly two decades through the 1960s and early 1970s amid increasingly massive domestic war protests. In June 1971, portions of the "Report of the Office of the Secretary of Defense Vietnam Task Force," otherwise known as the Pentagon Papers, were leaked to the New York Times, creating a national sensation about the lies the government told to the America people about the Vietnam War including the secret U.S. bombings carried out in Laos and Cambodia. Watergate followed in June 1972, and for more than two years, the United States was mired in one of the worst presidential scandals in its history. The regular drip of revelations about the secret use of governmental agencies against political opponents and illegal covert political operations and cover-ups directed by senior administration officials resulted in months of media reports, Congressional hearings, and ultimately the threat of impeachment in the House with near certain conviction in the Senate. President Richard M. Nixon finally resigned on August 9, 1974. Six months later, on April 30, 1975, the last few Americans still in Saigon were airlifted from the rooftop of the U.S. Embassy as the country fell to North Vietnamese forces.[64] Distrust of the federal government only grew. Six months later, in April 1976, the U.S. Senate Select Committee to Study Governmental Operations with Respect to Intelligence Activities, (also known as the Church Committee) began an investigation of many Central Intelligence Agency (CIA) foreign covert operations done in the name of anti-communism.[65]

If confidence in the capability and moral rectitude of the U.S. military and government leaders had reached a nadir by the mid-70s, the U.S. public was about to get another shock about its growing *economic* vulnerability, one that has continued into the twenty-first century. This economic vulnerability would eventually lead to the emergence of the thirteenth educational archetype—The Nation at Risk—which continues to be the dominant education archetype as of this writing.

THE NATION AT RISK ARCHETYPE—
EDUCATION FOR ECONOMIC SECURITY

The postwar economic boom enjoyed by the United States and other countries as well came at a strategic cost—an Arab oil squeeze. Even though U.S. domestic oil production soared since World War I, it could not keep up with world demand. By 1973, foreign oil imports constituted about one-third of all U.S. petroleum consumption.[66] Only about one-sixth of that one-third came from the Organization of Petroleum Exporting Countries (OPEC). However, the United States was vulnerable to supply-chain disruptions because domestic production could not be increased quickly enough to make up for any sudden shortfall.[67] This vulnerability in oil supply became a reality when, in October 1973, war broke out between Egypt, Syria, and Israel. Since the United States supported Israel with supplies, the Arab states of OPEC retaliated against the United States and its allies by placing an embargo on oil exports to them to gain leverage in postwar negotiations.[68] The result was a quadrupling of oil prices with severe oil shortages in the United States, causing long lines at the gas pumps.[69] Two months later, in November 1973, the United States fell into a two-year recession. To the average American, the very idea of a faraway Arab cabal of obscure Middle Eastern countries inflicting economic pain was a psychological shock. For the first time, a much weaker military adversary was able to directly attack the U.S. domestic population using *oil* as a weapon.[70] In response, Congress passed the Energy Policy and Conservation Act of 1975 (EPCA), which among other measures established the Strategic Oil Reserve to buffer oil supply disruptions. It would not be enough.

A second oil shock occurred in 1979, this time triggered by the Iranian Revolution against the reign of Shah Mohammad Reza Pahlavi. Shah Pahlavi had been installed as king in 1953 with help from the CIA as a bulwark against Soviet expansionism in the region.[71] By 1978, Iran had the world's fifth largest army, with the United States its principal supplier of arms since 1949.[72] Pahlavi kept himself in power with his infamous SAVAK, the Iranian secret police, who brutally tortured and killed thousands of his political opponents.[73] After four of his men deliberately locked 470 people inside the Cinema Rex movie theater in Abadan on August 19, 1978 and set it on fire according to anti-Shah protesters, uncontrollable masses of people demonstrated against his regime.[74] When the Shah fled Iran in January 1979, Iranian oil output suddenly dropped by 4.8 million barrels a day, which represented seven percent of the world's oil production. Sheikh Khomeini, who had been living in exile in France, took control of Iran as the Grand Ayatollah, establishing an anti-U.S. Islamic Republic.[75] Gilford John Ikenberry, a theorist of international relations, explained the impact of the oil embargoes:

> The remarkable postwar expansion of the advanced industrial economies was at an end; no longer could governments promise unlimited economic growth. Nor could they retain exclusive control over the management of the world economy; developing countries, particularly those rich in resources, had to be brought into the system. Most important, American postwar leadership, already perceived to be on the wane, looked to have been dealt another, perhaps decisive, blow. An era was ending. The shape of the new one remained to be negotiated.[76]

Seen from the United States' perspective, the postwar economic euphoria turned sour by the 1970s and early 1980s. During this time, there were four recessions. Inflation reached 13.6 percent. Unemployment reached 10.8 percent. The oil shocks of 1973 and 1979 made it clear to the American voter the threats to their *economic* security. No longer was the United States the singular economic power wholly self-sufficient; rather, it was connected to a global *political economy*. In some cases, one country or coalition of countries, such as OPEC, could have substantial asymmetrical leverage over the United States. However U.S. economic vulnerabilities were not limited to oil and Mideast geopolitics.

After World War II, Japan and Germany rebuilt their countries with substantial U.S. humanitarian and economic assistance.[77] By 1980, they had become economic powerhouses. This proved unsettling to many. Whereas the U.S. gross domestic product (GDP) rose five-fold from $543.3 billion in 1960 to $2.86 *trillion* in 1980, Japan's GDP rose *25-fold*, from $44.3 billion in 1960 to $1.11 *trillion* in 1980. Taken together, by 1980, Japan's and Germany's economies had risen from the ashes of World War II to equal 72 percent of the U.S. GDP.[78] A highly visible sign of Japan's and Germany's economic rebound was in passenger and commercial vehicle manufacturing.[79] In 1950, the United States produced more than eight million autos, Germany produced about 306,000, and Japan produced less than 32,000. But by 1981, Japan was producing three million more passenger and commercial vehicles compared to the United States. (11.18 million for Japan versus 7.9 million for the United States.)[80]

Clearly, the global political and economic order had changed dramatically since the end of World War II. If America was still first in the world in many categories, it no longer reigned supreme in all. Indeed, in some areas, such as automobile manufacturing, the United States had fallen behind other advanced countries. The punctuation mark to this dismal mood was the ill-fated rescue attempt on April 24, 1980, of the fifty-two Americans held hostage in the U.S. Embassy by Iran's Grand Ayatollah. The attempt known as Operation Eagle Claw ended in disaster when the rescue helicopter crashed in the desert, killing eight U.S. service members while failing to rescue any of the hostages.[81] In his acceptance speech for the Republican nomination for president on July 17, 1980, then-candidate Ronald Reagan summarized the mood of the country and provided his promise stating,

> Never before in our history have Americans been called upon to face three grave threats to our very existence, any one of which could destroy us. We face a disintegrating economy, a weakened defense and an energy policy based on the sharing of scarcity. . . . For those who've abandoned hope, we'll restore hope and we'll welcome them into a great national crusade to make America great again.[82]

Reagan won the November 1980 election in an electoral landslide with 489 votes to President Jimmy Carter's 49. On January 20, 1981, U.S. president-elect Ronald Reagan took the oath of office. Within the hour, Iran released all fifty-two hostages. Thus began the so-called "Reagan Revolution," which impacted all aspects of American life, especially education.

The connection between the condition of education and the perception of America facing increasing global economic competition and geopolitical vulnerability has defined the post-Carter era and drove federal and state policies accordingly. In January 1981, the same month as President Reagan's inauguration, the Southern Regional Education Board, a nonprofit group of sixteen southern governors and legislatures proclaiming itself as America's first interstate compact for education,[83] commissioned a task force to make recommendations to address the "quality crisis" in education and university teacher preparation programs. The report issued five months later, in June 1981, entitled "The Need for Quality" reflected "a growing public belief that educational quality is unacceptability low." The work of the task force was undertaken because "the region aspires to a leading economic role in the nation" and "there is an unprecedented need and opportunity to improve the quality of education, provide public support is marshalled to that end."[84]

Two months later, on August 5, 1981, President Reagan's Secretary of Education, Terrel H. Bell, appointed a National Commission on Excellence in Education to, among other things: "examine and to compare and contrast the curricula, standards, and expectations of the educational systems of several advanced countries with those of the United States."[85]

In April 1983, Secretary Bell's Commission issued its high-profile report entitled "A Nation at Risk: An Imperative for Educational Reform."[86] The Nation at Risk report echoed many of the recommendations of the SREB report but was much more forceful and alarming in tone and message. The Nation at Risk commissioners issued a blunt warning to the country, using Cold War-like rhetoric to describe foreign threats to America's economic security:

> Our Nation is at risk. Our once unchallenged preeminence in commerce, industry, science, and technological innovation is being overtaken by competitors throughout the world. If an unfriendly foreign power had attempted to impose on America the mediocre educational performance that exists today, we might well have viewed it as an act of war. As it stands, we have allowed this to happen to ourselves. We have even squandered the gains in student achievement made in the wake of the Sputnik challenge. Moreover, we have dismantled essential support systems which helped make those gains possible. We have, in effect, been committing an act of unthinking, unilateral educational disarmament.

The Nation at Risk report urged the country to set heightened expectations for *all* students to meet the demands of stiffer global competition.

> The risk is not only that the Japanese make automobiles more efficiently than Americans. . . . It is not just that the South Koreans recently built the world's most efficient steel mill, or that American machine tools, once the pride of the world, are being displaced by German products. It is also that these developments signify a redistribution of trained capability throughout the globe. Knowledge, learning, information, and skilled intelligence are the new raw materials of international commerce and are today spreading throughout the world. . . . If only to keep and improve on the slim competitive edge we still retain in world markets, we must dedicate ourselves to the reform of our educational system for the benefit of all—old and young alike, affluent and poor, majority and minority. Learning is the indispensable investment required for success in the "information age" we are entering.[87]

As we will show in part III, the Nation at Risk archetype is still the dominant and driving force behind national, state, and local education policy into the third decade of the twenty-first century. But we maintain that the rationale for its original purpose has been superseded by a still more profound change. As we will set forth in part IV, creating a more meaningful and contemporary archetype for the needs and challenges of the twenty-first century will require a new purpose of education. To understand why this will be a daunting task, we now turn to part II, where we expose the corrupting influences that have been the shadow side to the much-vaunted American dream.

NOTES

1. Upon witnessing the successful detonation of the first atomic bomb, physicist Robert Oppenheimer, the "father of the atomic bomb," recalled a line from the Bhagavad Gita, "Now I Am Become Death, the Destroyer of Worlds." See https://www.youtube.com/watch?v=n8H7Jibx-c0.

2. "Ships Hit During WWI," Uboat.net, accessed Feb. 1, 2023, https://www.uboat.net/wwi/ships_hit/losses_year.html?date=1917-11.

3. Cuthbertson, *The Halifax Explosion: Canada's Worst Disaster* (Toronto: Patrick Crean Editions, 2017), 37.

4. Nick Walker, "The Disaster that Reshaped a City," *Canadian Geographic*, December 6, 2017.

5. Cuthbertson, *The Halifax Explosion*, 173.

6. Alex Wellerstein, "Counting the Dead at Hiroshima and Nagasaki," *Bulletin of Atomic Scientists* (August 4, 2020), https://thebulletin.org/2020/08/counting-the-dead-at-hiroshima-and-nagasaki/.

7. Hans M. Kristensen and Matt Korda, "Nuclear Arsenals of the World," *Federation of American Scientists Nuclear Notebook,* accessed Feb. 1, 2023, https://thebulletin.org/nuclear-notebook/#post-heading.

8. Robert J. Watson, *History of the Office of the Secretary of Defense (Volume IV): Into the Missile Age, 1956–1960.* U.S. Department of Defense (Government Printing Office, 1997), 1.

9. John M. Logsdon, "R-7," *Encyclopedia Britannica*, May 17, 2015, https://www.britannica.com/technology/R-7.

10. John Foster Dulles, "The Strategy of Massive Retaliation," speech before the Council on Foreign Relations, January 12, 1954, http://msthorarinson.weebly.com/uploads/4/1/4/5/41452777/dulles_address.pdf.

11. Annie Jacobsen, *Operation Paperclip: The Secret Intelligence Program that Brought Nazi Scientists to America* (New York: Little, Brown & Company, 2014).

12. Franklin D. Roosevelt, "Letter to Vannevar Bush," November 17, 1944, National Science Foundation, https://www.nsf.gov/about/history/nsf50/vbush1945_roosevelt_letter.jsp.

13. Roosevelt, "Letter to Vannevar Bush."

14. David Hawkins, Edith C. Truslow, and Ralph Carlisle Smith, "Manhattan District History Project Y: The Los Alamos Project," Los Alamos Scientific Laboratory of the University of California Los Alamos, Dec. 1, 1961, https://www.osti.gov/opennet/manhattan-project-history/publications/LANLMDHProjectYPart1.pdf.

15. "National Science Foundation," Performance.gov, last updated Jan. 7, 2021, https://trumpadministration.archives.performance.gov/NSF/#:~:text=The%20National%20Science%20Foundation%20(NSF,people%20to%20create%20knowledge%20that.

16. National Science Foundation, *The First Annual Report of the National Science Foundation, 1950–1951*(Washington, DC: U.S. Government Printing Office), viii, https://www.nsf.gov/about/history/ann_report_first.pdf.

17. Merriam Hartwick Trytten, *Student Deferment in Selective Service: A Vital Factor in National Security* (Minneapolis, MN: University of Minnesota Press, 1952), 49–54, https://archive.org/details/studentdeferment0000tryt/page/54/mode/1up?view =theater.

18. Keith Olson, "The G. I. Bill and Higher Education: Success and Surprise," *American Quarterly* 25, no. 5 (Dec. 1973): 596–610.

19. Lawrence P. Blum, "Research News and Communications," *The Journal of Educational Research* 45, no. 1 (1951): 67–74, https://doi.org/10.1080/00220671 .1951.10881921.

20. Alan R. Blackmer et al., *General Education in School and College: A Committee Report by Members of the Faculties of Andover, Exeter, Lawrenceville, Harvard, Princeton, and Yale* (Cambridge, MA: Harvard University Press, 1952), 133–134.

21. Eric Rothschild, "Four Decades of the Advanced Placement Program," *The History Teacher* 32, no. 2 (February 1999).

22. "Summary of the Atomic Energy Act," United States Environmental Protection Agency, last updated on March 21, 2022, https://www.epa.gov/laws-regulations /summary-atomic-energy-act.

23. Barton J. Bernstein, "Sacrifices and Decisions: Lewis L. Strauss," *The Public Historian* 8, no. 2 (1986): 105–120, https://doi.org/10.2307/3377436.

24. Lewis L. Strauss, "Freedom's Need for the Trained Man: Remarks to Sixth Thomas Alva Edison Foundation Institute, November 24, 1955," *Hearings Before the Joint Committee on Atomic Energy, Congress of the United States, 1956* (Washington, DC: U.S. Government Printing Office), 40.

25. "Hearings Before the United States Senate Committee on Armed Services: The Preparedness Investigating Subcommittee Inquiry into Satellite and Missile Programs November 25, 25, 27, December 13,14, and 17, 1957, January 10,13,15,16,17, 20, 21 and 23, 1958," https://babel.hathitrust.org/cgi/pt?id=uc1.b5107082&view=page &format=plaintext&seq=46&q1=TellerNovember%2025.

26. "Hearings Before the United States Senate Committee on Armed Services," 20.

27. "Hearings Before the United States Senate Committee on Armed Services," 20.

28. "Hearings Before the United States Senate Committee on Armed Services," 24.

29. U.S. House, "National Defense Education Act of 1958," https://history.house .gov/HouseRecord/Detail/15032436195.

30. "Hearings Before the United States Senate Committee on Armed Services: The Preparedness Investigating Subcommittee Inquiry into Satellite and Missile Programs."

31. John G. Brainard, "Genesis of the ENIAC," *Technology and Culture* 17, no. 3 (July 1976): 482–488.

32. *History of Computing in the Twentieth Century* (Academic Press, Cambridge, Mass 1980), 525–550.

33. This includes bombs and warheads; guided and ballistic missiles; artillery, mortar, rocket, and small arms ammunition; all mines, torpedoes, and depth charges; demolition charges; pyrotechnics; clusters and dispensers; cartridge and propellant actuated devices; electro-explosive devices; clandestine and improvised explosive devices.

34. Anne C. Fitzpatrick, "Teller's Technical Nemesis: The American Hydrogen Bomb and Its Development within a Technological Infrastructure," *Society for Philosophy and Technology Quarterly* 3, no. 3 (Spring 1998): 119–123.

35. Jan Van der Spiegel, "ENIAC-on-a-Chip," University of Pennsylvania, updated December 27, 2012, https://www.seas.upenn.edu/~jan/pictures/eniacpictures/EniacChipPackaged.jpg.

36. Josef Taalbi, "Origins and Pathways of Innovation in the Third Industrial Revolution," *Industrial and Corporate Change* 28, no. 5 (October 2019): 1125–1148.

37. Darko Galinec, Darko Možnik, and Boris Guberina, "Cybersecurity and Cyber Defence: National Level Strategic Approach, *Automatika* 58, no. 3 (2017): 273–286, https://doi.org/10.1080/00051144.2017.1407022.

38. Michael J. Mazarr et al., *Hostile Social Manipulation: Present Realities and Emerging Trends* (Santa Monica, CA: RAND Corporation, 2019).

39. Cynthia Dion-Schwarz, David Manheim, and Patrick B. Johnston, *Terrorist Use of Cryptocurrencies: Technical and Organizational Barriers and Future Threats* (Santa Monica, CA: RAND Corporation, 2019).

40. "The Specialized High Schools Student Handbook 2011–2012," New York City Department of Education Office of Assessment and the Division of Portfolio Planning, https://testprepshsat.com/wp-content/uploads/2014/05/SHSAT_2011_HandbookFinal.pdf.

41. Elizabeth S. Auritt, "Harvard Accepts Record Low of 5.9 Percent to the Class of 2016," *The Harvard Crimson*, March 29, 2012.

42. Joshua Lederberg (1941), Nobel Prize in Physiology or Medicine, 1958; Robert Fogel (1944), Nobel Memorial Prize in Economic Sciences, 1993; Roald Hoffmann (1954), Nobel Prize in Chemistry, 1981; Richard Axel (1963), Nobel Prize in Physiology or Medicine, 2004.

43. "About," North Carolina School of Science and Mathematics, https://www.ncssm.edu/about.

44. "Best STEM High Schools 2022," *U.S. News & World Report*, https://www.usnews.com/education/best-high-schools/national-rankings/stem.

45. Drew Lindsay, "The Success Factory," *Washingtonian Magazine*, October 2009.

46. "Quick Facts: Fairfax County, Virginia," U.S. Census, https://www.census.gov/quickfacts/fairfaxcountyvirginia.

47. Cindy Wei, "Connections," *NCSSSMST Journal* 12, no. 2 (Spring 2007): 12–13.

48. "About," National Consortium of Secondary STEM Schools, last updated 2023, https://www.ncsss.org/about/.

49. The ranking criterion was a formula based on schools' number of advanced placement math and science courses and students' AP test scores.

50. "The Nuclear Testing Tally," Arms Control Association, Aug. 2022, https://www.armscontrol.org/factsheets/nucleartesttally.

51. "The Largest Bomb Ever Dropped," Military.com, Dec. 9, 2011, https://www.military.com/video/nuclear-bombs/nuclear-weapons/the-largest-bomb-ever-dropped/1318659315001.

52. "The Cuban Missile Crisis, October 1962," U.S. Department of State Office of the Historian, https://history.state.gov/milestones/1961-1968/cuban-missile-crisis.

53. Michael Ellman and S. Maksudov, "Soviet Deaths in the Great Patriotic War: A Note. *Europe-Asia Studies* 46, no. 4 (1994): 671–680.

54. H.G.W. Davie, "Soviet Casualties—Factors, Effects and Outcomes History of Military Logistics," History of Military Logistics [blog], Oct. 19, 2018, https://www.hgwdavie.com/blog/2018/10/6/soviet-casualties.

55. Francois Bourguignon and Christian Morrisson, "Inequality among World Citizens: 1820–1992," *The American Economic Review* 92, no. 4 (2002): 727–744. https://doi.org/10.1257/00028280260344443.

56. Bourguignon and Morrisson, "Inequality."

57. U.S. Census Bureau, "Real Median Family Income in the United States," updated Sep. 13, 2022, https://fred.stlouisfed.org/series/MEFAINUSA672N, Oct. 13, 2020.

58. U.S. Census Bureau, *Bicentennial Edition: Historical Statistics of the United States, Colonial Times to 1970* (Washington, DC: Bureau of the Census, 1975).

59. Ibid.

60. Keith W. Olson, Olson, "The G. I. Bill and Higher Education: Success and Surprise," *American Quarterly* 25, no. 5 (1973): 596–610, https://doi.org/10.2307/2711698.

61. National Center for Education Statistics, "120 Years of American Education: A Statistical Portrait," 77, https://nces.ed.gov/pubs93/93442.pdf.

62. Charles Maland, "Dr. Strangelove (1964): Nightmare Comedy and the Ideology of Liberal Consensus," *American Quarterly* 31, no. 5 (Winter 1979): 697–717.

63. "The Bay of Pigs," John F. Kennedy Presidential Library and Museum, https://www.jfklibrary.org/learn/about-jfk/jfk-in-history/the-bay-of-pigs.

64. "The Last Helicopter: Evacuating Saigon," *Newsweek*, April 26, 2015, https://www.newsweek.com/last-helicopter-evacuating-saigon-321254.

65. U.S. Senate, "Final Report of the Select Committee to Study Governmental Operations with Respect to Intelligence Activities," 1976, https://archive.org/details/ChurchCommittee/Church%20Committee%20Book%20I%20-%20Foreign%20and%20Military%20Intelligence/.

66. U.S. Energy Information Administration, "Oil and Petroleum Products Explained," updated Nov. 2, 2022, https://www.eia.gov/energyexplained/oil-and-petroleum-products/imports-and-exports.php.

67. Frank A. Verrastro and Guy Caruso, "The Arab Oil Embargo—40 Years Later," The Center for Strategic and International Studies (CSIS), Oct. 16, 2013, https://www.csis.org/analysis/arab-oil-embargo%E2%80%9440-years-later.

68. Canada, Japan, the Netherlands, the United Kingdom, and later extended to Portugal, Rhodesia and South Africa.

69. Greg Myre, "Gas Lines Evoke Memories of Oil Crises in the 1970s, National Public Radio, Nov. 10, 2012, https://www.npr.org/sections/pictureshow/2012/11/10/164792293/gas-lines-evoke-memories-oil-crises-in-the-1970s.

70. Greg Myre, "Gas Lines."

71. Central Intelligence Agency, "USSR-Iran Boundary, 1951," declassified report 4/17/2000, https://www.cia.gov/readingroom/docs/CIA-RDP79-00976A000200010003-4.pdf.

72. Comptroller General of the United States, "Report to Congress: Issues Related to U. S. Military Sales and Assistance to Iran, October 21, 1974," https://www.gao.gov/assets/120/111930.pdf.

73. Immigration and Refugee Board of Canada, "Iran: Information on SAVAK," accessed Oct. 14, 2020, https://www.refworld.org/docid/3ae6aaa724.html; and Jonathan C. Randal, "SAVAK Jails Stark Reminder of Shah's Rule," *Washington Post*, December 13, 1979, https://www.washingtonpost.com/archive/politics/1979/12/13/savak-jails-stark-reminder-of-shahs-rule/b2b37be2-356a-43e2-ba68-dd474e9023b0/.

74. The Cinema Rex fire was set ablaze on Aug. 19, 1978.

75. Jahangir Amuzegar, *The Dynamics of the Iranian Revolution: The Pahlavi's Triumph and Tragedy* (New York: SUNY Press, 1991).

76. G. John Ikenberry, *Reasons of State: Oil Politics and the Capacities of American Government* (Ithaca, NY: Cornell University Press, 1988), 1.

77. Nina Serafino, Curt Tarnoff, and Dick K. Nanto, "Report to Congress: U.S. Occupation Assistance: Iraq, Germany and Japan Compared," March 23, 2006, https://sgp.fas.org/crs/natsec/RL33331.pdf.

78. The World Bank, "GDP (current U.S.$): Germany, Japan, United States," https://data.worldbank.org/indicator/NY.GDP.MKTP.CD?locations=DE-JP-US.

79. Includes all trucks and buses: light trucks, such as pickups, sport utility vehicles, and minivans.

80. United States Department of Transportation, Bureau of Transportation Statistics, "Table 1–23: World Motor Vehicle Production, Selected Countries," https://www.bts.gov/archive/publications/national_transportation_statistics/table_01_23.

81. Mark Bowden, "The Desert One Debacle," *The Atlantic,* May 2006.

82. Ronald Reagan, "Address Accepting the Presidential Nomination at the Republican National Convention in Detroit, July 17, 1980," The American Presidency Project, https://www.presidency.ucsb.edu/documents/address-accepting-the-presidential-nomination-the-republican-national-convention-detroit.

83. Southern Regional Education Board, "65 Years Helping States Improve Education," 2013, https://www.sreb.org/sites/main/files/file-attachments/13e04_65_years.pdf?1458835252.

84. "The Need for Quality: A Report to the Southern Regional Education Board by Its Task Force on Higher Education and the School," June 1981, https://files.eric.ed.gov/fulltext/ED205133.pdf.

85. National Commission on Excellence in Education, "A Nation at Risk: An Imperative for Educational Reform," April 25, 1984, http://edreform.com/wp-content/uploads/2013/02/A_Nation_At_Risk_1983.pdf.

86. National Commission on Excellence in Education, "A Nation at Risk."

87. National Commission on Excellence in Education, "A Nation at Risk."

Part II

THE CORRUPTION OF PURPOSE

Filling the conscious mind with ideal conceptions is a characteristic of Western theosophy, but not the confrontation with the shadow and the world of darkness. One does not become enlightened by imagining figures of light, but by making the darkness conscious. The later procedure, however, is disagreeable and therefore not popular.

—Carl G. Jung[1]

We began this book by asking a few simple questions: What should we teach children in the twenty-first century, and how should they be taught? Given the pace of knowledge expansion and global change, can we teach forthcoming generations anything of lasting value? To begin to answer these questions, we outlined how 13 different aims of education emerged over the course of 400 years since the founding of the earliest American colonies. We sketched in broad strokes the many profound and unexpected changes that came into being and how new purposes of education emerged from them. We also stressed the reciprocal relationship between the aspirations and needs of the larger society in each era and the purposes of education that made those changes possible to be sustained. Thus, there could be no Industrial Revolution, for example, without inventors and industrially trained workers. Nuclear deterrence would not be sustainable without nuclear scientists, engineers, and a host of technicians. Fulfilling the aspirations and needs of society depends on raising new generations of young talent, laborers, and citizens. In turn, these hopes for the future shape the purposes of education. As we saw in part I, hope and change are inexorably linked with the purposes of education, each mutually influencing and making the other possible. Thus, the purposes of education that we described in part I have a certain gravitas as to why they came about and still exist.

At the same time, there are shadows associated with these purposes—dark sides of the American spirit that course underground through each era: the sense of entitlement that comes from wealth and privilege; nativism and xenophobia; the ideology of White Protestant Christian supremacy; and the irrational antagonisms against science and objective facts. Thus, the shadow of the Hampton Archetype is the sense of superiority that animated and justified the enslavement of Blacks. The Cold War of the Classroom's shadow was manifest in the many U.S.-Soviet proxy wars fought in Third World countries, such as in South and Central America, Vietnam, and Iran, where the rights to self-determination were trampled.

The origins of these shadows in the United States begin with European monarchs' horrific conquest of Indigenous peoples in the New World. These shadows are not events per se, but twisted psychologies emanating from ideologies and legal doctrines that have justified oppression, cruelty, forced assimilation, and cultural dominance. Their influence can be seen in a myriad of historical chronologies, which are too numerous to detail here and well beyond our scope. But the main point is that these shadows, these darker spirits, are still with us in the twenty-first century. Their continued presence corrupts the purposes of education and the nobler aspirations of younger generations.

The purposes of education—the collective raising of children—are replete with moral, social, and economic implications. Education is not an object, as if it were a detachable commodity that can be bought and sold, a uniform and objective *thing* that one can acquire or consume. Rather, as we have shown in part I, its defining purposes for the direction of new generations reflect historic changes and cultural aspirations attached to the larger issues and ethnos that define an era.

The American dream and the hope of education are in a symbiotic relationship; each is at once influenced by and dependent upon the other. If we are to move beyond our current Nation at Risk archetypal purpose to conceive a new purpose of education for the twenty-first century—a purpose that provides hope for diverse voices and equitable inclusion while reexamining priorities to make a more just and uplifting society—we must acknowledge and deal with these shadows. They are also part of the American story that demands, in the spirit of Jung's directive, to be brought to light if we want a more enlightened educational system and society. And they are still very much with us today, as the jarring rhetoric of public discourse reveals.

Part II is about shedding light on these shadows by using the very words and legal doctrines of those who have attempted and mostly succeeded in enforcing their will on others, thereby distorting the original purpose of an education archetype. In our experience trying to improve schools and education, we encountered their presence. They cannot be ignored and should not be feared but illuminated. Candid conversations are essential. We hope that the influence of these shadows can be minimized.

In the opening chapter of part 2, we look at the long shadow cast by extreme wealth inequality and White male privilege. We show how it impacts schools in counterproductive ways. Chapter 7 describes the demeaning nativist attitudes toward and fear of immigrants as far back as Benjamin Franklin and how it impacts schooling. Chapter 8 describes the long shadow of White supremacist structures as seen through the lens of America's two original sins: the near extermination of the American Indian and their forced assimilation and the stain of slavery and its creation of a near-permanent underclass. We conclude with chapter 9, where we examine the shadows of anti-science and superstition.

NOTE

1. Carl G. Jung, *Collected Works of C.G. Jung, Volume 13: Alchemical Studies* (United Kingdom: Princeton University Press, 1953), 265.

Chapter 6

Wealth, Education, and the Cycles of Privilege and Poverty

The people are turbulent and changing; they seldom judge or determine right. Give, therefore, to the first class a distinct, permanent share in the government.[1]

—Alexander Hamilton

EXTREME WEALTH INEQUALITIES

The wealthy, well-educated, and well-connected have sat atop the heap in the United States for centuries.[2] The extent of their influence belies their relatively small number. It has been so from the beginning. Consider Chester County, Pennsylvania, a mostly White, rural area situated between Philadelphia, Pennsylvania, and Wilmington, Delaware, and one of the three original counties that William Penn, Jr., established when he landed in Philadelphia in 1682.[3] An extensive study of the assessed taxable wealth in Chester County indicates that in 1693, the top tenth of all taxpayers held nearly *four* times the amount of wealth as the bottom tenth (24 percent versus 6 percent, respectively). Over the course of the next century, the number of taxpayers in Chester County grew twentyfold (from 257 to 5,291 taxpayers), and the disparity in wealth grew even wider. By 1782, the top tenth held over *thirty-three times* the amount of wealth held by the bottom tenth (33 percent versus 1 percent, respectively).[4]

Chester County was not unique. Disparities in wealth continued to widen elsewhere in the colonies, as evidenced by tax and estate probate records. For example, in Boston's Suffolk County, the top tenth of the population owned 42 percent of the wealth. In six Maryland counties, among adult males with estates, the top 10 percent owned nearly 66 percent of all the wealth.[5] In colonial cities, wealth inequalities were even greater. In Philadelphia, by the time of the signing of the Declaration of Independence, the city's top tenth in population held 72 percent of its taxable wealth.[6] Meanwhile,

> Everywhere the poor were struggling to stay alive, simply to keep from freezing in cold weather. All the cities built poorhouses in the 1730s, not just for old people, widows, crippled, and orphans, but for unemployed, war veterans, and new immigrants. In New York, at mid-century, the city almshouse, built for one hundred poor, was housing over four hundred. A Philadelphia citizen wrote in 1748: "It is remarkable what an increase of the number of Beggars there is about this town this winter."[7]

In the southern states, the disparities were even more severe. By the time of the adoption of the U.S. Constitution in 1790, slavery had already existed for 170 years in the colonies. As the most populous state, Virginia had 748,000 people, of whom 302,000 were slaves. Not only did slaves hold no wealth, but they were regarded as property and, as such, constituted a significant portion of White slaveholders' wealth. Yet wide wealth disparities existed even among White families. Nearly two in three southern White families did *not* own a slave, many of them being poor farmers or indentured servants themselves.[8] Figure 6.1 illustrates that of the 77,000 slaveholding families, only about 1,000 families had fifty slaves or more, and several dozen extremely wealthy families had over 200 slaves.[9,10]

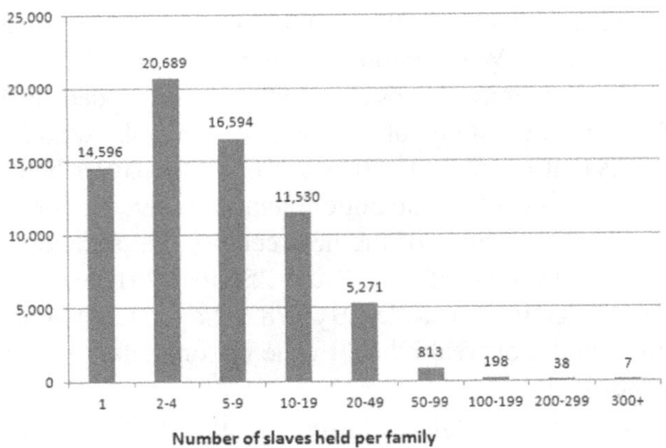

Figure 6.1   Number of Families Holding Slaves in Four Southern States in 1790 *Average share of wealth for each household out of 100s households. *Source*: U.S. Census, 1909.

WEALTH AND DEMOCRACY

The shadowy nexus between very wealthy White males and democracy dates back to the founding of the United States. Of the 103 people who either signed the 1776 Declaration of Independence or were delegates to the 1787 Constitution Convention, all were White men.[11] Most were wealthy by colonial standards. Many had slaves, George Washington among them, (although he released them upon his death).[12] Robert Morris, the Philadelphian financier who signed both documents, was one of the richest people in America at the time.[13]

The superior political status of wealthy White men was implicitly written into the original U.S. Constitution as well as the original thirteen state constitutions. While the U.S. Constitution stipulated that the "[U.S.] House of Representatives shall be composed of Members chosen every second Year by the People of the several States,"[14] it allowed each *state* legislature to determine *who* could vote in these elections.[15] As to the selection of U.S. Senators, the original U.S. Constitution left the decision to the *state* legislatures.[16] Except for New Jersey,[17] twelve states' early constitutions enfranchised only "freemen" who had paid taxes and established a length of residency. Pennsylvania's 1790 constitutional language was typical:

> In elections by the citizens, every freeman of the age of twenty-one years, having resided in the state two years next before the election, and within that time paid a state or county tax, which shall have been assessed at least six months before the election, shall enjoy the rights of an elector.[18]

Later in 1838, Pennsylvania amended its constitution to clarify that only *White* freemen could vote. The selection of the president was determined by the top vote-getter in the Electoral College, where each state was entitled to the number of presidential electoral votes, which corresponded to the state's total number of house representatives plus their two U.S. senators. However, the U.S. Constitution left it to the state legislatures to determine *how* to choose their presidential electors. In the first presidential election of 1788/1789, only six states chose their electors by popular vote, which totaled less than 50,000 votes nationwide.[19] This number represented only about 15 percent of the total number of free White males over the age of twenty-one. Entirely excluded were women, slaves, American Indians, and indentured servants. The remaining states either didn't choose presidential electors at all or left it up to their state legislatures. Of the 138 electoral votes cast, George Washington received exactly half; the remaining being split among twelve other candidates.[20]

Thus, the entire legal framework in the early years of the United States at the federal, state, and local levels gave effective control of affairs to an exceedingly small, privileged portion of the adult population who were White male landowners and who also happened to hold the bulk of the nation's wealth. Those who had high net worth could influence state legislatures and governors and, through them, the federal legislature or become candidates for office themselves. Some of our Founding Fathers possessed an unabashed sense of superiority, claiming it was their right to rule. The New York banker and delegate to the Constitutional Convention, Alexander Hamilton, succinctly expressed this view:

> All communities divide themselves into the few and the many. The first are the rich and well-born, the other the mass of the people. The voice of the people has been said to be the voice of God; and however generally this maxim has been quoted and believed, it is not true in fact. The people are turbulent and changing; they seldom judge or determine right. Give, therefore, the first class a distinct, permanent share in the government. They will check the unsteadiness of the second, and, as they cannot receive any advantage by a change, they therefore will ever maintain good government.[21]

Wealth inequality in the United States continues into the twenty-first century and has grown even more extreme, posing even greater threats to democracy. In 2020, the top 1 percent of households in the United States held more than 31 percent of the entire country's wealth.[22] By contrast, the bottom half of households held less than 3 percent. To illustrate this difference, imagine 100 people splitting up 100 apples. One person at the top gets to keep thirty-one apples all to themselves. The fifty people at the bottom get only three apples total.

The top 10 percent of households hold 68 percent of the nation's wealth. One advantage of being in the top 10 percent is the ability to afford private education and all the benefits that go with it: smaller class size, better teachers and faculty, better facilities and technologies, more academic and extracurricular opportunities, travel studies, and a safer environment compared to most public schools. In turn, better-educated children have a better chance of replicating their parents' wealth and privilege in a virtuous cycle—wealth begets more wealth.[23]

There is wealth, and then there is *extreme* wealth. To qualify for the Forbes 400 list of the richest Americans in 2022, the threshold was a net worth of $2.7 *billion*.[24] The spirit of the Hamiltonian upper class's right to rule is still with us in the twenty-first century. People in the Forbes 400 do not just buy private education for their children; they can in effect buy U.S. Senate and presidential candidates by giving tens of millions to political action committees (PACs) to campaign on their behalf, including funding the never-ending stream of negative political television ads.

Once their candidate is elected, this high-end donor class expects laws, regulations, and tax codes to be enacted that are favorable to their group. In addition to donating millions to favored PACs, individuals with extreme wealth have the means to buy entire cable media outlets, regional news stations, and online platforms to spread their message, reaching millions and even billions of people. They can fund academic think tanks and nonprofit advocacy research organizations that provide an appearance of legitimacy to their policy agendas, shaping national public opinion for or against issues and causes. They can undertake protracted legal actions to wear down their opponents and even influence the selection of federal judges, including U.S. Supreme Court justices! Finally, they have the resources to invent and amplify contrived cultural controversies in education, such as "Critical Race Theory," to stir up passions for or against political candidates. In her book *Dark Money: The Hidden History of the Billionaires Behind the Rise of the Radical Right*, Jane Mayer describes how conservative billionaires exert social and political influence. One example is brothers Charles and David Koch, whose estimated $90-billion fortune was made by owning thousands of miles of pipelines, oil refineries, and paper, coal, and chemical companies.[25] Mayer recounted how the Koch brothers spent some of their resources on a long-term quest to "destroy the prevalent statist paradigm":

> [The Kochs] subsidized networks of seemingly unconnected think tanks and academic programs and spawned advocacy groups to make their arguments in a national political debate. They hired lobbyists to push their interests in Congress and operatives to create synthetic grassroots groups. . . . In addition, they financed legal groups and judicial junkets to press their cases in court. Eventually, they added to this a private political machine that reviled, and threated to subsume, the Republican Party.[26]

Those who have extreme wealth have the ability to greatly amplify their social and political views by owning many media outlets so that contrary voices are excluded or misrepresented. In a 1978 article written by Charles Koch and published in a magazine he owned, he outlined his strong libertarian views, calling for a radical deregulation of business and the lifting of legal restrictions against certain personal behaviors, such as voluntary sexual activities. Koch argued that to promote liberty, "we need a movement. Only with a movement can we build an effective force for social change. Our movement should have as its goal the fulfillment of the ideals of the free and independent entrepreneur. . . . Our movement must destroy the prevalent statist paradigm and erect, in its stead, a new paradigm of liberty for all people."[27]

Extreme wealth can work to monopolize the means of communication and pump disinformation to targeted groups to create echo chambers where facts and evidence are discredited by attacking the messenger. While Mayer's book focuses on the interplay between extreme wealth and national politics, there is an analogous interplay between wealth and *education.*

THE INTERPLAY OF EXTREME WEALTH DISPARITIES AND EDUCATION

Extremely wealthy individuals or their foundations have exerted a major influence on the type and direction of attempted education improvements by making very large grants (e.g., $10 to $150 million) to school districts and politically connected think tanks. Unfortunately, this can lead to unintended negative consequences. We say this without questioning the sincerity of a person's philanthropic intent or diminishing their generosity. Nonetheless, we can identify four types of unintended consequences to educational projects funded by those with extreme wealth.

The first negative consequence is that very large grants to school districts to initiate changes can turn out to be ineffective, or worse, counterproductive. A second risk is that a school district's time and attention may be consumed with a benefactor's pet project, thereby crowding out other approaches that may have greater evidence of effectiveness. The third risk is that positive improvements may not be sustainable but instead dependent on the benefactor's continued largesse. The fourth risk is that the larger the grant, the more likely it will be involved in partisan politics. A case in point involved the Annenberg Challenge.

The Annenberg challenge was launched in December 1993 with a gift of $500 million from billionaire Walter H. Annenberg (1908–2002) to improve public schools. It was a five-year school reform effort that required a local match. Three of the largest awards were made to Philadelphia ($50 million), Chicago ($49.2 million), and Los Angeles ($53 million). Altogether, eighteen sites were funded.[28] The matching requirement generated another $600 million from private and public sources.[29] The Annenberg Challenge had three goals: (1) to improve education in the inner city; (2) to assist isolated rural schools; and (3) to demonstrate that the arts should be part of every child's education. All three goals were seen as vital to preserving American democratic values. However, the Annenberg Challenge was also entangled with national politics. President Clinton announced the program in the Rose Garden. The Chicago Annenberg Challenge was chaired by then Illinois State Senator Barack Obama. When Mr. Obama ran for president in 2008, he was attacked for his association with the project and with former anti-Vietnam protester William Ayers, who helped write Chicago's proposal to Annenberg. Partisan critics claimed Obama was out to radicalize students.[30] As might be expected, the Annenberg Challenge's eighteen sites were controversial, and the results were mixed. To the Annenberg Foundation's credit, they have been forthcoming about the lessons learned. Three of their many reports are instructive for anyone who attempts large-scale change in school districts.[31] Annenberg grants were not unique, but they illustrate how extremely wealthy people can steer educational agendas that crowd out more fundamental discussions as to the purposes of education.

LOCAL BEHAVIOR

Large wealth inequalities are felt most directly at the local level, where there is a vast divide between those who can afford to send their children to private schools or move to affluent, predominantly White suburban school districts and those who are trapped in poor, often dysfunctional communities without the financial means to escape. In between is a large multiracial suburban populace of modest means stuck with the schools they have. Urban districts get the most attention because they have large portions of students who consistently score below proficiency in reading, mathematics, and science. The battle over proposed solutions tends to be framed as a choice between either: (1) providing more resources to poorer districts in the name of fairness or (2) providing no additional resources to poor districts without greater accountability for the funds already provided. Both positions miss the mark.

An example of the first position is a ruling in a 1981 class action lawsuit, Abbott v. Burke, filed on behalf of twenty children attending public schools in four New Jersey towns. The case challenged New Jersey's system of financing public education under the Public School Education Act of 1975 (Chapter 212). The New Jersey Supreme Court ruled in Abbott's favor, reasoning as follows:

> This record proves what all suspect: that if the children of poorer districts went to school today in richer ones, educationally they would be a lot better off. Everything in this record confirms what we know: they need that advantage much more than the other children. And what everyone knows is that as children the only reason they do not get that advantage is that they were born in a poor district. For while we have underlined the impact of the constitutional deficiency on our state, its impact on these children is far more important. They face, through no fault of their own, a life of poverty and isolation that most of us cannot begin to understand or appreciate.[32]

From 1981 to 2017, there have been twenty-seven Abbott rulings in New Jersey,[33] which resulted in substantially more state funds going to poorer school districts.[34] While the Court's reasoning may make intuitive sense, many research studies, including ours, have consistently shown little evidence to support the belief that increased school spending *necessarily* leads to improved student performance. For example, Coate and Vanderhoff found no relationship between additional district expenditures and high school student achievement before and after the 1990 Abbott II court decision. Ritter and Lauver analyzed the same data and concluded that the higher funding received by Abbott districts did not seem to improve student outcomes.[35] Simple resources are likely to be a necessary but not sufficient condition for improving teaching and learning outcomes.[36,37]

Other studies show that "adequacy litigation" like Abbott v. Burke can play only a limited role in a comprehensive education reform strategy.[38] Peevely and Ray found that students in the school districts that prevailed in Tennessee's school-finance litigation showed no consistent pattern of greater gains than students in the rest of the state.[39] In our study, we looked for any relationship between levels of school expenditures across fifteen different expense categories and student state test scores across nearly 500 high schools. We found little to no association between levels of education expenditures and eleventh-grade student achievement after controlling for other variables. Instead, the strongest factor associated with state test scores and SAT scores was the percentage of adults in a district who had a four-year college degree. This is followed by the percentage of White students in a district and the percentage of students eligible for free and reduced lunch. Spending per pupil, regardless of expenditure category, had no association with student achievement on the Pennsylvania System of Student Assessment (PSSA), or at best only a weak positive or a weak negative correlation with student achievement.[40]

How does one reconcile the seeming contradiction between the New Jersey Supreme Court's reasoning in *Abbott v. Burke* and the research on how little additional expenditures for poorer school districts improve student achievement? We believe the Court's reasoning about the effects of poverty is correct but misplaced. The issue is not with poorly funded school districts as much as it is with low-income *households* and their surrounding *communities*. Students from low-income households live in poor communities. As a result, these children have multiple disadvantages even before birth: higher infant mortality and disabilities, higher cases of asthma and lead contamination, food deserts, and neighborhood crime.[41] Consider the impact of children with excessive blood lead levels and their test scores. Lead is a well-known neurotoxin that can have negative cognitive and behavioral consequences. At the 21st Century Partnership for STEM Education, we studied the relationship between children who live in Philadelphia zip codes with different percentages of lead contamination as defined by the Environmental Protection Agency (EPA) and the test scores on the Pennsylvania System of Student Assessment (PSSA). Our findings in figure 6.2 illustrate an association between the percentage of students with lead contamination in different zip codes and their schools' third-grade test results.[42] As the chart shows, the greater the percentage of students with elevated blood lead levels, the worse the students performed on their state tests in math and reading. Families with low incomes tend to live in lead-contaminated neighborhoods because they lack the means to move out.

In summary, wealth accumulation over generations gives beneficiaries greater stability compared to those whose income is limited to wages and salaries. People accumulate wealth not only from home ownership but also from income-producing assets such as rental properties, stocks and bonds, and commercial ventures that produce regular income over an extended period that is undiminished by sickness or disability. Furthermore, upon death, a person's wages and salary go to zero, but their wealth lives on and is passed on to their heirs. A study by the U.S. Bureau of Labor Statistics found that about 30 percent of households could expect to receive an inheritance that would amount to nearly 40 percent of their net worth.[43] Families that cannot accumulate wealth are stranded where they are. Thus, educating children is set within a larger family, community, and economic context.

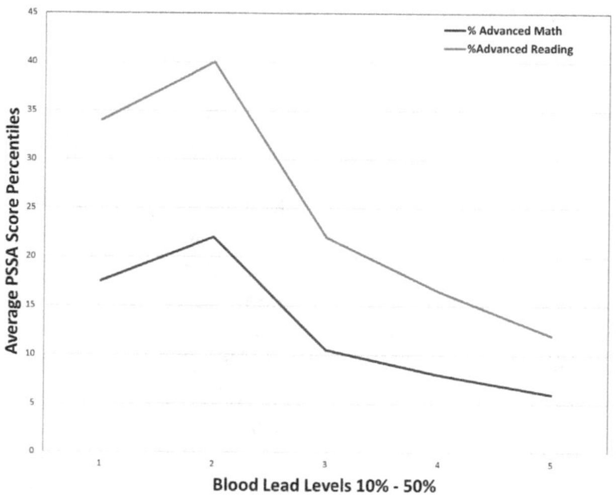

Figure 6.2 Third Grade 2005 PSSA Score Percentiles in Advanced Math and Reading by the Blood Levels in Children. *Blood lead levels are ranked 1 to 5 corresponding to 10 percent to 50 percent of a zip code having excessive blood lead levels. *Source:* From an unpublished study by the authors.

If we want to improve the chances of success in life for disadvantaged children, the crushing negative cycle must be interrupted. Family and neighborhood impoverishment leads to unsuccessful educational outcomes which in turn leads to poor life outcomes. To be sure, equitable school funding is necessary, but it will never be sufficient. At best, it can ameliorate deplorable conditions and inadequate facilities. At worst, arguments over equitable school funding can draw attention away from the larger consequences of extreme wealth inequalities, where the bottom half of families has only 3 percent of the nation's wealth among them, while the top half has 97 percent of the wealth.

Anyone who desires to improve public education within the current *Nation at Risk* purpose or develop a new purpose of education more attuned to the realities of the twenty-first century must contend with the corrupting influences of extreme wealth inequality. But that's not all. In the next three chapters, we illuminate three additional long shadows and their corrupting influences on the purposes of public education, each impairing progress in a different way.

NOTES

1. Alexander Hamilton, "Speech at the Federal Convention, June 18, 1787," in *The Works of Alexander Hamilton,* Vol. 1, ed. Henry Cabot Lodge (New York: Putnam, 1904), https://oll.libertyfund.org/title/lodge-the-works-of-alexander-hamilton-federal-edition-vol-1#Hamilton_0249-01_1098.

2. We use the term wealth (net worth) rather than income level because a household can have high income but also high amounts of debt, resulting in low or even negative net worth.

3. Pennsylvania Historical and Museum Commission, Chester County History, http://www.phmc.state.pa.us/bah/dam/rg/di/IncorporationDatesForMunicipalities/pdfs/chester.pdf?catid=15.

4. James T. Lemon and Gary Nash, "The Distribution of Wealth in Eighteen-Century America: A Century of Change in Chester County Pennsylvania 1693-1802," *Journal of Social History.* 2, no. 1 (1968): 1–24, https: doi:10.1353/jsh/2.1.1.

5. Jeffrey Williamson and Peter H. Lindert, "Long-Term Trends in American Wealth Inequality," in *Modeling the Distribution and Intergenerational Transmission of Wealth,* ed. James D. Smith (Chicago: University of Chicago Press, 1980), 9–94.

6. Williamson and Lindert, "Long-Term Trends," 78.

7. Howard Zinn, *The People's History of the United States* (New York: Harper Collins, 2010), 39. Chapter 3 describes the economic conditions in Colonial America.

8. W.S. Rossiter, "A Century of Population Growth: From the First to the Twelfth Census of the United States: 1790-1900" (U.S. Census, 1909): 135, https://www2.census.gov/library/publications/decennial/1900/century-of-growth/1790-1900-century-of-growth-part-1.pdf.

9. Rossiter, "A Century," 136.

10. Alice Hanson Jones, *Wealth of a Nation to Be: American Colonies on the Eve of the Revolution* (New York: Columbia University Press, 1980).

11. There were fifty-six signers of the Declaration of Independence and fifty-five delegates to the Constitutional Convention. Eight men were both signers in 1776 and Convention delegates in 1787.

12. See Henry Wiencek, *An Imperfect God: George Washington, His Slaves, and the Creation of America* (New York: Farrar, Straus, and Giroux, 2003).

13. Kevin Phillips, *Wealth and Democracy: A Political History of the Rich and Poor* (New York: Broadway Books, 2002).

14. U.S. Constitution, art. 1, sec. 2.

15. U.S. Constitution, art. 1, sec. 4.

16. U.S. Constitution, art. 1, sec. 3.

17. The New Jersey constitution was originally gender neutral, allowing "all inhabitants" to vote, thus theoretically allowing single or widowed females with property to vote. In 1807, the NJ Assembly passed a law limiting suffrage to "free white males." For more detail, see Judith Apter Klinghoffer and Lois Elkis, "The Petticoat Electors: Women's Suffrage in New Jersey, 1776-1807," *Journal of the Early Republic* 12, no. 2 (Summer, 1992): 159–193.

18. The 1790 Pennsylvania constitution was amended in 1838 to read: "ARTICLE III Section I. Election franchise. In elections by the citizens, every white freeman of the age of twenty-one years, having resided in the State one year, and in the election district where he offers to vote, ten days immediately preceding such election, and within two years paid a State or county tax, which shall have been assessed at least ten days before the election, shall enjoy the rights of an elector.

19. Michael J. Dubin, *United States Presidential Elections, 1788–1860: The Official Results by County and State* (Jefferson: McFarland Publishing, 2002).

20. U.S. Census Bureau, "Series Y 79-83: Electoral and Popular Vote Cast for President, by Political Party 1789-1968," *Historical Statistics of the United States: Colonial Times to 1970* (Census Bureau, 2003), 1073–1074.

21. Alexander Hamilton, "Speech at the Federal Convention."

22. Board of Governors of the Federal Reserve System, "Distribution of Household Wealth in the U.S. since 1989," https://www.federalreserve.gov/releases/z1/dataviz/dfa/distribute/table/#quarter:133;series:Net%20worth;demographic:networth;population:all;units:shares.

23. Edward N. Wolff and Maury Gittleman, "Inheritances and the Distribution of Wealth or Whatever Happened to the Great Inheritance Boom?" *The Journal of Economic Inequality* 12 (2014): 439–468.

24. Rob LaFranco and Chase Peterson-Withorn, "The Forbes 400 2022" (2023), https://www.forbes.com/forbes-400/.

25. "Charles Koch," Forbes.com, https://www.forbes.com/profile/charles-koch/?sh=27d17b7557d7.

26. Jane Mayer, *Dark Money: The Hidden History of the Billionaires Behind the Rise of the Radical Right* (New York: Doubleday, 2016), 6. The practice of fabricating a grassroots movement to sway public opinion is known as "astroturfing."

27. Charles Koch, "The Business Community: Resisting Regulation," *Libertarian Review* (August 1978): 34.

28. "The Annenberg Challenge," The Annenberg Foundation, https://annenberg .org/initiatives/the-annenberg-challenge/.

29. Dakari I. Aarons, "Backers Say Chicago Project Not 'Radical,'" *Education Week* (October 9, 2008).

30. Dakari I. Aarons, "Backers."

31. The Annenberg Foundation published three reports on the results of the Annenberg Challenge: "Research Perspectives on School Reform: Lessons from the Annenberg Challenge" (2003); "The Annenberg Challenge: Lessons and Reflections on Public School Reform" (2002); "The Arts and School Reform: Lessons and Possibilities from the Annenberg Challenge Arts Projects" (2003).

32. Abbott v. Burke, 119 N.J. 287 (NJ 1990).

33. See the Education Law Center, https://edlawcenter.org/litigation/abbott-v -burke/abbott-history.html.

34. Douglas Coate and James VanderHoff, "Public School Spending and Student Achievement: The Case of New Jersey," *Cato Journal* 19, no. 1 (1999): 85–99.

35. Gary W. Ritter and Sherri C. Lauver, "School Finance Reform in New Jersey: A Piecemeal Approach to a Systemic Problem," *Journal of Education Finance* 28, no. 4 (2003): 575–598.

36. W. N. Grubb, (2008). "Multiple Resources, Multiple Outcomes: Testing the "Improved" School Finance with NELS88," *American Educational Research Journal* 45, no. 1 (2008): 104–144.

37. William J. Glenn, "School Finance Adequacy Litigation and Student Achievement: A Longitudinal Analysis," *Journal of Education Finance* 34, no. 3 (2009): 247–266.

38. Michael A. Rebell, "Professional Rigor, Public Engagement and Judicial Review: A Proposal for Enhancing the Validity of Education Adequacy Studies," *Teachers College Record* 109, no. 6 (2007): 1303–1373.

39. Gary L. Peevely and John R. Ray, "Does Equalization Litigation Effect a Narrowing of the Gap of Value Added Achievement Outcomes Among School Districts?" *Journal of Education Finance* 26, no. 3 (2001): 319–332.

40. F. Joseph Merlino et al., "Are Educational Expenditures Associated with 11th Grade Student Achievement in Pennsylvania School Districts?" *The 21st Century Partnership for STEM Education* (November 2010).

41. Richard Rothstein, *Class and Schools: Using Social, Economic, and Educational Reform to Close the Black-White Achievement Gap* (New York: Teacher College Press, 2004).

42. The 21st Century Partnership for STEM Education, unpublished study.

43. Wolff and Gittleman, "Inheritances," 1.

Chapter 7

White Protestant Nativism and "Otherness"

E Pluribus Unum—Out of Many, One

—The Great Seal of the United States of America

The U.S. one-dollar bill is so commonly used that many people might assume the Great Seal on its reverse side is of minor significance. Yet this iconography succinctly summarizes the central idea of the Founders' aspirational vision for the United States of America. This vision continues to be one of the most important unfulfilled goals for our country in the twenty-first century. In this chapter, we explain why, and how the future of education is bound up with this original vision of "out of many, one."

On July 4, 1776, the Continental Congress of the newly formed United States passed a resolution to form a committee to design a seal for the new government. Leading the committee were Benjamin Franklin, John Adams, and Thomas Jefferson. Six years and several more committees later, the Great Seal of the United States was finally approved. It is adorned with much symbolism. Thirteen stars above the eagle's head symbolize the original thirteen states.[1]

The motto, *E Pluribus Unum,* Latin for "Out of Many, One," signifies the union of those thirteen states.

The meaning of *E Pluribus Unum* is central to the nation's identity, yet it contains inherent ambiguities. The motto originally referred to "out of many *states,* one *union"*—the United *States.* However, it is unclear whether the Founders also meant the motto to mean "Out of many, one union of *people.*" Our Founders expressed this second meaning in the preamble to the Constitution: "We the *People* of the United States, in Order to form a more perfect Union . . ."[2] But the "We" did not include American Indians, slaves, women, indentured servants, or unnaturalized immigrants who did not have voting and other legal rights. One of the first laws passed by Congress, the Naturalization Act of 1790, defined who could become a naturalized citizen: a free White person only.[3]

Out of four million people in 1790, Whites comprised 81 percent of the total population, excluding American Indians. Blacks represented 19 percent, of whom the vast majority (90 percent) were slaves. The country's White ethnic composition was overwhelmingly English and northern European. Nearly eight in ten Whites were either English, Scots Irish, Scottish, Irish, or Welsh.[4] Although the 1790 census did not collect data on religious affiliation, congregational records show that Protestant denominations constituted 98 percent of all the houses of worship in the United States (see table 7.1).[5] Seventy-four years later, in 1850, the number of congregations increased eleven-fold. Protestants continued to be the overwhelming majority, dominating religious, civic, and cultural life.

As we described in Chapter 1, fierce religious rivalries emerged between Protestant sects. These sectarian rifts were the impetus behind William Penn's 1682 Frame of Government and the Quaker archetype of education, which emphasized religious tolerance and separation of church and state. However, as the tide of new immigrants from different Northern European lands continued to flood prerevolutionary America, tensions rose. In the 1750s, none other than Benjamin Franklin wrote to a friend disparagingly about the influx of German immigrants into Philadelphia.

Those who come hither are generally of the most ignorant Stupid Sort of their own Nation, and as Ignorance . . . few of the English understand the German

Table 7.1   Congregations in the United States 1776 and 1850

	1776		1850	
Denomination	Number	Percent	Number	Percent
Congregational	668	20.7	1,725	4.5
Presbyterian	588	18.2	4,858	12.8
Baptist	497	15.4	9,563	25.1
Episcopal	495	15.3	1,459	3.8
Quaker	310	9.6	726	1.9
German Reformed	159	4.9	341	0.9
Lutheran	150	4.6	1,231	3.2
Dutch Reformed	120	3.7	335	0.9
Methodist	65	2	13,302	34.9
Other Protestants	176	3.6	3,247	8.5
Total Protestant	3,228	98	36,787	96.5
Roman Catholic	56	1.7	1,222	3.2
Jewish	5	0.02	36	0.01

Data from Rodney Stark and Roger Finke, "American Religion in 1776: A Statistical Portrait," *Sociological Analysis*, 49, no. 1 (Spring 1988): 39–51.

Language, and so cannot address them either from the Press or Pulpit, 'tis almost impossible to remove any prejudices they once entertain. Their own Clergy have very little influence over the people; who seem to take an uncommon pleasure in abusing and discharging the Minister on every trivial occasion. Not being used to Liberty, they know not how to make a modest use of it . . . Thus they are under no restraint of Ecclesiastical Government. . . . Few of their children in the Country learn English; they import many Books from Germany. . . . In short unless the stream of their importation could be turned from this to other Colonies, as you very judiciously propose, they will soon so outnumber us, that all the advantages we have will not [in My Opinion] be able to preserve our language, and even our Government will become precarious.[6]

In 1798, Congress, then located in Philadelphia,[7] passed a series of laws known as the Alien and Sedition Acts (later repealed) that made it lawful for the president "to order all such aliens as he shall judge dangerous to the peace and safety of the United States . . . to depart out of the territory of the United States."[8] Nonetheless, despite the fear of aliens, immigration continued and accelerated. Starting around 1820 (when official immigration records began to be kept), several waves of immigrants came to the United States. More than nine out of ten immigrants were from Northern Europe. While previously some immigrants to colonial America were Scots-Irish or Ulster-Irish *Protestants* from Northern Ireland, this time a new element came pouring in: nearly two million Irish *Catholics,* making them the largest group of immigrants. In the first wave of recorded Irish immigration from 1820 to 1827, over 30,000 came to the United States. In the decade that followed, Irish immigration increased *tenfold.*[9] Then, a third wave of Irish fled to the United States due to the potato famine beginning in 1845. By the start of the Civil War in 1861, upward to five million Irish immigrants had arrived. Many Protestants saw them as an existential threat to the ideals of the new republic.[10]

THE PHILADELPHIA BIBLE RIOTS OF 1844

The Protestant character of English colonial America was rooted in the bloody history and corruption of the Roman Catholic Church that precipitated the Reformation. American Protestants were resolute in their rejection of Rome and the Pope, whom they considered capable of imposing dominion over them in all aspects of their personal, spiritual, and public lives if the Pope were able to gain control. As evidence, Protestants cited various Papal encyclicals and decrees. On August 15, 1832, Pope Gregory XVI issued an encyclical letter addressed to all "Patriarchs, Primates, Archbishops, and Bishops," repudiating the main pillars of the U.S. Constitution and Bill of Rights, calling such principles the "dark conspiracy of impious men."

Freedom of the press, he wrote, was that "pest of all others most to be dreaded in a state," with its "unbridled liberty of opinion, licentiousness of speech and a lust of novelty, which . . . portend the downfall of the most powerful and flourishing empires." He went on, "Regarding that worst and never-sufficiently to be execrated and detested liberty of the press for the diffusion of all manner of writings. . . . Far other hath been the discipline of the Church in extirpating this pest of bad books, even as far back as the times of the Apostles, who we read committed a great number of books publicly to the flames."[11]

Self-government and freedom of religious expression were viewed by the Pope as, "the zeal of some to separate the Church from the State, and to burst the bond which unites the priesthood to the Empire. For it is clear that this union is dreaded by the profane lovers of liberty." Many U.S. Protestants saw Irish Catholic immigrants as holding allegiance to and potentially being secret agents of the Pope and therefore direct threat to American values. As a counterpoint to such papal positions, the Third U.S. Congress had added more conditions for new arrivals to become naturalized citizens: they had to renounce allegiance to "any foreign, prince, potentate, state or sovereignty" and relinquish any titles of nobility.[12]

This anti-immigrant impulse only grew stronger and more intense as Irish immigration swelled. Adding to the fear of Catholic immigrants undermining Protestant core values were economic concerns. The Panic of 1837, what has been called America's first Great Depression,[13] lasted six years and severely reduced labor demand. Within this contracted environment, Protestants resented the Irish Catholic immigrants as competitors for scarce jobs.

In Philadelphia, opposition to Irish Catholic immigrants intensified when aggressive Protestant gangs repeatedly assaulted Irish Catholics and Blacks. Adding fuel to the fire, in 1838, a year into the Panic, the Pennsylvania legislature mandated that the Protestant King James Bible be a daily part of the public school curriculum. The mandate was an attempt to force Irish Catholic children to assimilate into the Anglo-Protestant culture.[14] In November 1842, twenty-eight Philadelphia ministers formed the American Protestant Association (APA) with a mission to warn Protestants about the dangers of the Pope. Its founding documents included a thirty-page address crafted by a committee of Philadelphia Protestant clergy that proclaimed the Roman Catholic Church and its Pope represented no less than the Antichrist.

The ground on which the glorious Reformation was undertaken and achieved was that the Popery was the great *Antichrist* so minutely detailed in the prophecies of Daniel, in several of the Epistles, and in the Book of Revelation; and that this view has not only been adopted by the great body of Protestant

Commentators and Divines, but incorporated in the Creeds and Confessions of nearly all of the Reformed Churches.[15]

To Protestant clergymen, the goal of the Roman Pope was to systematically infiltrate and ultimately take a controlling interest in the United States of America, supported by unsuspecting Protestants:

> Seminaries [are] springing up in every part of the valley of the Mississippi and sustained mainly by Protestant families. . . . And now we see a gigantic scheme set on foot in Great Britain disseminating Popery here by planting large colonies of Papists in our Western states. . . . The church of Rome has determined to spare no effort or expense for the purpose of securing a controlling influence in the Valley of the Mississippi, and thereby, a political predominance in the country at large, and an expansion of her power and influence which would be felt throughout the world.[16]

Given these fears about the ultimate goals of the Vatican, the purpose of the APA was established to "awaken the attention of the community to the dangers which threaten the liberties, and the public and domestic institutions, of these United States from the assaults of Romanism." With this mandate, Native (Protestant) American clubs or "American Republic Associations" sprang up throughout Philadelphia to advocate for the Protestant Bible in public schools, the suppression of immigration numbers, and the tightening of requirements for naturalization. Philadelphia historian Sam Warner writes, "The platforms of these associations called for the lengthening of the waiting period for naturalization to twenty-one years, the restriction of public office to citizens born in the United States and the teaching of the Protestant version of the Bible in public schools."[17] Irish Catholics strongly objected to these Protestant positions. They had endured a long history of massacres and oppression at the hands of the English going back to the twelfth century.[18] Their Catholic Douay Bible symbolized their fight to preserve their culture and identity as distinct from English Protestants. Compromises were attempted, but by 1843, the Philadelphia School Board effectively cut off further debate by banning the Catholic Douay Bible from use in public schools because it had notes and commentary. It was clear that nativist Anglo-Protestants were using the King James Bible in Pennsylvania's public schools to force Irish Catholic immigrants to assimilate into their Protestant cultural norms.

In May 1844, a series of public speeches and demonstrations by Native Protestant American groups took place in the Nanny Goat Market in the Kensington area of Philadelphia, a working-class, predominantly Irish Catholic enclave. Violent clashes ensued between the two groups. At the time,

Philadelphia was merely a patchwork of semi-autonomous neighborhoods loosely held together by a fragmented and weak police force. Over the next two months, mayhem broke out, leaving twenty dead, one hundred injured, and thirty homes and two Catholic churches burned to the ground.[19] To cap the conflict, on July 4, 1844, a Grand Parade was staged in Philadelphia attended by nativist groups from twenty-six states. Their members marched, sat in horse-drawn barouches, and rode horses. Each group carried placards with political artwork and banners proclaiming their nativist Protestant principles, such as:

"The Bible the basis of Education and Safeguard of Liberty"
"Our fathers gave us the Bible; we will not yield it to a foreign land"
"Foreign influence is one of the most baneful foes of Republican government"
"Beware of Foreign Influences"
"America—Our Native Land"[20]

The 1844 Bible riots shocked the rest of Philadelphians into taking action to unify the police, establish a paid fire department, and consolidate the outlying industrial neighborhoods into a single city government. But it did not resolve the Bible impasse in public schools between Anglo-Protestants and Irish Catholics. As it would turn out, there was no reconciliation between the two groups. In the end, Philadelphia Catholic Archbishop Francis Patrick Kenrick abandoned efforts to allow the Catholic Bible to be used in public schools and instead pursued plans for a separate, privately funded, Catholic-controlled school system.

NATIVISM BECOMES A POLITICAL PARTY

A year after the nativist parade in Philadelphia, the first National Convention of the American Party was held on the fifth and seventh of July 1845, also in Philadelphia. This political party's extensive manifesto of Declarations and Principles echoed the same nativist spirit as the Protestant rectors' revolt against Catholicism and the Pope's alleged plan for U.S. domination. Here is an excerpt of the American Party's lengthy declaration that illustrates their demonization of European immigrants:

A large proportion of the foreign body of citizens and voters now constitutes a representation of the worst and most degraded of the European population, victims of social oppression, of personal vices, utterly divested by ignorance or crime, of the moral and intellectual requisites for political self-government. . . . numerous societies and corporate bodies in foreign countries have found it economical to transport to our shores, at public and private expense, the feeble, the imbecile, the idle, and intractable, thus relieving themselves of the burdens resulting from the vices of the European social systems, by availing themselves of the generous errors of our own.[21]

In 1851, Irish immigration reached a high point with 221,253 new arrivals, accounting for nearly six out of ten immigrants. As tens of thousands of German and other Central and Southern European immigrants also arrived, nativist resentments grew more public and overtly political. By "nativist resentments" we mean the dominant Protestant culture's sense of entitlement, privilege, social superiority, and cultural ownership, all of which were seen as being impinged upon by foreigners: Catholics, Jews, and those from non-English countries of origin.[22]

Whatever the political form, nativism has regularly stepped out of the shadows in full public view to oppose each new wave of immigrants. For example, from 1900 until the start of World War I, nearly 13.4 million immigrants came to the shores of the United States. Two-thirds of these new immigrants originated from Italy, Central Europe, or Tsarist Russia,[23] reinvigorating the usual nativist reactions. Political cartoons portrayed these immigrants as "riffraff" and a menace to American ideas and institutions. In truth, the successive waves of immigrants have acted time and again to uphold the American ideals of freedom, equality, opportunity, and merit-based advancement. Their belief in these ideals is what drew them to America in the first place. Immigrants were the ones most willing to work hard in menial and dangerous jobs and serve in the U.S. armed forces. In the Civil War, immigrants, mostly Irish and German, made up a quarter of Union soldiers and another 18 percent had a foreign-born parent.[24] In World War I nearly one in five U.S. soldiers was born overseas. Thirteen of these immigrant soldiers received the Medal of Honor.[25] This underscores the fact that many immigrants, particularly the children of immigrants, *wanted* to assimilate into the dominant culture—to become *Americanized.*

From 1820 until 2021, the United States admitted over eighty-seven million legal immigrants.[26] Until about 1940, eighty percent to 98 percent of all immigrants were from either Europe or Canada and consisted predominantly of predominantly White Christians. Despite Anglo-Protestant nativist reactions toward these European/Canadian newcomers, their assimilation and acceptance eventually occurred after several generations. However, the acceptance of Catholics and Jews by the dominant Anglo-Protestant culture has been more problematic. During Senator John F. Kennedy's 1960 presidential campaign, for example, a coalition of evangelical Protestants and conservative business people and politicians dispersed hundreds of anti-Catholic articles and publications throughout the country warning of the dangers of a Vatican-controlled White House.[27] Only two American presidents out of forty-six have been Irish Catholics (Kennedy and Biden), and no Italians, Hispanics, Jews, or Muslims have held that office to date.

NATIVISM 2.0

By 1980, the percentage of European and Canadian immigrants to the United States dropped precipitously to only about 10–15 percent.[28] In their place, Hispanic, Asian, and African immigration grew dramatically. Since 1980, there have been about ten million new immigrants every decade, the vast majority of whom were neither White nor Protestant. As a result, nativists in the twenty-first century have constructed even more fearful images of *others* to sow fear among Whites, particularly Christian evangelicals. Instead of Germans, Irish and Italian Catholics, and Jews, the new "menace" is comprised of alleged rapists from Mexico, drug gangsters from Colombia, Islamic terrorists from Somalia, anti-Christian turban-headed Sikhs from Punjab, hijab-wearing Muslims from the Middle East, and so on down the list. Compounding the "otherness" of these new immigrants is the fear that Whites will soon be overrun and become a minority group in their own country.

In the twenty-first century, the White percentage of the U.S. population will indeed dip below 50 percent. The declining percentage of White Protestants in the United States is due to the raw numbers of new immigrants and their birthrate, which is outpacing the birthrate of Whites. Figure 7.1 shows that in 2020, for the first time, the number of non-White children under eighteen years of age was equal to the number of White (non-Hispanic) children. If current trends continue, by 2060, White children will constitute only about 36 percent of the total.

At the same time, unprecedented and rapid changes in *adult* demographics are also occurring. Whites have consistently constituted 85 to 90 percent of the U.S. population since 1790, the year of the first U.S. Census (excluding American Indians). The other 10–12 percent of the population has been predominantly Black. But since 1980, the population share of Whites has been steadily *declining*. The U.S. Census projects the White (non-Hispanic) population in the United States will no longer be dominant by 2045. Whites will be in the *minority* for the first time.[29]

The major drivers of these demographic changes are the growth in immigration by Hispanic, Asian Indian, and other non-European ethnicities along with U.S. domestic births of children from these same ethnic groups. With a population of eighty-seven million, Hispanics now make up the largest minority group in the country. While Hispanic is a category used by the U.S. Census, Hispanic immigrants come from more than twenty different

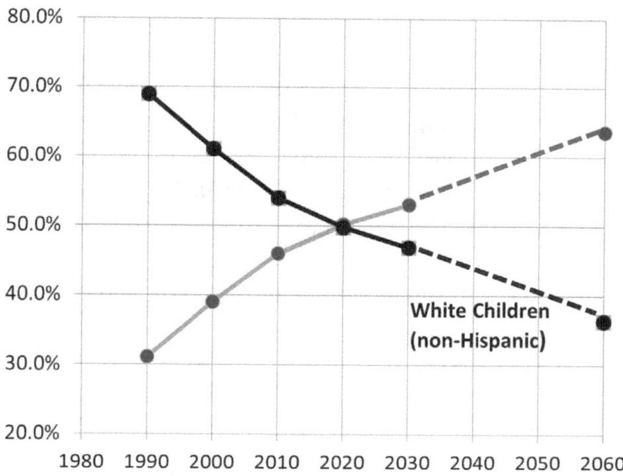

Figure 7.1 Percent of White (Non-Hispanic) and Children of Color Under Eighteen Years of Age. Dotted lines represent the projected portion of school children by race from 2030 to 2060. *Source*: Data sourced from U.S. Census Bureau, "2017 National Population Projections Tables: Main Series," accessed May 13, 2023, https://www.census .gov/data/tables/2017/demo/popproj/2017-alternative-summary-tables.html.

Table 7.2 Hispanic Immigrants' Countries of Origin

Central American	2010 Census	South American	2010 Census
Mexican	31,798,258	Argentinean	224,952
Puerto Rican	4,623,716	Bolivian	99,210
Cuban	1,785,547	Chilean	126,810
Dominican	1,414,703	Colombian	908,734
Costa Rican	126,418	Ecuadorian	564,631
Guatemalan	1,044,209	Paraguayan	20,023
Honduran	633,401	Peruvian	531,358
Nicaraguan	348,202	Uruguayan	56,884
Panamanian	165,456	Venezuelan	215,023
Salvadoran	1,648,968	Other South Amer.	21,809
Other Central Amer	31,626	Spaniard	635,253
Sub-total	43,620,504	All other	3,452,403
		Sub-total	6,857,090

Adapted from Sharon R. Ennis et al., "The Hispanic Population: 2010," Table 4 (May 2011), 8 https://www. census.gov/content/dam/Census/library/publications/2011/dec/c2010br-04.pdf

countries, as shown in table 7.2. They are not a monolithic group in terms of educational attainment, economic class, culture, or politics.[30]

Many Protestant Whites find these new demographic realities alarming. Most Hispanics are Catholic. Most other immigrants are non-White, and many are non-Christian. This new demographic reality provides a ready-made rationale for the rebirth of Protestant nativism with its religious demigods, craven politicians, and media pundits who would exploit divisions along ethnic, racial, religious, and cultural lines for their own purposes—money and votes. Consider, for example, the nativist passion expressed by one reader's comments appended to an August 2010 *Smithsonian Magazine* article about the changing demographics of America:

> We did, in fact, at one time, used to be the greatest nation in the world. We had the best educational system in the world, the highest standard of living, number one in most industries and the most technically advanced nation in the world. Of course, these things were in the pre-diversity days of America, when the old red, white, and blue was roaring like a lion and national identity and patriotism was strong. These things have gradually eroded over the past 45 years to where they no longer exist. It is obvious to all but the most dimwitted that we are in terminal decline and have been for some time. An extra 100 million, mostly illiterate third worlders added to the population will exacerbate that decline much more quickly, although I find it hard to believe that we won't crash long before we reach that number.[31]

How does the rest of the American public feel about these demographic trends? It depends on whom you ask.

In 2018, the Pew Research Center surveyed the U.S. population involving a representative sample of 2,524 adults on their views about America's future.[32] When asked whether having a majority of the U.S. population made up of Hispanics, Blacks, Asians, and other racial minorities by the year 2050 will strengthen or weaken American customs and values, *half* (46 percent) of Whites believed that having a majority non-White population will *weaken* American values. This compares with only 18 percent of Blacks and 25 percent of Hispanics who hold the same opinion. Conversely, 40 percent of Blacks and 46 percent of Hispanics said diversity will *strengthen* America. But only 23 percent of Whites agreed.

The Pew Research Center asked another question: "Are you optimistic or pessimistic about America's future over the next 30 years?" Again, there was a sharp difference along racial and ethnic lines. Seventy percent of Blacks and 67 percent of Hispanics were either somewhat or very *optimistic* about America's future. This contrasts with only 51 percent of Whites.

This is a curious finding. As we noted in the previous chapter, people of color generally fall into the lowest rungs of wealth and income. In addition, data on nearly every other measure of well-being—educational attainment, health condition, job prospects, and public safety—show vast inequalities between Whites and people of color. Why would people of color be optimistic about the future? One might expect that if any group should feel pessimistic about America's future, it would be groups that have been historically marginalized. And yet, Whites are much more pessimistic about America's future over the next thirty years than people of color. Why is that?

The Pew Center report did not delve into the reasons for Whites' pessimism about America's future. One theory is that different subpopulations of Whites foresee different kinds of depressing news. Some may worry about not meeting the global challenges such as reversing climate change and preventing global conflicts. Other noncollege, educated Whites may foresee that more jobs shifting overseas robbing them of the earning power that they once had. Still, a third group of Whites may be pessimistic about the future because they perceive hordes of non-White immigrants streaming into the country.

Older White people remember a time when the United States was close to 90 percent White. For nearly four centuries, the burden was on new immigrants to adjust and adapt to the dominant White Protestant culture. And many gladly did so. Now, in the twenty-first century, it is the *White Protestants* who feel they are being forced to deal with a shifting demographic reality. The dramatic diversification of the United States has left many Whites feeling like a foreign invasion is occurring. Cable news channels and social media platforms regularly show thousands of migrants camping along the southern border. These images and others like them enable media pundits and politicians to whip up nativist sentiments with frightening images—the more threatening the better—for advertising dollars and political contributions.[33] The United States is not only becoming more racially and ethnically diverse, but its geographic distribution throughout the country is also becoming lumpy; that is, different racial and ethnic groups are not uniformly distributed geographically. Whites in certain regions do not experience the rich diversity in America and see it as an asset. Instead, they feel threatened by non-Whites encroaching on their territory. Cable news shows and social media propagate conspiracies like the "Great Replacement" and "White Extinction" theories.[34]

This fear has led to vigorous legislative efforts to enact more restrictive immigration and naturalization laws and cries to build a two-thousand-mile wall along the southern border. In the meantime, many older Whites retreat to retirement villages or outer-ring suburban and rural areas where the local population is still more than 80–90 percent White. Ironically, it was a violent horde of *White* people who stormed the United States Capitol on January 6, 2021, in an attempt to prevent the peaceful transfer of presidential power.

THE PEOPLE ON THE FRONT LINES—TEACHERS AND PRINCIPALS

How can "we, the people" form a more perfect union when there is such vitriolic divisiveness over its increasing ethnic and racial diversity? The people on the front lines of this issue are the nearly 6.7 million public school teachers, school administrators, instructional aids, and support staff working in nearly 100,000 public schools.[35] Each school day, they face a wide diversity of students in terms of race, ethnicity, language, culture, religion, socioeconomic status, learning readiness, and behavioral and cognitive challenges. Each day, they make choices about how to engage and teach all of them. It is not easy. Research, for example, shows that teachers tend to pay more attention to boys than girls. Black students are more likely to be punished than White students for the same offense.[36] Teachers must be sensitive to gender roles and orientations and neurological and personality spectrums.

In 1975, Congress passed the Education for All Handicapped Children Act[37] to support states and localities in protecting infants, toddlers, children, and youth with disabilities and their families. This law led to the Individuals with Disabilities Education Act (IDEA), which governs how states and public agencies provide services to more than 7.5 million eligible children and youth with disabilities.[38] Under the IDEA, students must be placed in the "least restrictive environment" and in regular classrooms with appropriate support whenever possible. *Otherness* has also been addressed to some degree in Title IX legislation protecting people in federally funded educational programs from discrimination based on sex.

It is the duty of adults who work in public schools to exemplify kindness and acceptance of children with disabilities and provide them with the best education possible. This requires *inclusive leadership* from school boards and administrators, teachers, coaches, and parents. A healthy school and peer culture where bullying is disdained and children are not made the butt of cruel jokes requires the artful nurturing and disciplining of children where restorative justice and community norms and sanctions constrain abusive behaviors.[39] To our good fortune, we have witnessed classrooms in which children who are visually impaired, deaf, disabled, disfigured, or even dressed out of the norm are treated inclusively. This is the spirit of education for all.

Yet, in the twenty-first century, public schools and those who work in them are surrounded by a larger socio-political environment of divisiveness over diversity where politicians and media agitators use schools as pawns in their culture wars. The poisonous vapors of nativism and violence toward others seep into public schools, corrupting their purpose. According to school safety surveys, 22 percent of students have been bullied, with the most being reported in rural schools. In 2020–2021 there were forty-three mass school shootings and another fifty shootings with injuries.[40]

Public schools are indispensable to the cultivation of character and social/emotional competencies that help provide the cohesive bonding to unite a diverse people. The great challenge for school teachers and university faculty is to try to understand, appreciate, and find ways to teach students who are different from themselves and/or who come from social and economic environments unfamiliar to them. An equitable and safe school environment encourages student learning, creativity, and social responsibility where conflicts are resolved through restorative justice practices. But to do this sort of cultivation, to achieve the dream of "Out of many people, one nation," we need to reckon with an even darker and longer shadow than nativism that goes to our very origins. This shadow is the subject of our next chapter.

NOTES

1. U.S. Department of State, "The Great Seal of the United States," https://usa.usembassy.de/etexts/gov/great_seal.pdf.

2. "The Constitution of the United States," National Archives, https://www.archives.gov/founding-docs/constitution-transcript.

3. "Naturalization Acts of 1790 and 1795," George Washington's Mount Vernon, https://www.mountvernon.org/education/primary-source-collections/primary-source-collections/article/naturalization-acts-of-1790-and-1795/.

4. Thomas L. Purvis, "The European Ancestry of the United States Population 1790: A Symposium," *The William and Mary Quarterly* 41, no. 1 (January 1984): 85–101. English 59.7 percent, Scots Irish 10.5 percent [Ulster Ireland Protestant], German 8.9 percent, Irish 5.8 percent, Scottish 5.3 percent, Welsh 4.3 percent, Dutch 3.1 percent , French 2.1 percent, and Swedish 0.3 percent.

5. Rodney Stark and Roger Finke, "American Religion in 1776: A Statistical Portrait," *Sociological Analysis* 49, no. 1 (Spring 1988): 39–51.

6. "From Benjamin Franklin to Peter Collinson, May 9, 1753," Founders Online, National Archives, https://founders.archives.gov/documents/Franklin/01-04-02-0173. [Original source: *The Papers of Benjamin Franklin*, vol. 4, July 1, 1750, through June 30, 1753, ed. Leonard W. Labaree (New Haven: Yale University Press, 1961), 477–486.

7. Robert Fortenbaugh, *The Nine Capitals of the United States* (York: Maple Press, 1948).

8. "Alien and Sedition Acts (1798)," National Archives. The Sedition Act also made it a crime for American citizens to "print, utter, or publish . . . any false, scandalous, and malicious writing" about the government.

9. U.S. Census Bureau, "Series C 89-119: Immigrants, by Country: 1820 to 1970," *Historical Statistics of the United States: Colonial Times to 1970* (Census Bureau, 2003), 105.

10. L. J. McCaffrey, *The Irish Catholic diaspora in America* (Washington, DC: Catholic University of America Press, 1997).

11. Pope Gregory XVI, *Mirari Vos: On Liberalism and Religious Indifferentism, August 15, 1832* (Kansas City: Angelus Press, 1998).

12. . United States Naturalization Act of 1795 (1 Stat. 414, enacted January 29, 1795), para. 4.

13. Alasdair Roberts, *America's First Great Depression: Economic Crisis and Political Disorder After the Panic of 1837* (Ithaca, NY: Cornell University Press, 2012).

14. Anthony S. Bryk, Valerie E. Lee, and Peter B. Holland, *Catholic Schools and the Common Good* (Cambridge: Harvard University Press, 1993).

15. American Protestant Association, *Address of the Board of Managers* (1843), 14, https://babel.hathitrust.org/cgi/pt?id=umn.31951001508384m&view=1up&seq=5.

16. American Protestant Association, *Address,* 18.

17. Sam Bass Warner, *The Private City: Philadelphia in Three Periods of its Growth* (Philadelphia, PA: University of Pennsylvania Press, 1968), 144.

18. John Gillingham, "The Beginnings of English Imperialism," *Journal of Historical Sociology* 5, no. 4 (December 1992): 392–409, https://doi.org/10.1111/j.1467-6443.1992.tb00033.x.

19. Melissa Mandell, "The Kensington Riots of 1844," Historical Society of Pennsylvania, http://www.philaplace.org/story/316/.

20. John Hancock Lee, *The Origin and Progress of the American Party in Politics; Embracing a Complete History of the Philadelphia Riots in May and July, 1844, with a Full Description of the Great American Procession of July Fourth, and a Refutation of the Arguments Founded on the Charges of Religious Proscription and Secret Combinations* (Philadelphia: Elliot & Gihon, 1855), 136–140, https://archive.org/details/originprogressof00leejuoft.

21. John Hancock Lee, *The Origin,* 235–236.

22. Norman L. Friedman, "Nativism," *Phylon* 28, no. 4 (1967): 408–415.

23. U.S. Census Bureau, "Series C 89-119."

24. Don H. Doyle, *The Cause of All Nations: An International History of the American Civil War* (New York: Basic Books, 2015).

25. U.S. Citizenship and Immigration Services, "The Immigrant Army: Immigrant Service members in World War 1," accessed May 9, 2023, https://www.uscis.gov/about-us/our-history/history-office-and-library/featured-stories-from-the-uscis-history-office-and-library/the-immigrant-army-immigrant-service-members-in-world-war-i#:~:text=Foreign%2Dborn%20soldiers%20composed%20over,patriotism%20for%20their%20new%20country.

26. United States Department of Homeland Security, "Yearbook of Immigration Statistics 2022, Table 1."

27. John Huntington, "The Kennedy Speech that Stoked the Rise of the Christian Right," *Politico*, March 8, 2020, https://www.politico.com/news/magazine/2020/03/08/the-kennedy-speech-that-stoked-the-rise-of-the-christian-right-123369.

28. Campbell Gibson and Kay Jung, "Historical Census Statistics on Population Totals by Race, 1790 to 1990, and by Hispanic Origin, 1790 to 1990, for the United

States, Regions, Divisions, and States," https://www.census.gov/content/dam/Census /library/working-papers/2002/demo/POP-twps0056.pdf.

29. U.S. Census Bureau, "2017 National Population Projections Tables: Alternative Scenarios," accessed May 13, 2023, https://www.census.gov/data/tables/2017/ demo/popproj/2017-alternative-summary-tables.html.

30. Sharon R. Ennis et al., "The Hispanic Population: 2010," U.S. Census Bureau, May 2011, https://www.census.gov/content/dam/Census/library/publications/2011/ dec/c2010br-04.pdf.

31. Joel Kotkin, "The Changing Demographics of America," *Smithsonian Magazine,* August 2010, https://www.smithsonianmag.com/travel/the-changing-demographics-of-america-538284/.

32. Kim Parker et al., "Looking to the Future, Public Sees an America in Decline on Many Fronts Majorities," Pew Research Center, March 21, 2019, https://www .pewresearch.org/social-trends/2019/03/21/public-sees-an-america-in-decline-on -many-fronts/.

33. Stephanie Ewert, "U.S. Population Trends: 2000 to 2060," U.S. Census, Oct. 15, 2015, https://pdf4pro.com/view/u-s-population-trends-2000-to-2060-5f9c6e .html.

34. Jason Wilson and Aaron Flanagan, "The Racist 'Great Replacement' Conspiracy Theory Explained," May 17, 2022, Southern Poverty Law Center, https:// www.splcenter.org/hatewatch/2022/05/17/racist-great-replacement-conspiracy-theory-explained.

35. National Center for Education Statistics, "Digest of Education Statistics, Table 105.50," https://nces.ed.gov/programs/digest/d21/tables/dt21_105.50.asp.

36. Travis Riddle and Stacey Sinclair, "Racial Disparities in School-Based Disciplinary Actions Are Associated with County-Level Rates of Racial Bias," *Proceedings of the National Academy of Sciences* 116, no. 17 (April 2019): 8255–8260, https://doi.org/10.1073/pnas.1808307116.

37. "A History of the Individuals with Disabilities Education Act," U.S. Department of Education, accessed May 11, 2023, https://sites.ed.gov/idea/IDEA-History#:~ :text=On%20November%2029%2C%201975%2C%20President,and%20locality %20across%20the%20country.

38. "A History of the Individuals with Disabilities Education Act."

39. Gerry Johnstone and Daniel W. Van Ness (Editors), *Handbook of Restorative Justice* (London: Taylor & Francis, 2013).

40. Véronique Irwin et al., "Report on Indicators of School Crime and Safety: 2021," Institute of Education Sciences, June 2022, https://nces.ed.gov/pubs2022 /2022092.pdf.

Chapter 8

The Doctrine of Discovery and the Shadow of White Supremacy

Perhaps there is no more urgent and difficult domestic task than achieving social reconciliation and moral redemption from the legacy of our country's two original sins: the 300-year war against and near eradication of the American Indian and the 244 years of U.S. domestic enslavement of Africans and their children. As James Baldwin observed, "The whole process of education occurs within a social framework and is designed to perpetuate the aim of society."[1] Today, there are seventy-five million children in school, the majority of whom are children of color. Given such diversity, what should be the aim of society in this new era? The answer will determine the future character of the nation and the purposes and processes of education. A reckoning will need to occur sooner or later. Attempts have been made.

Since the Great Society legislation of the mid-1960s, there has scarcely been a federal program, private foundation initiative, or social/education project that did not have as one of its goals to bring about the advancement of those in poverty and educational disadvantage. Yet extreme wealth and education disparities continue to create a negative cycle of dysfunction for the bottom half of the population, especially among people of color. In 2020, one in six children still lived in impoverished families.[2] Parental education matters. Sixty-two percent of Black children who live in poverty have parents who did not complete high school.[3] But for Black families in which at least one parent has an associate degree (one or two years of college), only 22 percent live in poverty. Yet, for *White* families where at least one parent has an associate degree, only 8 percent live in poverty. Why is there a difference?

James Baldwin's answer to this "Negro problem" was to regard it as a White problem of racism.[4] Racism has two levels, prejudice at the personal level and racism at the systems level, as in the judicial system, the health care system, the education system, and so on.[5] Systemic racism may be

difficult for many Whites to recognize. A 2020 University of Massachusetts poll of 1,000 adults asked whether Black children are systematically
disadvantaged in the American education system. Forty-one percent of
Whites said "No, they have the same chance," whereas only 10 percent of
Blacks believed Black children had the same chance.[6] The same poll found
similar patterns of responses between Whites and Blacks in other areas. For
example, when asked whether Blacks were treated fairly by the police in
their community, nearly half of Whites agreed (46 percent), whereas only
15 percent of Blacks agreed. How are we to reconcile these differences in
perceptions?

When David Hornbeck was the Superintendent of the School District of
Philadelphia beginning in the mid-1990s, he accused the Pennsylvania General Assembly of perpetuating a "racist system" of school funding. But many
Pennsylvania legislators interpreted Hornbeck's accusations of systematic
racism as being leveled against them *personally*, provoking their resentment.
In 2000, Hornbeck resigned after serving six turbulent years as superintendent of the district.[7] These legislators' unwillingness to consider that Mr.
Hornbeck might have a legitimate point is an example of *White fragility*, a
term Robin DiAngelo coined to describe "a state in which even a minimum
amount of racial stress becomes intolerable, triggering a range of defensive
moves."[8] Why should there be such fragility and defensiveness? The answers
might be found at a deeper level, where systemic racism is a subset of a
supremacist system.

ELEMENTS OF A SUPREMACIST SYSTEM

The paradox of a supremacist system is that it can be so pervasive and all-
encompassing that those to whom it confers an advantage are unconscious
of its existence, much less its harmful effects on others. This is the point of
Baldwin's "paradox of education," that as one begins to become conscious of
one's social context, one begins to examine the society in which one is being
educated. We offer the following four elements of a supremacist system:

1. *Hierarchical ideologies* comprised of myths, half-truths, lies, and/
   or legends that rank people from the highest (those who have been
   anointed by a Divine creator) to the lowest (those regarded as sub-
   human and animal-like). Hierarchical ideologies, rooted in human psychology, are simple enough to understand that large numbers of people
   can be induced to believe and act upon them. Hierarchical ideologies
   can be thought of as vertically ordered as opposed to horizontal ideologies, such as the proposition that all people are created equal.

2. *Unequal laws and governing rules are applied* in keeping with a hierarchical ideology. At the highest level, there are few if any laws for the lawgivers, as they believe they are above the law. Thus, any standard to which they proclaim to hold for themselves one day can be reversed the next day. Different privileges and prerogatives descend according to the ranks within the hierarchy, with those at the bottom rung having none, not even any rights over their bodies which can be used by those above as they please, including subjugation, enslavement, execution, and forcing women to carry children at the risk of their lives.

3. *Communication controls* are the means to create and disseminate myths, half-truths, lies, and/or legends. Cause and effect are routinely reversed or invented whereby victims of the hierarchy are pronounced as the *cause* of whatever calamity or ills befall them, thus rendering them deserving of their fate. Blaming women for a rapist's behavior is a classic example. At the same time, contrary thoughts and information are suppressed and/or discredited. Those that give voice to them are silenced by whatever means necessary.

4. *Coercive mechanisms* to enforce the first three elements. The key to holding the ideological hierarchies in place is to completely control and suppress the bottom-most rung using a variety of coercive mechanisms such as instilling a psychological sense of inferiority and dependency in children, selective denial of information and/or education, restricted property rights, access to capital, and legal representation, and/or use of physical force including secret police, imprisonment, enslavement, and mass murder.

Supremacist systems can involve any racial, ethnic, or religious group anywhere from any era. In the Americas, we recount the emergence of a White Christian supremacist system through two origin myths taught to nearly all public school children and celebrated as holidays: Columbus Day and Thanksgiving Day. Through the lens of these four supremacist elements, we then describe how the long shadow of White Christian supremacy continues to particularly disadvantage students of color in the public education system and block reform efforts, but not in the way some might suppose.

CHRISTOPHER COLUMBUS AND THE DOCTRINE OF DISCOVERY

Our first origin myth was that the New World was an uninhabited wilderness discovered in 1492 by a daring and noble explorer, Christopher Columbus, whose discovery eventually led to the founding of the United States. In truth, the Americas were invaded and conquered.[9] Some scholars have estimated as many as one hundred million Indigenous peoples were living in the Americas before Columbus' arrival.[10] These Indigenous peoples had discovered, settled in, and filled out the New World at least 16,000 years before any Europeans set foot on it.[11] Moreover, in the eyes of European monarchs at the time, it was not Columbus who "discovered" *North* America. It was another Venetian navigator, Giovanni Caboto, AKA John Cabot. This is not simply a technicality. As we shall see, Cabot's landing, not Columbus', is what the U.S. Supreme Court would later use to justify the United States' title to land occupied by millions of American Indians. The court's justification was based on the European *Doctrine of Discovery*.

It is true that the existence of the Americas, ensconced between two vast oceans, was largely unknown to the rest of the world except as lore.[12] The same was not true of the Orient, as Europeans had been engaging in recorded trade with the Han Dynasty as early as the third century BC.[13] Over the centuries, traders continually worked around periodic Euro-Asian political obstacles and upheavals to explore and utilize different trading routes across the Euro-Asian landmass. By the beginning of the fourteenth century, five major east–west routes were well established, including a sea-land-sea route (across the Mediterranean Sea, up the Nile River, overland through Egypt to the Red Sea, and out to the Indian Ocean to India and China).[14] The Atlantic Ocean proved to be a more formidable barrier to exploration and trade.

Beginning in the early fifteenth century, the Portuguese embarked on a program of systematically exploring the west coast of Africa and establishing a lucrative trade market, including slave trading, with local tribes. The proceeds from this trade were reinvested to continue exploring and exploiting the southwestern African coastline and islands.[15] However, for this trade to remain profitable, Portuguese King John II had to protect his African sea routes from his chief maritime rivals, King Ferdinand II of Aragon and his wife Queen Isabel I of Castile, who with their marriage in 1469, united as the Kingdom of Spain. To establish peace, Spain and Portugal signed the Treaty of Alcáçovas in 1479 whereby Spain agreed to stay out of Portugal's African trading territories. Portugal's program of finding an all-sea route to India paid off when in 1488 explorer Bartholomew Dias successfully circumnavigated the southern tip of Africa, thus demonstrating that India was not landlocked and setting up Vasco da Gama's groundbreaking voyage to India ten years later.[16,17,18]

Since the Treaty of Alcáçovas excluded Spain from exploring a possible *eastern* sea route to India, the idea of sailing *westward* to India was intriguing. This imagined western sea route across the Atlantic Ocean was not a new notion, as legendary tales of earlier Atlantic voyages had long circulated in Europe.[19] Through a series of well-placed intermediaries, Christopher Columbus,[20] in

January 1486, managed to get an audience with Spain's Isabel I, whereupon she referred the matter to a committee for an extended period of review—nearly seven years. Finally, on April 30, 1492, King Ferdinand and Queen Isabel, believing the potential rewards of a westward exploration were worth the risks, granted the following "Privileges and Prerogatives" to Columbus:

> For as much of you, Christopher Columbus, are going by our command, with some of our vessels and men, to discover and subdue some Islands and Continent in the ocean, and it is hoped that by God's assistance, some of the said Islands and Continent in the ocean will be discovered and conquered by your means and conduct, therefore it is but just and reasonable, that since you expose yourself to such danger to serve us, you should be rewarded for it.[21]

The key words here are "subdue," "conquer," and "reward." Columbus signed a commercial agreement with the King and Queen known as the Santé Fe Capitulation to receive one-tenth of the sale of "pearls, precious stones, gold, silver, spices" and other goods that were transferable to his heirs in perpetuity.[22] Five months later, on the morning of October 12, 1492, Columbus landed his three ships on the Bahamian island of Guanahaní, about fifty miles east of Florida, renaming it "San Salvador" (Holy Savior).

When he returned home to Spain, he accidentally landed in Lisbon, Portugal. Upon learning of Columbus' exploits, Portugal's King John II, perceiving Columbus's voyage had violated the terms of the Treaty of Alcáçovas, threatened conflict with Spain. Since both Spain and Portugal had previous territorial disputes where they sought Papal mediation, they asked Pope Alexander VI to intervene. In May 1493, the Pope issued the *Inter Caetera* Bull, a diplomatic settlement that divided "the discovered and yet to be undiscovered" New World between Spain and Portugal, exclusively. The dividing line was a meridian drawn from the North Pole to the South Pole that went through the eastern part of Brazil. All newly discovered lands east of this meridian would belong to Portugal. Everything West would belong to Spain. The Inter Caetera also contained the key proviso that "We make, appoint, and depute you and your said heirs and successors lords of them [islands] and mainlands not previously in the possession of any Christian ruler with full and free power, authority, and jurisdiction of every kind."[23]

This proviso is the essence of the *Doctrine of Discovery*: The God-given right of European monarchs (who, at that time, were all Catholic) to conquer, subdue, rule over, and convert to Christianity, forcibly, if necessary, any of the non-Christian Indigenous people in these newly discovered lands. There were only two requirements: 1) the people to be conquered were not already Christian, and 2) they were not under the dominion of another European power. Aside from that, they were fair game.

A little more than a year after Pope Alexander decreed the Inter Caetera, Portugal and Spain signed a formal treaty in the town of Tordesillas in central Spain. The 1494 Treaty of Tordesillas paralleled the language of the Inter Caetera by stipulating that it was entered into by both parties "for the purpose of discovering and seeking any mainlands or islands, or for the purpose of trade, barter, or *conquest* of any kind."[24] And conquer they did. As Columbus had written in his diary of his first voyage to the New World, there was much to be exploited: "There I found very many islands, filled with innumerable people, and I have taken possession of them all for their Highnesses, done by proclamation and with the royal standard unfurled, and no opposition was offered to me."[25]

On his second of four voyages to the Americas, Columbus led seventeen Spanish ships to begin the conquest of Hispaniola and the nearby islands.[26] We need not go into the subsequent Spanish conquistadors' treatment of the Indigenous peoples of Central America and western South America. Bartolome de las Casas, a Dominican friar and later the Bishop of Chiapas, has amply chronicled in graphic detail the many extreme moral depravities and atrocities the Spaniards committed. Nor is it our intent here to recount Spain's more than three centuries of repressive rule over these Indigenous people and their forced conversions to Catholicism,[27] which finally ended with Spanish America's wars of independence in the early nineteenth century.[28] Rather, our point is that arguments about whether we should honor Columbus are a diversion from confronting our actual supremacist origins, the foundation of which goes back directly to the Doctrine of Discovery.

JOHN CABOT CLAIMS NORTH AMERICA FOR ENGLAND

Concurrently with Spain's commissioning of Columbus's voyages, Henry VII, King of England and France and lord of Ireland, as he referred to himself, paid no heed to the Treaty of Tordesillas. The king sought his own Northwest Passage to the Orient. Records indicate that from 1491 to 1498, English explorers periodically sailed from the port of Bristol, taking two to three vessels a year to seek out new land west of Ireland.[29] Not unlike the language of the "Privileges and Prerogatives Granted By Their Catholic Majesties to Christopher Columbus," King Henry VII granted Letters of Patent on May 5, 1496, to an Italian navigator Giovanni Caboto (John Cabot) and his three sons to "seek out, discover and find whatsoever isles, countries, regions, or provinces of the heathen and infidels whatsoever they be . . . [that you] may subdue, occupy and possess all such towns, cities, castles and isles."[30] A year later, in June 1497, after an initial aborted voyage west, Cabot sailed again from Bristol, England, with one small ship, the *Matthew*, with eighteen crewmen. This time Cabot succeeded in finding what historians believe was Newfoundland.[31] Cabot left behind no men on Newfoundland, nor ship's logs or personal diaries. A few details are provided in three Italian newsletters published in London. On his third voyage, Cabot is believed to have disappeared at sea. Nonetheless, exploration of the North American continent continued. After Cabot's discovery, patents for discovery were given to other English voyagers, including Cabot's son, Sebastian, to further explore the east coast of North America. Indeed, as one historian has reflected about the significance of English voyagers:

> It is a virtual certainty that, even had Columbus never left the small port of Palos in search of a water route to the Orient, and thereby discovered a New World, other European voyagers of the late fifteen century would soon have touched upon American shores. Basques, Bretons and Bristolmen were as motivated by greed and geographical inquisitiveness as Columbus and were active in westward voyaging even before 1492.[32]

None of the founding documents of the United States mentioned the Doctrine of Discovery. It was assumed that Great Britain had the right to the land over the Indians. However, this assumption was formally tested more than three centuries after Cabot's voyages. In 1823, a case was presented to the Supreme Court on this question: Do the hundreds of American Indian nations and tribes have title to the land they occupy? If the Court answered in the affirmative, then upon what legal grounds would the United States of America have to exist? If Indians had no right to their land, what was the legal justification for seizing it?

Chief Justice John Marshall wrote the opinion justifying denying Indian title to the land they occupied. It was not the Indian's land. The Court based its reasoning on the Doctrine of Discovery. Chief Justice Marshall's lengthy opinion is instructive and fascinating from both a historical and legal perspective. We provide only selected excerpts of his opinion, starting with his opening account of European nations' real motivations for acquiring land in the New World and how they rationalized the conquest of American Indians:

> On the discovery of this immense continent, the great nations of Europe were eager to appropriate to themselves so much of it as they could respectively acquire. Its vast extent offered an ample field to the ambition and enterprise of all; and the character and religion of the inhabitants afforded an apology for considering them as a people over whom the superior genius of Europe might claim an ascendency . . . convincing themselves that they made ample compensation to the inhabitants of the new, by bestowing on them civilization and Christianity.

Chief Justice Marshall continues by explaining how the European powers would manage this territorial acquisition based on the principle of who first discovered and claimed it. We include only a small segment of his extensive historical narrative:

> As they all were in pursuit of nearly the same object, it was necessary, in order to avoid conflicting settlements, and consequent war with each other, to establish a principle, which all should acknowledge, as the law by which the right of acquisition, which they all asserted, should be regulated as between themselves. This principle was that discovery gave title to the government by whose subjects, or by those whose authority, it was made, against all other European governments, which title might be consummated by possession.

> The exclusion of all other Europeans necessarily gave the nation making the discovery the sole right of acquiring the soil from the natives and establishing settlements upon it. The rights thus acquired being exclusive, no other power could interpose between them [the discover and the natives]. . . . The history of America, from its discovery to the present day, proves, we think, the universal recognition of these principles.

Marshall goes on to describe how the Discovery Doctrine was used to justify European colonialism throughout the Americas. But how did the English colonists obtain rights to the Indian-occupied territories? Marshall argues:

> So early in the year 1496, [England's] monarch granted a commission to the Cabots, to discover countries then unknown to *Christian people*, and to take possession of them in the name of the King of England. Two years afterward, Cabot proceeded on this voyage and discovered the continent of North America, along which he sailed as far south as Virginia. To this discovery the English trace their title. . . .

> By the treaty which concluded the war of our revolution, Great Britain relinquished all claim, not only to the government, but to the "propriety and territorial rights of the United States," whose boundaries were fixed by the second article. By this treaty, the powers of government, and the right to soil, which had previously been in Great Britain, passed definitively to these States.[33]

KILL THE INDIAN, SAVE THE MAN

Our second origin myth is the Thanksgiving story. The Pilgrims fled persecution in England, sailed across the Atlantic, and landed at Plymouth Rock in November 1620, where they were greeted by friendly American Indians.

After suffering a brutal winter, the Pilgrims managed to plant crops, with the help of the Indians, and then celebrated the harvest the following November by giving thanks. The record shows there is some truth to this story. According to a letter written in December 1621 by Edward Winslow, one of the original Pilgrims,

> Our corn did prove well, and God be praised, we had a good increase of Indian corn, and . . . many of the Indians coming amongst us, and among the rest their greatest King Massasoit, with some ninety men, whom for three days we entertained and feasted, and they went out and killed five deer, which they brought to the plantation and bestowed on our governor, and upon the captain, and others. . . . We have found the Indians very faithful in their covenant of peace with us; very loving and ready to pleasure us.[34]

This idyllic image, however, is but a snapshot of the actual nature and scope of the relationship between European Whites and American Indians over nearly five centuries. The story is actually an instance of the Doctrine of Discovery, obscured by the Thanksgiving mythology. Between Columbus's voyages and the Pilgrims' landing is almost 130 years—the entire sixteenth century—that is absent in our collective memory. Yet it was in this century that the earliest supremacist system in North America took root: *White over Red.*

During the century between John Cabot's discovery of Newfoundland in 1497 and the Plymouth colony's founding in 1620, four major European powers (England, Spain, Portugal, and France) sent voyagers on a race to try to map the North American continent. After Cabot, Portugal sent Gaspar Corle Real (1501) to retrace Cabot's route. Spain sent Juan Ponce de León to Florida (1513) and Francisco Gordillo to explore the Georgia, South Carolina, North Carolina, and Virginia coasts (1521), and Cabrillo along the California coast (1541). France hired another Italian navigator, Giovanni de Verrazano (1523), to explore the Carolinas up to New England. Later, Francis I of France sent Jacques Cartier and his crew to penetrate Canada inland along the St. Lawrence River (1534).[35]

The mapping and the detailed sea logs served to establish each European monarch's right of dominion over any part of the New World they "discovered." These voyagers' narratives, along with the Indians they managed to kidnap and bring back to Europe, were critical to demonstrating to their monarchs and investors that the territory they claimed to have explored was a real place with rich resources and trade possibilities, such as gold, gems, and furs. For example, when King James of England granted the First Charter of Virginia in 1606 to a group of would-be colonists, he specified the exact latitudes of the land to be granted, that is, between the thirty-fourth and forty-fifth parallels (roughly from Wilmington, North Carolina, to Bangor, Maine) based on the data from the sea logs.[36]

During the sixteenth century, no permanent European settlements were successfully established. It was not for lack of trying. As early as 1541, France's Cartier set up a makeshift fort at what is now Quebec City, only to abandon it two years later after attacks by the Huron Indians. In 1584, Queen Elizabeth issued a patent to Sir Walter Raleigh to set up a colony on Roanoke Island, North Carolina, but the colony disappeared after he left.[37] In 1607, the Popham colony consisting of 125 settlers attempted to build a settlement near Bath, Maine, only to leave fourteen months later due to deaths, harsh weather conditions, and food scarcity.[38]

The full stories of the first two permanent English settlements, Jamestown in 1607 and Plymouth in 1620, are emblematic of the divergent motivations behind English colonization and Indian relations. The Jamestown settlement was run by a private group of investors, the Virginia Company of London, searching for gold, silver, copper, and other gems.[39] The Pilgrims of Plymouth, in contrast, were searching for a New Israel. Whereas the Wampanoag tribe of New England collaborated with the Pilgrims and shared their food, the Powhatan tribes of Virginia displayed hostility to the Jamestown colony from the beginning. When the Powhatan tribes refused to sell food to the colonists during the harsh winter of 1610, approximately 400 of the 500 colonists starved to death.[40] In 1622, the Powhatan-led tribes attacked and killed 350 White men, women, and children. In April of 1644, another series of Virginia Indian attacks left nearly 500 colonists dead.

The violence between European settlers and the many Indian tribes shaped their relationship for the next 300 years. In each case, the supremacist ideology of the Doctrine of Discovery served as the justification for colonists to claim Indian lands and occupy them by force if necessary. White Christian civilization was superior to "Red heathen savagery"; therefore, European monarchs had the right to subdue and conquer Indians and possess their land. As President Andrew Jackson, a slayer of Indians in Alabama and Georgia, would later state in his address to Congress more than two centuries later,

Humanity has often wept over the fate of the aborigines of this country, and philanthropy has been long busily employed in devising means to avert it, but its progress has never for a moment been arrested, and one by one have many powerful tribes disappeared from the Earth. To follow to the tomb the last of his race and to tread on the graves of extinct nations excite melancholy reflections. But true philanthropy reconciles the mind to these vicissitudes as it does to the extinction of one generation to make room for another. . . . The tribes which occupied the countries now constituting the Eastern states were annihilated or have melted away to make room for the whites.[41]

As mentioned previously, every supremacist system must have a means of enforcing its ideology. In this respect, there were three irresistible forces the American Indians could not overcome. The first was the growing difference in population between the European colonists and the Indian tribes. After the establishment of settlements in Massachusetts and Virginia, Northern Europeans continued to arrive by the boatload. In our first chapter, we described the exponential growth in the colonial population from a few thousand in 1620 to nearly four million by 1790. By 1850, the White population had increased to nearly twenty million. At the same time, ever since Columbus and other Europeans arrived, the indigenous population was devastated by the introduction of diseases for which they had no natural resistance.[42] For example, in the three years prior to the Pilgrims' arrival, 1616–1619, nearly 90 percent of some New England tribes had already been wiped out due to an epidemic.[43] The Puritans interpreted these deaths as divine intervention on behalf of their New Israel.[44] But after John Cabot's voyage to Newfoundland in 1497, Indians began to have contact with European explorers and fishermen prior to the Puritans' settlement in 1620. The Indian, Samoset, for example, was the first to greet the Puritans and he did so in English.[45]

The second force was the intense inter-Indian tribal conflict over trade and territory. There was no governmental framework that could unite the many eastern Indian tribes and arbitrate disputes among them. The closest entity, perhaps, was the Iroquois[46] Confederacy of five nations in northern New York. This confederacy, which had a constitution, emerged after decades of vicious inter-tribal warfare. The confederacy was inspired by the legendary peacemaker, Hiawatha, and his spiritual guide Deganawidah.[47] The Iroquois were a formidable threat to other tribes and the French fur traders. The English colonists skillfully exploited these rivalries, playing one against the other.

The third force working against the American Indian was gun trafficking. European arms dealers traded guns, shot, and powder for Indian-supplied goods, such as furs. Historian David J. Silverman summarizes the volume of European Indian gun trafficking:

The founders of the later colonies, such as Pennsylvania and Georgia, arrived to find indigenous people already furnished with the best gun technology Europe could produce and keen to acquire more. Except under the rarest circumstances, no one state authority had the ability to choke Indians from guns, powder and shot. There were just too many rival imperial powers and colonies in North America, their governments were weak, and the trade ran through a labyrinth of unofficial channels such as itinerant fur traders, native middlemen, and smugglers. Indians often wielded better weapons than Euro-American, including their armed forces.[48]

In short, before there was a wild, wild *west* there was a wild, wild *east*. Battles among tribes and European rivals for control of the eastern seaboard continued for some 170 years until the revolution against England resulted in the independence and unification of the thirteen former British colonies.

Civilize or Exterminate

The three founding documents of the U.S. government—the Declaration of Independence, the Constitution, and the Bill of Rights—make no mention of any religion, race, or ethnic group save one, the Indians. The U.S. Constitution gave the exclusive right to the federal government to execute treaties with all Indian nations and tribes. Seen from a Jacksonian supremacist ideology, there were only three options for dealing with the American Indians: (1) eliminate them either by killing them (e.g., Sand Creek and Old Kettles massacres), starving them, spreading fatal diseases, or stoking inter-tribal warfare; (2) remove and confine them to a desolate place by persuasion or threat of force, such as with the Indian Removal Act of 1830 and the establishment of reservations, and/or (3) try to assimilate them to the European Christian White culture, beginning with their children. All three options were deployed. A fourth option promoted by William Penn, to try to live peacefully among the Indians, which he managed to do, was abandoned after Penn's death.

Secretary of the Interior Alexander H. H. Stuart, a Virginian serving under President Fillmore, summed up the situation in a November 1851 report to Congress on the state of Indian Affairs. Stuart stated that the influx of Whites populating California and Oregon, along with the southwestern territories acquired from Mexico, had effectively surrounded the Indians. He put the federal government's choice of what to do next with the American Indian in stark terms:

> Heretofore, our settlements being confined to the eastern portion of our continent, we have been gradually forcing the Indian tribes westward, as the tide of population flowed in that direction. By this means they have accumulated in large numbers on our western frontier. The results have been injury to the Indians, by crowding them together in such numbers that the game is insufficient for their support; and injustice to the western States, whose security is endangered by the proximity of their savage neighbors. But since the acquisition of California and Oregon, and the establishment of large settlements on the coast of the Pacific and in Utah, a new flow of white population is advancing upon them from the west. The pressure is, therefore, increasing upon them from both sides of the continent. On the north and south they are also hemmed in by civilized communities. They are thus encompassed by an unbroken chain of civilization; and the question forces itself upon the mind of the statesman and the philanthropist, what is to become of the aboriginal race? The policy of removal, except

under peculiar circumstances, must necessarily be abandoned; and the only alternatives left are, to civilize or exterminate them.[49]

Stuart recommended manual-labor schools where agriculture and the ways of peace would be taught so that the Indians could look forward to the day "when they may be elevated to the dignity of American citizenship." This policy, clear evidence of supremacist hierarchical thinking, would later be adopted in the form of federally run Indian industrial boarding schools throughout the country. Many Indian children, as young as five, were forcibly taken from their parents and tribal cultures and put in distant boarding schools. In these schools, many of which were run by missionaries, young Indians were stripped of all vestiges of their native culture. Their hair was cut, clothes taken, native tongue forbidden, and religious traditions banned.

The first such school was the Carlisle Indian Industrial School established in 1879 and located on the grounds of the Army War College in Carlisle, Pennsylvania. The idea of industrial education for Indians paralleled the New York Trade School archetype. However, we consider the Carlisle Indian Industrial School and those like it to be a perversion of the industrial school archetype. When the students returned to the reservation, there were no industries where they could employ their skills. The real intent of the school was to erase the students' Indian identity. The Carlisle school was run by Army Captain Richard H. Pratt, whose motto was "Kill the Indian, save the man." Addressing an 1891 national convention, Pratt declared, "A great general has said that the only good Indian is a dead one, and that high sanction of his destruction has been an enormous factor in promoting Indian massacres. In a sense, I agree with the sentiment, but only in this: that all the Indian there is in the race should be dead. Kill the Indian in him, and save the man."[50] Over three decades, the Carlisle Indian Industrial School enrolled approximately 10,000 students. Diseases were rampant. Nearly 200 children were buried on the grounds, and only recently have some of the remains been returned to the original tribal home.[51] A similar program of forced assimilation was installed in Canada.

The full text of Captain Pratt's and Secretary Stuart's reports suggests that they felt their plan was an enlightened way to deal with the Indian problem. Given the choice between education or eradication, it seemed that it was the far more humane choice to attempt to assimilate Indian children into the White Christian culture, even if they had to be forced to do so. To show Washington, D.C., policymakers the promise of Indian industrial boarding schools, Pratt hired a photographer to take before and after photos of the visible transformation of the Carlisle Indian Industrial School's children. (See figure 8.1.)

The approximately 140 boarding schools that were established in the United States were part of a de facto eradication program of American

Figure 8.1 Carlisle Indian School in 1884 with Its 375 Students. *Source*: Cumberland County Historical Society, Carlisle, PA.

Indians and their culture that had already been largely accomplished through war, disease, and removal to reservations. By 1890, the U.S. Census recorded an American Indian population of less than 250,000 out of a total U.S. population of sixty-three million, or about four Indians per 1,000 people. The boarding schools, however well intended, represented the longstanding official government policy that any vestiges of Indian culture had to be erased, save for ceremonial events and sideshows.[52] As David Treuer, author of *The Heartbeat of Wounded Knee,* put it, "Education was something that was done *to* us, not something that was done *for* us."[53]

The result of this supremacist ideology as applied to the estimated seven to eighteen million aboriginal natives living in North America before Cabot[54] was summarized in the opening paragraphs of an 847-page Rockefeller Foundation report submitted to the U.S. secretary of the interior in 1928 on "The Problem of Indian Administration," referred to as the "Merriam Report":

An overwhelming majority of the Indians are poor, even extremely poor, and they are not adjusted to the economic and social system of the dominant white civilization. The poverty of the Indians and their lack of adjustment to the dominant economic and social systems produce the vicious circle ordinarily found among any people under such circumstances. Because of interrelationships, causes cannot be differentiated from effects. The only course is to state briefly the conditions found that are part of this vicious circle of poverty and maladjustment.[55]

The recurring theme of the "dominant white civilization" is evident throughout the Bureau of Indian Affairs' official yearly reports to Congress and the detailed annual Indian ethnographic reports by the Smithsonian Institution's Bureau of American Ethnology.[56]

WHITE OVER BLACK

As with the American Indian, the history of relations between the "dominant White civilization" and African slaves and their descendants cannot be captured in a chapter or series of books. Like the story of the American Indian, it is too massive a story. For our purposes, we will confine ourselves to making only a few points. The same White Christian supremacist ideology that relegated the American Indian to heathen savage status did the same to the Africans who were captured, chained, traded, and brought to the New World. Perhaps the most profound and pristine promulgation of this supremacist ideology was written in 1857 by Roger Taney, Chief Justice of the United States Supreme Court in the infamous case of Dred Scott. We excerpt an extended passage from Chief Justice Taney's majority opinion because of the boldness of its supremacist ideology.

> We think . . . [Negroes] were not intended to be included, under the word "citizens" in the Constitution, and can therefore claim none of the rights and privileges which that instrument provides for and secures to citizens of the United States. On the contrary, they were at that time considered as a subordinate and inferior class of beings who had been subjugated by the dominant race, and, whether emancipated or not, yet remained subject to their authority, and had no rights or privileges but such as those who held the power and the Government might choose to grant them.

> They had for more than a century before been regarded as beings of an inferior order, and altogether unfit to associate with the White race either in social or political relations, and so far inferior that they had no rights which the White man was bound to respect, and that the negro might justly and lawfully be reduced to slavery for his benefit. He was bought and sold, and treated as an ordinary article of merchandise and traffic whenever a profit could be made by it. This opinion was at that time fixed and universal in the civilized portion of the White race. It was regarded as an axiom in morals as well as in politics which no one thought of disputing or supposed to be open to dispute, and men in every grade and position in society daily and habitually acted upon it in their private

pursuits, as well as in matters of public concern, without doubting for a moment the correctness of this opinion.

And in no nation was this opinion more firmly fixed or more uniformly acted upon than by the English Government and English people. They not only seized them on the coast of Africa and sold them or held them in slavery for their own use, but they took them as ordinary articles of merchandise to every country where they could make a profit on them and were far more extensively engaged in this commerce than any other nation in the world.[57]

The Taney court did not stop with the question of Dred Scott's citizenship. It also ruled *in the same case* that the Missouri Compromise was unconstitutional, that Congress cannot ban slavery in the new territories from which new states would be formed, and that the federal government could not free slaves that had been brought into the territories as slaves. These judicial rulings were critically important to slaveholders since "virtually every Southern spokesman believed that slavery must expand or die."[58] Northerners also believed that limiting slavery to only the existing slave states would kill it, "as a poisoned rat dies of rage in its hole."

The numbers make it clear what was at stake with the ruling of the Taney Court. By 1850, 348,000 slaveholding families held more than 3.2 million slaves.[59] No slaveholding families were listed in New England and only 1,000 in the middle states. While the number of slaveholding families had increased in the southern states, slave holdings increased even more dramatically in the *new territories*, the location of over 42 percent of all the slaves, which the Taney decision upheld. With the Dred Scott ruling, the Southern states believed the slave question was finally settled. The Supreme Court had ruled in favor of White supremacists. Thus, people of African descent, enslaved or free, were not U.S. citizens; could never be U.S. citizens; and were the property of their slave masters who could buy, sell, and keep them as they wished including in the new territories.[60] Abolitionists were outraged.

Black abolitionist Frederick Douglass, in a speech delivered before the American Anti-Slavery Society in New York in 1857, prophesied the following:

I have sought, in my humble way, to penetrate the intervening mists and clouds, and, perchance, to descry, in the dim and shadowy distance, the white flag of freedom, the precise speck of time at which the cruel bondage of my people should end, and the long entombed millions rise from the foul grave of slavery and death. But of that time I can know nothing, and you can know nothing. All is uncertain at that point. One thing, however, is certain; slaveholders are in earnest, and mean to cling to their slaves as long as they can, and to the bitter end. . . . The State governments, where the system of slavery exists, are complete slavery organizations. . . . All that is merciful and just, on Earth and in Heaven, will execrate and despise this edict of Taney.[61]

The end of slavery did come, and it was indeed bitter. More than a million soldiers lay dead, maimed, or wounded. The southern states were laid to waste, their slaves set free. An assassin's bullet could not stop the ratification of the Thirteenth Amendment to the U.S. Constitution in December 1865, forever abolishing slavery and involuntary servitude in the United States. The first civil rights laws followed the next year, becoming the basis for the Fourteenth Amendment defining citizenship as birth in the United States or naturalization, and guaranteeing due process of law and equal protection under the law.[62] Two years later suffrage was granted to former slaves when the Fifteenth Amendment was ratified, prohibiting the denial of citizens the right to vote on account of race, color, or previous condition of servitude.

REVISITING MR. HORNBECK'S CHARGE OF A "RACIST SYSTEM"

The Thirteenth, Fourteenth, and Fifteenth Amendments were only the beginning of the dismantling of the White supremacist legal system. There remained a vast web of federal laws, administrative regulations, and state and local laws still to be deconstructed. Jim Crow laws, for example, kept Blacks segregated and effectively subordinated. Selective omissions of equal protection allowed more than 5,000 instances of domestic terrorism in the form of lynchings and burnings to go unpunished. Justice cannot be done here, in this brief accounting, to the struggle for racial equality that continues into the twenty-first century. Much is still left to do.

Although the culturally destructive Indian boarding schools, as physical schools, may no longer be operational, the supremacist shadows of the "dominate White civilization" still haunt the American Indian[63] as they do other people of color. From our experience, the forced assimilation of children of color and those with special needs into a White-dominant curriculum and assessment system is the heart of the "racist education system,"—not only a state's funding formula. Why, for example, should student achievement on Algebra 1 tests be the principal measure of students' intellectual ability, overshadowing the value of all other types of subjects, save for English reading and writing?

Research on the reasons students drop out of high school does not cite schools' lack of resources. They cite a boring and irrelevant curriculum, stultifying teaching methods, and the type of rank-ordering assessments they perceive are designed to confirm their inferiority rather than affirming their assets.[64] American Indian novelist David Treuer asks about schools: "Are we going to be a country where a person goes to get rich, or are we going to be a country that empowers and emboldens and supports its more vulnerable citizens? What kind of force in the world do we want to be?"[65] We would include among these more vulnerable students those with special needs or unique physical or mental challenges who do not fit the mold of the mainstream.

How can our educational system emerge from this supremacist shadow? Some of the most valuable answers come from the aforementioned groups. The National Academy of Science's *How People Learn II: Learners, Contexts and Cultures* summarizes a substantial body of research on how different social, emotional, and cultural contexts influence different ways of thinking and learning.[66] These research findings have found supporting voices coming from Indigenous groups and more vulnerable learners. For example, *Atlantic* education columnist Kristina Rizga writes:

> In 1994, the Alaska Natives Commission, a federal and state task force, cited the dismal outcomes of Native students in the system founded by outside experts. The Commission called for all future efforts related to Alaska Native education to be initiated from *within* the Native community. This prompted a variety of Native-led projects, such as the Alaska Native Curriculum and Teacher Development Project, Alaska Rural Systemic Initiative, and Alaska Native Knowledge Network, that developed and disseminated culturally responsive curricula, oral histories, language materials, and relevant research.[67]

Rizga emphasizes that these new systems are about "playing to the strengths of both Western and Native models—helping students learn how to thrive locally while participating in a global society." Furthermore, to underscore the importance of Alaskan Native culture, the Alaska State Department of Education requires courses in Alaskan studies and culture for certification of all K-12 teachers.

Another example is Hawaii's Kamehameha school system consisting of preschools, K-12 schools, and continuing education statewide. One of its foundational goals is its commitment to Hawaiian identity—creating a world-class, culture-based educational experience through its curriculum, faculty, staff, *'āina* (love of the land and its people), and most importantly its *haumāna* (students).[68] Additionally, since 1980 there has been a Hawaiian Studies Program that provides the support and resources needed, among other things, to support teachers and cultural personnel resources in gaining knowledge of Hawaiian Studies content which includes the culture, history, places, and language of Hawaii.[69] Lastly, the work of Dr. Temple Grandin, a well-known autistic professor of animal behavior, argues for curricula and teaching methods that support and build on the different ways children think and learn.[70] Her arguments, like those of many Native American educators, are supported by the findings in *How People Learn II*.

The shadow of the Doctrine of Discovery hinders the widespread use of multi-layered culturally relevant teaching methods and neuroscience-based approaches to learning. This is not to say schools are ignoring equity issues. Across the country, there are school leaders and teachers who have become alert to the subtle biases of low expectations and how they affect student confidence and motivation. In one case, the superintendent of a greater-metropolitan-area district in Minnesota, a state that persistently has one of the widest racial opportunity gaps in the nation, prioritized raising student achievement levels. Knowing that people in the past had made pessimistic predictions of low achievement based on racial stereotypes, the superintendent approached his job with a commitment to raise achievement so that his district would become "the most demographically unpredictable school district in Minnesota."[71] At the time of this writing, the district's public high school consistently posts ACT scores higher than the Minnesota state average and boasts a 91 percent graduation rate for Black students and a 95 percent graduation rate for Hispanic students,[72] significantly higher than the statewide averages of 70 percent and 69 percent, respectively.[73]

In the next chapter, we illuminate one last shadow.

NOTES

1. Baldwin James, "A Talk to Teachers," *The Saturday Review*, Dec. 21, 1963, 42.

2. Véronique Irwin, Josue De La Rosa, Ke Wang, Sarah Hein, Jijun Zhang, Riley Burr, Ashley Roberts, Amy Barmer, Farrah Bullock Mann, Rita Dilig, and Stephanie Parker, "Report on the Condition of Education 2022 (NCES 2022-144)" (Washington, DC: U.S. Department of Education, 2022), https://nces.ed.gov/pubsearch/pubsinfo.asp?pubid=2022144.

3. National Center for Education Statistics, "Characteristics of Children's Families," Figure 5 (Washington, DC: U.S. Department of Education, 2022), https://nces.ed.gov/programs/coe/indicator/cce/family-characteristics.

4. Beau Fly Jones, "James Baldwin, The Struggle for Identity," *The British Journal of Sociology* 17, no. 2 (June 1966): 107–121.

5. William H. Barber et al., "What Courage to Change History Looks Like," *New York Times*, June 19, 2020.

6. Joshua J. Dyck and John Cluverius, "Survey of American Adults," Center for Public Opinion, University of Massachusetts-Lowell, 2020, https://www.uml.edu/docs/2020-Nat-Survey-RJ-Topline_tcm18-330167.pdf.

7. Robert C. Johnston, "Hornbeck Quits as Power Shifts in Philadelphia," *Education Week*, June 14, 2000.

8. Robin DiAngelo, "White Fragility," *International Journal of Critical Pedagogy* 3, no. 3 (2011): 54.

9. Francis Jennings, *The Invasion of America* (Chapel Hill, NC: University of North Carolina Press, 1975).

10. Douglas H. Ubelaker, "Patterns of Demographic Change in the Americas," *Human Biology* 64, no. 3 (June 1992): 361–379.

11. Elizabeth Prine Pauls, "Native American," *Encyclopedia Britannica*, accessed June 12, 2021.

12. John L. Allen, "From Cabot to Cartier: The Early Exploration of Eastern North America, 1497–1543," *Annals of the Association of American Geographers* 82, no. 3 (Sep. 1992): 500–521.

13. Debin Ma, "The Great Silk Exchange: How the World was Connected and Developed" in *Pacific Centuries; Pacific and Pacific Rim History Since the 16th Century*, D. Flynn, Lionel Frost, and A.J.H. Latham, eds. (New York: Routledge Press, 1998).

14. A.H. Lyber, "The Ottoman Turks and the Routes of Oriental Trade," *The English Historical Review* 30, no. 120 (October 1915): 577–588i.

15. Ulf Christian Ewert, "Exploration of Markets at Distant Shores: Knowledge, Investment and Governance in 15th Century Portuguese Trade with West Africa," working paper prepared for the 10th European Historical Economics Society Conference, 2013.

16. Over the next three-and-a-half centuries Portugal would dominate the East–West long-haul trade until the construction of the Suez Canal in Egypt in 1869 opened up another shipping option.

17. Albert Howe Lybyer, "The Ottoman Turks and the Routes of Oriental Trade," *The English Historical Review* 30, no. 120 (October 1915): 577–588.

18. Janina Z. Klawe, "Bartholomew Dias and the Voyage of Christopher Columbus," *Organon* 24 (1988): 129–137.

19. John L. Allen, "From Cabot to Cartier."

20. Roger M. McCoy, *On the Edge: Mapping North America's Coasts* (Oxford: Oxford University Press, 2012), 10.

21. "Privileges and Prerogatives Granted by Their Catholic Majesties to Christopher Columbus: 1492," Lillian Goldman Law Library, Yale Law School, https:// avalon.law.yale.edu/15th_century/colum.asp.

22. Filson Young, *Christopher Columbus and the New World of His Discovery*, Vol. 2 (Philadelphia, PA: Lippincott): 336.

23. "Inter Caetera, Pope Alexander VI, 1493," Papal Encyclicals Online, accessed April 17, 2021, https://www.papalencyclicals.net/alex06/alex06inter.htm.

24. "Treaty of Tordesilla, June 1494," UNESCO, https://en.unesco.org/memoryoftheworld/registry/613.

25. Christopher Columbus, *Epistola Christofori Colom* (Letters of Christopher Columbus) (Rome: Stephan Plannck, Rare Book and Special Collections Division, Library of Congress), https://www.loc.gov/exhibits/exploring-the-early-americas/ columbus-and-the-taino.html.

26. Library of Congress, "Exploring the Early Americas," accessed April 12, 2021, https://www.loc.gov/exhibits/exploring-the-early-americas/columbus-and-the-taino.html.

27. National Humanities Center, "Requirement: Pronouncement to be Read by Spanish Conquerors to Defeated Indians, 1510," http://nationalhumanitiescenter.org/pds/amerbegin/contact/text7/requirement.pdf.

28. John Lynch, *The Spanish American Revolutions, 1808-1826*, 2nd ed. (Woodstock, VT: W. W. Norton & Company, 1986).

29. President of the Royal Geographical Society. "Fourth Centenary of the Voyage of John Cabot, 1497," *The Geographical Journal* 9, no. 6 (June 1897): 604–615.

30. National Archives, "John Cabot," https://www.nationalarchives.gov.uk/education/resources/significant-people-collection/john-cabot/.

31. President of the Royal Geographical Society.

32. John L. Allen, "From Cabot to Cartier: The Early Exploration of Eastern North America, 1497-1543," *Annals of the Association of American Geographers* 82, no. 3 (Sep. 1992): 500–521.

33. Johnson & Graham's Lessee v. McIntosh, 21 U.S. 543 (1823).

34. Caleb Johnson's Mayflower History, "Letter of Edward Winslow, 11 December 1621," http://mayflowerhistory.com/letter-winslow-1621.

35. John L. Allen, "From Cabot to Cartier."

36. John L. Allen, "From Cabot to Cartier," 514.

37. Scott Dawson, *The Lost Colony and Hatteras Island* (Cheltenham, Gloucestershire: The History Press, June, 2020).

38. Myron Beckenstein, "Maine's Lost Colony: Archeologists Uncover an Early American Settlement that History Forgot," *Smithsonian Magazine*, Feb. 2004.

39. William Waller Hening, ed., *The Statutes at Large; Being a Collection of All the Laws of Virginia from the First Session of the Legislature, in the Year 1619* (New York: R. & W. & G. Bartow, 1823), 88.

40. David A. Price, "Jamestown Colony," *Encyclopedia Britannica*, updated Feb. 3, 2023, https://www.britannica.com/place/Jamestown-Colony.

41. President Andrew Jackson Second Annual Message to Congress, Dec. 6, 1830, https://millercenter.org/the-presidency/presidential-speeches/december-6-1830-second-annual-message-congress.

42. Russell Thornton, "Population History of Native North Americans," in *Population History of North America*, Michael R. Haines and Richard H. Steckel, eds. (New York: Cambridge University Press, 2000).

43. J. S. Marr and J. T. Cathey, "New Hypothesis for Cause of Epidemic Among Native Americans, New England, 1616-1619," *Emerging Infectious Diseases* 16, no. 2 (2010): 281–286.

44. Gordon Harris, "Historic Ipswich: The Great Dying 1616-1619, 'By God's Visitation, a Wonderful Plague,'" accessed May 17, 2021, https://historicipswich.org/2021/04/21/the-great-dying/.

45. Dwight B. Heath, ed., *Mourt's Relation: A Journal of the Pilgrims at Plymouth* (Bedford, MA: Applewood Books, originally published in 1622).

46. The Iroquois was a name given by the French. Officially they are Haudeno-saunee, meaning "people of the longhouse."

47. Daniel K. Richter and James H. Merrell, ed., *Beyond the Covenant Chain—The Iroquois and Their Neighbors, 1600–1800* (University Park, PA: Penn State University Press, 2003).

48. David J. Silverman, "Guns, Empires and Indians," Aeon, Oct. 13, 2016, https://aeon.co/essays/how-did-the-introduction-of-guns-change-native-america.

49. Alexander H. H. Stuart, "Report of the Secretary of the Interior," in First Session of the Thirty-Second Congress (Washington, DC: Boyd Hamilton, 1852), 502, https://www.govinfo.gov/content/pkg/SERIALSET-00612_00_00/pdf/SERIALSET-00612_00_00.pdf.

50. Richard H. Pratt, Captain, "The Advantages of Mingling Indians with Whites," in Proceedings of the National Conference of Charities and Corrections at the Nineteenth Annual Session in Denver, Colorado, June 23–29, 1982 (Boston, MA: George H. Ellis), 46.

51. Joseph Cress, "Army to Disinter Remains of Six Carlisle Indian School Students in June," *The Sentinel*, March 3, 2022, https://cumberlink.com/news/local/history/.

52. David Wallace Adams, *Education for Extinction American Indians and the Boarding School Experience, 1875-1928* (Lawrence, KS: University Press of Kansas, 1995).

53. Alia Wong, "The Schools that Tried—But Failed—to Make Native America's Obsolete," *Atlantic Magazine,* March 5, 2019, https://www.theatlantic.com/education/archive/2019/03/failed-assimilation-native-american-boarding-schools/584017.

54. John D. Daniels, "The Indian Population of North America in 1492," *The William and Mary Quarterly* 49, no. 2 (April 1992): 298–320.

55. Lewis Meriam, *The Problem of Indian Administration* (Baltimore, MD: Johns Hopkins Press, 1928), 3.

56. J. W. Powell, Charles C. Royce, and Cyrus Thomas, "1899—Eighteenth Annual Report of the Bureau of American Ethnology—1896-97, Part 2," https://digitalcommons.csumb.edu/hornbeck_ind_1/2/.

57. Scott v. Sanford, 60 U.S. 393 (1857).

58. Frederick Douglass, "Speech on the Dred Scott Decision," May 14, 1857, https://www.utc.edu/sites/default/files/2021-01/fddredscottspeechexcerpt2018.pdf.

59. U.S. Census, "Statistics of the United States Slave Population of the United States," (1850), 82, accessed Feb. 16, 2023, https://www2.census.gov/library/publications/decennial/1850/1850c/1850c-04.pdf.

60. Stuart A. Streichler, "Justice Curtis Dissent in the Dred Scott Case: An Interpretative Study,*" Hastings Constitutional Law Quarterly* 24, no. 2 (Winter 1997): 529.

61. Frederick Douglass, "Speech on the Dred Scott Decision," May 14, 1857, http://www.libraryweb.org/~digitized/books/Two_Speeches_by_Frederick_Douglass.pdf.

62. Ratified on July 9, 1868.

63. The National Native American Boarding School Healing Coalition. Minneapolis, MN, https://boardingschoolhealing.org/education/impact-of-historical-trauma/

64. Deborah L. Feldman et al., *Why We Drop Out: Understanding and Disrupting Student Pathways to Leaving School* (New York: Teachers College Press, 2017).

65. Ali Wong, "The Schools That Tried—But Failed—to Make Native Americans Obsolete," *The Atlantic,* March 5, 2019, https://www.theatlantic.com/education/archive/2019/03/failed-assimilation-native-american-boarding-schools/584017/.

66. National Academies of Sciences, Engineering, and Medicine, *How People Learn II: Learners, Contexts, and Cultures* (Washington, DC: The National Academies Press, 2018).

67. Kristina Rizga, "The Alaska Native Teacher Upending the Legacy of Colonial Education," *The Atlantic*, April 4, 2020, https://www.theatlantic.com/education/archive/2020/04/teaching-native-culture-in-alaskas-classrooms/609292/.

68. "Cultural Principles and Education Framework Cultivate Strong Hawaiian Identity in KS Learners," Kamehameha Schools, Jan. 9, 2017, https://www.ksbe.edu/article/cultural-principles-and-education-framework-cultivate-a-strong-hawaiian-ide/.

69. "Hawaiian Studies," Hawai'I State Department of Education, http://www.hawaiipublicschools.org/TeachingAndLearning/StudentLearning/HawaiianEducation/Pages/HSP.aspx.

70. Temple Grandin, "Different Kinds of Minds," filmed on May 27, 2011 at TEDxDU, Denver, CO, video, https://www.youtube.com/watch?v=aF4sP-uC-yI.

71. "About St. Louis Park Schools," St. Louis Park Schools, 2022, https://mnschooljobs.org/company/st-louis-park-schools/#:~:text=Student%20Achievement-,St.,unpredictable%20school%20district%20in%20Minnesota.

72. "About St. Louis Park Schools."

73. Minnesota Department of Education, "83.3 Percent of Minnesota's Class of 2021 Graduate in Four Years," https://content.govdelivery.com/accounts/MNMDE/bulletins/311010e.

Chapter 9

Religionists' Claims Against Science and Other Deniers

> If we are seeking to serve the God of truth then we should really welcome truth from whatever source it comes. We shouldn't fear the truth. . . . The crucial thing is to be honest.
>
> —John Polkinghorne, Physicist and Anglican Priest[1]

Puritan John Cotton, considered the preeminent minister and theologian of the Massachusetts Bay Colony, wrote in his *The Powring Out of the Seven Vials* (1642), "The more learned and witty you bee . . . the more fit to act for Satan will you bee."[2] Puritans took their Bible seriously. Taken out of context, Reverend Cotton's quote might be seen as an admonishment against learning rather than a warning to avoid prideful elitism. Unfortunately, Protestant fundamentalism took the former interpretation to reject any non-Biblical learning that may be construed as contradicting a literal interpretation of the Bible. As historian Richard Hofstadter has described, there has been a deep river of anti-intellectualism in America:

> The American mind was shaped in the mold of early modern Protestantism. Religion was the first arena for American intellectual life, and thus the first arena for an anti-intellectual impulse. . . . The disdain for doctrine and for refinements in ideas, the subordination of men of ideas to men of emotional power or manipulative skill are hardly innovations of the twentieth century; they are inheritances from American Protestantism.[3]

The Enlightenment ideals of reason and evidence that guided the Protestant Founding Fathers' framing of law and government were in competition with colonial preachers bellowing that unconverted heathens were bound for eternal torment in hell. In 1741, Anglican minister Jonathan Edwards, leader of the Great Awakening, preached his famous "Sinners in the Hands of an Angry God." It soon became the earthly standard for fire and brimstone, bound-for-hell-unless-you-repent preaching. On the question of disciplined learning, Edwards said: "There is this clear evidence that men's own wisdom is no security to them from death; that if it were otherwise we should see some difference between the wise and politic men of the world, and others, with regard to their liableness to early and unexpected death: but how is it in fact? Eccl. 2:16. 'How dieth the wise man? even as the fool.'"[4]

Many passionate, well-meaning people have struggled to reconcile different truths claimed by literal interpreters of scripture, Biblical archeologists, and people of science. Religious fundamentalists, like Edwards, preached an outright antagonism toward reason and scientific evidence. This latent American anti-intellectualism has been fueled and expertly exploited by modern Protestant fundamentalist preachers, craven politicians, and media pundits who purposefully sow doubt and division by promoting frightening superstitions and half-truths wrapped in conspiracy theories. It is one thing to preach the Bible on questions of God, values, and the meaning of life and death; it is quite another to misuse the Bible to take direct aim against the findings of objective science and censor science education. In this chapter we tell the story of the depth and breadth of religionists' claims against science and their attempt to reassert the political potency of Protestant fundamentalism into the larger American society through the door of public schools. This shadow of anti-intellectualism and anti-science is what most educators must deal with sooner or later, to one degree or another.

As we saw in the three previous chapters, White Protestant Christianity has dominated American life since the early colonial era. But by the mid-twentieth century, this Protestant cultural dominance had weakened in many parts of the country through increased educational attainment and repeated court challenges. As the noted historian Conrad Henry Moehlman admonished his fellow Protestant Christians in his book, *School and Church*, published in 1943:

Although the Protestant Age in American history ended in principle with the adoption of the First Amendment in 1791, there are many among us who refuse to admit that fact even today. The content of that amendment was so radical and so revolutionary at the time of its approval that serious men the world over predicted anarchy and dissolution for the newly organized union. . . . Utterly unaware of what has taken place among us during the last hundred and fifty years, various religious groups are conducting a vigorous propaganda for the return of the formal teaching of religion to the public classroom. If one looks more closely, he seems to discover ultimate objectives such as state support for private schools, the securing of "release time" at the expense of the efficiency of the public schools, the signing over to public education what ought to be the job of the family and the churches. And these pressure groups seem oblivious of the damage their programs are doing to the churches they desire to maintain and advance.[5]

Five years after the publication of Moehlman's book, the U.S. Supreme Court issued a landmark ruling in *McCollum v. Board of Education,*[6] which banned *all* Bibles and sectarian religious education in public schools. Subsequent U.S. Supreme Court decisions in the second half of the twentieth century likewise struck down other schemes for state support of sectarian religious instruction. Yet despite legal setbacks, certain Protestant pressure groups, as Professor Moehlman termed them, whose membership predominately consisted of White fundamentalists, persisted in seeking to reassert their lost cultural dominance. Their influence in education and society might have faded entirely from view if not for certain developments that came from an unlikely source: advances in geology and biology science. Ironically, science has given renewed cultural clout to Protestant fundamentalism. And a major source of this cultural clout can be found in heated debates over the content of the public school curriculum as it pertains to science spanning the last two centuries.

NEW VERSUS OLD EARTH, FULLY FORMED HUMANS VERSUS EVOLUTION

It all begins with Genesis. Here in succinct authoritative form is the purported answer to the fundamental questions about our origins. As one fundamentalist theologian stated,

> The Book of Genesis . . . contains the authoritative information given to the race concerning these questions of everlasting interest: the Being of God; the origin of the universe; the creation of man; the origin the soul; the fact of revelation; the introduction of sin; the promise of salvation; the primitive division of the human race; the purpose of the elected people.[7]

In the eighteenth century, in the absence of empirical evidence to the contrary, it was intellectually convenient and emotionally reassuring to assume Genesis told the natural history of the Earth and the origin of all life. Thus, when the Church of Ireland's Anglican Archbishop James Ussher published his massive, 1,600-page *Annuals of History* in 1650, in Latin, which dated the beginning of the world to 9:00 a.m. on the morning of October 23, 4,004 BC, it was widely accepted among the educated classes.[8] The publication of

Bishop Ussher's *Annuals* coincided with the dawn of the Enlightenment with its advances in astronomy, physics, and mathematics which so captivated the imaginations of Johannes Kepler and later Benjamin Franklin and his contemporaries. Scientific advances would soon occur in other fields as well.

By the late 1700s and early 1800s, a new science—geology—had emerged. One of the first empirical studies to determine the age of the Earth was conducted by James Hutton of Scotland, considered by many as the founder of modern geology.[9] In 1788, Hutton published his *Theory of the Earth*[10] which detailed the layered fossil records within the Earth's strata. Hutton concluded that these fossils showed a very old Earth dating millions of years ago—vastly older than Archbishop James Ussher's claim of 4,004 BC. Many more empirical geological studies soon followed. In 1808, the Geological Society of London, the oldest geological society in the world, was established with thirteen members. By 1818, its membership had grown to 400.[11] Their impact was monumental. As the modern-day geologist Reverend Michael Roberts sums up this revolution in thinking about Earth and Genesis: "In three decades geology was transformed from speculation about the Flood to a historical reconstruction of the world. In 1790 it was just possible for an 'up-to-date' geologist to accept 4,004 BC as the date of creation, but by 1810 all geologists accepted a vast age."[12] Still, there were some people of science who continued to believe in a literal interpretation of Genesis, advocating instead for a "young Earth" view that was scripturally based. One example was Dr. Andrew Ure, a medical doctor, professor of physics, and member of the Geological and Astronomical Societies of London. Ure's 700-page tome, *A New System of Geology,* published in 1829, argued that:

> With regard to the antiquity of our Earth, nothing can be known except what the Eternal Spirit has deigned to reveal. The date of its creation, according to the Chronology of the Hebrew Bible, was 4,004 years before the Birth of our Saviour. . . . If it [Earth] was formed for the dwelling place of Man, what use is there for imagining a more distant beginning? Why build a mansion in the wilderness of space, long ere tenants are prepared to occupy it? It appears therefore that neither Reason nor Revelation will justify us in extending the origin of the material system beyond 6,000 years from our own days. The world then received it substance, form, and motions, form the volition of the Omnipotent.[13]

Adherents to a literal interpretation of Genesis soon found themselves defending it on another front, this time from advances in evolutionary biology led by Charles Darwin's seminal publication, *The Origin of Species by Means of Natural Selection*[14] in 1859, and later his *Descent of Man* published in 1871.[15] For some scientists, even highly respected ones, it was difficult to relinquish the literal notion of human origins as described in Genesis that

God created man *fully formed* in a manner distinct from other animals. For example, consider the distinguished Sir William Dawson (1820–1899), a Fellow of the Geological Society of London and the Royal Society. Dawson was the first president of the Royal Society of Canada, president of the Geological Society of America, and president of both the American and British Associations for the Advancement of Science. In a glowing eulogy to him upon his death in 1899, there were remarks about Dawson's tendency toward Biblical literalism:

> As may be inferred from their titles, many of his books display a strong theological bias. Sir William was a Presbyterian of the old school and strongly opposed to all theories of the evolution of man from brute ancestors, nor would he allow anything more than a very moderate antiquity for the species. He held that there is no adequate reason for attributing the so-called "Neolithic" man to any time older than that of the early eastern empires, while he thought the time for Paleolithic man need not be more than twenty or thirty centuries in addition, man having thus made an abrupt appearance in full perfection.[16]

Yet many other clergy and theologians in the nineteenth century saw no conflict between an old Earth/evolutionary biological view and Genesis, so long as the Bible was not taken literally as science.[17] As Reverend Roberts concluded:

> It is easy to overstate the importance of the "Anti-geologists" as they had a high profile and attracted much attention, particularly in retrospect. The "Anti-geologists" were not representative of Christians as they were attacked most vigorously by other Christians, as is shown by the response to Ure's *A New System of Geology* (1829) . . . reports of warfare between geology and Genesis are greatly exaggerated. In fact, the converse is true, as from 1790 to 1860 the majority of educated Christians, including most Evangelicals, positively embraced geology and rejected Biblical literalism.[18]

BANNING THE TEACHING OF SCIENCE

The controversy over Biblical literalism and science might have remained an academic or private matter were it not for the explosion in high school enrollment in the United States in the early twentieth century. Between 1890 and 1920, high school enrollment climbed from 300,000 to over 2.4 million students. Nearly 30 percent of students in the first decade (1900–1910) had an Earth science course.[19] For Protestant fundamentalists who had seen their cultural influence steadily erode, the teaching of modern "old Earth" geology in Earth science courses provided a new opening to reassert their influence via a culture war fought in the public schools. The fundamentalists argued that the teaching of old Earth geology was tantamount to promoting atheism because it contradicted Genesis. By 1928, the percentage of secondary students enrolled in an Earth science course had plummeted to less than 3 percent.

The teaching of evolution stirred similar opposition at the same time. In 1928, Arkansas voters passed a ballot initiative banning the teaching of evolution in public schools. It read:

> It shall be unlawful for any teacher or other instructor in any university, college, normal, public school or other institution of the state which is supported in whole or in part from public funds derived by state or local taxation to teach the theory or doctrine that mankind ascended or descended from a lower order of animals, and also it shall be unlawful for any teacher, textbook commission or other authority exercising the power to select text-books for above-mentioned institutions to adopt or use in any such institution a text-book that teaches the doctrine or theory that mankind descended or ascended from a lower order of animals.

Violators were subject to a $500 fine and dismissal from state service. The ballot measure was approved in a landslide vote of 63 to 37 percent, making Arkansas the first state to make teaching of evolution a crime in public schools through popular vote.[20]

Legislators in other states attempted to enact similar anti-evolution laws, and in some cases succeeded. In a notoriously celebrated case that drew international attention, John Scopes, a twenty-four-year-old algebra and physics teacher who occasionally taught biology, was tried and convicted in 1925 of violating Tennessee's recently enacted "Monkey law," which banned the teaching of evolution. Such anti-evolution laws were in force for the next forty years until Susan Epperson, a Little Rock, Arkansas, biology teacher, won a U.S. Supreme Court decision that struck down the anti-evolution Arkansas law as unconstitutional. Writing for the majority in 1968, Justice Fortas opined:

> The law must be stricken because of its conflict with the constitutional prohibition of state laws respecting an establishment of religion or prohibiting the free exercise thereof. The overriding fact is that Arkansas' law selects from the body of knowledge a particular segment which it proscribes for the sole reason that it is deemed to conflict with a particular religious doctrine; that is, with a particular interpretation of the Book of Genesis by a particular religious group.[21]

Faced with this and other U.S. Supreme Court defeats involving the insertion of Protestant fundamentalism into public schools, one might have thought that a "renaissance of the [anti-evolutionism] movement is most unlikely."[22]

But this interest group has displayed remarkable persistence throughout the centuries, adapting to defeat and mutating their positions into different lines of argument. Instead of trying to legally reassert the cultural primacy of a literal interpretation of Genesis into education, a new tactic was employed: "creation science."

CREATION SCIENCE

As a way around U.S. Supreme Court rulings, "creationism"[23] was (and still is) touted as a scientific alternative to evolutionary science that should be accorded equal status because, it is argued, both are *theories* and, therefore, *both* theories should be taught in public schools. This literal Biblical view still is held by a substantial portion of the public even into the twenty-first century. The strong persistence of the belief in creationism was evidenced in a 2019 national Gallup survey of 1,015 adults. The survey found that 40 percent of Americans believe that God created humans in their present form at one time within the last 10,000 years.[24]

Given the modern public's beliefs about God and evolution, it is a relatively simple matter for determined partisan groups to claim that if creationism is left out of their local public schools, biology teachers are, in effect, promoting atheism. This is a politically potent claim, and the continued popular appeal of creationism should not be underestimated. The 2019 Gallup poll revealed sharp divisions between different groups. Among people who identify as conservatives, 54 percent believe in *a young Earth and that humans were created fully formed at one time within the last 10,000 years*, versus 29 percent of liberals. Likewise, when analyzed for levels of education, the survey found that for people with only a high school degree, 51 percent agree while 23 percent of college graduates agree that humans were created fully formed at one time within the last 10,000 years.[25]

For college graduates, this is a curious result. Either modern high school biology courses simply do not teach evolution, it is not taught very well, or students' active misconceptions of evolutional biology are far more deeply rooted than is commonly supposed. There appears to be some truth in all three explanations. In a representative sample of 926 public high school biology instructors conducted in 2007 and again in 2019,[26] Pennsylvania State University researchers Eric Plutzer and Michael B. Berkman found that more than one-third of biology teachers surveyed disagreed that evolution was the unifying theory of biology. They also found that about 13 percent of biology teachers teach creationism as a "valid scientific alternative to Darwinian explanations for the origin of species." As one Minnesota teacher commented: "I don't teach the theory of evolution in my life science classes, nor do I teach the Big Bang Theory in my Earth science classes. We do not have the time to do something that is at best poor science."[27] As a Pennsylvania teacher explained, students should make up their minds "based on their own beliefs and research. Not on what a textbook or on what a teacher says."[28] In a 2019 replication of the 2007 high school biology teacher survey, a similar percentage (17 percent) did not spend any time teaching about human evolution.[29] This view runs counter to the National Research Council's recommendations for the teaching of evolution, which calls for introducing evidence that evolution occurred and crafting lesson plans with evolution as a unifying theme of biology.[30]

Are some teachers' reluctance to teach evolution a matter of poor science or poorly *understood* science? Berkman and Plutzer also found that only a few of the "cautious 60 percent" group of biology teachers felt they had a strong understanding of evolution. This last finding is consistent with a series of research reports on the large number of college biology majors who harbor misconceptions about natural selection, evolution, and the scientific facts that support it.[31] If today's college biology students who graduate and become high school teachers have misconceptions about evolution, how can they enlighten their high school students who bring their own ideas, misconceptions, and religious biases to school?

PUBLIC SCHOOLS AS AN ARENA FOR CULTURE WARS

Since the mid-nineteenth century, resistance to the teaching of old Earth geology and evolutionary biology has become a surrogate for continued Protestant fundamentalist influence in public schools and the wider political and social culture. These groups have managed to leverage public misunderstanding of both science and Christianity to create a powerful negative feedback loop: Biblical literalism blocks the understanding and acceptance of science; the lack of understanding and acceptance of science creates a vacuum easily filled by Biblical literalism. Despite repeated U.S. Supreme Court setbacks, these interest groups can survive by drawing their energy from a large pool of the voting public who are caught in this negative feedback loop. Given this significant segment of the public who have negative views of science vis-a-vis the Bible, some state and local public school board members risk inciting a public backlash if their schools teach the facts and theory of evolution. Yet to teach evolution *with* reference to God's active involvement (a belief that represents the majority of the public's opinion) has been ruled unconstitutional.[32] Even though Protestant fundamentalist groups have been repeatedly defeated in courts, they can still assert cultural dominance through the *court of public opinion*—provided there is a threshold level supporting their cause. Texas is an example of this political dynamic.

THE CASE OF TEXAS

Texas enrolls nearly 5.7 million students, second to only California with over 6.7 million students.[33] Together, these two states account for one in five students nationwide. Both states adopt textbooks statewide, thus providing publishers a lucrative market for their textbooks if they can get them approved by their respective state boards of education. The Texas State Board of Education (SBOE) is an elected fifteen-member board, each from one of fifteen geographical areas. (In contrast, the California SBOE has eleven members, all of whom are appointed by the governor.)

In the 2012 Texas general election, nearly eight million Texans voted for the U.S. president, and over 90 percent of those voters *also* voted for a state school board candidate. Republican candidates dominated their races for state school board, winning ten out of fifteen seats. According to a Pew study, 39 percent of Texans believed the Bible to be "literally true, word for word" and the same percentage believed humans were created fully formed.[34] Therefore, to win their primary races, Republican candidates must appeal to those who strongly believe in the literal interpretation of the Bible. An example is Republican Marty Rowley.

In Rowley's hotly contested 2012 primary election, he advertised himself as a "Conservative Republican candidate," attorney, and pastor of an 8,000-member church. Rowley stated his position on the teaching of evolution, "I do think if our teachers are given the freedom to teach the strengths and the weaknesses of evolution, then what we're going to do is allow our students to look at all aspects and to make a well-reasoned decision as to what they believe with regard to a particular theory."[35] Rowley won his primary fight against his Republican opponent, Anette Carlisle, by only one percentage point—50.5 versus 49.5 percent. Despite narrowly winning his Republican primary election in the November 2012 general election, Rowley trounced his Democratic opponent 76 to 24 percent for the District 15 Texas State School Board seat. In sum, in those Texas districts that are either heavily Republican or heavily Democratic, the real races are in the primary elections that tend to produce more extreme candidates because they must appeal to a narrower base of voters.

Shortly after the November 2012 general election, the new Texas SBOE appointed an expert panel to review science textbooks for statewide purchase. Not surprisingly, given the ten-to-five Republican majority on the Texas school board, the board was criticized for packing the panel with creationists, evolution skeptics, and others, such as Rowley, with little background in science education. One panel member wrote this in a letter to the Texas SBOE about his fellow review panelists:

> It would seem that the selection process for reviewers is lacking, at best—politically motivated at worst. . . . I fully expected that as a doctoral student at the University of Texas at Austin I would be the least-qualified member on the panel. My fears of inadequacy would soon subside; it seems that I was in fact one of only two *practicing* scientists present; indeed, I was among a small minority of panelists that possessed any postsecondary education in the biological sciences. . . . It is impossible to conclude that the teams reviewing textbooks were anything other than grossly skewed and obviously biased. The net result of having a huge raft of non-scientists on the panels . . . [was that] I was put into the position of having to painstakingly educate other panel members on past and current literature.[36]

There has not been much change in Texas since 2013. Of the nine Republicans on the 2022 Texas School board, six tout their Protestant (Baptist, Pentecostal) church positions as pastors, deacons, music directors, and/or members. The Texas example provides an illustration of how a small percentage of White Christian fundamentalists can concentrate their energies on the *primary* election process to leverage statewide political dominance disproportionate to their numbers. While the impact of primary elections in Texas has obvious implications for schooling policy in Texas, what may be less obvious is that because of the huge Texas market for textbooks and the investment of publishers to meet this market, the Texas version is heavily marketed nationally. Thus, a small primary election in Texas may have national implications for school textbook sales.

BIBLICAL LITERALISM AND ANTI-SCIENCE BIAS

Political opportunists can readily exploit large segments of the population who passionately believe the Bible is true, "word for word." For Biblical literalists, science and scientists are not to be trusted. The resistance to accepting science is not just about the content of science. It is also about the *process* of science as well. Science is not divinely revealed nor is it about beliefs or opinions. New scientific knowledge and more powerful theoretical frameworks to understand reality are driven by evidence.

When new evidence appears that contradicts old ways of thinking, there is always a certain degree of mental and emotional adaptation that needs to occur, even among scientists. When scientific advances are revolutionary, as Thomas Kuhn has described in his seminal book, *The Structure of Scientific Revolutions,* even men and women of science can have great difficulty accepting evidence that requires changing deep-seated views. For example, from the earliest reports of the novel COVID-19 pandemic, there were public complaints that scientists were changing their views about the virus. The Centers for Disease Control and Prevention (CDC) published a growing library of studies on the *novel* coronavirus. But to an impatient public clamoring for definitive information and guidance, the CDC guidelines seemed constantly shifting and confusing. One day facial masks were unnecessary, the next day they were mandated. Each COVID-19 study focused on only a portion of the pandemic. Only over time did a more complete understanding of the virus emerge.[37] These public complaints reveal a misunderstanding of the process of science, which sadly reinforces the mistrust of science and scientists. But the process of science can take time to get it right.

To understand science as a *process of learning* is to appreciate the time-consuming struggle to develop understanding of new phenomena. Without appreciating the process of science, different research findings can be mistaken for partisanship rather than as the often-messy search for truth. As Kenneth R. Lutken, Dean of the College of Engineering and Professor of Biomedical Engineering at Boston University, remarked, "Anti-scientists believe that if the data does not convey the message desired, then just dismiss the data."[38] According to Anthony Fauci, former Director of the National Institute of Allergy and Infectious Diseases, "One of the problems we face in the United States is that unfortunately, there is a combination of an anti-science bias [by which] people . . . for reasons that sometimes are . . . inconceivable and not understandable . . . just don't believe science and they don't believe authority."[39] Lutken agrees, stating, "For years, conservative media and conservative politicians have attacked basic ideas of science from evolution to climate change," and currently (in 2020), "the U.S. is gripped not only by the coronavirus pandemic, but also an anti-science pandemic."[40]

From denials about evolution to the efficacy of vaccinations to evidence for human-induced climate change, anti-science sentiment remains staunch among certain sectors of the public. The implications for science education are even more problematic. As the Texas example illustrates, a relatively small but determined fundamentalist political group can play a major role in subverting science education nationwide. The lack of science literacy among the public provides the political leverage to influence state and local education policy and instructional practices, which in turn have the effect of perpetuating the very same scientific illiteracy among teachers, students, and community members. In so doing, this provides a continual wellspring of political energy for reactionary conservative forces to advance their agenda of establishing an American political and social culture in their image while the rest of the world is teaching authentic science, not religious theology as a substitute for science.

Unless educators and policymakers are more explicit in defending the teaching of evidence-based science, our states and nation will suffer the consequences of American students being ill-informed and not intellectually prepared to lead in creating the medical, health, and economic breakthroughs that keep us competitive (and alive) in the global economy. There are ways of mitigating the corrupting influence of Biblical literalism on science education and public policy. One way is to improve teachers', students', and the public's understanding of the principles and processes of science.

SCIENCE EDUCATION IMPROVEMENTS

The U.S. Department of Education has required states to certify that they are graduating "highly qualified" science and math teachers. One way is to require secondary teacher candidates to also graduate with a bachelor's degree in their subject.[41] Among disciplinary science faculty at universities across the country is a large and growing movement called Discipline Based Education Research.[42] This movement uses insightful assessments to uncover student misconceptions in different subjects so that instruction can be adjusted accordingly. Many universities have developed faculty development programs based on research on the scholarship of teaching and learning[43] so that science teacher candidates do not harbor misconceptions and know how to teach children important basic scientific understandings. The National Science Teachers Association, for instance, has authored a set of science teaching standards, which are designed to help universities focus on specific areas of improvement.[44] And many states have adopted new and improved science content, process, and practices standards.[45]

Another mitigation effort is providing more and better training for school board members. In two groundbreaking studies sponsored by The Iowa Association of School Boards known as the Lighthouse Inquiry Study I and II,[46] researchers found that "school boards in high-achieving districts are significantly different in their knowledge and beliefs than school boards in low-achieving districts. This difference appears to carry through among administrators and teachers throughout the districts." The National School Boards Association has issued a summary report based on the Lighthouse studies that describes eight characteristics of effective school boards.[47] Various state school boards associations have made concerted efforts to train their members about their roles, such as the California School Boards Association.[48] Also, in many communities and states, reform movements are focusing on the election of school board members as nonpartisans. The impact of this movement is not definitive, but it indicates an increasing awareness by poli-cymakers of the importance of taking school governance out of the political arena.[49]

Public Understanding of Science

There is a growing movement to better coordinate and fund formal and infor-mal science programs. For example, a group of private corporate and founda-tion donors have supported the creation of one hundred and eleven "STEM Learning Ecosystems."[50] These ecosystems connect schools, museums, science centers, and other community resources and organizations so that teachers, stu-dents, and their families can see and experience science, technology, engineer-ing, and mathematics all around them. These science, technology, engineering, mathematics (STEM) Ecosystems strive to create multiple opportunities for students to experience science through collaborative and rigorous activities outside of the classroom. They also provide valuable resources to help teach-ers and families develop the capacity to support their children. Although the STEM Ecosystems' emphasis is on kids, it could easily be shifted to include family science activities around everyday subjects such as cooking and feeding the hungry of all ages, from babies to the elderly with chronic conditions.

A significant funder of informal science education is the National Sci-ence Foundation's *Advancing Informal STEM Learning* (AISL) program.[51] Over the past thirty-five years, National Science Foundation has made over 2,100 AISL awards to museums, universities, and other nonprofit organiza-tions totaling nearly $3.5 billion.[52] Additionally, there are a growing number of "citizen science" projects throughout the world.[53] These projects take advantage of the global reach of the internet and involve almost all branches of science. The projects engage citizen scientists of all ages and abilities in authentic research through observation and data collection, the hallmarks of the scientific method.

Public Dialogues Between Scientists and Theologians

Far from the bustle of the media's stoking the fires of in-your-face shouting matches and wild accusations are quieter conversations that explore the nexus between science and faith. We offer three examples below, but many more have occurred and are occurring nationally and internationally. In the 1990s, a series of five international research conferences on science and religion was cosponsored by the Vatican Observatory in Rome and the Center for Theology and the Natural Sciences at the University of California at Berkley. The sec-ond conference, for example, produced a series of fifteen papers that explored the implications of modeling complex systems, like weather forecasting, for issues regarding God's divine action in the world.[54] Even Pope Francis in a 2015 interview entertained the possibility of intelligent alien life on other planets, yet saw no necessary conflict with Catholicism: "Until America was discovered we thought it didn't exist, and instead it existed. . . . In every case I think that we should stick to what the scientists tell us, still aware that the Creator is infinitely greater than our knowledge."[55] Another example is the work of the Metanexus Institute, a not-for-profit organization founded in 1997 that is "dedicated to promoting scientifically rigorous and philosophically open-ended explorations of foundational questions." Its board, staff, research agenda, and programs reflect the interweaving of both science and religion.[56] A third example is the National Association of Evangelicals (NAE) teaming up with the American Association for the Advancement of Science (AAAS), the largest general science association in the world, "to study, dialogue and resource together." In partnership with AAAS, the NAE produced a set of ten essays entitled "When God and Science Meet: Surprising Discoveries of Agreement" to help church leaders address their congregants' curiosity and concerns about science. Within the first two weeks, nearly 4,000 copies were downloaded or ordered.[57] At the same time, more resources and attention can be devoted to countering science illiteracy and the prevalence of false theories circulating virally on social media.

These kinds of initiatives all provide a way to reframe science and religion away from an us-versus-them standoff to one that helps explicate the purposes and limitations of both without dogmatic judgments and misplaced accusations. Neither is the desired state in a nation committed to freedom of expression and responsible behavior.

As Dr. Reverend Polkinghorne reminded us, "If we are seeking to serve the God of truth then we should really welcome truth from whatever source it comes. We shouldn't fear the truth. . . . The crucial thing is to be honest." In part III that follows, we explore the illusions of education reform to bring some honesty to the more intractable problems of student learning. Then, in part IV, we describe a breakthrough in education we helped to develop in an unlikely place—Egypt.

NOTES

1. See for example one of John C Polkinghorne's books on physics and theology, *Quantum Physics and Theology: An Unexpected Kinship* (New Haven, CT: Yale University Press, 2007).

2. John Cotton, "The Powring Out of the Seven Vials: Or An exposition, of the 16. Chapter of the Revelation, with an Application of it to Our Times" (1642), accessed Oct. 21, 2020, https://quod.lib.umich.edu/e/eebo2/A80630.0001.001?view=toc.

3. Richard Hofstadter, *Anti-Intellectualism in American Life* (New York: Alfred A. Knopf, 1963), 55.

4. Jonathan Edwards, "Sinners in the Hands of an Angry God" (1741), section 3, http://www.jonathan-edwards.org/Sinners.pdf.

5. Conrad Henry Moehlman, *School and Church: The American Way, A Historical Approach to the Problem of Religious Instruction in Public Education* (New York: Harper & Brothers, 1944), ix.

6. McCollum v. Board of Education, 333 U.S. 203 (1948).

7. Dyson Hague, "The Doctrinal Value of the First Chapters of Genesis," in *The Fundamentals: A Testimony to the Truth,* Volume 8 (Chicago: Testimony Publishing, 1910), 74.

8. James Ussher, "The Annals of the World: The Origin of Time, and Continued to the Beginning of the Emperor Vespasian's Reign and the Total Destruction and Abolition of the Temple and Commonwealth of the Jews," 1650, https://archive.org /details/TheAnnalsOfTheWorld1658EditionPartOne4004To176BC/The%20Annals %20Of%20The%20World%20%281658%20Edition%29%20Part%20One%20 %284004%20to%20176%20BC%29/.

9. Sir Edward B. Bailey, "James Hutton, Founder of Modern Geology (1726–1797)," *Proceedings of the Royal Society of Edinburgh, Section B. Biology* 63, no. 4 (January 1949): 357–368.

10. James Hutton, "Theory of the Earth; or an Investigation of the Laws Observable in the Composition, Dissolution, and Restoration of Land upon the Globe," *Transactions of the Royal Society of Edinburgh* I, Part II (1788): 209–304.

11. The Geological Society, "History," http://www.geolsoc.org.uk/en/About/ History.

12. Michael Roberts, "Genesis and Geology Unearthed," *The Churchman* 112, no. 3 (October 1998): 225–255.

13. Andrew Ure, *A New System of Geology in which The Great of the Earth and Animated Nature are Reconciled at Once with Modern Science and Sacred History* (London, 1829), 13–15.

14. Charles Darwin, *On the Origin of Species by Means of Natural Selection, or the Preservation of Favoured Races in the Struggle for Life* (London: John Murray, 1859).

15. Charles Darwin. *The Descent of Man, and Selection in Relation to Sex* (London: John Murray, 1871).

16. Frank D. Adams, "Sir William Dawson," *The Journal of Geology* 7, no. 8 (Nov.–Dec., 1899): 727–736.

17. Much early work in empirical geology was led by two ministers, the Reverends Adam Sedgwick and William Buckland.

18. Michael Roberts, "Genesis," 248.

19. U.S. Census Bureau, "Series H 545-571: "Public Secondary Day Schools—Percent of Pupils Enrolled in Specified Subject: 1890 to 1965," *Historical Statistics of the United States Colonial Times to 1970* (Census Bureau, 2003), 377.

20. R. Halliburton, Jr., "Arkansas Anti-Evolution Referendum," *Proceedings of the Oklahoma Academy of Science* (1964): 159–166.

21. Epperson v. Arkansas, 393 U.S. 97 (1968).

22. R. Halliburton, Jr., "Arkansas' Anti-Evolution," 165.

23. Henry M. Morris, *Scientific Creationism* (San Diego, CA: C.L.P. Publishers, 1974): 12. Morris is the Founder and President Emeritus of the Institute for Creation Research. Two of the tenets of creationism state: a) "Each of the major kinds of plants and animals was created functionally complete from the beginning and did not evolve from some other kind of organism. Changes in basic kinds since their first creation are limited to "horizontal" changes (variations) within the kinds or "downward" changes (e.g., harmful mutations, extinctions)"; and b) "The first human beings did not evolve from an animal ancestry, but were specially created in fully human form from the start." These tenets have recently been adopted by the staff of the Institute for Creation Research and incorporated permanently in its By-Laws as posted at http://www.icr.org/article/168/.

24. Megan Brenan, "40% of Americans Believe in Creationism," July 26, 2019, https://news.gallup.com/poll/261680/americans-believe-creationism.aspx.

25. Brenan, "40% of Americans."

26. Michael B. Berkman et al., "Evolution and Creationism in America's Classrooms: A National Portrait," *PLOS Biology* 6, no. 5 (May 20, 2008), https://doi.org/10.1371/journal.pbio.0060124.

27. Eric Plutzer and Michael B. Berkman, "Defeating Creationism in the Courtroom, But Not in the Classroom," *Science* 331, no. 6016 (Jan. 28, 2011): 404–405, https://www.science.org/doi/10.1126/science.1198902.

28. Berkman et al., "Evolution," 405.

29. Eric Plutzer et al., "Teaching Evolution in U.S. Public Schools: A Continuing Challenge," *Evolution: Education and Outreach* 13, no. 14 (June 9, 2020), https://evolution-outreach.biomedcentral.com/articles/10.1186/s12052-020-00126-8.

30. National Research Council, *National Science Education Standards* (Washington, DC: National Academy Press, 1996).

31. Ross H. Nehm and Leah Reilly, "Biology Majors' Knowledge and Misconceptions of Natural Selection," *BioScience* 57, no. 3 (March 2007): 263–272, https://doi.org/10.1641/B570311.

32. Kitzmiller v. Dover Area School District, 400 F. Supp. 2d 707 (M.D. Pa. 2005).

33. National Center for Education Statistics, "Enrollment in Public Elementary and Secondary Schools, by Region, State, and Jurisdiction: Selected Years, Fall 1990 Through Fall 2023, Table 203.20," https://nces.ed.gov/programs/digest/d13/tables/dt13_203.20.asp.

34. Pew Research Center, "Religious Landscape Study: Adults in Texas," 2014, https://www.pewresearch.org/religion/religious-landscape-study/state/texas/.

35. Jacob Mayer, "Evolution Tops State Board of Education Debate Topics," *Amarillo Global News*, Oct. 17, 2012, https://www.amarillo.com/story/news/local/2012/10/18/evolution-tops-debate-topics/13110954007/.

36. Brian Tashman, "Texas Textbook Reviewer Sheds Light on Creationist Efforts to Undercut Science Education," Right Wing Watch, September 12, 2013, https://

www.rightwingwatch.org/post/texas-textbook-reviewer-sheds-light-on-creationist
-efforts-to-undercut-science-education/.

37. For the Centers for Disease Control and Prevention COVID-19 Science Updates from 2020 through 2022, see https://www.cdc.gov/library/covid19/scienceupdates.html?Sort=Date%3A%3Adesc.

38. Kenneth R. Lutchen, "Years of Anti-Science sentiment has Left America in a Terrifying Predicament," *Business Insider*, Sep. 17, 2020, https://www.businessinsider.com/american-anti-science-sentiment-comes-back-hurt-us-wildfires-pandemic-2020-9.

39. Jacqueline Howard and Veronica Stracqualursi, "Fauci Warns of 'Anti-Science Bias' Being a Problem in US," CNN Politics, June 18, 2020, https://www.cnn.com/2020/06/18/politics/anthony-fauci-coronavirus-anti-science-bias/index.html.

40. Kenneth R. Lutchen, "Years."

41. See U.S. Department of Education Highly Qualified Teacher (HQT) requirements by state, https://www2.ed.gov/programs/teacherqual/hqtplans/index.html.

42. National Research Council, *Discipline-Based Education Research: Understanding and Improving Learning in Undergraduate Science and Engineering* (Washington, DC: The National Academies Press, 2012), https://doi.org/10.17226/13362.

43. See, for example, the journal published by the Humboldt State University Center, *Scholarship of Teaching and Learning, Innovative Pedagogy*.

44. National Science Teaching Association, "Position Statement: Science Teacher Preparation," https://www.nsta.org/nstas-official-positions/science-teacher-preparation.

45. Next Generation Lead States, *Next Generation Science Standards: For States, by States* (Washington, DC: The National Academies Press, 2013), https://doi.org/10.17226/18290.

46. Iowa Association of School Boards, Leadership for Student Learning: The School Board's Role in Creating School Districts Where All Students Succeed (Des Moines: Iowa Association of School Boards, 2016), 6, https://www.ia-sb.org/docs/default-source/iasb-general/books-pubs/leadershipforstudentlearningbookupdatedd82bca6a-de70-4321-aa3c-0df32d0fbe97.pdf?sfvrsn=703da278_3.

47. Chuck Dervarics and Eileen O'Brien, "Eight Characteristics of an Effective School Board," Center for Public Education, 2019, https://www.nsba.org/-/media/NSBA/File/cpe-eight-characteristics-of-effective-school-boards-report-december-2019.pdf.

48. California School Boards Association, "The School Board Role in Creating the Conditions for Student Achievement," May 2017, https://www.csba.org/GovernanceAndPolicyResources/~/media/CSBA/Files/GovernanceResources/Reports/201705BoardResearchReport.ashx.

49. Evan Crawford, "How Nonpartisan Ballot Design Conceals Partisanship: A Survey Experiment of School Board Members in Two States," *Political Research Quarterly* 71, no. 1 (March 2018): 143–156.

50. STEM Ecosystems, "Why Cultivate STEM Learning Ecosystems?" https://stemecosystems.org/what-are-stem-ecosystems/.

51. National Science Foundation, "Advancing Informal STEM Learning (AISL), Aug. 17, 2022, https://www.nsf.gov/funding/pgm_summ.jsp?pims_id=504793.

52. National Science Foundation Awards, https://www.nsf.gov/awardsearch/simpleSearchResult?queryText=AISL&ActiveAwards=true&ExpiredAwards=true.

53. "List of Citizen Science Projects," Wikipedia, April 13, 2023, https://en.wikipedia.org/wiki/List_of_citizen_science_projects#:~:text=Citizen%20science%20projects%20are%20activities%20sponsored%20by%20a,at%20home%20or%20in%20the%20field%20for%20eBird.

54. Robert John Russell et al., *Chaos and Complexity: Scientific Perspectives on Divine Action* (The Vatican Observatory, 1996).

55. Elise Harris, "Do Aliens Exist? Pope Francis Tackles This (and Other Things) in New Interview," *Catholic News Agency*, Oct. 15, 2015, https://www.catholicnewsagency.com/news/32820/do-aliens-exist-pope-francis-tackles-this-and-other-things-in-new-interview.

56. "People," Metanexus Institute, https://metanexus.net/people/.

57. Sarah Kropp Brown, "Are Evangelicals Anti-Science?" National Association of Evangelicals, Sep. 22, 2015, https://www.nae.net/evangelicals-anti-science/.

Part III

THE PROMISES AND ILLUSIONS OF EDUCATIONAL REFORM

The cover of the December 8, 2008, issue of *Time Magazine* featured the lead article "How to Fix America's Schools." In this part of the book, we examine the promises and illusions of "fixing America's schools." In trying to improve student learning in hundreds of secondary schools and scores of colleges and universities within the current Nation at Risk archetype, we have become aware of many illusions. The notion that schools can be "fixed," as if schools were broken like a piece of machinery, is one of them. Time magazine's headline writers, along with others, might be excused for having this illusion. The metaphor of schools being something mechanical is pervasive in our post-industrial society. This notion of "fixing" has become almost imprinted in U.S. culture. Using this metaphor, schools are regarded as merely a complex assembly of parts that can be taken out, discarded, repaired, and replaced if they are not "working." But students, teachers, principals, and staff are not like so many interchangeable mechanical parts. They are living beings who live in relation to each other and move about in their local geographic, economic, and cultural environment, or ecosystem. Moreover, these actors have different perspectives, passions, and beliefs, both positive and negative, based on their experiences. So, while you might fix a tire, you do not fix a tomato plant. You *cultivate* it.

The inappropriate use of metaphors and analogies, like the mechanical metaphor of schooling, has consequences leading to certain policies rather than others. If schools are to be repurposed for a new era, it is important to be aware of how language is used to conjure false imagery. Consider, for example, what happened during the Great Recession of 2008–2011. States and school districts saw their tax revenues plummet. As part of the federal government's $832 billion stimulus package, $100 billion was allocated to rescue state public education budgets from bankruptcy. Three billion was

175

allocated for one of the largest federally funded interventions, the School Improvement Grants (SIG), to try to lift student achievement in chronically low-performing schools.[1]

The SIG program might have started with the question about repurposing schools involving a more relevant curriculum, using more engaging teaching methods, and/or administering mixed assessment measures. Instead, millions of dollars were granted to school districts to implement one of four prescribed "school intervention models" labeled: *transformation, turnaround, restart,* or *closure.* In simple terms, these models came down to either (1) firing the principal; (2) firing the principal and half of the teachers; (3) restarting the school as a charter; or (4) closing down the school altogether. To use an analogy, if the school buses are moving too slowly, either (1) fire the drivers; 2) (fire the supervisor and replace half of the drivers; (3) form a new bus company; or (4) have the passengers find alternative transportation. It didn't matter if the roads had potholes, the bridges were jammed, the buses had bald tires, the engines were smoking, and there were too many passengers. It's the drivers' fault. Fire them! The result, according to a study, was that the SIG-funded models had no significant impact on test scores, high school graduation, or college enrollment, nor did the SIG programs have an impact on the use of instructional practices promoted by the program.[2] What went wrong?

Imagine you have been asked by a superintendent who had received a SIG grant to help "fix" a school's chronic problems of low student math and reading scores on state tests after the principal and half of the teachers were fired and replaced. What if the approach had been to cultivate students' learning rather than trying to fix things? The SIGs might have started with the question about the purpose of schools; the kinds of curriculum taught; why only reading and math were usually tested; the importance of other subjects like the arts and entrepreneurship; the development of a child's personality, sense of responsibility, and social skills, and so on. We might then notice how the shadows discussed in part II overlay schools, from lead poisoning to low expectations. Suddenly, the idea of "fixing schools" becomes a mirage. As you try to grasp for interventions that might "work," they instead turn to wisps of air. There is a deeper reality at play.

Part III describes some of the more significant illusions of education reform we have encountered. We then pivot to findings from educational research that can lead to new solutions. In the next chapter, the Promises and Illusions of College and Career Success, we expose the consequences of school leaders using the percentage of their students admitted to colleges and universities as the singular measure of a school's success. In chapter 11, "The Math Wars," we unveil the illusion that the value of various educational interventions can be judged using math test scores. In chapter 12, "The Illusion That Activity Equals Progress," we explore the illusion that adding more plans and programs without due regard for their implementation will somehow translate into educational progress. Finally, in chapter 13, "The Turning Point," we describe illusions about teaching, learning, and assessment and share how we and others have confronted them and gone beyond to more engaging and authentic student learning.

These chapters are a necessary prelude to our story about Egypt in part IV.

NOTES

1. Alyson Klein, "Remember When K-12 Education Got a $100 Billion Windfall from Washington?" *Education Week*, February 18, 2019, https://www.edweek.org/policy-politics/remember-when-k-12-education-got-a-100-billion-windfall-from-washington/2019/02.

2. Lisa Dragoset et al., "School Improvement Grants: Implementation and Effectiveness: Executive Summary (NCEE 2017-4012)," Institute of Education Sciences, U.S. Department of Education, January 2017, https://ies.ed.gov/ncee/pubs/20174013/pdf/20174012.pdf.

Chapter 10

The Promises and Illusions of "College and Career Success"

The Nation at Risk Archetype was interpreted by many policymakers as a call to increase college enrollment; for example, the National Governors Association issued the following statement:

> Postsecondary education is more important to states than ever before. Within the next decade, nearly two-thirds of the jobs in the U.S. will require some form of college credential. To meet that demand, states must lead efforts to graduate more students from high-quality certificate and degree programs with the resources available.[1]

This call for increased college enrollment, however, presented policymakers with a dilemma about what to do with traditional vocational education that by law had been designed to be separated from general academic education. If the United States had indeed committed an act of unilateral educational disarmament as the Nation at Risk report contended, was vocational education exempt from the need to increase the number and rigor of core academic subjects? The rhetorical way around this dilemma was to promote the idea that all students should be ready to go to college *or* enter the workforce upon graduation. Implementing the Nation at Risk report's recommendations would serve both pathways for students. Thus, "college and career readiness" became the guiding mantra of state and federal policymakers ever since the Nation at Risk report was issued in 1983. Underscoring the perceived importance of college and career readiness to a state's economy in 1996, an independent nonprofit organization, Achieve Inc., was created by a bipartisan group of governors and business leaders to promote college and career readiness through several corporate and private foundation-funded initiatives.[2]

We maintain that the idea of college and career readiness is largely an illusion that distracts us from deciding what the prime purpose of high school, *in and of itself*, should be in this new era as opposed to considering it merely as a stepping stone to yet more academic education. The illusions about postsecondary education have consequences for colleges, secondary schools, and even elementary schools. In this chapter, we identify three of these illusions and their consequences.

THE ILLUSION OF COLLEGE PREPARATION PROGRAMS

In secondary schools, our experience has been that college preparation is of paramount concern to students, parents, teachers, and school administrators. Any educational change that is perceived to lessen students' chances for admission to and success in college is fiercely opposed by vocal parents at local school board meetings and on social media. One uppermost concern of many parents is their child's opportunity to get into college. Some parents push for more advanced academic courses in English, science, mathematics, and social studies, since the more the better, as the thinking goes, with advanced placement (AP) and honors courses being the pinnacle. The late Clifford Adelman's work provides some evidence for the relationship between academic high school course-taking and later college success.[3] Adelman found that a student's "academic intensity" in high school, such as taking more advanced math courses, was predictive of later college success. For example, if students completed calculus in high school, they had about an 80 percent chance of completing a four-year college degree. In contrast, a student without any algebra had little more than a 2 percent chance of earning a four-year college degree.[4]

Research findings like Adelman's led governors to enact policies to encourage students to complete at least an Algebra 2 course under the theory that Algebra 2 was a "gateway course" to college.[5] By 2009, nearly 76 percent of all students had earned at least half a credit in Algebra 2 or higher.[6] But what exactly is meant by "Algebra 2"? Each state has somewhat different interpretations as reflected in their respective state exams. In the mid-2000s, governors wanted a standard Algebra 2 test by which progress toward college readiness could be measured. In 2005, with funding from the Gates Foundation, Achieve, Inc. developed and enlisted states to voluntarily administer a pilot test version of a *common* end-of-course Algebra 2 exam to nearly 90,000 students. When the participating states experienced large percentages of students in wealthier school districts performing poorly on this pilot exam, however, the states withdrew from the project.[7] Given this result, how does

"Algebra 2" success lead to college success? If large numbers of affluent students failed this pilot Algebra 2 exam, perhaps we need to explore what is meant by Algebra 2 and its causal connection to college success.

THE MEANING OF ALGEBRA

There is a wide difference of opinion among mathematicians and math educators about the meaning of algebra. For some, algebra is about performing complex symbol manipulations to arrive at an answer, namely $x^5 - 2x^3 = 8$; find the value of x. For others, algebra is a way to represent real-world factors to make sense of their relationship. The latter is often referred to as "mathematizing" a problem. The Mathematics Association of America uses the term "quantitative literacy" or QL.[8] Here is an example of a middle school level QL type question: "If you wanted to get the best buy on a jar of peanut butter, would you buy a 12-ounce jar for 30 cents an ounce for a total cost of $3.60, or a 20-ounce jar at 25 cents an ounce for a total cost $5.00? Explain your reasoning." This question is assessing whether students understand the concept of "unit pricing." At another level, this question also probes students' understanding of bulk buying, that is, the unit cost of an item is usually lower if bought in bulk because of efficiencies in mass production, even though the total cost is higher.

If algebra is just a set of abstract procedures to be performed, you get one kind of test. Achieve Inc.'s Algebra 2 pilot test favored performing complex symbol manipulations. Alternatively, if algebra is instead a *way of thinking* about real-world problems such as the peanut butter question, you get another, very different kind of test. If there are two very different approaches to the meaning of Algebra 2, how is Algebra 2 a gatekeeper to student success in college? What is the causal connection? Is one kind of algebra better than the other? Adelman could not determine the *causal* relationship between specific high school courses, such as Algebra 2, and later college success. It could be the case that advanced academic course-taking in high school, such as calculus courses, is rather a proxy, or in medical jargon a *marker*, for motivational characteristics, smaller class sizes, more inspiring teachers, or the availability of more private resources. Adelman had to work within the existing configuration of most high school courses and schools. His was a *retrospective* analysis—not an experiment. In a follow-on study, Adelman stated that the factors he found,

> do not ascribe cause or pretend to predict. They recognize that what is associated with degree completion in one generation may not be associated with it in the next, or that the strength of association may change. Conditions and populations

change, after all. Rigid prediction is a risky call, and besides, that's not what the data and statistical standards allow one to do.[9]

The Causal Problem

Adelman's research pointed to the idea that college completion was more dependent on "academic intensity" as measured by the number of core academic high school subjects a student completed. At the top of the intensity list are AP courses. The number of students sitting for AP exams has risen sharply in the twenty-first century. When the AP exams debuted in 1955–1956, a mere 1,229 high school students took them spread across 103 high schools. The growth in the number of students taking the AP exams administered by the College Board, a nonprofit organization, has been nothing short of phenomenal. In 2022, more than 2.6 million high school students took nearly 4.8 million AP exams, with calculus and English leading the way.[10] The growth in AP course-taking is indicative of the strongly held belief among students and parents that taking AP exams helps one get accepted into college, better prepares one for the rigors of college studies, shortens the time to complete college, and saves money. Why not endure taking AP courses in high school and pay the relatively small price to take the placement exams to avoid spending thousands on a college course that covers the same material?

College Board psychometricians have only shown an *association* between AP exams and *first-year* college success and retention. Opening an umbrella is *associated* with rain, but it does not *cause* rain. In educational research, as well as medical research and many other areas, distinguishing between the true *cause* of something versus what is merely associated with it is the gold standard for truth-seeking. Is it truly the case that taking higher levels of mathematics courses in high school or taking AP courses *causes* greater rates of college success?

Researchers at the University of Texas analyzed the non-AP course background of 28,000 Texas high school graduates who attended thirty-one four-year Texas public universities.[11] They found that once other factors are taken into consideration, AP course-taking *itself* does not reliably predict students' first-semester college grades or their retention into the second year of college. How could this be? Surely taking AP calculus and scoring well must better prepare students for high-level college math courses. Yet in an analysis of actual student placement across fourteen colleges, researchers found that only 22 percent of AP calculus takers scoring a "3" or better went on to take more advanced calculus classes at any time in their college career.[12] In a two-year study, committees of the National Research Council issued a 589-page report on the AP program and the International Baccalaureate program. They concluded that "colleges and universities should not automatically award AP to students with specified AP scores and assume that they will be success-ful."[13] Perhaps more telling is the decision by eight private Washington, DC, area schools to stop offering AP courses altogether, stating, "We believe a curriculum oriented toward collaborative, experiential, and interdisciplinary learning will not only better prepare our students for college and their professional futures, but also result in more engaging programs for both students and faculty."[14] It is not possible to determine from Adelman's work whether *other* curricular content and pedagogical approaches reflecting different purposes to a high school education could be equally influential to a student's later college and career success. So where does this leave us in terms of college preparation?

IS HIGH SCHOOL PREPARATION FOR COLLEGE POSSIBLE?

The National Survey of College Graduates lists thirty broad areas of study.[15] Related to these areas are some 438 postsecondary instructional programs.[16] Given the number and diversity of these programs, how can a high school education prepare students to be successful in college? A second problem is how to prepare high school students if they later decide to switch their major to another instructional program? According to a National Center for Education Statistics (NCES) report, "A total of 48 percent of bachelor's degree students and 69 percent of associate degree students who entered science, technology, engineering, and mathematics (STEM) fields between 2003 and 2009 had left these fields by spring 2009. Roughly one-half of these leavers switched their major to a non-STEM field, and the rest of them left STEM fields by exiting college before earning a degree or certificate."[17] Attrition rates in *non-STEM* fields were as high as or higher than those in STEM fields. "At the bachelor's degree level, students in humanities, education, and health sciences had higher attrition rates (56–62 percent) than did those in STEM fields (48 percent), and students in business and social/behavioral sciences had comparable attrition rates (50 and 45 percent, respectively) as did students in STEM fields."[18] It could be argued that the job of a high school is not so much to prepare a student for a *particular* collegiate field of study, but instead to instill in students certain habits of mind such as critical thinking, problem-solving, creativity, and communicating and collaborating with others.[19] These "soft skills," also sometimes referred to as twenty-first century skills, which employers say are lacking in many college and high school graduates. Other researchers cite certain behaviors as being associated with college success such as time management, goal setting, self-responsibility, self-initiative, persistence, having realistic expectations, and engaging with peers and faculty.[20]

It may well be true that the above skills and characteristics are needed to be successful in college or vocations. The question remains, however, what should be the *content* of their high school education? Thinking creatively is not something that can be done apart from what one should think creatively *about*. Twenty-first-century skills and other behavioral characteristics cannot be taught or instilled in a person apart from the specific objects of knowledge and experiences that are the occasion for their development and expression. We believe the more difficult question is what makes high school meaningful and worthwhile for students so that they *want* to learn. However the pursuit of college for some parents and students may not be about higher learning at all; rather, it is the pursuit of prestige and what it brings.

College Admission and the Pursuit of Prestige

In March 2019, the United States Department of Justice brought federal racketeering, money laundering, and obstruction of justice charges against William "Rick" Singer of Newport Beach, California. Along with Singer were federal indictments of thirty-three parents and thirteen coaches and associates of Singer's businesses. Also included were two Scholastic Assessment Test (SAT) and American College Test (ACT) administrators. Code-named "Operation Varsity Blues," the U.S. Attorney's Office for the District of Massachusetts announced that "between approximately 2011 and February 2019, Singer allegedly conspired with dozens of parents, athletic coaches, a university athletics administrator, and others to use bribery and other forms of fraud to secure the admission of students to colleges and universities including Yale University, Georgetown University, Stanford University, the University of Southern California, and Wake Forest University, among others."[21] Singer's criminal conspiracy was composed of three schemes to nearly guarantee admission to prestigious colleges and universities for parents who could pay tens and even hundreds of thousands of dollars to his "charity." The first scheme involved cheating on college entrance exams by arranging for others to take the exams in place of the student or altering the student's answers after the exams. This was done by bribing psychologists to claim a student had a learning disability which would allow the student more time and/or travel to a place where a corrupt SAT or ACT proctor could doctor the exam answers. The second scheme was to bribe university athletic coaches and administrators to recruit a student for their sports team, thus guaranteeing admission since each sport is granted a number of admission slots reserved for athletes. The third scheme involved Singer creating a nonprofit charitable organization to which parents contributed as a means of laundering their payments and paying out bribes.[22] For example, actress Lori Loughlin and her husband, the fashion designer Mossimo Giannulli, were convicted and sent to prison for paying bribes to get their two daughters accepted as recruits for the rowing team at the University of Southern California, even though neither took part in the sport.[23] In San Diego, two prominent families were accused of paying $875,000 in bribes to get their sons and daughters admitted to elite universities.[24]

Why would extremely well-off parents who could afford to give their sons and daughters every educational advantage—from private schools and tutors to enrichment activities and travels abroad—feel it necessary to engage in a criminal conspiracy to guarantee their child's admission to an elite college or university of their choice? In 2021, Netflix released a documentary on the Operation Varsity Blues scandal including interviews with the accused defendants and various college admission officers not involved in the scandal. When asked what motivated these very wealthy parents to cheat, one commentator cited the "pursuit of prestige." Jon Reiner, a former Stanford University admissions officer, offered his perspective:

> Over the last three of four decades higher education has become increasingly a commodity, something that you purchase, a product. It's a goal in and of itself, rather than the goal being to get an education. . . . Prestige is actually a French word. In the original French it means deceit, something people don't realize is imaginary; it's an illusion, yet people believe in it.[25]

One explanation offered to account for this behavior is the theory of social reproduction, the idea that some parents are driven to maintain or advance their social and economic status through their children. If they went to a prestigious college or university, then they want the same status for their children by any means necessary; anything less represents a step down. Admittedly, few parents have the financial means to engage in a six-figure college bribery scheme, and perhaps fewer still would be so unethical even if they had the means. But the pursuit of prestige is still a seductive motivator for some parents and their ambitious progeny. Parents and students, however, are not the only ones who pursue admission to prestigious colleges and universities. Most high schools, especially elite private and exclusive charter schools, claim bragging rights when their graduates are accepted to various prestigious colleges as evidence of the school's quality. It is an irresistible temptation.

The Illusion of Prestige

What makes a college or university "prestigious" is defined by commercial media such as the *U.S. News and World Report*,[26] *Wall Street Journal*,[27] and *Princeton Review*[28] among many other entities that advertise their brand and particular method for ranking higher education institutions. And who wouldn't want to go to the "best college or university"? After all, we tend to rank almost everything else, although, according to readership surveys of college aspirants, only about 10 percent of them cite news/magazine college rankings as "very important" in making their college choices. The 10 percent who do use college rankings tend to be from families with high socioeconomic status whose family members know how colleges operate and who can pay for private college counselors.[29] Another 30 percent said rankings are "somewhat important." In other words, students who come from upper-middle-class and upper-class backgrounds are expected to attend a "good" college, one that is ranked commensurate with or above their parent's socioeconomic class. Each year various media companies such as *U.S. News and World Report* publish their ranking of the "best" colleges and universities.[30] All of the best are ranked as the "Most Selective" and are very expensive private universities. Their tuition, fees, room, and board average $75,000 a year (in 2021 dollars) or about $300,000 for four years. Their average undergraduate enrollment for the top ten is about 6,000 students.[31]

How does one get admitted to these selective colleges short of bribery? According to the National Association for College Admission Counseling survey of 220 admission officers, the factors having "Considerable Importance" are: 1) grades in all courses (75 percent), 2) grades in college prep courses (73 percent), 3) strength of curriculum (62 percent), and 4) SAT/ACT exams (46 percent). Twelve other factors trailed far behind.[32] So it is all about getting the "A." One way for students to boost their grade point average (GPA) is to take AP courses. High schools often give greater weight to AP courses when calculating students' GPAs, thus tipping these students' GPAs toward the upper end.

The pursuit of prestige colleges does have unintended consequences. One negative effect is the resistance to changing the high school curriculum. If high school GPA and school rank are important to get into elite universities, then those students who have been successful in the established system will tend to resist any change to a high school's curriculum, pedagogy, or assessments. They want predictability. But to succeed in an evolving knowledge-based economy, graduates must have the ability to think and reason about complex problems that do not have obvious solutions. In real life, there are tradeoffs, ambiguities, and dilemmas. The college professors we have known lament that many of their freshman students do not want to *think*. They want to be told the answer so they can memorize it for an exam to get an "A." Second, parents of "A" students often feel threatened by any proposed changes that are meant to help "B" or "C" students, fearing the curriculum will be "dumbed down."

Another unintended consequence of college rankings is the distorting effects it has on higher education institutions. Recognition and reputation are the combined currency that motivates many college faculty and administrators. As Don Hossler, Distinguished Provost Professor Emeritus at the University of California, notes:

> There is increasing evidence that rankings are having a pernicious effect on the policies and practices of colleges and universities. Although most college administrators decry rankings and their methodologies, many of these same institutions tout their ranking in their recruitment literature. In addition, colleges and universities are changing their admissions procedure, manipulating data to cast their institutions in the best light and sometimes putting pressure on academic programs and faculty for the sole purpose of improving their ranking.[33]

THE ILLUSIONS OF COLLEGE LIFE AND CAREER SUCCESS

There are close to 18 million undergraduate college students at two- and four-year colleges[34] in the United States and a large portion of them suffer from exhaustion, anxiety, and depression. A 2019 national survey (pre-COVID-19) of over 54,000 undergraduate college students from ninety-eight postsecondary schools found that over the past twelve months: 76 percent felt exhausted; 61 percent felt very sad; 51 percent felt overwhelming anxiety; 49 percent felt things were hopeless; 37 percent felt so depressed that it was difficult to function; 13 percent seriously considered suicide, and 2 percent attempted it.[35] Students attending elite colleges and universities may feel particularly stressed due to pressures from their academic workload and fears of academic and social failure. Additional sources of stress include food and housing insecurity and school safety concerns.[36]

Upon enrolling in postsecondary institutions, students can experience a rude awakening, finding that many of their undergraduate courses are being taught by adjuncts or part-time lecturers. This is especially the case at the more expensive, private, nonprofit, four-year colleges where 60 percent of the instructional staff is part-time or "contingent" faculty.[37] It's not that contingent faculty are necessarily inferior teachers, but they may not be fully available to mentor or advise students. Only two in five part-time instructors at private institutions have an office or an institution-provided computer, phone, or email account.[38] In addition, many college students become disillusioned about the time it takes to complete their degree.

A UCLA survey of over 190,000 first-time, full-time students entering 283 four-year U.S. colleges and universities of varying levels of selectivity and type found that fully 83 percent expected to graduate with a bachelor's degree within *four* years from the time they entered.[39] However, more than half (56 percent) of all students entering a four-year degree program took longer than four years to complete their degree.[40] A case in point is Cambridge High School[41] located in an affluent, predominantly White Philadelphia suburb where 60 percent of the local residents have a college degree. In the study the authors conducted, out of a Cambridge senior graduating class of 2,111 students, almost all said they intended to go to college. But four years later, as shown in figure 10.1, only 681 (32 percent) of Cambridge's high graduates had completed college.[42]

The fate of Cambridge high school graduates is not an outlier. The National Student Clearinghouse (NSC) tracks the college status of nearly all high school graduates in the United States who enroll in college.[43] Thus, it is now possible for every school district to obtain college completion data for nearly every one of its graduates who enroll in college. The aggregate results can be shared with parents and voters. In the case of Cambridge, we went one step further. We combined prior *high school* transcript data for every high school student and linked it to their college outcomes via the NSC data. We collected eight years of secondary and postsecondary course-taking data for every student in eight high school graduating classes. Our report showed what types of courses and course grades were associated with later college success or failure.

Tallying the number of students enrolled among six programs—academically assisted, college prep, honors, advanced honors, transferred, and special education (including gifted)—the largest percentages of Cambridge

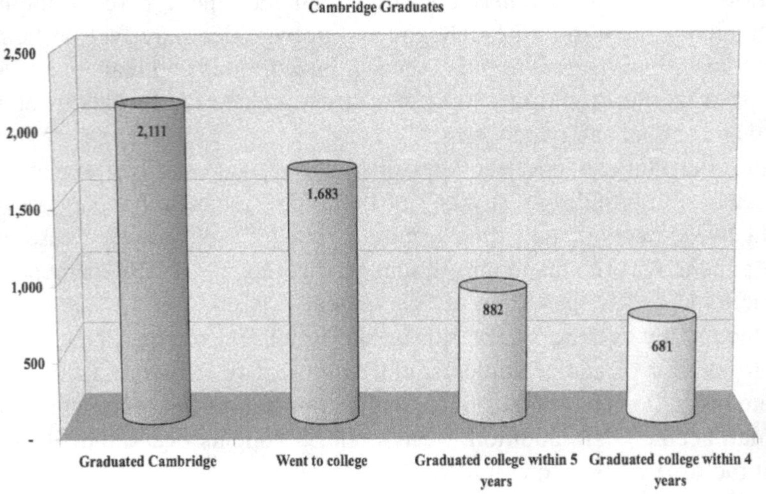

Figure 10.1   Outcome of Cambridge Graduates. Our eight-year study documented the number of high school graduates who attended college and time taken to complete their four-year degrees. *Source:* The 21st Century Partnership for STEM Education, "Cambridge High School Report Summary," February 2009, https://www.21pstem.org/_files/ugd/bf6da2_99b345b0a34e4f40bc287a0d03617c72.pdf.

graduates who attained STEM degrees in college were in the advanced honors (21.9 percent) and special education (20.0 percent) tracks.[44]

Going back to our question about Algebra 2 as a marker for college success, we presented the report to Cambridge administrators showing how a reform math program was statistically superior to a traditional approach; however, they discontinued the reform math program citing parental fears. Publicly, they continued to cite the number of their graduates *intending* to go to college rather than the students' later collegiate outcomes. The same reaction of administrators occurred when we presented our analysis to another affluent New Jersey suburban school district.

PARENT AND GUARDIAN CONCERNS ABOUT COLLEGE AFFORDABILITY AND EMPLOYMENT

Students are not the only ones who may become disillusioned with the time to complete college. Seventy-three percent of parents with children under the age of 18 years cite "college savings" as their top financial worry—a higher percentage than any other financial category among any sub-group.[45] For the academic year 2020–2021, college tuition, fees, and room and board costs for full-time undergraduates living on campus were $54,500 per year for four-year private institutions and $25,700 for four-year public ones. The least expensive option at $9,700 per year was for a student attending a public two-year college and living at home.[46] Fortunately, federal grants and other scholarships can reduce this financial burden. Nonetheless, the real costs of college (adjusted for inflation): tuition, fees, books, and room and board have more than doubled for all types of postsecondary institutions since 1990–1991 when the average total real costs of colleges of all types was $10,648. By 2021, the real costs were $25,910 per year—an increase of more than 100 percent.[47] Meanwhile, median household incomes have not kept pace. During the same period (1991–2021), median household income increased by only 21 percent.[48] As a consequence, middle- and lower-income families are caught in an ever-tightening financial squeeze to afford higher education. Student college debt has more than tripled from $480 billion in 2006 to close to $1,800 billion in 2022.[49] At this scale, student debt impacts the entire nation. To make matters worse, more than half of undergraduate students do not graduate within four years and a quarter of those who graduate require six or more years to do so.[50] The result is added college expenses plus loss of employment earnings. Thus, financial considerations are a major reason why many don't attend or complete college. In a Pew survey among adults who do not have a bachelor's degree and are not currently enrolled in school, 42 percent cite college affordability as a major reason why they have not received a four-year college degree.[51]

It could be argued that a student's stress and college debt load are part of the price to pay for the prospect of future job earnings. This presumes there is a match between a college degree and a career path. Even if a young person were to obtain a four-year college degree, there is no assurance that college prepares one for finding work that requires a college degree. Economic analysts at the Federal Reserve Bank of New York have reported that roughly two-fifths of recent college graduates are working in jobs that do *not* require a college degree. These *under*employment numbers have remained fairly consistent since 1990.[52] Furthermore, graduates in certain majors have extraordinarily high underemployment. More than 70 percent of college graduates who majored in performing arts and criminal justice, for example, are working in occupations that do not require a college degree.[53]

At the same time, workforce researchers have found mismatches between the skills employers say they want and what employers perceive is lacking in college graduates. In a 2020 survey of more than 400 employers conducted on behalf of the American Association of Colleges and Universities, for example, 60 percent of employers thought it was "very important" for their employees to have "critical thinking skills" but judged only 39 percent of college graduates to have these skills.[54] In a 2022 survey of manufacturers, "attracting and retaining a quality workforce" is listed as their top concern.[55] By "quality workforce" they do not necessarily mean college graduates. Nearly eight in ten job openings in the next ten years will *not* require a four-year college degree, according to the U.S. Bureau of Labor Statistics (BLS). The BLS tracks over 800 occupations in the United States and collects many categories of information about each occupation: the number employed, expected openings each year, average compensation, and educational attainment required for an entry-level position according to surveys of employers. The BLS also has a "staffing matrix" that crosses these 800 occupations with about one-hundred business sectors and subsectors. Only about 20 percent of the expected job openings will require a four-year college degree.[56] There *is* a lack of qualified workers to fill many skilled technical positions in emerging industries such as battery and semiconductor manufacturing. However, these jobs do not require a four-year college degree. Likewise, the traditional skilled trades, the backbone of middle-class America, are suffering from a shortage of workers. This shortage is what many cite as a challenge for American growth in advanced manufacturing.[57] For example, in 2021 71 percent of the total employment in 2021 was for workers without bachelor's degrees. The annual average for the next ten years is projected to be 79 percent for the same population sector. In other words, the relative demand for bachelor's degrees and above will be *decreasing* over the coming years. The idea that one must go to a four year college to get a better job may not be viable. So where does this leave us?

Creating a College and Career Feedback Loop

We might be able to salvage the notion that high school should be about preparation for college and career success if boards of education followed their high school graduates into college and the workforce. Their high school courses, grades, and other experiences could then be correlated with their later college and career outcomes to determine the most influential school factors for their success or lack of success. In turn, the high school curriculum and extracurricular experiences could be iteratively revised to provide better preparation for college and career success. Such a feedback system might yield surprising findings. Politically, however, the establishment of such a feedback system would appear highly unlikely. What school board would voluntarily tell their parents and local taxpayers that only 30 percent of their district's graduating seniors completed college in four years? Far better to boast that 90 percent of the senior class *intends* to go to college! Likewise, how many parents would let their high-achieving child forego AP courses for a project-based internship unless they could be assured that the latter would give their children a leg up in admission to a highly competitive college? We are left in the grip of a vicious cycle. Underwhelming college and career outcomes are partly due to an inadequate K-12 education system. That system, in turn, is unable to correct its shortcomings due to the political risk of discovering one's school district does not live up to its image— the shinier the image, the more politically risky to present evidence to the contrary.

Philadelphia high schools demonstrate the problem of using "college and career success" as the rationale for a high school education. In a study that tracked the 1999 cohort of the City of Philadelphia's ninth-grade students into college, only 23 percent managed to enter college and only 10 percent finished any type of college within six years.[58] More recently, the Pennsylvania Department of Education established a cohort methodology that tracks entering ninth-grade students in each Local Education Agency and counts whether they graduated within four, five, or six years. The 2021–2022 figures for the Philadelphia School District showed that 69 percent of its ninth graders graduated on time in four years. For Hispanic and multi-race students, the graduation rate was under 60 percent.[59] What good is an academic "college preparation" program that leads to neither high school nor college completion, nor career success? What did high school prepare them for?

THE PROBLEM OF PURPOSE

College and career success may be well intended but it is also a distraction. The difficult questions about the purpose of high school for a new era are put off. What *should* be the purpose of high school education? Can the fulfillment of this purpose be determined by the *end* of high school? College and career successes are not purposes of education but *outcomes* that flow from defining a compelling purpose that has meaning and value in the lives of adolescents as they are in the present moment. The reason to learn something should be readily apparent. Call it the high school "engagement proposition." What do young people wonder about? What are they struggling to understand? Do they want to know who they are, their purpose in life, how to make money, or what to do if they are arrested, involved in an accident, or dealing with dangerous situations? High school programs and learning experiences need to be anchored in a real purpose so that students *want* to learn more. Learning to read is necessary for college, but its primary value is not measured by college success alone. It has value in its own right.

By no means are we arguing that college is of little value and that its pursuit should be abandoned; on the contrary. Higher education and further learning should be pursued and made affordable at any point in a person's lifetime if done for the right reasons. To be sure, postsecondary education is necessary for certain kinds of occupations. But higher education has a social calling more than, and in addition to, job preparation. We started this chapter with a quote from the National Governor's Association on the importance of a college credential for job seekers. We end with an excerpt from a report by a Harvard committee convened immediately after the defeat of Nazism and fascism in World War II. The committee's report was titled "General Education in a Free Society." In the introduction, James Conant, president of Harvard, wrote:

> The heart of the problem of a general education is the continuance of the liberal and humane tradition. Neither the mere acquisition of information nor the development of special skills and talents can give the broad basis of understanding which is essential if our civilization is to be preserved. No one wishes to disparage the importance of being "well informed." But even a good grounding in mathematics and the physical and biological sciences, combined with an ability to read and write several foreign languages, does not provide a sufficient educational background for citizens of a free nation. . . . The student in high school, in college and in graduate school must be concerned, in part at least, with the words "right" and "wrong" in both the ethical and the mathematical sense.[60]

Conant's introduction to the Harvard report on the role of "General Education in a Free Society" could just as easily be applied to primary and secondary education as it was to the university. One should not wait until college for a young person to be taught what is ethical, the difference between "right" and "wrongful" behavior toward self and others, to acquire a sense of duty and responsibility. These cannot be done with courses alone—they must be imbued throughout the character of the school. This is the social and moral dimension of a school's purpose that cannot wait for college and career success. Our proposals for how to integrate these aspects of education are discussed in part IV.

In the next chapter, we take on the Math Wars and the illusions and misconceptions that have sustained it. We show how these wars have prevented progress in defining a more compelling purpose of education for the new era.

NOTES

1. National Governors Association, https://www.nga.org/bestpractices/post-secondary-education/.

2. "Contributors," Achieve, last modified 2021, https://www.achieve.org/contributors.

3. Clifford Adelman, "Answers in the Tool Box: Academic Intensity, Attendance Patterns, and Bachelor's Degree Attainment," U.S. Department of Education, June 1999, https://eric.ed.gov/?id=ED431363.

4. Adelman, "Answers," 17.

5. See Achieve's American Diploma Project (ADP) to develop specifications for a common end-of-course exam in Algebra 2, http://www.achieve.org/adp-network.

6. National Center for Education Statistics, "Table 225.40: Percentage of Public and Private High School Graduates Taking Selected Mathematics and Science Courses in High School, by Selected Student and School Characteristics: Selected Years, 1990 through 2009," https://nces.ed.gov/programs/digest/d19/tables/dt19_225.40.asp?current=yes.

7. Sean Cavanagh, "New Algebra 2 Test Suggests States Face High Hurdles," *Education Week,* August 27, 2008, http://www.edweek.org/ew/articles/2008/08/27/01achieve.h28.html.

8. Mathematics Association of America, "Quantitative Reasoning for College Graduates: A Complement to the Standards," https://www.maa.org/programs/faculty-and-departments/curriculum-department-guidelines-recommendations/quantitative-literacy/quantitative-reasoning-college-graduates#TOC.

9. Clifford Adelman, "The Toolbox Revisited: Paths to Degree Completion from High School Through College," U.S. Department of Education, 2006, 13.

10. College Board, "AP Data and Research, Class of 2022," https://apcentral.collegeboard.org/about-ap/ap-data-research.

11. Kristen Klopfenstein and M. Kathleen Thomas, "The Link between Advanced Placement Experience and Early College Success," *Southern Economic Journal* 75, no. 3 (January 2009): 873–891.

12. William Lichten, "Whither Advanced Placement?" *Education Policy Analysis Archives* 8, no. 29 (June 24, 2000), https://doi.org/10.14507/epaa.v8n29.2000.

13. National Research Council, *Learning and Understanding: Improving Advanced Study of Mathematics and Science in U.S. High Schools* (Washington, DC: The National Academies Press, 2002), 194.

14. Brad Mielke and Kelly McCarthy, "8 Schools in the Washington, DC, Area Announce Plan to Eliminate AP Program," *ABC News*, June 20, 2018, https://abc-news.go.com/US/schools-washington-dc-area-announce-plan-eliminate-ap/story?id=56027089.

15. National Center for Science and Engineering Statistics (NCSES), *National Survey of College Graduates: 2021. NSF 23-306* (Alexandria, VA: National Science Foundation, 2022), https://ncses.nsf.gov/pubs/nsf23306/.

16. U.S. Department of Education, National Center for Education Statistics, "The Classification of Instructional Programs 2020," https://nces.ed.gov/ipeds/cipcode/browse.aspx?y=56.

17. Xianglei Chen and Matthew Soldner, "STEM Attrition: College Students' Paths Into and Out of STEM Fields (NCES 2014-001)," Institute of Education Sciences, U.S. Department of Education (November 2013): iv, http://nces.ed.gov/pubs2014/2014001rev.pdf.

18. Chen and Soldner, "STEM Attrition," iv.

19. David T Conley, *College and Career Ready: Helping All Students Succeed Beyond High School* (Indianapolis: Jossey-Bass, 2011).

20. George D. Kuh et al., "What Matters to Student Success: A Review of the Literature Symposium on Postsecondary Student Success," National Postsecondary Education Cooperative (NPEC), July 2006, https://nces.ed.gov/npec/pdf/Kuh_Team_Report.pdf.

21. U.S. Attorney's Office, District of Massachusetts, "Arrests Made in Nationwide College Admissions Scam: Alleged Exam Cheating & Athletic Recruitment Scheme," March 12, 2019, https://www.justice.gov/usao-ma/pr/arrests-made-nationwide-college-admissions-scam-alleged-exam-cheating-athletic.

22. U.S. Attorney's Office, District of Massachusetts, "Arrests Made."

23. Kate Taylor, "Lori Loughlin and Mossimo Giannulli Get Prison in College Admissions Case," *The New York Times,* August 21, 2020, https://www.nytimes.com/2020/08/21/us/lori-loughlin-mossimo-giannulli-sentencing.html.

24. Kristina Davis and Gary Robbins, "University of San Diego, Local Families Caught Up in College Admissions Scandal," San Diego Union-Tribune, March 12, 2019.

25. *Operation Varsity Blues: The College Admissions Scandal*, directed by Chris Smith (Netflix, 2021), 00:12:50 and 00:14:04, https://www.netflix.com/title/81130691.

26. "U.S. News Best Colleges," *U.S. News and World Report*, 2022, https://www.usnews.com/best-colleges.

27. "The College Rankings List," *Wall Street Journal*, 2022, https://www.wsj.com/articles/college-rankings-list-2022-11632246093.

28. "The Best 388 Colleges," *Princeton Review,* 2023, https://www.princetonreview.com/college-rankings/best-colleges.

29. Patricia M. McDonough, "Democratized College Knowledge for Whom?" *Research in Higher Education* 39, no. 5 (October 1998): 513–537.

30. See for USNWR methodology Robert Morse and Eric Brooks, "How U.S. News Calculated the 2022 Best Colleges Rankings," *U.S. News and World Report,* September 12, 2021, https://www.usnews.com/education/best-colleges/articles/how-us-news-calculated-the-rankings.

31. National Center for Education Statistics, "Undergraduate Enrollment: Condition of Education," May 2023, https://nces.ed.gov/programs/coe/indicator/cha.

32. Melissa Clinedinst, "2019 State of College Admission," Association for College Admission Counseling, 16, https://nacacnet.org/wp-content/uploads/2022/10/soca2019_all.pdf.

33. Don Hossler, "The Problem with College Rankings," *About Campus*, 5, no. 1 (2000): 20–24, https://doi.org/10.1177/108648220000500105.

34. National Center for Education Statistics, "Undergraduate Enrollment."

35. American College Health Association, *American College Health Association-National College Health Assessment II: Undergraduate Student Executive Summary Spring 2019* (Silver Spring: American College Health Association, 2019), https://www.acha.org/documents/ncha/NCHA-II_SPRING_2019_UNDERGRADUATE_REFERENCE%20_GROUP_EXECUTIVE_SUMMARY.pdf.

36. Katharine M. Broton and Clare L. Cady, *Food Insecurity on Campus Action and Intervention* (Baltimore, MD: Johns Hopkins University Press, 2020).

37. Ellen Bara Stolzenberg et al., "Undergraduate Teaching Faculty: The HERI Faculty Survey 2016–2017," Higher Education Research Institute at UCLA, 2019, https://heri.ucla.edu/monographs/HERI-FAC2017-monograph.pdf.

38. Ellen Bara Stolzenberg et al., "Undergraduate."

39. Ellen Bara Stolzenberg et al., "The American Freshman: National Norms Fall 2019," Higher Education Research Institute at UCLA (2020), https://heri.ucla.edu/monographs/HERI-FAC2017-monograph.pdf.

40. Erin Dunlop Velez et al., "Baccalaureate and Beyond (B&B:16/17): A First Look at the Employment and Educational Experiences of College Graduates, 1 Year Later (NCES 2019-106)," National Center for Education Statistics, 3, https://nscresearchcenter.org/completing-college/.

41. A pseudonym.

42. The 21st Century Partnership for STEM Education, "Cambridge High School Report Summary," February, 2009, https://www.21pstem.org/_files/ugd/bf6da2_99b345b0a34e4f40bc287a0d03617c72.pdf.

43. J. Causey et al., "Completing College: National and State Report on Six-Year Completion Rates for Fall 2015 Beginning Cohort," National Student Clearinghouse Research Center, February 2022, https://nscresearchcenter.org/wp-content/uploads/Completions_Report_2021.pdf.

44. The 21st Century Partnership for STEM Education, "Cambridge," 23.

45. Jefferey Jones, "M.U.S. Parents' College Funding Worries Are Top Money Concern," April 20, 2015, https://news.gallup.com/poll/182537/parents-college-funding-worries-top-money-concern.aspx.

46. National Center for Education Statistics, "Winter 2020–21 Student Financial Aid Component" and "Fall 2020 Institutional Characteristics Component," Digest of Education Statistics 2021, Table 330.40, https://nces.ed.gov/programs/coe/indicator/cua/undergrad-costs#fn4.

47. National Center for Education Statistics, "Average Undergraduate Tuition, Fees, Room, and Board Rates Charged for Full-time Students in Degree-Granting Postsecondary Institutions, by Level and Control of Institution: Selected Years, 1963-64 through 2020–21," Table 330.10, https://nces.ed.gov/programs/digest/d21/tables/dt21_330.10.asp.

48. Federal Reserve Bank of St. Louis, "Real Median Household Income in the United States," accessed February 3, 2023, https://fred.stlouisfed.org/series/MEHOINUSA672N.

49. Federal Reserve Bank of St. Louis, "Student Loans Owned and Securitized," accessed February 3, 2023, https://fred.stlouisfed.org/series/SLOAS.

50. Erin Dunlop Velez et al., "Baccalaureate and Beyond."

51. Katherine Schaeffer, "10 Facts About Today's College Graduates," accessed February 3, 2023, https://www.pewresearch.org/fact-tank/2022/04/12/10-facts-about-todays-college-graduates/.

52. The Federal Reserve of New York, "The Labor Market for Recent College Graduates," accessed February 3, 2023, https://www.newyorkfed.org/research/college-labor-market/index#/underemployment.

53. The Federal Reserve of New York, "The Labor Market."

54. Colleen Flaherty, "What Employers Want: AAC&U Survey of Employers Shows Liberal Arts Skills Are Valued and Sought Out in the Workplace but Raises Questions about Student Preparation," *Inside Higher Education* (April 6, 2021): 16.

55. The Manufacturing Institute, "The Future Skill Needs in Manufacturing: A Deep Dive," October 2022, https://www.themanufacturinginstitute.org/wp-content/uploads/2022/10/NAM_Rockwell-PTC-Study.pdf.

56. U.S. Bureau of Labor Statistics, "Employment Projections, Table 1.7," https://www.bls.gov/emp/.

57. Asutosh Padhi et al., *The Titanium Economy: How Industrial Technology Can Create a Better, Faster, Stronger America* (New York: Public Affairs, 2022).

58. OMG Center for Collaborative Learning, "College Access and Success in Philadelphia Part II: College Enrollment Activity," October 29, 2010, https://search.issuelab.org/resource/college-access-and-success-in-philadelphia-part-ii-college-enrollment-activity.html.

59. Pennsylvania Department of Education, Division of Data Quality, "Cohort Graduation Rates 4-year 2021-22," https://www.education.pa.gov/DataAndReporting/CohortGradRate/Pages/default.aspx.

60. The Committee on the Objectives of a General Education in a Free Society, *General Education in a Free Society: Report of the Harvard Committee* (Cambridge: Harvard University Press, 1950), viii, https://ia902606.us.archive.org/34/items/generaleducation032440mbp/generaleducation032440mbp.pdf.

Chapter 11

The Math Wars

There is nothing more difficult to take in hand, more perilous to conduct, or more uncertain in its success, than to take the lead in the introduction of a new order of things. Because the innovator has for enemies all those who have done well under the old conditions, and lukewarm defenders in those who may do well under the new.

—Niccolo Machiavelli, 1532, *The Prince*[1]

The introduction of a new order of things in education is indeed difficult, perilous, and uncertain. The scale of difficulty in making educational changes increases dramatically when the proposed changes are linked to the wider social and political context. For example, the 2019-22 COVID-19 pandemic led to heated reactions to school mask and vaccine mandates for students and school staff. In October 2021, U.S. Attorney General Merrick Garland issued a memorandum to the Federal Bureau of Investigation and the ninety-four assistant U.S. attorneys, wherein he stated, "In recent months, there has been a disturbing spike in harassment, intimidation, and threats of violence against school administrators, board members, teachers, and staff who participate in the vital work of running our nation's public schools."[2]

In this chapter, we reveal the inner dynamics of another visceral educational controversy, one that is intimately connected to the illusions of college and career success discussed in the previous chapter and the dark shadows of wealth, racism, rankings, and elitism outlined in part II. The controversy centers around mathematics.

We contend that mathematics has become one of the linchpins of the entire academic structure of the Nation at Risk archetype. Regardless of efforts to improve greater equity in schools or initiate new education programs, if the math curriculum, instruction, and assessments remain basically the same as they did in the 1980s and 1990s, perhaps with newer branding, nothing or very little will have really changed. Some might respond by saying that math is math; it is unchanging and true everywhere in the world, regardless of country, culture, or era. Is there not universal agreement that $2 + 2 = 4$? Were it that simple. In truth, math is not singular but plural. There is not math, but *maths*. The many domains of mathematics are not static but evolving. Consider all the scientific and technological advances since the 1980s. Most visible is the revolution in computing and data science from smartphones to complex computer simulations and artificial intelligence. The kind of mathematics typically taught in school is but a fraction of what could be taught and learned. Instead, the world of mathematics has been truncated to just "math" as if it were a packet of instant oatmeal rather than a buffet table.

MATH STIRS PASSIONS

The subject of math stirs passions as few subjects do. Ask anyone at any gathering. Many will say they are no good at math or are anxious about it or downright *hate* it with a passion. We once gave a three-question survey to 1,300 students from an average suburban New Jersey high school. Call it Pine Hill High School. We asked the students to write down their thoughts about the following: (1) If math were a food, what would it be for you and *why*? (2) If math were an animal, what would it be for you and *why*? (3) If math were a color, what would it be for you and *why?*

The "why" part is critical. Here is a sample of students' negative responses:

"If math were a food, it would be broccoli, because I hate broccoli."
"If math were an animal, it would be a wolverine, ready to slash my grades."
"If math were a color, it would be midnight blue, because
 as hard as I try, I can never see the light."

Some students thought of mathematics in a very positive light.

"If math were a food, it would be pizza. I love pizza."
"If math were an animal, it would be a lion because it is strong and the king of all."
"If math were a color, it would be yellow, like sunshine."

We then had research teams rate the 1,300 students' responses to these three questions on a scale of one to five, from "hate" to "love." We could have simply asked students to rate their feelings about math, but we would not have captured their passionate reasons why they felt as they did. More than one in six students intensely hated math. A lesser proportion loved it. We further analyzed the students' responses by the level of math course and whether the students were in the upper or lower academic tracks.[3] When we separated the responses of the students by math course type, we found a stark contrast in their feelings. In the "Career Math" course, which contained the lower track, half of the thirty-one students hated math. In the calculus course, none hated math.[4] Does higher-level math bring greater love of math, or does greater love of math bring a willingness to study more of it? We also surveyed, in person, hundreds of high school math teachers from dozens of high schools. We asked them to rank their concerns about their students from greatest to least. The teachers' top concern was "Low Student Motivation." We then asked the teachers to rate their students on a scale of one to ten for their math motivation level. The teachers rated the top one-third of their math students at 7.0 and the lower two-thirds at 3.3. But when we asked teachers about the degree to which their high school students were *intrinsically* motivated to study math, the ratings fell to 6.1 and 0.8 respectively.

In sum, the upper one-third of students either loved, liked, or were neutral about math, with a good percentage of them having a fairly high level of intrinsic motivation to study it, whereas the lower two-thirds of students either hated, disliked, or were neutral about math and had virtually no intrinsic motivation to study it. When asked why their students had such low motivation to learn math, virtually none of the teachers cited the curriculum or the way they taught it. Instead, most teachers blamed the students. But why should a lack of love for math be a problem? Not everyone enjoys or is intrinsically motivated to learn to play the piano or speak French. What makes math so special?

THE SPECIAL STATUS OF MATHEMATICS

Math's special status extends beyond its intrinsic value as a subject to that of a proxy for three other things of high value.

College Admissions and Placement

As we discussed in the previous chapter, admission officers at highly selective colleges and universities regard grades in the higher-level core academic courses to be the most important factor in their decision-making. Honors precalculus and calculus are prominent members of this club. Another important factor is scores on the Scholastic Assessment Test (SAT) or American College Test (ACT).[5] The SAT is comprised of two tests: "Verbal" (also known as "Reading and Writing") and "Mathematics."[6] The SAT Mathematics test is a timed, eighty-six-minute test (two forty-three-minute modules) consisting of fifty-four exam items, for an average of about 1.5 minutes per question.[7] However, the questions are not just a list of calculations. They require a careful reading of the math problem (often in the form of a short essay question), discerning what is actually being asked, focusing on the relevant information while disregarding distracting text, thinking about how to formulate an answer, and selecting the correct answer from three others that are incorrect, but which might appear correct at first glance. The goal is to separate students so that the total body of students will have a sufficient range of scores to be ranked for college admission purposes. Those who are motivated enough to persevere through tedious mathematical questions or have the benefit of private tutoring will do better than others who cannot afford tutoring or who have more serious concerns on their mind, such as homelessness, family strife, or unsafe neighborhoods.[8]

To underscore the associations of family income and race with SAT and ACT scores, a 2013 study found a wide gap in SAT Mathematics and Verbal scores between Black and White students with the same family income (see table 11.1). The study also found wide differences in scores according to family income level regardless of race. The widest differences in SAT math scores (the perfect score is 800) were between Black test takers whose family income was less than $10,000 (382) and White test takers whose family income was greater than $100,000 (568).[9,10]

In line with these research findings, on October 12, 2019, California governor Gavin Newsom vetoed a bill that would have allowed California school districts to substitute the SAT and ACT exams for the state's test. The governor's reasons for his veto were as follows:

Encouraging students' access to college and reducing the student testing burden in high school are laudable goals. However, I am concerned that replacing the state's high school assessment with the Scholastic Aptitude Test (SAT) or American College Test (ACT) will have the opposite effect. Specifically, their use exacerbates the inequities for underrepresented students, given that performance on these tests is highly correlated with race and parental income, and is not the best predictor for college success.[11]

Two months later, a coalition of students, nonprofit organizations, and a school district filed a lawsuit (*Kawika Smith v. Regents*) against the

Table 11.1   SAT scores by Race and Family Income

Family Income	Black Test-Takers' Average Score		White Test-Takers' Average Score	
	Math Score	Verbal Score	Math Score	Verbal Score
Less than $10,000	382	381	478	480
$20,000 to $25,000	409	413	493	495
$50,000 to $60,000	441	450	516	514
More than $100,000	490	495	568	557

Source: Data from Ezekiel J. Dixon-Román, et al., "Poverty and SAT Scores: Modeling the Influences of Family Income on Black and White High School Students' SAT Performance," Teachers College Record 115, no. 4, (2013): 14.

University of California Board of Regents over the use of SAT and ACT exams in admission decisions.[12] Eighteen months later, in May 2021, a settlement was reached whereby the Board of Regents agreed to no longer use SAT and ACT scores for college admission decisions.[13] Even where the SAT or ACT is not required for admission, students must still take English and math placement tests, and the problem isn't just at the four-year university level. A major reason for students dropping out of community college is their failure to pass the required remedial college math courses, known as "developmental math," a rehash of middle school and high school math.[14] Upwards of 40 percent of all college students are enrolled in community colleges. The issue is the degree to which a particular domain of math is used as a gatekeeper for higher learning in other fields that do not require higher-level math.

State Graduation Requirements, State Testing, and Federal Funding

Prior to the 1983 *A Nation at Risk* report, the controversy over math in the 1970s was about whether to go "back to basics." Algebra and calculus were reserved for a relatively small portion of college-bound students. The rest would get "general math." The 1983 *A Nation at Risk* report roundly criticized this condition:

> Secondary school curricula have been homogenized, diluted, and diffused to the point that they no longer have a central purpose. In effect, we have a cafeteria style curriculum in which the appetizers and desserts can easily be mistaken for the main courses. . . . This curricular smorgasbord, combined with extensive student choice, explains a great deal about where we find ourselves today. We offer intermediate algebra, but only 31 percent of our recent high school graduates complete it. Calculus is available in schools enrolling about 60 percent of all students, but only 6 percent of all students complete it. Twenty-five percent of the credits earned by general track high school students are in physical and health education, work experience outside the school, remedial English and mathematics, and personal service and development courses, such as training for adulthood and marriage.[15]

The *Nation at Risk* commissioners recommended longer school days, up to seven hours a day, and longer school years, up to 220 days a year. They recommended more academic courses rather than courses about cooking and health, despite the potential infusion of math and science into those courses. The commissioners also recommended that grades be the indicator of academic achievement, that states should adopt standardized tests of achievement, and that colleges and universities should raise their admissions requirements. Regarding mathematics, the commissioners issued a one-paragraph recommendation:

> The teaching of *mathematics* in high school should equip graduates to: (a) understand geometric and algebraic concepts; (b) understand elementary probability and statistics; (c) apply mathematics in everyday situations; and (d) estimate, approximate, measure, and test the accuracy of their calculations. In addition to the traditional sequence of studies available for college-bound students, new, equally demanding mathematics curricula need to be developed for those who do not plan to continue their formal education immediately.[16]

Implicit in the Commission's recommendations for mathematics learning was that higher levels of math were meant for *all* students, not just those bound for selective colleges.

In response to the 1983 *Nation at Risk* report, states adopted substantially stricter graduation requirements and increased the number and rigor of core academic courses. The structure of most public high school curricula is based on core academic courses: English, math, social studies, and science. The graduation requirements commonly include three to four years of mathematics. The content of these courses is based on College and Career Readiness Standards and the Common Core State Standards,[17] even for vocational education students. The overriding purpose is "college and career readiness." The report did not question the primary purposes of education or how to make the curriculum more meaningful and motivating to a larger number of students.

The central role played by mathematics in college admissions, state standards, and state assessments has the effect of crowding out other purposes of education that may be more relevant to a young person's life in this new era. Whether true or not, algebra is seen as the "gateway" to more "rigorous" high school courses, such as AP and honor calculus, which are valued by selective college admissions officers. Math enjoys unquestioned status as an indispensable element of the SAT and ACT exams. Algebra is a requirement for high school graduation in most states and is a prominent part of state exams. Consequently, algebra plays an outsized role as part of student academic outcome measures. If one wants to introduce a new purpose to public education for a new era, we must understand the fervid controversies known as the math wars[18] and why a new math war will break out if math is changed, different areas emphasized or deemphasized, or new topics introduced that are more relevant to the new era.

DIFFERENT APPROACHES TO THE MATH PROBLEM

The First Approach, More of the Same Is Better

The Commission's recommendations were acted upon in two ways. First, federal and state policymakers, with few exceptions, focused on enacting educational regulations that could be readily seen and measured: more instructional time for core academic courses, longer school days and school years, higher levels of academic courses, tougher graduation requirements, more testing of students tied to federal funding, more requirements to license teachers, and greater school, principal, and teacher accountability. To reach a consensus for this policy direction, on September 27 and 28, 1989, President George H.W. Bush, in collaboration with the National Governors' Association (NGA), convened an Education Summit in Charlottesville, North Carolina. The Summit was surrounded by much fanfare. At the end of the summit, six national education goals were adopted.[19] President Bush announced these education goals in his January 31, 1990, State of the Union Address before the U.S. Congress:

1. By the year 2000, every child must start school ready to learn.
2. The United States must increase the high school graduation rate to no less than 90 percent.
3. In critical subjects—at the fourth, eighth, and twelfth grades—we must assess our students' performance.
4. By the year 2000, U.S. students must be the first in the world in math and science achievement.
5. Every American adult must be a skilled, literate worker and citizen.
6. Every school must offer the kind of disciplined environment that makes it possible for our kids to learn. And every school in America must be drug-free.[20]

These six goals became the legislative framework to implement the Nation at Risk archetype. Given the context of the times, they sounded reasonable. In 1994, President Bill Clinton, who had been co-chair of the NGA's education task force, signed both the Goals 2000: Educate America Act and the Improving America's Schools Act, a reauthorization of the 1965 Elementary and Secondary Education Act. Both laws were crafted to help states implement these six goals.

In 2001, President George W. Bush continued the spirit of the Charlottesville Education Summit by significantly strengthening school-accountability policies with the enactment of the No Child Left Behind (NCLB) Act of 2001. While NCLB had the effect of bringing increased attention and accountability to address the chronic underachievement of certain groups of students, the chief indicators used to measure "Annual Yearly Progress" or "AYP" were math and English scores on state-developed tests. As a result, many school districts chose to constrict their curricula to focus on state-mandated math and reading tests. Science teaching time, for example, was reduced to allow more time for math instruction and test preparation. More interesting approaches to teaching were replaced with repeated "benchmark testing," as if repeatedly weighing an undernourished child would make them gain weight.

In 2015, President Obama and the U.S. Congress continued where President Bush left off by enacting the Every Student Succeeds Act of 2015 (ESSA).[21] This policy requires states to continue to demonstrate student performance to receive federal funding. States must administer annual state-wide assessments to all students in reading/language arts and mathematics in grades three through eight and once in high school. Science assessments are to be administered in each grade span for all students. For all English learners, annual English language proficiency assessments are to be given in all grades K-12. ESSA requires that states establish college- and career-ready standards and maintain high expectations when assessing all students against those standards.[22] Thus, there has been a consistent bipartisan policy, through Republican and Democratic administrations, to implement the framework set forth in Charlottesville based on the Nation at Risk archetype, which is measured via math, science, and English testing. But it was not always this way, nor must it remain so.

A Second Approach, Math 2.0.

The *Nation at Risk* Commission called on national nonprofit organizations such as the American Association for the Advancement of Science and the National Council of Teachers of Mathematics (NCTM) to "revise, update, improve, and make available new and more diverse curricular materials." These organizations focused on parts "c" and "d" of the *Nation at Risk's* math recommendations: "(c) apply mathematics in everyday situations; and (d) estimate, approximate, measure, and test the accuracy of their calculations. In addition to the traditional sequence of studies available for college-bound students, new, equally demanding mathematics curricula need to be developed for those who do not plan to continue their formal education immediately."[23]

In 1989, the same year the Charlottesville Education Summit was held, the Mathematical Sciences Education Board (MSEB) of the National Research Council issued its seminal report, *Everybody Counts: A Report to the Nation on the Future of Mathematics Education.*[24] While acknowledging much of the economic justification for mathematics contained in the *Nation at Risk* report, the MSEB's *Everybody Counts* went further by articulating what *about* mathematics learning was critical for all students to achieve:

> Jobs that contribute to this world economy require workers who are mentally fit workers, who are prepared to absorb new ideas, to adapt to change, to cope with ambiguity, to perceive patterns, and to solve unconventional problems. It is these needs, not just the need for calculation (which is now done mostly by machines), that make mathematics a prerequisite to so many jobs. More than ever before, Americans need to think for a living; more than ever before, they need to think mathematically.

But what exactly is meant by "thinking mathematically"? Here is an example. Suppose we ask a child to add 15 + 10 + 1. They would usually be taught a certain procedure or "algorithm" to come up with the one correct answer, in this case, twenty-six. But suppose we instead ask a child, "How many ways can you use pennies, nickels, dimes, and quarters to make twenty-six cents?" What if we grouped three or four children at a table with a pile of play coins and asked each child to come up with a different way to add the coins up to twenty-six cents? Then each group would show the rest of the class how they reached their answer. How much more interesting and enlightening would it be for children to *play* with math. By extension, what if we then used pennies, nickels, and dimes to teach Roman numerals (i.e., I, V, X) using the same problem?

What if math topics recommended in the *Nation at Risk* report (algebraic concepts, probability and statistics, and geometric concepts) were presented in the context of both "everyday situations" and situations involving "unconventional problems" that required children to use their creativity? This was the essential idea behind the publication of the NCTM *Curriculum and Evaluation Standards* released in the same year as MSEB's *Everybody Counts*. Soon after these publications were released, the National Science Foundation (NSF), in accordance with the *Nation at Risk's* call to "revise, update, improve, and make available new and more diverse curricular materials," began funding the development of new mathematics curricula materials.

The NSF, with funding from Congress, would eventually support the development of thirteen new K-12 curriculum projects with titles like *Everyday Math, Math in Context, Connected Math, Interactive Math, Contemporary Math in Context, and Mathematics: Modeling our World.* All these new curriculum materials were developed by university mathematics professors and math educators, practicing math teachers, and related nonprofit organizations. These NSF curriculum projects were extensively field-tested in schools and revised accordingly. Funds were also provided for substantial teacher professional development in the use of the new materials. To support these efforts, from 1985 to 2005, the NSF made some 2,400 instructional materials development and teacher enhancement awards totaling over $2.1 billion. Another $874 million was awarded to 310 state, urban, and rural "systemic change initiatives" to align their curriculum and assessment systems to the new standards. In short, what the MSEB, NCTM, and NSF were advocating, as distinct from that of the governors, was to develop agile mental capacity in children needed to deal with the change and ambiguity of a modern world that would require new and unconventional solutions.

To see the practical implications of these two different approaches and why they might lead to a math war, let's return to the coin example. On one side, we have a procedure to teach a child how to add $10 + 15 + 1$. Some called this "traditional math," or basic math. We'll call it Math 1.0. Here the teacher is instructing the class how to add. Children complete it by themselves at their desks. No calculators are allowed. The teacher collects the students' work and marks whether or not the answers are correct. At the end of the marking period, the grades of all homework assignments, quizzes, and tests are added together to get a final course grade, either as a percentage score of 0–100 or converted to a letter grade A to F. Most notably, Math 1.0 permits fast grading and a clear ranking of students. Students who can follow rules and procedures and quickly perform calculations based on them should do well on these tests.

In contrast, in a math reform classroom, the teacher may arrange the class into groups of four students at a table. She provides the play coins at each table and explains to the students what they are to figure out. She gives a few simple rules: a nickel is worth five pennies, a dime is equal to ten pennies, and a quarter equals twenty-five pennies. She then gives the students a short time limit to come up with as many ways as possible to arrange the coins to equal twenty-six pennies. Directing them to a piece of blank chart paper attached to the wall, she then asks each table to come up and present their solutions. The rest of the class is asked to comment on the solutions and state if they are correct and why. The teacher assesses their understanding based on the students' presentations. Quizzes and tests are given less frequently and more as a review of what was presented. Some have called this "reform math" or "constructivist math." We'll call it Math 2.0.

Both NCTM and MSEB argued that children have natural abilities to learn to count and develop more complex mathematical concepts. By actively creating their own math ideas, children would increase their mathematical power and come to see math all around them, such as in shapes, angles, ratios, and proportions. In short, *structured play* is critical to learning and novel problem-solving. In *Everybody Counts,* the authors argued that math curriculum and teaching should cultivate a child's mathematical faculties as opposed to instruction that drilled math facts and procedures:

> In reality, no one can teach mathematics. Effective teachers are those who can stimulate students to learn mathematics. Educational research offers compelling evidence that students learn mathematics well only when they construct their own mathematical understanding. To understand what they learn, they must enact for themselves verbs that permeate the mathematics curriculum: "examine," "represent," "transform," "solve," "apply," "prove," "communicate." This happens most readily when students work in groups, engage in discussion, make presentations, and in other ways take charge of their own learning.[25]

THE ATTACK ON MATH 2.0, THE MATH WARS

The earlier adoption of the 1985 California Math Framework[26] anticipated much of the later MSEB and NCTM reports released in 1989. It also stirred a strong reaction among a small group of self-styled critics of Math 2.0. Since California is the most populous state in the union, the choice of textbooks it adopts has a ripple effect across the country, just like Texas' impact. As the NCTM standards and new NSF curriculum materials started to make their way into California classrooms beginning in the early 1990s, local opposition to these math reforms began to intensify. Then something happened to trigger an explosion of opposition to Math 2.0 nationally.

In 1994, Congress directed the U.S. Department of Education's Office of Educational Research and Improvement to establish "panels of appropriate qualified experts and practitioners." The purpose was to evaluate educational programs and recommend those programs that should be designated as exemplary or promising to the secretary of education.[27] In October 1999, an expert math panel published its list of exemplary and promising math programs, many of which had been developed with funding from the NSF. It was greeted by a firestorm of opposition. Leading the way was a group of nearly 200 research mathematics professors who published an open letter to U.S. Education Secretary Richard Riley in the form of a full-page advertisement in the *Washington Post*.[28] The ad was funded by the Packard Humanities Institute run by Hewlett-Packard computer heir David W. Packard. The thrust of the ad complained that there were no research mathematicians on the expert panel that had recommended the exemplary and promising mathematics textbooks. Chief among this group's criticisms was that not enough emphasis was placed on certain topics, such as the division of fractions and the use of paper and pencil tasks to solve long division problems using standard algorithms, for example divide 125,674 by 281.[29]

Many of the signers of the 1999 *Washington Post's* anti-Riley ad became advisors to local school opposition groups via the new communications technologies—the World Wide Web and email. The professors used their university credentials to provide savvy media support to vocal parents and recalcitrant teachers to resist and/or repeal Math 2.0 reform efforts. Their strategy was simple: sow seeds of fear, uncertainty, and doubt (the "FUD factor") about what was new and unfamiliar. As Machiavelli warned about change, "the innovator has enemies in all those who profit by the old order, and only lukewarm defenders in all those who would profit by the new order."

THREE ATTACK STRATEGIES ON MATH 2.0

Three strategies were used by critics of Math 2.0. The first strategy was to claim, without evidence, that these new NSF curricular materials had "dumbed down" the traditional math curriculum so that lower-ranked students could succeed, thus harming higher-achieving students. If everyone is equal, then no one is ahead. For parents of students who succeeded in the traditional Math 1.0 approach, the fact that otherwise lower-achieving students were now doing better *had* to mean the curriculum was being dumbed down, otherwise, how could *those* kids be succeeding? Since class rank is one of the factors in college admissions decisions, having lower-ranked students doing better could mean less separation from the higher-ranked students.

A second strategy was to call Math 2.0 "Fuzzy Math," claiming it lacked rigor and precision. The nature of the Math 2.0 curriculum required students to think more for themselves about novel and applied problems rather than memorize math procedures as taught by the teacher. Students thinking for themselves implied ambiguity about the correct answer or that there could be more than one right answer. This fuzzy labeling created anxiety for college-bound students who feared they would not be adequately prepared for college math.

At the time, few, if any, quality research studies were available to quell parental fears about their children enrolled in Math 2.0 courses. To help address these concerns, we conducted the Cambridge High School (our pseudonym for a school in an affluent suburban Philadelphia school district) study discussed in Chapter 10. We compared the first four high school graduating classes that had taken traditional Math 1.0 against four subsequent cohorts who took Math 2.0 high school courses. The results were remarkable. The four Math 2.0 cohorts did statistically significantly *better* at college *completion* in four years than the four previous Math 1.0 cohorts; 36 percent completed college in four years versus 28 percent who took Math 1.0.[30]

The problem of "what causes what" led President George W. Bush and Congress in 2002 to establish the Institute of Education Science (IES) within the U.S. Department of Education.[31] Congress limited the IES to: "(iv) making claims of causal relationships only in random assignment experiments or other designs (to the extent such designs substantially eliminate plausible competing explanations for the obtained results)."[32] Since 2003, IES has funded hundreds of studies to test various education interventions using randomized control trials according to its "scientifically based research standards." The results of many such studies are contained in the U.S. Department of Education's "What Works Clearinghouse"[33] and/or published in peer-reviewed educational research journals that are publicly available. Nonetheless, those who abide by facts and research findings have a difficult time overcoming the shadows of race, rankings, and elitism described in part II.

The third strategy of critics of Math 2.0 was to *transpose* cause and effect; that is, the *solution* to a problem became the *cause* of the problem. Suppose a new cancer treatment is introduced where only 30 percent of patients died rather than the usual 60 percent. Would this cancer treatment be labeled a failure for not preventing all the deaths? No, it would likely be hailed as a medical breakthrough. It could certainly not be said that the new cancer treatment *caused* those remaining patients to die since twice that number were *already* dying before the new treatment was introduced. Yet such was the logic of the critics of Math 2.0. Suppose 60 percent of high school graduates fail to pass a community college math placement exam for algebra. Then suppose a new curriculum is introduced where the failure rate decreases to 30 percent. Nonetheless, negative anecdotes from the 30 percent of students who continue to fail were used to create the illusion that the entire reform curriculum is hurting students' chances at college. This illusion was possible because parents, students, and the public were unaware of what was occurring with high school graduates *prior* to Math 2.0 being implemented. We encountered this transposed reasoning in many of the districts we worked with—blaming the new remedy for pre-existing failures.

The emergence of new digital technologies in the mid-1990s enabled critics of Math 2.0 to accelerate the spread of disinformation. Misleading statements and half-truths were simply asserted as true based on the preeminence of the person making them. The sheer volume, speed, and repetition of these anti-Math 2.0 reform messages created the impression that what was stated must be true. It became virtually impossible to rebut every half-truth and misstatement that continually popped up at school board meetings and on the Internet.

NEW MATH WARS

In November 2021, the math wars erupted again, this time over a draft of an updated version of the 2013 California Math Framework (CMF).[34] The newer version of the math framework is many hundreds of pages long. It mirrors many of the themes found in the 1983 *Nation at Risk* and 1989 *Everybody Counts* reports but with more recent math education research and cognitive science research to support it. Like these earlier reports, the CMF urges greater efforts and different strategies for engaging traditionally underrepresented groups to grasp the power of thinking and reasoning mathematically. But it goes further in that it also recommends multiple pathways to higher-level mathematics beyond the traditional algebra-geometry-trigonometry-calculus sequence.

The updated CMF was quickly greeted with a torrent of criticism in the late fall of 2021 that echoed the rhetoric used in earlier math wars. In an open November 2021 Google blog post, with the names of accomplished university and corporate professionals attached, two unfounded charges were leveled against the CMF. The first charge was that "such frameworks aim to reduce achievement gaps by limiting the availability of advanced mathematical courses to middle schoolers and beginning high schoolers."[35]

The updated CMF did no such thing. The second erroneous charge implied that the CMF is part of "another deeply worrisome trend [to devalue] essential mathematical tools such as calculus and algebra in favor of seemingly more modern 'data science.'"[36] Once again, the charge was unfounded. Indeed, the updated framework recommended what these critics said should be done. Namely, "There cannot be a 'one size fits all' approach to K-12 mathematical education. Students should be offered multiple pathways and timelines to explore mathematics."[37]

These math debates miss a larger point. What is the purpose of education in the first place? What are the likely realities young people will face and the competencies they will need to thrive in this new era? Why should forcing all children to solve decontextualized quadratic equations be privileged over more useful mathematical knowledge? There are certainly plenty of mathematics to explore such as fractals and risk analysis. Is it possible to design such a curriculum? Our answer is "yes." There is evidence both in schools in the United States and in other nations that a curriculum can be designed that elevates the level and practicality of mathematics learned by students.

In part IV, we will show how we linked mathematics to other subjects to provide students with the practical, real-world contextualization necessary to deeply engage them and provide purpose and meaning. If we are to find a new purpose of education for a new era, we will need a Math 3.0 version.

But before we get to part IV and Egypt, we need to dispel the illusion that activity equals progress.

NOTES

1. Niccolo Machiavelli, *The Prince*, https://fulltextarchive.com/book/The-Prince.

2. United States Attorney General, "Partnership Among Federal, State, Local, Tribal, and Territorial Law Enforcement to Address Threats Against School Administrators, Board Members, Teachers and Staff," U.S. Department of Justice, October 4, 2021, https://www.justice.gov/ag/page/file/1438986/download?utm_medium=email&utm_source=govdelivery.

3. Jinfa Cai and F. Joseph Merlino, "Metaphors: A Powerful Means for Assessing Students' Mathematical Dispositions," in *73rd Yearbook: Motivation and Disposition: Pathways to Learning Mathematics*, Daniel J. Brahier and William R. Speer, eds. (Reston: National Council of Teachers of Mathematics, 2011), 147–156.

4. Unpublished internal data.

5. National Association for College Admission Counseling, "Counseling Trends Survey, 2018-19," https://files.eric.ed.gov/fulltext/ED608316.pdf.

6. The College Board, "Inside the Test," accessed May 28, 2023, https://collegereadiness.collegeboard.org/sat/inside-the-test.

7. The College Board, "2023 SAT Suite of Assessments Downloadable Full-Length Practice Tests," https://satsuite.collegeboard.org/digital/digital-practice-preparation/practice-tests/linear.

8. Michele Wages, *The Achievement Gap: A Poverty Crisis, Not an Education Crisis* (Rowman and Littlefield, 2018).

9. Ezekiel J. Dixon-Román et al., "Race, Poverty and SAT Scores: Modeling the Influences of Family Income on Black and White High School Students' SAT Performance," *Teachers College Record* 115, no. 4, (2013): 1–33, https://www.cs.jhu.edu/~misha/DIReadingSeminar/Papers/DixonRoman13.pdf.

10. Note that the same pattern is apparent in the Verbal scores.

11. Office of the Governor, "Memorandum to the Members of the California Assembly," October 12, 2019, https://www.gov.ca.gov/wp-content/uploads/2019/10/AB-751-Veto-Message.pdf.

12. Lauren Camera, "Lawsuit Against University of California System Challenges SAT, ACT Admissions Requirement," *U.S. News and World Report*, December 10, 2019.

13. Nanette Asimov, "UC Settles Student Lawsuit, Agrees Not to Use SAT, ACT Scores in Admissions," *San Francisco Chronical,* May 14, 2021, https://www.sfchronicle.com/local/article/UC-settles-student-lawsuit-agrees-not-to-use-16178677.php.

14. Adnan Moussa and Susan Bickerstaff, "Creating Accelerated Pathways for Student Success in Mathematics," Community College Research Center, Teachers College, Columbia University, October 2019, https://www.luminafoundation.org/wp-content/uploads/2019/11/accelerated-pathways-student-success-mathematics.pdf.

15. National Commission on Excellence in Education, "A Nation at Risk," April 1983, https://archive.org/details/nationatrisk0000unse/page/24/mode/2up?view =theater.

16. National Commission on Excellence in Education, "A Nation at Risk," 25.

17. National Governors Association Center for Best Practices and the Council of Chief State School Officers Common Core State Standards Initiative, 2009, http://www.corestandards.org/.

18. Alan H. Schoenfeld, "The Math Wars," *Education Policy* 18, no. 1 (January 2004): 253.

19. Maris A. Vinovskis, *The Road to Charlottesville: The 1989 Education Summit,* National Education Goals Panel, September 1999, https://govinfo.library.unt.edu /negp/reports/negp30.pdf.

20. George H. W. Bush, "The State of the Union," January 31, 1990, http://webarchive.loc.gov/congressional-record/20160311160455/http://thomas.loc.gov/cgi-bin/query/F?r101:33:./temp/~r10172Du5a:e0:.

21. "An Original Bill to Reauthorize the Elementary and Secondary Education Act of 1965 to Ensure that Every Child Achieves," *Public Law* 114–95, December 2015, https://www.congress.gov/bill/114th-congress/senate-bill/1177/text.

22. U.S. Department of Education, "Every Student Succeeds Act, Assessments under Title I, Part A & Title I, Part B: Summary of Final Regulations," https://www2 .ed.gov/policy/elsec/leg/essa/essaassessmentfactsheet1207.pdf.

23. National Commission on Excellence in Education, "A Nation at Risk," 25.

24. National Research Council, Everybody Counts: A Report to the Nation on the Future of Mathematics Education (Washington, DC: The National Academies Press, 1989), 1.

25. National Research Council, Everybody Counts, 58.

26. Mathematics Framework for California Public Schools, Kindergarten Through Grade Twelve.

27. U.S. Department of Education Math and Science Education Expert Panel, "Exemplary and Promising Mathematics Programs," 1999, 5, https://files.eric.ed.gov /fulltext/ED434033.pdf.

28. Richard Riley, "An Open Letter to United States Secretary of Education," November 1999, http://www.mathematicallycorrect.com/riley.htm.

29. Jeffrey Mervis, "Packard Heir Signs Up for National 'Math Wars,'" *Science* 287, no. 5455 (February 11, 2000): 956–959.

30. The 21st Century Partnership for STEM Education, "Cambridge High School Report Summary," February 2009, https://www.21pstem.org/_files/ugd/bf6da2_99b 345b0a34e4f40bc287a0d03617c72.pdf.

31. *Education Sciences Reform Act of 2002.* Pub. L. No. 107-279. ESRA also provides the legislative authority for the four IES Centers (NCER, NCES, NCEE, and NCSER) and for most IES programs.

32. *Education Sciences Reform Act of 2002,* Section 102 18 B iv, https://www .congress.gov/107/plaws/publ279/PLAW-107publ279.pdf.

33. U.S. Department of Education, Institute of Education Science, What Works Clearinghouse, accessed May 28, 2023, https://ies.ed.gov/ncee/wwc/.

34. California Department of Education, "Mathematics Framework," modified July 14, 2022, https://www.cde.ca.gov/ci/ma/cf/.

35. "Open Letter on K-12 Mathematics," K-12 MathMatters, para. 2, accessed May 28, 2023, https://sites.google.com/view/k12mathmatters/home.

36. "Open Letter," para. 3.

37. "Open Letter," para. 7.

Chapter 12

The Illusion That Activity Equals Progress

Intractability is the hallmark of problems for which customary assumptions and axioms are no longer valid. The problem is not technical. Nor is it motivational. Nor is it moral. The problem inheres in your unreflective acceptance of assumptions and axioms that seem so obviously right, natural, and proper that to question them is to question your reality.

—Seymour B. Sarason[1]

Education has a number of problems that seem to be intractable despite great efforts and activities to overcome them. Schools set goals, and when they fall short of them, the reaction tends to be to try harder, install more programs, employ different administrators and teachers, or test more. Seymour Sarason's observations resonate with our experience in trying to improve teaching and learning. Before attempting to repurpose education for a new era, it may be worthwhile to examine customary assumptions and axioms to see if they are still valid.

CRITICAL THINKING AND LIFELONG LEARNING

The ability to think critically is one of those cherished educational goals people are fond of citing. But how do we go about measuring critical thinking ability? What does it mean in this new era of digitalized social media with deep fakes and disinformation generated by ill-intended foreign and domestic actors aided by stunning advances in artificial intelligence? In the largest study of its kind on critical thinking applied to digital social media content, 3,446 high school students were given six online tasks where they

215

were asked to tell the difference between authentic and fake information. Nearly all struggled. More than half of the students believed that a fake Facebook video provided "strong" evidence of voter fraud. Only three students tracked down the original source of the manipulated video, a BBC News video showing that the people of *Russia*—not the United States—were committing voter fraud. Ninety-six percent were ignorant about a climate change website's connection to the fossil fuel industry. The vast majority of students accepted as true information from websites based on the site's appearance or the content of its "About" page. Less than 10 percent were able to critically evaluate information by checking its source, seeking corroboration from reliable sources, or questioning the logic of the information. Two-thirds were not able to recognize the difference between news stories and ads on a website.[2]

One reason why critical thinking is difficult to develop in students is their intractable misconceptions, superficial judgments, and faulty reasoning that remain unchanged even after explicit instruction is provided and contrary evidence is presented. This inflexible cognitive condition allows young people to be easily exploited later in life. Casinos know that many gamblers have a naïve understanding of the fundamentals of probability, thus ensuring that once they are enticed to play, in the long run, the house always wins. For example, if a coin is tossed five times and comes up heads each time, a common gambler's fallacy is the belief that on the sixth time, tails is due to come up because it is "tails' turn." Yet the probability of a coin coming up tails on the sixth toss is the same as it was on the first: fifty-fifty (assuming a fair coin).

Superficial judgments about cause and effect abound without giving due regard to counterfactual evidence. For instance, many students, even Harvard graduates, believe that the cause of a hot summer July in Boston is because the Earth is closer to the Sun. If this were true, then everywhere on Earth would be hotter, including South America, where it is actually winter in July. The first step to critical thinking is to become awakened to contradictions within one's thinking and to be open to evidence that challenges one's positions. This is the ideal of science and a liberal education.

Another largely illusionary goal of schools is for students to become "lifelong learners." Yet, the attitudes of most high school students seem to be that they can't wait to graduate, never wanting to open a serious book again. Others simply drop out. In 2015, before the COVID-19 pandemic, a survey was conducted involving over 21,000 high school students on their feelings about school. The study was directed by the Yale Center for Emotional Intelligence and the Yale Child Study Center.[3] The sample of students came from all fifty states and was diverse in terms of gender identity, socioeconomic status, race and ethnicity, geography, and public or private schools. The students were asked, "How do you typically feel when you are in school? List up to three feelings."

The online survey contained blank text boxes for students to enter. The study reported the top ten feelings, nearly three-quarters of which were negative. "Tired," "stressed," and "bored" topped the list. Only one in four students reported feeling "happy," and only one in twenty reported being "excited." Those who listed tired and bored indicated they felt these feelings the great majority (up to 80 percent) of the time. These negative feelings were present across all demographic groups. Positive feelings were more frequently reported by older male students from higher socioeconomic-status families enrolled in private schools. We can only speculate as to why. If this and other similar studies are indicative of the true feeling of high school students, why should we expect those who are bored, tired, and stressed to want to become "lifelong learners"?

The late Seymour Sarason, an esteemed professor of psychology and founder of the Yale Psycho-Educational Clinic in 1961, recounted his first encounter with high school geometry:

> On the second or third day of my geometry class in high school, the teacher drew two connecting lines on the blackboard and said "That is an obtuse angle." Why is it called *obtuse*? Why *that* word and not some other word? Why a word that I had never heard of before? Why should I care about obtuse angles or, for that matter, geometry? What does geometry *mean*? Who invented the curse of geometry and what relation did it have to anything in my life. . . . One secure conclusion resulted: only under threat of death would I take another math class.[4]

Mr. Sarason's experience in his 1940s math class was not unique at the time, nor have geometry classes changed much for many students in the intervening years, apparently. Boredom, stress, and tiredness are still the dominant experiences for the vast majority of those attending high school, public, or private. Teachers told us that their high school students' lack of motivation was their leading problem. Yet, they tell us they feel helpless to counter it. Why do young children begin school so excited and eager to learn[5] and end their tenure so bored and eager to leave? Why does a lack of motivation seem so intractable?

HAS THE UNITED STATES BECOME THE WORLD LEADER IN MATH AND SCIENCE EDUCATION?

As mentioned in the previous chapter, one of the six goals emerging from the 1989 Charlottesville, Virginia, education summit led by President George H.

W. Bush with the nation's governors was to be "first in the world in math and science achievement by the year 2000." In 1994, this goal was codified in the Goals 2000: Educate America Act.[6] So did we reach this goal by the year 2000?

In 1995, the largest, most comprehensive international assessment was launched: the Trends in International Math and Science Study (TIMSS). This study tests a sample of students from different countries in grades four and eight every four years using a testing framework that emphasizes two dimensions: subject-matter content knowledge and thinking processes. In December 2000, the TIMSS results were released. Despite all the federal and state efforts since the 1983 *Nation at Risk* report, including the Goals 2000 Act and the adoption of new math and science standards, U.S. eighth graders ranked *nineteenth* in mathematics and *eighteenth* in science out of thirty-eight industrialized countries—far from first.

Falling short of the lofty goal of being first in the world in math and science by the year 2000 could be dismissed as the usual unrealistic promises of elected officials. After all, what sounds better: setting the goal of being first in the world by the year 2000 or being somewhere in the middle of the pack? In our conversations with teachers and school administrators, the country's lackluster performance on international assessments like TIMSS is rationalized in several ways, e.g., the test was not representative of the U.S. curriculum; other countries excluded their poorer-performing students; or the United States has to teach a wider diversity of students. The usual villains were also cited, such as uncaring or missing parents, teacher unions, lack of adequate school funding, lack of student discipline, and unmotivated and underprepared students. Only once did we hear from a school district's administrators that they were okay to be nineteenth in the world—that was good enough.

Perhaps it is in the United States' DNA to always strive to be the best, the world's leader in everything. Harken back to May 25, 1961, when newly elected U.S. president John F. Kennedy addressed a special joint session of Congress and set forth a bold new national goal:

I believe that this nation should commit itself to achieving the goal, before this decade is out, of landing a man on the moon and returning him safely to earth. No single space project in this period will be more exciting, or more impressive, or more important for the long-range exploration of space; and none will be so difficult or expensive to accomplish. . . . Let it be clear that I am asking the Congress and the country to accept a firm commitment to a new course of action, a course which will last for many years and carry very heavy costs. . . . If we are to go only halfway, or reduce our sights in the face of difficulty, in my judgment it would be better not to go at all.[7]

Landing a man on the moon has become the gold standard, so it seems, by which all other grand public goals have been measured, national education goals being no exception. The nation's governors did indeed make a firm commitment to achieving these national education goals by 2000. States mandated new graduation requirements. New math and science content standards were adopted. Teacher certification requirements were toughened. Yet using the standard of landing a man on the moon for social change is an illusion. The engineering feat of going to the moon and back, while technically complex, is more straightforward than achieving great leaps in educational improvement. The latter goal has a different kind of complexity because education is set within a human context and often a disabling one at that: chronic poverty, two-parent households on the decline, income and wealth inequities, systemic racism in institutions including education and healthcare, and implicit bias in a predominantly White teaching and administrative system, all of which interfere with learning. Adding to the challenge is tremendous variability across and within states of support for preparing and supporting high-quality teachers and quality schooling generally. Engineering a moonshot does not have to contend with these problems but the task of educating children does.

A NATION AT RISK 2.0

The United States entered the third millennium with a string of upheavals, beginning with the threat of a worldwide banking and government collapse from the so-called "Y2K bug." Fears spread that computer programs would not be able to deal with the year 2000 since previous computer programs only used the last two digits for the date and thus could not tell the difference between 1901 and 2001. Governments and companies raced to fix the "millennium bug," spending some $100 billion.[8] A rapid succession of political upheavals followed. First, there was a bitterly contested November 2000 presidential election following only the second impeachment of a president in history. Then, on September 11, 2001, nineteen al-Qaida terrorists simultaneously hijacked four passenger jets crashing them into the World Trade Center towers and the Pentagon, with a fourth diverted from the U.S. Capitol by nosediving into the ground in Shanksville, Pennsylvania, a small town seventy-five miles southeast of Pittsburgh. In response, the United States invaded Iraq and Afghanistan, the latter war lasting twenty years.

The same period saw economic crises. The dot.com bubble burst in March 2000, igniting a stock-market crash. Five trillion dollars in market value was lost and the economy slid into an eight-month recession.[9] As in the early 1980s, there was renewed alarm over the United States' perceived inability to compete in a global economy. This time it was not the spectacular rise in Japan's and Germany's manufacturing power, but the spectacular growth in China's and India's economies along with the rise in the "Asian Tigers"—South Korea, Taiwan, Singapore, and Hong Kong.[10]

During the 2000 decade, at least thirty-one national reports were issued stressing the urgent need to respond to these new economic challenges from Asia and India.[11] But these challenges differed from those of the 1970s and 1980s that motivated the original *Nation at Risk* report. Now the risks were falling behind a global, digitized, internet-driven, knowledge-based *innovation* economy. Perceived shortages in American scientific and engineering talent and lagging innovation capacity were seen as threats to both national security *and* future economic prosperity. For example, in 2005, the Council on Competitiveness report, *Innovate America,* asserted in its preamble that "Innovation will be the single most important factor in determining America's success through the 21st century."[12] In 2007, The National Academies of Science report entitled *Rising Above the Gathering Storm* warned, "Without high-quality, knowledge-intensive jobs and the innovative enterprises that lead to discovery and new technology, our economy will suffer and our people will face a lower standard of living."[13] In 2007, the National Governors Association issued a call to action entitled *Innovation America,* claiming that "Innovation is a hallmark of a successful economy, and it drives economic growth and the creation of new jobs . . . the challenge for the United States is to innovate at a faster rate and more effectively than its rivals."[14]

The main thrust of these reports was their emphasis on developing *innovative and knowledgeable* talent. Increased levels of educational attainment in math and science courses, while necessary were insufficient. The updated 2000 report by the Secretary's Commission on Achieving Necessary Skills emphasized five core worker competencies. These included the basic skills of mathematics and science but also "thinking skills involving creativity, problem-solving and reasoning" and "systems understanding and design."[15] As shown in figure 12.1 from a report by the Federal Reserve Bank of St. Louis, the increasing employment prospects of workers who possess the ability to deal with "nonroutine" cognitive and/or nonroutine manual tasks contrast with those who perform only routine tasks since the latter can be overtaken by automation, including robots and artificial intelligence.[16] For example, most bank tellers' tasks involving routine cognitive skills have been supplanted by ATM machines and online banking apps. Nonroutine tasks, on the other hand, typically involve the application of knowledge to identify and diagnose problems and formulate solutions that cannot as yet be easily automated. These include both white-collar professions, such as law, medicine, and counseling services, and blue-collar occupations, such as plumbing and electrical services.

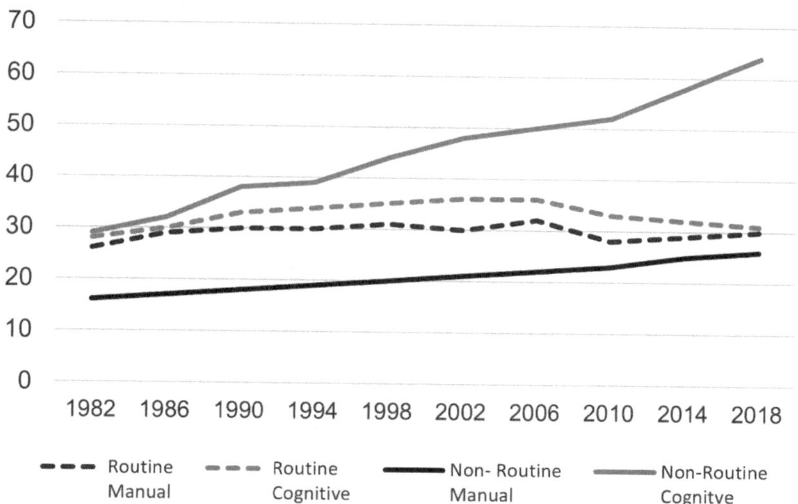

Figure 12.1   Jobs: Routine vs. Non-routine and Cognitive vs. Manual. Jobs in Non-routine Occupations, Both Manual and Cognitive, Have Steadily Increased While Jobs in Routine Occupations Have Been Stagnant. *Source*: Data from Maximiliano A. Dvorkin, "Jobs Involving Routine Tasks Aren't Growing," Federal Reserve Bank of St. Louis, January 4, 2016.

To underscore the importance of workers' ability to solve problems on the job, economists Eric Hanushek from Stanford University and Ludger Wößmann from the University of Munich published findings in 2008 that quantified how cognitive skills—as measured by international assessments—related to economic growth. Their analysis showed that it is the *quality* of learning, not only the length of schooling or attainment, which makes the difference. "Cognitive skills are related, among other things, to both the quantity and quality of schooling. But schooling that does not improve cognitive skills, measured here by comparable international tests of mathematics, science, and reading, has a limited impact on aggregate economic outcomes and economic development."[17] If this is true, states' push to merely raise the number of core academic courses needed to graduate is based on an illusion that more courses equal quality learning. But how can we be sure this is an illusion?

The TIMSS and PISA International Assessments in the Twenty-First Century

In the world of comparative international assessments, there are two widely respected sources. The first is the quadrennial TIMSS assessments, mentioned earlier in this chapter, organized by the International Association for the Evaluation of Educational Achievement, headquartered in Amsterdam, in partnership with Boston College's Lynch School of Education and Human Development. The second is the triennial Program of International Students Assessment (PISA) from the Organisation for Economic Cooperation and Development (OECD) located in Geneva.

TIMSS

We now have mountains of student performance data from TIMSS and PISA gathered during the first two decades of the twenty-first century, more than we've ever had in the past. Did U.S. students perform any better on the 2019 TIMSS tests twenty years after the 1999 TIMSS study that showed U.S. students ranking nineteenth in math and eighteenth in science? The short answer is no, not really, although it might appear so. Yes, the United States did move up in the 2019 TIMSS math rankings from nineteenth to twelfth and in science rankings from eighteenth to eleventh. But the mix of countries that participated in the 2019 TIMSS was *different* from the countries that participated in the 1999 TIMSS.

If you compare the United States to only those twenty countries that participated in *both* the 2019 and the 1999 TIMSS assessments, the U.S. ranking in math turned out to be the same: ninth out of twenty. As for science, the United States ranking of tenth in 2019 was essentially unchanged from that in 1999 among the same twenty countries. And, while the United States did increase its 2019 average score in math and science from the 1999 TIMSS, *so did most of our competitors.* The Asian rim countries and the Russian Federation continued to have superior scores in 2019 as they did in 1999 compared to that of the United States.[18] (See table 12.1.)

What do these TIMSS scores mean in terms of the *quality* of learning? To measure quality, the TIMSS assessments are divided into four "benchmarks:" The higher the benchmark level, the more complex and nonroutine the tasks. Figure 12.2 contains a summary of the benchmark levels for math and science, with the top line reflecting U.S. student math performance at the highest benchmark, which involves nonroutine problems. This shows a steady rise in scores over the years among the highest performing U.S. students, those in the ninetieth percentile.[19] However, the students in the lowest benchmark have seen scores about the same as they were in 1999. Moreover, in 2019 the gap between the highest and lowest benchmark groups had never been wider, a separation in performance by 256 points.

Table 12.2 illustrates that there is also a wide gap in average scores between racial and ethnic groups within the United States. Asian Americans have consistently scored much higher than all other groups, a gap that has only widened over time.

In terms of how the top-scoring U.S. students compared with other countries in math, the 2019 TIMSS showed that 14 percent of U.S. students scored

Table 12.1 Top Ranked TIMSS Scores by Country 1999 and 2019

TIMSS Math	Rank	1999	TIMSS Math	Rank	2019	2019–1999 Gain/Loss
Singapore	1	604	Singapore	1	616	12
Korea, Rep. of	2	587	Chinese Taipei	2	612	27
Chinese Taipei	3	585	Korea, Rep. of	3	607	20
Hong Kong SAR	4	582	Japan	4	594	15
Japan	5	579	Hong Kong SAR	5	578	(4)
Hungary	6	532	Russian Federation	6	543	17
Russian Federation	7	526	Lithuania	7	520	38
Malaysia	8	519	Hungary	8	517	(15)
United States	9	502	United States	9 tied	515	13
England	10	496	England	9 tied	515	19
New Zealand	11	491	Cyprus	11	501	25
Lithuania	12	482	Italy	12	497	18
Italy	13	479	New Zealand	13	482	(9)
Cyprus	14	476	Romania	14	479	7
Romania	15	472	Malaysia	15	461	(58)
Jordan	16	428	Iran, Islamic Rep.	16	446	24
Iran, Islamic Rep.	17	422	Chile	17	441	49
Chile	18	392	Jordan	18	420	(8)

Source: Country rankings data from TIMSS 2019 international results in mathematics and science. From Ina V. S. Mullis et al., TIMSS 2019 International Results in Mathematics and Science," International Association for the Evaluation of Educational Achievement (2020), 151.

at the Advanced Benchmark and 38 percent scored at the High Benchmark level. As shown in table 12.3, these rankings were still well behind the participating Asian rim countries. The U.S. TIMSS science results are similar to those in math.

What about the extent to which students like learning math? The TIMSS study collects a host of ancillary data on teachers, school environments, and student attitudes toward math and science. In the 2019 TIMSS study, only 17 percent of U.S. eighth-grade math students "very much liked learning math." Forty-five percent did not like learning it.[20] This data confirms our interview finding about student motivations to learn math as discussed in the math wars chapter.[21]

PISA

In 2000, the OECD inaugurated the PISA to test fifteen-year-old students. In the United States, the modal grade level is tenth grade. The purpose of PISA is to measure students' ability to think and reason mathematically and

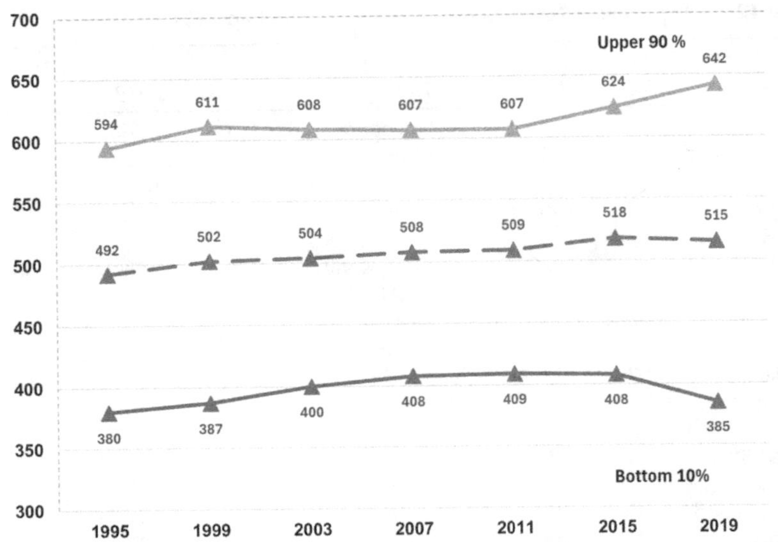

Figure 12.2 Trends in Average Scores and Selected Percentile Scores of U.S. Grade Eight Students on the TIMSS Mathematics Scale, Selected Years 1995–2019. *Source*: Data from the National Center for Education Statistics Blog Editor, "New International Data Show Large and Widening Gaps Between High- and Low-Performing U.S. 4th- and 8th-Graders in Mathematics and Science," February 10, 2021.

Table 12.2   U.S. TIMSS Trends in Mathematics Eighth Grade

Race	1995	1999	2003	2007	2011	2015	2019
Asian	—	—	—	549	568	585	591
White	516	525	525	533	530	541	548
Multiracial	—	—	—	506	513	521	540
U.S. Average	500	502	504	508	509	518	515
Hispanic	443	457	465	475	485	492	486
American Indian/ Alaska Native	—	—	—	—	—	477	483
Black	419	444	448	457	465	462	445

scientifically in a real-world context. This ability is referred to as math and science *literacy*. Reading and financial literacy are also tested. About two-thirds of students across OECD countries score between 400 and 600 points out of 1000. The first PISA assessments began in 2000 for reading, in 2003 for math, and in 2006 for science.

The 2018 PISA assessment included thirty-seven OECD countries and forty-two partner countries and economies.[22] Despite the goal of being first in the world in math and science by the year 2000, in the 2018 PISA, U.S. students ranked thirty-seventh out of seventy-nine countries in math literacy.

Table 12.3 TIMSS 2019 Math Percent of Students Reaching Benchmarks

	Country	Advanced (625 score)	High (550 score)
1	Singapore	51	79
2	Chinese Taipei	49	75
3	Korea, Republic of	45	74
4	Japan	37	71
5	Hong Kong SAR	32	66
6	Russian Federation	16	48
7	Israel	15	40
8	United States	14	38

Source: Data from Ina V. S. Mullis et al., TIMSS 2019 International Results in Mathematics and Science," International Association for the Evaluation of Educational Achievement (2020), 175.

As with TIMSS, the Asian rim countries were at the top by a wide margin. As for science literacy, U.S. students ranked eighteenth out of seventy-nine countries. In reading literacy, U.S. students ranked thirteenth. The U.S. students' scores have remained remarkably consistent since PISA's first assessment in 2000 despite all of the national reports and federal and state reform efforts in the first two decades of the twenty-first century.

These TIMSS and PISA results do not mean that the U.S. public education system is "failing." The U.S. student international rankings are not terrible. But U.S. students have clearly and consistently fallen far short of being the best in the world. PISA rankings mean more than bragging rights. In 2010, OECD published an economic analysis showing how various OECD members' Gross National Product could be substantially *increased* in the long run by boosting students' cognitive abilities as measured in the PISA assessments. Relatively small improvements in workers' ability to deal with "nonroutine" tasks can have large economic impacts. The OECD analysis showed, for example, that if the United States could raise its PISA scores to that of Finland, the top-ranked OECD country, an additional \$103 *trillion* would accrue to the U.S. gross domestic product over a worker's lifetime.[23]

According to A Nation at Risk 2.0, one of the primary purposes of education is to teach children so they can be competent and innovative workers to compete and win in a global economy competition. If so, according to data from TIMSS and PISA, we have fallen short of that goal after nearly forty years of trying. What should we do next? Do we want to continue trying or take a different tack?

REVISITING THE PURPOSES OF EDUCATION

The question before us is this. Is the Nation at Risk 2.0 archetype still *the* most important overarching purpose of K-12 public education in the twenty-first century? Even if the United States had achieved its goal of being first in the world in math and science, does it mean it *should* continue as the leading educational purpose in this new era? We contend that today there are purposes for education that are more vital to young peoples' future. Consider, for example, the Level 5 benchmark for the PISA reading literacy assessment: "Students can comprehend lengthy texts, deal with concepts that are abstract or counterintuitive, and establish distinctions between fact and opinion, based on implicit cues pertaining to the content or source of the information."[24] Only about one in seven U.S. fifteen-year-olds attained this level and only about one in ten achieved this level across the other OECD countries. This means that the vast majority of adolescents in the United States and many OECD countries around the world cannot distinguish fact from fiction, cannot comprehend lengthy texts even if they had the desire to read them, and cannot deal with abstract concepts or those that go against their pre-conceived ideas. These PISA findings are consistent with the findings from the Civic Online Reasoning survey described at the outset of this chapter. As the PISA report warns:

> The demands placed on the reading skills of 15-year-olds have fundamentally changed. The smartphone has transformed the ways in which people read and exchange information and digitalisation has resulted in the emergence of new forms of text, ranging from the concise, to the lengthy and unwieldy. In the past, students could find clear and singular answers to their questions in carefully curated and government-approved textbooks, and they could trust those answers to be true. Today, they will find hundreds of thousands of answers to their questions online, and it is up to them to figure out what is true and what is false, what is right and what is wrong.[25]

The threat to democracy from unregulated social media platforms is real. Media professor Sarah Oakes, writing in the journal *Digital Wars,* contends that social media platforms are being weaponized as part of "information wars," a fifth theater of war along with air, sea, land, and space threatening democracy worldwide.[26] By the term "social media" we're not talking about a neighborhood gossip telephone line. Facebook alone is a $1.5 trillion[27] global behemoth with 2.9 billion users.[28] Frances Haugen, the former lead product manager for Civic Misinformation and Counterespionage for Facebook, provided stunning and riveting testimony before the United States Senate Committee on Commerce, Science and Transportation on October 4, 2021, describing how Facebook allows its platform to be weaponized for the sake of profits:

> I saw that Facebook repeatedly encountered conflicts between its own profits and our safety. Facebook consistently resolved those conflicts in favor of its

own profits. The result has been a system that amplifies division, extremism, and polarization—and undermining societies around the world. In some cases, this dangerous online talk has led to actual violence that harms and even kills people. In other cases, their profit optimizing machine is generating self-harm and self-hate—especially for vulnerable groups, like teenage girls. These problems have been confirmed repeatedly by Facebook's own internal research. This is not simply a matter of some social media users being angry or unstable. Facebook became a $1 trillion company by paying for its profits with our safety, including the safety of our children. And that is unacceptable.[29]

Haugen provided a large set of internal Facebook documents to Congress dubbed the "Facebook Papers" showing how Facebook's engineers use sophisticated data algorithms to feed users content, whether true or false, that repeatedly reinforces their pre-existing beliefs, even leading them to an alternate universe of false reality. Moreover, these algorithms give greater weight to provocative content that stokes anger and conflict to maximize viewer engagement.[30] As a result of these kinds of omnipresent social platforms, twenty-first-century communication technology has provided domestic and foreign agents with the unprecedented ability to sow division and discord among vast swaths of a country's population, and not just in the United States. These illiberal forces poison gullible and uncritical minds with conspiratorial falsehoods and half-truths threatening the disintegration of democracy, posing new risks to this nation that were unimaginable when the original *Nation at Risk* report was issued four decades ago.

If the viability of our democracy in both the short and long term depends on achieving a far greater level of critical thinking in our young people, we had better get it right, and soon. If we are to avoid violent discord, choices about educational priorities must be reevaluated. Even national science and mathematics educational organizations claim that the study of their disciplines is necessary for an informed citizenry.

One could argue that revising the purpose of education to address the dangers of disinformation and uncritical thinking will go for naught in the end, that little will change. After all, wasn't this chapter all about the illusions of progress? Indeed, Charles M. Payne in his 2017 book, *So Much Reform, So Little Change*,[31] recounts the decades of mostly futile urban education reform efforts launched after the 1983 *Nation at Risk* report. We know these reform efforts well. We directed a series of large National Science Foundation projects over two decades that were contemporaneous with other reform efforts as described by Payne. Despite not achieving the degree of success we originally envisioned, much has been learned and developed: new instructional materials, new standards, new assessments, and much educational research into what is and is not effective. While these advances are noteworthy, we have concluded that what has been missing is defining a new purpose of education. The *Nation at Risk* archetype is exhausted and obsolete for the realities facing young people in this new era. It is one of the reasons educational activity has not equaled much progress. School administrators and policymakers kept layering one reform initiative upon another as if on a supermarket shopping spree rather than questioning education's more fundamental purpose: how to connect schooling to student interest and the chief concerns of our time.

In the next chapter, we describe illusions from decades of educational research about how people learn and what the best teachers do.

Then in part IV, we describe how we used our lessons learned from these earlier projects to help engineer a breakthrough in Egypt. We describe how the Egyptians defined a new purpose for education, how we assisted their realization of it, and how we can apply the same reform processes on behalf of students in the United States.

NOTES

1. Seymour B. Sarason, *The Predictable Failure of Education Reform* (San Francisco: Jossey-Bass, 1990), 148.

2. Joel Breakstone et al., "Students' Civic Online Reasoning: A National Portrait," *Education Researcher* 50, no. 8 (2021): 505–515.

3. Julia Moeller et al., "High School Students' Feelings: Discoveries From a Large National Survey and an Experience Sampling Study," *Learning and Instruction* 66 (April 2020), https://doi.org/10.1016/j.learninstruc.2019.101301.

4. Sarason, *The Predictable Failure*, 160.

5. National Research Council, *Early Childhood Development and Learning: New Knowledge for Policy* (Washington, DC: The National Academies Press, 2001).

6. Goals 2000: Educate America Act. Pub. L. No. 103–227, § 102, 108 Stat. 130.

7. John F. Kennedy, "Special Message to Congress on Urgent National Needs," May 25, 1961, JFK Library, https://www.jfklibrary.org/asset-viewer/archives/JFK-WHA/1961/JFKWHA-032/JFKWHA-032.

8. Francine Uenuma, "20 Years Later, the Y2K Bug Seems Like a Joke—Because Those Behind the Scenes Took It Seriously," *Time Magazine,* December 30, 2019.

9. Kevin L. Kliesen, "The 2001 Recession: How Was It Different and What Developments May Have Caused It?" Federal Reserve Bank of St. Louis, 2003, https://files.stlouisfed.org/files/htdocs/publications/review/03/09/Kliesen.pdf.

10. Paulina Restrepo Echavarria and Maria A. Arias, "Tigers, Tiger Cubs and Economic Growth," Federal Reserve Bank of St. Louis, May 25, 2017, https://www.stlouisfed.org/on-the-economy/2017/may/tigers-tiger-cubs-economic-growth.

11. Project Kaleidoscope, "Transforming America's Scientific and Technological Infrastructure, Recommendations for Urgent Action," January 2006, https://www.pkallsc.org/resources/report-on-reports-ii/.

12. Council on Competitiveness, "Innovate America: National Innovation Initiative Summit and Report," 2005, 7, https://competeorg.wpengine.com/wp-content/uploads/ncf-reports/nii-innovate-america-2005.pdf.

13. National Academy of Sciences et al., *Rising Above the Gathering Storm: Energizing and Employing America for a Brighter Economic Future* (Washington, DC: The National Academies Press, 2007), 1, https://doi.org/10.17226/11463.

14. Erika Fitzpatrick, "Innovation America: A Final Report," The National Governors Association, July 2007, 1, http://eric.ed.gov/?q=Innovation+America&id=ED504101.

15. U.S. Department of Labor, "Skills and Tasks for Jobs: A SCANS Report for America 2000," 1991, https://eric.ed.gov/?id=ED350414.

16. Maximiliano A. Dvorkin, "Jobs Involving Routine Tasks Aren't Growing," Federal Reserve Bank of St. Louis, January 4, 2016, https://www.stlouisfed.org/on-the-economy/2016/january/jobs-involving-routine-tasks-arent-growing.

17. Eric A. Hanushek and Ludger Woessmann, "The Role of Cognitive Skills in Economic Development," *Journal of Economic Literature* 46, no. 3 (2008): 607–668.

18. From Ina V. S. Mullis et al., TIMSS 2019 International Results in Mathematics and Science," International Association for the Evaluation of Educational Achievement, 2020, 151, https://timss2019.org/reports/wp-content/themes/timssandpirls/download-center/TIMSS-2019-International-Results-in-Mathematics-and-Science.pdf.

19. National Center for Education Statistics Blog Editor, "New International Data Show Large and Widening Gaps Between High- and Low-Performing U.S. 4th- and 8th-Graders in Mathematics and Science," February 10, 2021, https://nces.ed.gov/blogs/nces/post/new-international-data-show-large-and-widening-gaps-between-high-and-low-performing-u-s- -and- -graders-in-mathematics-and-science.

20. From Ina V. S. Mullis et al., "TIMSS 2019 International Results in Mathematics and Science," International Association for the Evaluation of Educational Achievement, 2020, 430, https://timss2019.org/reports/wp-content/themes/timssandpirls/download-center/TIMSS-2019-International-Results-in-Mathematics-and-Science.pdf.

21. We used the most recent pre-Covid-19 scores for TIMSS and PISA so as to not distort country-by-country comparisons due to different school effects from COVID-19. Between 2019 and 2023, US math scores dropped 18 points for fourth graders and 27 points for eighth graders. A decline of 30 points roughly equals a year of learning. In science, declines weren't statistically significant but were in the same direction. The post COVID-19 scores for TIMSS and PISA show the relative ranking of the Unites States compared to other countries to be approximately the same as as pre-COVID-19 rankings.

22. The Organisation for Economic Co-operation and Development (OECD), *PISA 2018 Results: Combined Executive Summaries Volumes 1, II & III* (2019), https://www.oecd.org/pisa/publications/pisa-2018-results.htm.

23. Organisation for Economic Co-Operation and Development (OECD), "The High Cost of Low Educational Performance," 2010, https://read.oecd-ilibrary.org/education/the-high-cost-of-low-educational-performance_9789264077485-en#page1.

24. Organisation for Economic Co-Operation and Development (OECD), *PISA 2018 Results (Volume I): What Students Know and Can Do* (2019), 85, https://doi.org /10.1787/5f07c754-en.

25. Organisation for Economic Co-Operation and Development (OECD), *PISA 2018 Results (Volume I),* 3.

26. Sarah Oates, "The Easy Weaponization of Social Media: Why Profit Has Trumped Security for U.S. Companies," *Digital War* 1 (2020): 117–122, https://doi .org/10.1057/s42984-020-00012-z.

27. "Facebook Ad Revenue," Oberrlo, accessed May 30, 2023, https://www.oberlo .com/statistics/facebook-ad-revenue#:~:text=According%20to%20a%20recent %20report,a%20slowdown%20in%20growth%20rates.

28. "Leading Countries Based on Facebook Audience Size as of January 2023," Statista, https://www.statista.com/statistics/268136/top-15-countries-based-on-num-ber-of-facebook-users/.

29. United States Senate Committee on Commerce, Science and Transportation, "Statement of Frances Haugen," October 4, 2021, 2, https://www.commerce.senate .gov/services/files/FC8A558E-824E-4914-BEDB-3A7B1190BD49.

30. Christina Lima, "Facebook Under Fire: A Whistleblower's Power: Key Take-aways from the Facebook Papers," *The Washington Post*, October 21, 2021.

31. Charles M. Payne, *So Much Reform, So Little Change* (Cambridge, MA: Harvard University Press, 2017).

Chapter 13

The Turning Point

Over the past thirty years, from the 1989–1990 to 2019–2020 school years, the United States spent a total of $11.3 trillion on public education, or about $17,000 per pupil per year (in constant 2021–2022 dollars, including capital outlays and interest on debt).[1,2] Much good was derived for millions of students in public schools. And yet, as we saw in the last chapter, according to our 2018 Trends in International Mathematics and Science Study (TIMSS) and Program of International Students Assessment (PISA) scores, we haven't moved the needle much and are still far from our goal of being the global leader in mathematics and science education. It is clearly time to move on. As poet Amanda Gorman, in "New Day's Lyric," envisions:

Someday we can venture beyond it,
To leave the known and take the first steps.[3]

Leaving the known, however, can be difficult. In our experience with thousands of teachers, we have witnessed that teachers resist changing their traditional practices based on the belief that the best way students learn new material is through expert lecturing. The belief is that if students do not learn the material presented, either they lack the motivation to learn or they have such weak preparation that they are hopelessly behind. Administrators, for their part, blame teachers for their lack of content knowledge or poor pedagogy. Accordingly, many education reform efforts try to enhance teachers' content knowledge, prod students' motivation, or provide student remediation sessions. These efforts are superficial at best—window dressings for a dated archetype. As Gorman goes on to urge:

So let us not return to what was normal,
But reach toward what is next.

But what is next, and how can we get there? Dissatisfaction with traditional *teacher-centered*[4] practice is not new. In an 1880 report on a national survey conducted by the American Association for the Advancement of Science about the teaching of science in schools, the authors provided a scathing summary of the woeful state of physics teaching:

> The scientific method is simply a systemic exercise in truth seeking and is the only mode of using the human mind when it is desired to attain the most accurate and perfect form of knowledge. Our public schools, unhappily, make but little use of this method in the work of mental cultivation. They have grown up in conformity with the ideal that a school is a place where knowledge is got from books by the help of teachers. As a consequence, the science teaching in the public schools is generally carried on by instruction. The pupil is filled up with information in regard to science. . . . They are not made the means of cultivating observing powers, stimulating inquiry, exercising judgment in weighing evidence, nor of forming original and independent habits of thought. The pupil does not know the subject he professes to study by actual acquaintance with the facts and he therefore becomes a mere passive accumulator of second-hand statements. . . . This mode of teaching has been denounced by all eminent scientific men as a "deception," "a fraud," an "outrage upon the minds of the young," and "an imposture in education."[5]

It is hard to change traditional teacher-dominated instructional methods[6] without providing teachers with a clear vision of what is next—of how students could learn without the teacher always doing the instruction. Despite disappointing prior attempts at reforming schools as discussed in the last chapter, we now have the tools to build on what we and others have learned about teaching and learning.

The What Works Clearinghouse, described in chapter 11, has reviewed hundreds of studies about various reform efforts and found little to no effect for many of them when subjected to a scientific analysis. Uninspiring, boring, and sometimes alienating teaching is one of those great intractable problems of education. To be sure, we have also witnessed many teachers who inspired their students, sometimes quite profoundly. But why are there not more of them? What makes the difference?

Research studies on teacher quality tend to look at readily measurable characteristics of teachers—their certifications, advanced degrees, and years of teaching experience.[7] Researchers then try to draw associations between these quantifiable teacher characteristics and student achievement scores on state math and reading tests. In this chapter, we pull back this illusionary veil to focus on teaching *practices*—the way teachers interact with students, design lessons, and choose and utilize their teaching strategies.

Since the mid-1980s, an ever-increasing body of cognitive psychology and neuroscience research on human learning has been amassed.[8,9,10] It demonstrates that certain practices are more likely to inspire and motivate students to understand subject-matter content more deeply than traditional teacher lectures, but measures of learning, as exemplified on state achievement tests, are often limited to surface features of knowledge: facts and procedures. Newer assessments, however, have been developed that require students to engage in deeper levels of thinking such as analysis, synthesis, and evaluation in the disciplines.[11]

Based on research in educational psychology, cognitive science, and experience from hundreds of educational reform projects, we contend that four intertwined classroom components must be present to inspire students: a purposeful curriculum, skillful student-centered teaching, authentic and informative assessment, and a trust-filled learning environment.

TEACHING AND LEARNING

The Traditional Approach

While Gorman's poem implores us to understand what is *next,* when applied to education it is important to get a sense of where we are at present—our current *normal.* We have observed both teacher-centered and *student-centered* approaches. We have observed many K-6 classrooms, for example, using a student-centered approach. Children tend to be actively engaged in their learning—making things, using materials, and working together. "Teacher talk" is brief. Instead, teachers prompt children with many questions to elicit their engagement, thinking, problem-solving, and creative processes. This harkens back to the teaching of the 26-cent math problem described in chapter 11. By eighth grade, students are more likely to be sitting in less interactive, teacher-centered classrooms. The TIMSS video study of eighth-grade classrooms from around the world bears out this observation.[12] Students "sit and git" as teachers talk, do practice exercises at their desks or work on problems in which the content is prescribed and fact-based. Brazilian educator and philosopher Paolo Freire called this the "banking" model of education, in which teachers deposit information into students as if they are empty receptacles with no innate knowledge, creativity, or agency.[13] Classroom tests emphasize the recall of facts from lectures, explanations, and textbooks. While some learners get good grades in this traditional instruction because they are good memorizers, there are limitations to their learning. Even students who do well on college admissions tests may lack the skills and habits of mind needed to grasp more complex college-level material and the demands of the new era. College instruction, mostly conducted by contract lecturers,[14] also suffers from teacher-centered classrooms. So why is the traditional model of teaching so common, so limiting, and off-putting to students as Sarason experienced in high school? The following is what we noticed in many classrooms.

No Pre-assessment of Student's Conceptual Readiness

Traditionally, teachers start a lesson *without* checking for the learner's prior *understanding* of the new concept to be learned.[15] Instead, many teachers will simply give students a cursory pre-test for their knowledge of *facts or procedures*. If gaps are discovered, teachers are caught in a dilemma. How much should they review or reteach? Did students forget what was taught or was it poorly understood? If teachers choose to reteach the material and students do not retain what was taught, the problem is perpetuated for the next teacher. When should teachers press on to "teach" new material?

Instructional Approach (Teaching as I Was Taught)

Many adults we have encountered believe that without direct instruction, students cannot possibly learn. They assume that the teacher's or textbook authors' way of structuring and explaining knowledge is appropriate and sufficient for all learners. By structuring knowledge, we mean how various bits of information or data are organized, how evidence is used to validate it, and how information and data in one area relate to information and data in another. The way an expert organizes their understanding of a subject may seem eminently logical and reasonable to them. As we shall see below, however, this teacher-centered approach has critical limitations.

Traditional teacher-centered classrooms give students the impression that the source of knowledge resides in the teacher. This perception of authority ignores or minimizes what students bring to the classroom in terms of their interests, experiences, culture, and values.

In traditional classrooms, one observes teachers telling, explaining, or asking students questions and then quickly answering questions themselves, not allowing time for students to think or respond. In these classrooms, the average observed "wait time" (the time between the end of teachers' questions and their expectation of student response) is less than two seconds, the time to take a breath (1.5 seconds, to be exact).[16,17] But the average time to inhale and exhale is three seconds![18] In teaching this way, the traditional teacher unintentionally suppresses students' time to think, ultimately silencing students' voices, especially those of a different race/ethnicity than themselves.

Assessment of Learning

In traditional teacher-centered classrooms, the teacher generally conducts few or no assessments *during the learning process* to inform their instruction in real-time. Instead, the teacher tests students after a period of instruction. The test questions are likely to require the student to recall and replicate what the teacher or textbook covered. Traditional grading, especially in math and science, is about counting the number of right and wrong answers and calculating the percentage correct. More advanced cognitive skills[19] are rarely tested. Not only are assessments of higher-order skills more challenging for the students, but such tests are also more challenging for the teacher to construct and evaluate.

Cookbook Laboratory Activities

Laboratories in the traditional approach are usually designed as demonstrations or confirmations of already existing knowledge. However, when activities do not produce the predicted results, teachers and students often get frustrated and turn away from the laboratory and return to the comfort of the book. Many teachers are unprepared or hesitant to engage their students in sleuthing out the causes of these unexpected results and developing a better understanding of what they are studying as a result. While students often practice and master necessary laboratory procedures like lighting a Bunsen burner, such practices alone do not lead to an understanding of the underlying scientific concepts inherent to the laboratory activity. As visionary educator John Dewey[20] lamented in 1938 and is still much the case today, school lab activities usually cover isolated topics without building a coherent sequence resulting in a deeper conceptual engagement of students. While many students enjoy the hands-on aspect of lab work even in traditional classrooms, it is often deadening for them because it favors a "recipe" over inquiry. A 2006 study by the Committee on High School Science Laboratories provides hopeful evidence that research into student learning has begun to turn toward laboratory experiences that support relevant goals in science education.[21]

Failure to Address Students' Misconceptions

A growing body of recent formal and informal educational research has uncovered students' underlying preconceptions and misconceptions of different subject matter. Teachers who are not aware of this research may leave the learner caught between two views of reality: that version of reality as *told* by the teacher and that as *believed* by the learner. These beliefs are often developed from ordinary life experiences. For example, everyday language describes the Sun rising in the East and setting in the West. This statement implies the Sun revolves around the Earth, which is also supported by our untutored daily observations. It is possible for a person to correctly recite the scientific fact of Earth's rotation on its axis, but at the same time believe and feel that the Sun is going around the Earth every day. This is but one of hundreds of such examples of naïve beliefs.[22]

Forgetting

We have all heard lectures (or sermons) and thought we understood, only to find later that we have forgotten or cannot explain or use the ideas presented. In the moment we followed the speaker because they had a clear, well-developed mental organization (schema) of the material, but as mere listeners, we were not actively engaged in developing our own schemas. Students may retain what has been taught only long enough for the next test, but research in cognitive science shows such knowledge rarely is retained over time to remain robust enough for later applications.[23] Without actively reflecting on our own "understanding," our new knowledge is surprisingly transitory. This transitory learning from lectures applies not only to the development of higher-level concepts but also to the teaching and learning of manual skills. Better to learn by actively doing than passively listening.

TEACHING FOR CONCEPTUAL CHANGE

If a swimmer consistently loses in competition, a good coach studies different aspects of the swimmer's stroke and kick to determine how to improve the swimmer's performance. The coach doesn't simply admonish the swimmer to "swim faster." If a young violinist struggles with a difficult passage, the effective music teacher studies the youth's arm and hand position to determine adjustments needed to get those fingers aligned for a more fluid and accurate placement on the strings. Practice alone does not make perfect if what is being practiced is not correct. In some cases, a performer needs to unlearn old habits.

But what happens when the task is the acquisition of knowledge and the ability to apply it? For students to develop more complete and correct concepts of the world, they too may have to *unlearn* some of what they previously thought before they can arrive at a more correct understanding or technique. The process of unlearning can be unsettling because it forces learners to confront the fact that they were wrong, thereby threatening their existing conceptual framework.

An understanding, empathetic, and skilled teacher can help students overcome anxiety and confusion. Teachers do this by asking students probing questions to uncover their reasoning. If, for example, the student is going in an unproductive direction, the teacher, wondering what is blocking the student from developing a correct understanding, may ask, "Some people say . . . [insert the *correct* idea] . . . what do you think of that?" When coupled with lots of wait time, this provides the student with an alternative idea to consider and also helps the teacher understand the student's thought processes.

Alternatively, the teacher may sense the students are on the right path but rather than simply confirming their nascent concept, the teacher probes deeper to determine the strength of their students' reasoning about the concept in question. This probing can be done by posing a contrary thought such as, "Some people say . . . [insert an *incorrect* idea] . . . what do you think of that?" Eleanor Duckworth, a revered teacher educator at Harvard, describes this latter strategy as tossing in a "monkey wrench"[24]—a process by which the teacher provides a seemingly persuasive but incorrect explanation. The teacher is indirectly challenging the student to dispute the suggested incorrect idea through a reasoned explanation. This process prompts students to analyze their thinking while at the same time helping the teacher assess the tenacity of the students' ideas.

The kind of learning in which students grapple with ideas and observations of the natural and man-made worlds that conflict with their existing understanding is the essence of *deep* learning. Working through such conflicts often results in satisfaction and provides a source of motivation to learn more. True lifelong learners are alive with questions, explorations, and reflections on what they find, even if it conflicts with prior assumptions. This process prompts more questions, perhaps uncovering more misconceptions, and thus a cycle of learning is created. Alternatively, if people have become deadened to new learning, they just go through the motions of being a student.

Educational researchers Watson and Konicek[25] provide a seminal description of how the process of teaching for conceptual change looks in a real classroom. They describe a masterful elementary teacher, Deb O'Brian, working with young learners grappling with observations that conflict with their preconceptions. The authors describe Ms. O'Brian's classroom in which her fourth-grade students wrestle with their naïve beliefs that hats and sweaters are inherently warm—a belief that may have been inadvertently reinforced by adults who admonish the children to put on their "warm sweaters" or "warm hats!" She thoughtfully nurtures her students' curiosity by encouraging them to state and test their theories about why sweaters and hats keep a person warm.

The authors describe the children's confusion and growing curiosity about their observations when they put thermometers in sweaters on the shelf but saw no change in temperature. When they thought the thermometers hadn't been in the sweaters long enough, Ms. O'Brian encouraged them to test their ideas by leaving the thermometers in overnight. When that didn't cause the anticipated rise in temperature, one student thought air circulation might be the problem. She encouraged them to figure out how they could test that idea. So her students put the sweaters in plastic bags but were later dumbfounded when the temperature was still constant. The breakthrough didn't come until a boy suggested putting thermometers on their heads under the hats. When the thermometer reading rose, he had an "aha" moment. Now he was finally ready to work on developing a new theory. The authors explained that even though most children eventually stated the correct ideas (that hats and sweaters are not inherently warm but are good heat insulators), some still reverted to their original ideas when asked to explain their thinking. The degree to which children can hold onto their incorrect concepts is not to be underestimated!

What may be confounding to the teacher is that telling learners the right answer does not convince them of it. The surprise arising from the observation being different from the expectation has been described by Piaget,[26] Festinger,[27] Duckworth,[28] and others as *disequilibrium* or *cognitive dissonance*. Letting go of old, familiar ideas is not easy, even in the face of contradictory evidence. Not letting go of incorrect ideas is not unique to children; it rings true for adults as well, sometimes even more so.[29] Even when the learner does embrace new concepts, these new ideas may be tenuous and not strong enough to apply to different situations. For new concepts to become fully integrated into the learner's psyche, the learner must have opportunities to use this new knowledge in different ways. An observer of Ms. Deb O'Brian's class may have wondered why she had not simply corrected the children's misconceptions about sweaters and then tested the students on the right answer. Without the opportunity to revise their naïve schemas, the students would not begin to build the foundation of the general concept of insulation.

Ms. O'Brian's class is a classic example of teaching for conceptual change in which learners are encouraged to investigate, test their ideas, and reflect on the results. These are the "Let's see" or "Let's figure it out!" moments when intellectual struggle is productive and meaningful. Persevering through initial failure as a normal and necessary part of learning is what psychologist Carol Dweck calls a *growth mindset.* This is opposed to a *fixed mindset* in which children and adults tend to regard *themselves* as failures to learn by thinking "I'm a failure, why bother?"[30] In such a case, failure results in a lack of further effort—a dead end.

Teaching for conceptual change in students is messy and challenging for both the teacher and the learner. The learner rarely moves from a naïve idea to a new and better one in a linear pathway. Teachers who recognize the power of productive struggle organize engaging learning experiences for their students by recognizing common misconceptions and providing ways for their students to overcome them. Teachers must also recognize the psychological vulnerability of learners when they face roadblocks. Teachers need to provide emotional support to students to learn new ideas. The results are students who attain a sense of empowerment along with the love, fun, and satisfaction of learning.

Teachers' Conceptual Change About Teaching

Misconceptions are not limited to students. When author Deborah Pomeroy taught high school, she learned tough lessons about teaching by confronting her misconceptions about teaching and learning. This experience ultimately led to a new path in her education and teaching career. The turning point came after she had been teaching high school chemistry for about fourteen years.

Deborah enjoyed a reputation as a very good teacher. The students in her advanced placement (AP) chemistry classes generally scored very well on AP chemistry exams. She knew that some of them later went on to careers in science and engineering. But she discovered a misconception of her own a little over halfway through the school year in the mid-1980s. After the bell rang to start the AP chemistry class, her students settled in, ready to start a laboratory. The lab activity was from the students' lab textbook. It was a traditionally designed activity that would demonstrate a very important chemical principle they were currently studying. Because of the high expectations Deborah had set, the students had prepared their lab notebooks with the statement of purpose, procedures, and data tables. The sequence was always the same—do the required procedures and calculations and answer a few follow-up questions to apply the concept the students were learning. Happy chatter filled the room; the students always enjoyed lab work. But as she walked around the room greeting them and checking their work, she sensed an air of complacency that caught her by surprise. Was it the routineness? Perhaps. She realized she needed to change her approach. As she walked back to her desk, she decided to throw out her plan for the day and try something she had never done before with her students.

She asked them to take off their lab aprons and put away their equipment. She then told them they would be approaching this lab not so much as a demonstration of a principle as designed in their textbook, but *as a test of the principle.* They needed to work with their partners to frame a hypothesis, describe how they would test it, and fill in their prepared data tables by predicting all the observations and results they would expect based on their hypothesis.

Furthermore, they had to describe their reasoning. Their assignment for the next day would be to create new data tables for their actual results.

Calculators and reference books came out, scratch paper appeared, and animated discussions ensued among the students. She walked around listening to their discussions and smiling to herself. This activity took up an entire class period—the same amount of time as if they had done the actual lab work. The next day, her students came in eager to see if their results would match their predictions. In some cases, they did not. Generally, the reasons were minor, but they had to analyze their work to determine if there was a problem with their hypotheses, predictions, or procedures. Her surprise was the level of engagement and discussion among the lab partners.

Following clean-up and inspired by a recent workshop she had taken in writing-across-the-curriculum, Deborah had them ignore the traditional questions at the end of the lab. Instead, she asked them to work with their partners to write a scientific essay in which they described *why* they had done this work (in terms of their thinking about chemistry), their hypotheses, predictions, tests, results, and a discussion of the importance and application of their findings. On day three, they came into class begging for more time. When she asked them what was going on, they said, "This is hard!" When pressed as to why it was hard, one student said laughingly, "We have to really think!" Taken aback, Deborah asked the class if they hadn't been thinking all year. Most agreed that they'd been learning, but not having to *think*. For Deborah, the students' responses to her question gave her an intriguing and disturbing insight. Before this activity, Deborah had mistakenly thought she had been challenging her students all along to think.

What Deborah saw in those three days was a group of students eagerly digging into the work by grappling with new ideas as opposed to preparing their more formulaic lab reports of "purpose, procedures, filling in the blanks, and answering follow-up questions." They worked hard on their essays and clearly loved both the novelty and difficulty of the task. One student figured out how to meet all the requirements of the assignment and turn it into a detective story! Not only did they have to explain their reasoning and analyze their results, but they had to figure out how to incorporate chemical equations and data tables into their essays. While these students had been reading chemistry textbooks with such inclusions, they had never been challenged to write in such a manner. Some students examined different texts to see different styles of incorporating data tables and chemical and mathematical equations. With Deborah's support, they turned their assignment into a technical writing exercise. Although these very bright students could answer difficult test questions, they had not been prompted to think about chemical concepts as *ideas to be tested* and written about creatively and analytically.

The extra days spent both before and after the actual lab work paid off in time saved later. Having the students conduct investigations and analyses rather than memorizing a textbook enabled them to more easily recognize and then use this important chemical principle throughout the rest of the course. Needless to say, she had to do a lot of her own thinking, too—about teaching and learning.

Deborah's turning point, going from a teacher- and textbook-centered classroom to one in which she activated students to have a deeper intellectual and emotional engagement with the material, did not happen overnight. She had already started to think her teaching had become too comfortable and routine. Now she began a long, slow examination of her assumptions about teaching and learning. Occasionally she wrongly assumed that her students understood a chemical concept only to find later that nearly the whole class struggled on a unit test. Deborah also realized she had had a naïve, unquestioned, and unconscious assumption that the college prep curriculum and her teaching would be valued by all students no matter their backgrounds and previous life and school experiences. She realized that she had more to learn about teaching. Her "turning toward what is next" set her on a new path culminating in her attaining a doctoral degree at the Harvard Graduate School of Education.

Deborah was already an experienced teacher before her turning point. As the adage says, old habits die hard. Even years later, she'll admit there have been times, unintentional or more often caused by circumstances beyond her control, when she taught in a more traditional teacher-centered manner. Even so, she cringed at the time because she had come to understand the very real and substantial limitations of students' learning when taught this way. In over fifty years of teaching, she has undergone some big conceptual changes of her own about education through examining and reflecting on her struggles, failures, and successes.

While Deborah's story has unique elements, it is an example of how conceptual change occurs through self-examination and reflection as the teacher becomes the learner. When Deborah began examining her teaching practices, she was fortunate to find other educators who were engaging in similar reflection and research. These teachers, too, were questioning their ideas that traditional teaching is best because it is the way they learned and were taught to teach, and because it was the most comfortable mode of instruction in terms of preparation, delivery of instruction (notice the often-used term *delivery*), and management of the classroom. There are now groups of teachers such as those in the National Writing Project[31] and Critical Explorers[32] who are doing classroom-based research on ways to improve their classroom instruction and student outcomes.

Teaching for Conceptual Change

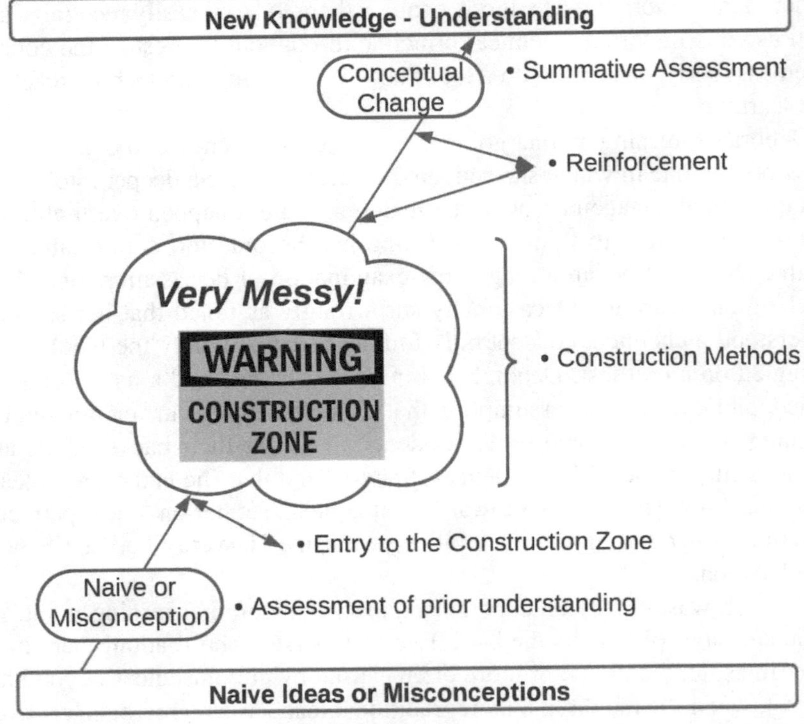

Figure 13.1 The Bottom-Up Process of Developing Conceptual Change. *Source*: Deborah Pomeroy.

MODELS OF STUDENT-CENTERED TEACHING PRACTICES

Conceptual Change

Stories of conceptual change are affirmed by the work of seminal cognitive developmental psychologists and constructivist educators[33] among others. Figure 13.1 illustrates some of the key characteristics and processes of effective student-centered teaching to facilitate students' conceptual change.

The Starting Point (Assessment of Prior Understanding)

As shown in the lower section of figure 13.1, teaching for conceptual change begins when teachers take the time to uncover students' naïve ideas and misconceptions that can be a barrier to learning. For example, if Deb O'Brian had not paid attention to her students' incorrect ideas about warm hats, she would never have had the opportunity to engage her students in an investigation to arrive at a correct understanding of thermal insulation. One strategy teachers can use to uncover how children and adolescents think is to ask students to predict the outcome of an event and explain *why*. The *why* is critical because it reveals a child's reasoning and naive ideas. Taking the time to probe students' prior ideas about a subject allows the teacher to adapt instructional activities that will help challenge any misconceptions and move the learner to a more correct or deeper level of understanding. Without such opportunities, students may simply parrot the teacher's explanation while still harboring their previous misconceptions and naïve ideas.

Entry to the Construction Zone

Change does not start until the learner experiences situations in which their prior understandings, theories, or paradigms do not work. Like Deb O'Brian, the teacher may have to provide students with multiple opportunities to test their naïve or mistaken ideas before they are ready to consider alternative ideas. As the change process begins, there comes a point of vulnerability as students open to the possibility that their ideas may not be correct, making it critical that teachers create a classroom environment that is safe physically, mentally, and emotionally.

Process (The Construction Zone)

It takes time for learners to replace their naïve ideas or misconceptions with more correct ones because they may be reluctant to let go of previously held beliefs without a strong new concept in place. Student-centered teachers are patient with the process. Imagine a trapeze artist who must let go of one trapeze to fly through the air and catch the outstretched hands of their partner on a second trapeze. The second trapezist artist must be clearly in sight and trusted. Mid-leap is a vulnerable moment. Letting go of a prior concept without a strong new concept in place can shake one's confidence because it brings into question the learner's error. To reduce the vulnerability of such leaps, the teacher, or *a more knowledgeable adult*, makes the leap as small as possible. This is much like a builder using scaffolding to reach higher levels of construction. Psychologist Lev Vygotsky calls this vulnerable but potentially rewarding area the *zone of proximal development*.[34] Rather than rewarding learners' new ideas and immediately moving on, effective teachers challenge learners to evaluate and apply their nascent ideas/skills. In this way, almost every student's response to a question or task becomes an opportunity for the teacher to assess the student's learning process and adjust instruction accordingly. These reinforcing activities and different experiences not only help anchor new ideas to students' conceptual frameworks but provide students the opportunity to gain comfort with the learning process which can otherwise feel very shaky. In a classroom in which the teacher understands the conceptual change process, these students' "ah ha" moments become self-reinforcing. They want to learn more.

Validation of Student Learning

Effective student-centered teachers do not simply tell students "Good job," or "Excellent work" because it would be the *teacher* validating or correcting (whether the student's response is good or bad) as opposed to students learning *how* to assess the validity of their ideas and those of others. As in the case of Deborah's chemistry students, when they could validate an idea on their own, without depending on her, it became transformative because it derived from the students making careful observations, weighing evidence, and recognizing and resolving contradictions. This leads to their ability to analyze a new problem, synthesize problem components, or make creative use of the new knowledge or skills.[35]

In student-centered classrooms, teachers use alternative end-of-course assessments that allow students multiple ways to demonstrate their ability to use and apply new concepts and/or skills, not just repeat what has been taught. This can occur through such things as projects, presentations, essays, or open-ended tests that require students to show or explain their problem analysis and solving.

Not all learning, however, involves conceptual change. Certain kinds of information have to be told to students: how to follow safety procedures, directions to a location, a person's name, definitions, jargon, accepted conventions, or the terminology of a discipline. There are also other times when the learner is not impeded by a misconception but simply does not know something.

TEACHING FOR CONCEPTUAL DEVELOPMENT

Conceptual change discussed in the previous section involves the correction of prior ideas resulting in the restructuring of a learner's schema. Think back to Deb O'Brian's students. They needed to replace their previous idea that sweaters and hats are inherently warm and replace it with the idea that sweaters are insulators that keep our bodies from losing heat. This is the messy construction zone we illustrated. Once this new idea of trapping body heat is accepted by the learner, it can lead to much broader applications of the idea of thermal insulation and ultimately to a generalization of the concept of insulation to other areas. Clearly, the learner's ideas about insulation are expanding in these latter instances, but it is not a revolutionary change so much as it is the further development of a correct, basic idea. This is the type of extended learning we call *conceptual development.*

There are other times when a student simply has no prior knowledge of something. A student's encounter with something new does not necessarily put the student into a conceptual conflict. It can arouse curiosity and invite investigation. It is an effective way for teachers to start a lesson and introduce and develop a new concept. This, too, is conceptual development.

Student-centered conceptual development involves further exploration of a concept, perhaps through mathematical analysis, new tools, or new techniques; extending it to new depths; applying it in both familiar and unfamiliar instances such as in projects; or using it to explain or analyze other observations. Both instances—of correct basic concepts and no prior concepts—are also best served through the process of student-centered learning as opposed to the traditional teacher-centered model. This also includes scaffolding of learning as discussed above, the opportunity to ask and explore new questions that arise, and the opportunity to incorporate the new knowledge into their existing knowledge structures by making strong connections to existing ideas. Of course, there may be instances of teachers providing explanations, but in a student-centered classroom, these are kept to a minimum.

As noted in figure 13.2, and as with any good instruction, the plan starts with an assessment of student learning. If students' conceptual foundations

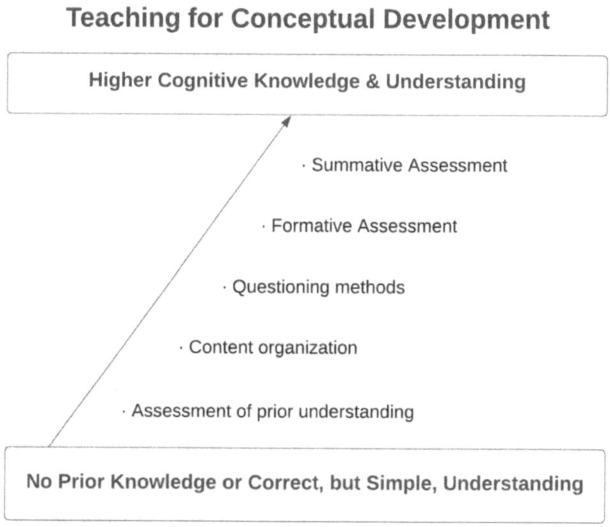

Teaching for Conceptual Development

Figure 13.2   Phases of Conceptual Development. *Source*: Deborah Pomeroy.

are good, but perhaps limited, the teacher can proceed with conceptual development. Content is structured by the teacher and sometimes by the students' questions to build upon the students' correct prior understanding by creating activities in which students are prompted to explore, generalize, apply, analyze, or synthesize concepts to master higher cognitive demand and use of skills. Teachers function as guides and resources for the students, prompting and supporting them as they wrestle with more complex or challenging concepts, higher cognitive demand, and the use of more challenging skills. Again, this can be thought of as building scaffolding on a firm foundation with pieces incrementally built up and filled in to achieve the goal. Upon achieving the goal, the learner has reached a level where there is now a newer, wider view of the world and the ability to see relationships to other concepts and skills that were not possible at the foundational level.

Such building of new knowledge can be done alone, but facilitated by a teacher, it is much easier—false steps can be avoided, and essential and meaningful components are less likely to be missed. These kinds of teaching methods are not just good ideas; they have been moved from theoretical to research based on the results of extensive studies.[36,37,38]

As with the conceptual change model, the teacher creates opportunities for multiple checks of student understanding and skill development throughout the learning process. The teacher provides students with feedback that is timely, objective, and clear, and includes suggestions as to what they can do to strengthen their performance. On the flip side, the results of these checks on student progress provide feedback to the teacher on the effectiveness of the instruction, enabling the teacher to adapt going forward as needed. Ideally, as in the conceptual change model, summative (final) assessments consist of some sort of complex performance or task in which students are required to demonstrate the ability to use higher cognitive skills and deeper understandings.

CYCLE OF MODELS

The process of learning is not a smooth, steady, straight-line accumulation of knowledge. Rather, deep learning is often punctuated by disruptive periods of conceptual change as shown in figure 13.3. Consider the author's story of relearning about teaching. She had been gaining/developing knowledge of teaching through years of formal education and teaching experience. But only when she tried a different teaching approach did she encounter a major discrepancy between what she expected and what she observed. This put her into a disruptive period of conceptual change about what it meant to be an effective teacher, which launched a course of self-study and ultimately

Cycle of Models

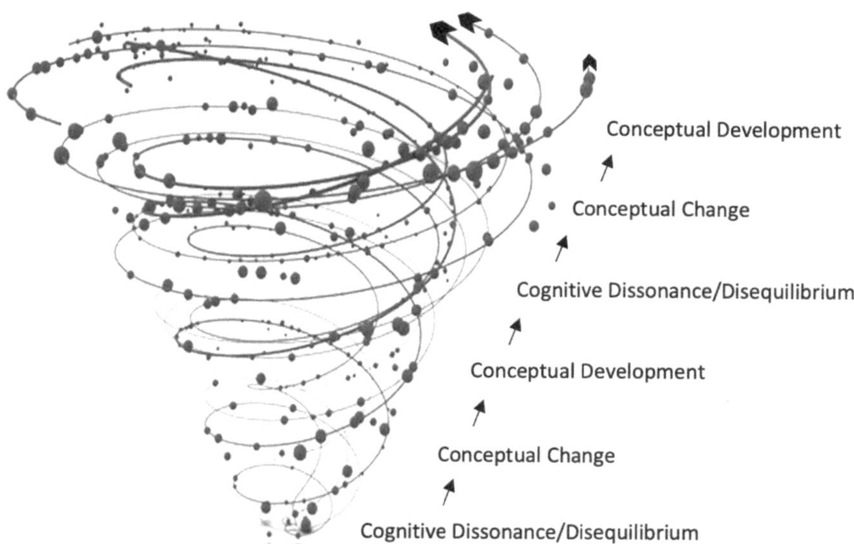

Figure 13.3 The Cycle of Models. *Source*: Deborah Pomeroy.

further formal study developing and refining her ideas and skills as an educator.

Master teachers have learned to discern the best methods to utilize these different instances of information exchange, conceptual change, and conceptual development for the benefit of their students. Effective administrators, likewise, have learned how to help teachers gain insight into effective student-centered teaching practices. Schools, as institutions, may also need to go through change to better serve their communities. All components of the education system are interrelated and can be mutually reinforcing when working well or poorly. When traditional instructional methods and curriculum fail to produce desired results, it is time to reexamine the foundational beliefs, purposes, and practices upon which they were built. However, parents, educators, and policymakers must first be convinced that their old ideas are no longer working, that student-centered instruction is not "pandering" to young people as some might suggest, but rather that rigorous teaching is more effective and engaging for the learner. Thus, begins entry into the messy construction zone in which new ideas about education can spring forth and new purposes of education defined.

If we are to prepare students to solve future problems, many yet unimagined, we must leave the old normal of traditional teaching practices[39] and curricula behind and create a new normal. In part IV, we describe how we helped the Egyptian Ministry of Education employ these better teaching practices in twenty-one new, advanced public STEM high schools in Egypt. We tell the story of the amazing opportunity we had in Egypt to help Ministry officials, school leaders, teachers, and ultimately students work through the process of their conceptual change and development. The result was a revolutionary, exciting, and purposeful approach to education—a breakthrough—for students living in the twenty-first century as they and we "reach toward what is next."

NOTES

1. National Center for Education Statistics. (2023). Public School Expenditures. Condition of Education. U.S. Department of Education, Institute of Education Sciences. Table 236.10. Retrieved November 29, 2023, from https://nces.ed.gov/programs/coe/indicator/cmb.

2. https://nces.ed.gov/fastfacts/display.asp?id=66.

3. Amanda Gorman, "New Day's Lyric," CNN, December 29, 2021, https://edition.cnn.com/style/article/amanda-gorman-new-days-lyric-poem-cec/index.htmlInstagram

4. By *teacher-centered* we mean lectures, explanations, and even problems or activities that are designed around the teacher's or textbook authors' understanding of how material should be taught instead of designing instruction around students' understanding, interests, abilities, and motivations.

5. Charles K. Wead, "Aims and Methods of the Teaching of Physics," *Circulars of Information*, no. 7 (1884): 672.

6. Note, not all problematic teaching is the fault of teachers. In the math wars described in chapter 11, change was impeded by administrators, parents, and some policymakers.

7. Laura Goe and Leslie M. Stickler, "Teacher Quality and Student Achievement: Making the Most of Recent Research," *TQ Research and Policy Brief*, 2007, https://eric.ed.gov/?id=ED520769.

8. National Research Council, *How People Learn: Brain, Mind, Experience and School* (Washington, DC: National Academies Press, 1999).

9. National Research Council, *How People Learn: History, Mathematics and Science in the Classroom* (Washington, DC: National Academies Press, 2005).

10. National Research Council, *How People Learn II: Learners, Contexts and Cultures* (Washington, DC: National Academies Press, 2019).

11. Susan R. Singer, Natalie R. Nielsen, and Heidi A. Schweingruber, eds., *Discipline-Based Educational Research: Understanding and Improving Learning in Undergraduate Science and Engineering* (Washington, DC: National Academies Press, 2012), https://www.nap.edu/catalog/13362/discipline-based-education-research-understanding-and-improving-learning-in-undergraduate.

12. The Third International Mathematics and Science Study (TIMSS), "1999 Video Study," accessed February 17, 2023, http://www.timssvideo.com/.

13. Paolo Freire, *Pedagogy of the Oppressed* (New York: Bloomsbury, 1970/2000).

14. National Center for Education Statistics, "Characteristics of Postsecondary Faculty," 2022, accessed December 1, 2022, https://nces.ed.gov/programs/coe/indicator/csc.

15. In this respect, we use the term *concept* to denote ideas and the term *skills* to denote mental or physical processes.

16. Mary Budd Rowe, "Wait Time: Slowing Down May be a Way of Speeding Up," *American Educator* 11 (Spring 1987): 38–43, 47.

17. Mary Budd Rowe, "Wait-Time and Rewards as Instructional Variables, Their Influence in Language, Logic, and Fate Control" (presentation, National Association for Research in Science Teaching, Chicago, 1972).

18. Susannah Fleming et al., "Normal Ranges of Heart Rate and Respiratory Rate in Children from Birth to 18 Years of Age: A Systematic Review of Observational Studies." *Lancet* 19, no. 377 (March 19, 2011): 1011–1018, https://doi.org/10.1016/S0140-6736(10)62226-X. PMID: 21411136; PMCID: PMC3789232.

19. For example: application, synthesis, evaluation, creation, testing, and disputing as described in Dr. Norman Webb's Depth of Knowledge (DOK) system. See https://www.webbalign.org/about/dok-explained.

20. John Dewey, *Experience and Education* (Kappa Delta Pi, 1938; New York: Free Press, 1997), 35.

21. National Research Council, *America's Lab Report: Investigations in High School Science* (Washington, DC: The National Academies Press, 2006).

22. See, for example, Harvard's "The Private Universe," https://www.learner.org/series/a-private-universe/1-a-private-universe/.

23. Henry Roediger, "Retrieval Practice Enhances Long-Term Retention of Science Learning," The 21st Century Center for Research and Development in Cognitive Science and Instruction, accessed February 17, 2023, http://cogscied.org/henry-roediger/.

24. Eleanor R. Duckworth, *The Having of Wonderful Ideas and Other Essays on Teaching and Learning*, 2nd ed. (New York: Teachers College Press, 1996), 133.

25. Bruce Watson and Richard Konicek, "Teaching for Conceptual Change: Confronting Children's Experience," *Phi Delta Kappan* 71, no. 9 (May 1990): 680–685.

26. Herbert P. Ginsburg and Sylvia Opper, *Piaget's Theory of Intellectual Development*, 3rd ed. (Englewood Cliffs, NJ: Prentice Hall, 1987).

27. Leon Festinger, *A Theory of Cognitive Dissonance* (Stanford, CA: Stanford University Press, 1962).

28. Eleanor R. Duckworth, *The Having of Wonderful Ideas*, 161.

29. During the Covid-19 pandemic, for instance, television provided a steady diet of information that many adults struggled with or even resisted, unable to let go of prior understandings or beliefs about vaccines despite overwhelming evidence of their safety and efficacy.

30. Carol Dweck, *Mindset: Changing the Way You Think to Fulfil Your Potential* (Boston, MA: Little, Brown, 2017).

31. National Writing Project, https://www.nwp.org/.

32. Critical Explorers, https://criticalexplorers.org/.

33. Jean Piaget, Lev Vygotsky, Eleanor R. Duckworth, and Richard A. Duschl.

34. In anatomy, the term *proximal* applies to the more central, body end of a bone of an appendage. Vygotsky metaphorically uses this term to describe the process of securely attaching new knowledge or skills to one's existing body of knowledge. See an overview at https://www.sciencedirect.com/topics/psychology/zone-of-proximal-development.

35. "Webb's DOK Explained," WebbAlign, accessed February 25, 2023, https://www.webbalign.org/about/dok-explained.

36. J. D. Bransford et al., eds., *How People Learn: Brain, Mind, Experience, and School*, expanded edition (Washington, DC: National Academy Press, 2000).

37. Robert J. Marzano, Barbara B. Gaddy, and Ceri Dean, *What Works in Classroom Instruction* (Aurora, CA: Mid-continent Research for Education and Learning, 2000). https://www.researchgate.net/publication/265663591_What_Works_In_Classroom_Instruction.

38. Robert J. Marzano, Debra Pickering, and Jane E. Pollock, *Classroom Instruction that Works: Research-Based Strategies for Increasing Student Achievement*, 1st ed. (Alexandria, VA: Association for Supervision and Curriculum Development, 2005).

39. We have illustrated teaching practice as an either/or dichotomy with classrooms described as either teacher-centered or student-centered. It is perhaps more realistic that these pedagogical characteristics are best represented as the opposite ends of a continuum, with many teachers and teaching materials falling somewhere in between.

Part IV

REPURPOSING EDUCATION FOR A NEW ERA

No subject of human thought has perhaps received more attention than that of education.

—Joseph Henry, 1856[1]

A most serendipitous event happened to the authors in the summer of 2011. It was an invitation to participate in a dream of repurposing education for a new era. It began near the end of our nine-year (2003–2012) National Science Foundation (NSF) project in the Greater Philadelphia area involving 200 secondary schools and 13 colleges and universities. Our project was the tenth largest out of 142 such projects known as Math Science Partnerships (MSPs). The goals were to increase student achievement in math and science, develop better teachers, and learn how best to do it. The NSF had given us extraordinary freedom to customize a variety of teaching and learning interventions to suit each of our schools' and university partners' aspirations and circumstances. We tried to implement the latest curricular innovations, instructional methods, and realistic assessments. We provided hundreds of hours of professional development to thousands of math and science teachers as well as principals. We consulted with scores of central office administrators. We awarded more than a dozen sub-grants to nearly a hundred university faculty members to experiment with improving their math and science teacher preparation programs. Everyone learned. We cultivated a broad network of experienced colleagues. We were part of a national community of learners. From our external evaluators' perspective, our MSP project seemed to be a success. Yet we still felt something was missing, something we did not see until the project was nearing its end.

If we had to boil it down to one main lesson learned, it was that teachers and schools needed a clear purpose for what they were teaching. Teaching and learning must be *intentional.* It must have a compelling reason to engage and motivate students. As Sarason had asked, "Why geometry?" Moreover, why *this* branch of geometry and not another? This is what we found to be lacking in educational reform efforts and missing in the two decades' worth of educational conference sessions we attended, in the papers we read, and in the many education reform projects we implemented.

We asked countless teachers why they were teaching this or that particular topic within their subject. If the essence of mathematics, for example, is patterns and relationships, an essential feature to all of nature and the man-made world, why are you teaching how to factor trinomials? What is the bigger point? Why do biology teachers begin with cells? Why not zoology, which is far more relatable to youth, or, if you must start with cells, why not begin with interesting questions, such as, "how do people grow" or "why do people get sick"? Few teachers could give a compelling answer as to *why* they taught what they taught. Most said it was because the students needed it for the final exam, the next course, or to graduate, or they needed it for the Scholastic Assessment Test or American College Test or for college or the state exam, or because it was a state standard. However, rarely did they address what *students* found intriguing to learn.

The question of purpose did not end with the individual teacher. It was characteristic of departments and entire schools. What passed for a school's purpose was the usual rhetoric: "college and career readiness," "life-long learning," "critical thinking," "citizenship," or "fulfilling a student's potential." We knew these phrases were mere rhetoric because it was difficult to see how they affected curricular and instructional choices. If schools were really designed to instill in students a desire for lifelong learning, why were so many students bored? Moreover, if school leaders were genuinely interested in preparing all students for college success, why did they shrink from using readily available data on how their graduates fared in college when we presented such data to them? In our experience, nearly every intractable internal issue of schooling has its roots in the inability to adequately define a relevant core purpose that is situated in the realities of the profound sociopolitical, economic, demographic, and technological changes of this new era.

The question about the purpose of education for a new era is what propelled us to research and chronicle the material for part I of this book. What were the earliest purposes of education and how did the profound changes in society lead to new purposes? What *should* the purpose be for our times? How have the historical and contemporary shadows of extreme wealth inequality, nativism, racism, and anti-science sentiments dimmed the learning opportunities for today's children? At the end of our MSP in 2010, we began to write this book on our lessons learned about the need for a new purpose in education and why reform efforts were so difficult. Then something unexpected happened.

In August 2011, author F. Joseph Merlino, president of 21PSTEM, received a call from the Philadelphia International Visitor's Center (IVC), with whom we had no previous contact. One of IVC's roles was to arrange and escort delegations of international visitors on "study tours" supported by the U.S. Agency for International Development (USAID). In this case, USAID had awarded a small contract to World Learning, Inc. to introduce an Egyptian delegation to several U.S. science, technology, engineering, and mathematics (STEM) schools and STEM educators. The city they chose to visit was Philadelphia. The ten-person Egyptian delegation was led by the Egyptian Minister of Education, Dr. Ahmed Gamal El-Din Moussa. Other high-level education officials included Dr. Reda Abouserie, the First Deputy Education Minister, and Ms. Hala Elserafy, an education program officer at USAID-Egypt.

World Learning contacted IVC to arrange the study tour, but IVC had no experience with STEM schools, so they did an online search of "STEM in Philadelphia" and found 21PSTEM. IVC requested our assistance to help World Learning prepare for the Egyptian delegation's Philadelphia visit and we accepted, though we had no experience with USAID or Egypt. On the first day of their visit to Philadelphia, the minister explained that he wanted to develop a new model of education in Egypt. Their country's education system had been the subject of a mammoth years-long national effort to overhaul it but with limited success. The delegation visited several STEM schools in Philadelphia during the next few days and concluded their visit with a technical briefing from 21PSTEM on what we had learned from our twenty years of implementing math and science reform projects. We invited two of our U.S. partners to give a briefing as well: Frederic Bertley, vice president of The Franklin Institute (TFI), and Janice Morrison, president of Teaching Institute for Excellence in STEM (TIES).

Near the end of the briefing, the minister announced he was planning to open the first public model Egyptian STEM boarding high school the following month, in September 2011. The minister had a much grander vision than simply establishing a new high school. This new school and others to be built like it were to serve as models for a new *system* of education in Egypt. These high schools would represent a new approach to education that was not bound by tradition or existing standards or assessments. But there was major work to do. The new school's curriculum and assessment system had not been developed. The school had no books or labs. None of the teachers had received any professional development, and the acting principal had just been fired and replaced. Nonetheless, the new residential high school was to open in September 2011 with about 150 academically talented tenth-grade boys chosen from all over Egypt.

As it would turn out, the opportunity to repurpose education for a new era would come not in the U.S., but in Egypt. Within a few months of the Philadelphia meeting, USAID-Egypt awarded a short-term contract to World Learning to do a "strength and needs assessment" of the STEM school and provide emergency professional development to its teachers who were using a makeshift curriculum for the first semester. World Learning turned to its three STEM partners it had recently met in Philadelphia to do the technical work: 21PSTEM, TFI, and TIES. And so, in January 2012, we (Bertley, Morrison, and author Merlino) found ourselves in Cairo.

With USAID funding that would eventually total more than $54 million, we were afforded the extraordinary opportunity to take all we had learned in the United States to help Egyptians define a new purpose of education for their new era. We were given the freedom to work with Egyptian educators to design and implement an entirely new integrated curriculum and assessment system that would be exempted from the national exams and existing standards. Ultimately, the credit for the establishment of these new schools belongs to the Egyptian Ministry of Education.

One Egyptian model STEM public residential high school has since grown to twenty-one schools[2] spread throughout Egypt. Students from these schools have won as many international awards as never before. Hundreds of Egyptian STEM students have received full scholarships to attend respected domestic and international universities, many in the United States. As a result, these new model schools are influencing the rest of education in Egypt. In chapters 14, 15, and 16, additionally co-authored with Dr. Reda and Ms. Hala, we describe our role in this still unfolding story and show its relevance to schools in the United States and elsewhere.

In chapter 17, we describe how we helped repurpose education in Bosnia and Herzegovina and started the same process in the Greater Philadelphia area. In our concluding chapter, we offer practical ways to initiate and sustain the repurposing of education for a new era that can bring renewed hope for the future of education and our country.

NOTES

1. Joseph Henry, "Philosophy of Education." *The American Journal of Education*, Ed. Henry Barnard, 1856, Volume 1, p. 43, https://openlibrary .org /books / OL7081980M/The_American_journal_of_education.

2. This is the number of Egyptian Model STEM high schools as of 2024

Chapter 14

Welcome to the Dream

Co-authored with Reda Abou
Serie and Hala El-Serafy

Hope lies in dreams, in imagination and in the courage of those who dare to make dreams into reality.

—Jonas Salk, developer of the Polio vaccine[1]

OUR ARRIVAL

We did not know what to expect when we left Philadelphia in January 2012. A representative from World Learning greeted us in the lobby of our Cairo hotel and broke the news that there had been a change in leadership in the Ministry of Education. Fortunately, before he left, the minister whom we had met in August had issued a decree (an administrative edict) to establish the 6 October STEM School for Boys on the outskirts of Cairo.[2] His first deputy minister, Dr. Reda Abouserie, who had been a member of the Egyptian delegation, would carry on and oversee the new model STEM school.

The next morning a driver took us to the new school.[3] The school, originally planned to be used as an advanced technical high school, was located on a large tract of barren land thirty miles west of Cairo. There was nothing around except sand. Because of its remote location, the residential school was limited to boys. By the time of its opening, the Government of Egypt had constructed the school's new dorms and buildings. We were waiting in the principal's office wondering what would come next when Dr. Reda burst through the door beaming and smiling. With arms wide open, he exclaimed, "Welcome to the dream!"

A YOUNG COUNTRY WITHIN AN OLD CIVILIZATION

Egypt is an ancient civilization, but in 2010 nearly two in three Egyptians were under thirty years of age.[4] The sheer volume of youth in any country can be both a blessing and a challenge. It is a blessing because it gives a country the vigor and freshness to break away from old ways that have kept it stuck. With a youthful workforce, a country's labor force can stretch into the future for many decades without the burden of supporting a large aging population as is the case with more advanced countries, such as Japan. But a young country also presents huge risks if this large number of youth cannot find employment and life-sustaining wages. As Ghada Barsoum, a sociologist in the Department of Public Policy and Administration at the American University in Cairo, remarked about the relationship between the quality of the labor supply and the demand side:

> Egypt currently has its largest cohort of youth in its history and equipping this large group with the skills necessary to compete in a globalized knowledge economy is a formidable task within an overly burdened and under-funded education system. On the labor demand side, the slow pace of job creation in the formal economy, and persistent low productivity and underemployment within the informal economy are limiting young people's options.[5]

The underlying economic and political conditions that had led to Egypt's revolution were many and intertwined. Youth discontentment was a factor.[6] The jobless rate for youth between the ages of eighteen and twenty-nine was nearly 60 percent.[7] Against this backdrop, when we toured the 6 October STEM school and met the students, its promise and potential were palpable.

The Egyptian Human Capital Crisis

A key driving force behind the STEM schools was the urgency for Egypt to develop the talents of its human capital, which was predominantly young. Human capital is defined as "the skills and capacities that reside in people and that are put to productive use" and can be more important for long-term economic prosperity than virtually any other factor.[8] An economic analysis done by the Organization for Economic Cooperation Development (OECD) argues that it is the *kind* of education youth receive that is connected to economic development, not merely the level of education attainment. Using historical data from the Program of International Student Assessment (PISA) discussed earlier, economists projected each OECD member country's gains in their gross domestic product (GDP) for each incremental rise in their country's PISA scores. The conclusion was that "relatively small improvements in the skills of a nation's labour force (human capital) can have very large impacts on future well-being . . . which far outstrip(s) the value of the short-run business-cycle."[9]

Before the establishment of the STEM schools, Egypt's Global Competitiveness Index ranked seventieth out of 133 countries. A survey listed an inadequately educated workforce as the third most problematic factor in doing business in Egypt. The quality of Egypt's educational system and the quality of math and science education ranked 123rd and 124th, respectively.[10] Dr. Ahmed Zewail, the first Egyptian scientist to win a Nobel Prize in Science (1999) and a man greatly revered throughout Egypt, had warned that "Human resources are just tremendous in Egypt, but we need the science base; we need the correct science base. . . . Investing in science education and curiosity-driven research is investing in the future."[11]

A related national problem was the small pipeline of high school and university science graduates who could help drive economic growth. While many Egyptian students aspire to go to universities, there was an oversupply of Egyptian university graduates for the labor market to absorb. Humanities majors usually graduate without acquiring employable skills. Accordingly, many Egyptian university graduates were unemployed or underemployed.[12]

The TIMSS Shock

In 2003, Egyptian eighth graders participated for the first time in the Trends in International Math and Science Study (TIMSS). The results were a shock. The Egyptian TIMSS scores for both math and science were not only below the international average, but below other Middle East and North African (MENA) countries' scores as well.[13] In addition to Egypt's eighth-grade students performing below many other MENA countries, a majority of them scored at the lowest level in math[14] (see figure 14.1). Compared to the rest of the world's students who participated in TIMSS, Egypt scored 406 in math and 421 in science when the international average was 467 and 474 respectively.

The 2007 TIMSS eighth-grade results were even worse (math 391, science 408).[15] Ninth-grade students were reluctant to pursue the science track in high school; only 10 percent did so. The rest pursued either vocational education or the literary (humanities) track,[16] but most of the higher-paying occupations require some degree of technical expertise in STEM. In addition, Egyptian students graduated from high school with almost no skills in doing independent research, presentations, issue-based problem-solving, or working cooperatively in teams—all highly valued twenty-first-century skills.[17] How could things be turned around?

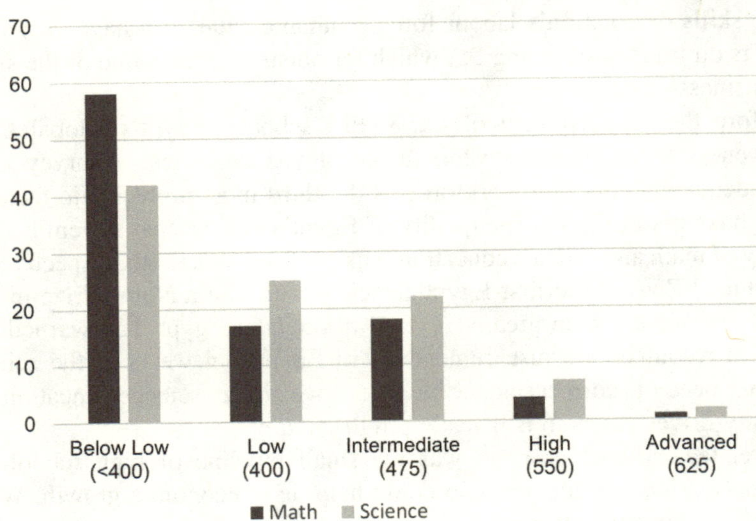

Figure 14.1   Preparatory Level Pupils' Performance on TIMSS (2003). *Source*: National Strategic Plan for Pre-University Reform in Egypt 2007. Annex 2, Figure 9 p. 67.

AN EDUCATION SYSTEM IN NEED OF REFORM

To conduct an adequate strength and needs assessment of the new 6 October STEM school, we had to understand how it was situated in the context of Egypt's K-12 education system. The system is managed by a massive, centralized institution, the Ministry of Education and Technical Education (MOETE). In 2010, Egypt had an enrollment of 18.4 million students in nearly 54,000 schools,[18] making it the largest K-12 education system in the MENA region.

A critical function of the MOETE is to administer a series of national exams at the end of twelfth grade known as the *Thanaweya Ammas*.[19] Students must pass these exams to be awarded a high school certificate. If a student desires to attend a university, they are matched to an available university determined by a centralized computerized algorithm based on a student's residence, subjects of interest, and their Thanaweya Amma scores. Egypt provides qualifying students a free education at twenty-six public universities (except for some modest fee-based special programs.) The particular public university where a student is permitted to enroll, and their course of study is based on a single composite score on a series of these Thanaweya Ammas.

As might be expected, Egyptians are conflicted about this arrangement. On one hand, the exams are objective, thereby minimizing the possibility of corruption. Everyone has a right to take the exams and access copies of previous exams. The process for admission to universities is fair and provides equal opportunities to all students. Everyone knows the rules. On the other hand, this system creates an extremely high-stakes testing environment that puts enormous pressure and stress on students and their families. And there are other negative consequences.

National High School Curricula

The unique importance of the national Thanaweya Ammas exams lends itself to the use of national high school curricula and common textbooks. Parents and students want certainty as to what will be on the exams. For this reason, the national exams closely follow the national textbooks. In a sense, the curricula *are* the textbooks. Because of the need for certainty as to *the* correct answers, the textbooks emphasize definitions and sets of procedures that can be memorized rather than novel problem-solving. In turn, the Thanaweya Ammas are constructed to require the recall of facts and definitions and the demonstration of procedures and calculations. But these questions must be detailed and difficult enough to get a sufficient spread of scores so that students can be ranked for university placement.

Unlike the Scholastic Assessment Test (SAT), the Thanaweya Ammas are the sole determination of a young person's future educational pathway increasing the pressure even more. About four in five parents hire private tutors. Many twelfth-grade math teachers, for example, report poor student attendance as their students are busy receiving tutoring for the national math exam. Indeed, many teachers hire themselves out as tutors for the extra pay! Overall private expenditures on education were estimated at 3.7 percent of GDP in 2004–2005, over 60 percent of which goes to tutoring.[20] Indeed, total household expenditures for private tutoring exceeded total public expenditures for education across all levels.[21]

Given this iron triangle of high-stakes national exams, nationally aligned textbooks, and pervasive private tutoring, how could the system be changed to improve student performance, especially in math, science, and technological literacy?

THE NATIONAL STRATEGIC PLAN FOR PRE-UNIVERSITY EDUCATION REFORM

In year 2006, the Egyptian Ministry of Education convened working groups involving participation of over 160 individuals from diverse groups of stakeholders including national and international education experts, universities, civil society, parents, teachers, and donor organizations. Together they researched and compiled a 575-page "National Strategic Plan for Pre-University Education Reform in Egypt 2007–2012."[22] This plan aimed to reform pre-university education through twelve main programs, but perhaps most importantly it underscored the critical problem with the national exam system and use of national textbook-based curricula, concluding that "Ultimately, Egypt will have to upgrade, modernize, and revamp its entire exam system, including the Thanaweya Amma."[23] The National Plan further promised reforms in curriculum, active learning, and new forms of assessment "aimed at encouraging and measuring the development of cognitive skills, critical thinking, and problem-solving strategies required for lifelong learning."[24]

The "guiding principle" for accomplishing these outcomes would be the use of technology.[25] But the average class size of forty students in the public schools did not help matters.[26] Still, the elephant in the room was the Thanaweya Amma exam system. The National Plan covered everything *except* how to replace this system with a different nationally standardized examination system that would support the above goals of the National Plan. In short, the Thanaweya Amma national exams and their relationship to university admissions was the linchpin to Egypt's entire secondary and postsecondary system. As long as this linchpin was in place, any secondary improvement efforts would be extremely difficult to achieve.

An Important Attempt to Reform the Thanaweya Amma

Following the government's approval of the strategic plan, the MOETE started an effort to reform the Thanaweya Amma with the Ministry of Higher Education. The two ministries established joint committees, which worked very hard for over a two-year period (2008 and 2009) to come up with a proposal to reform the Thanaweya Amma. Almost all donor agencies, including the United States Agency for International Development (USAID), participated in these efforts by providing technical assistance, national and international experts and sharing international best practices. The theme of the reform was "reforming secondary schools' system and admission to universities."

These huge efforts concluded with specific recommendations for reforming the Thanaweya Ammas. Chief among them was that students passing the high school exit exam successfully should not be the single criterion for admitting students to universities. Instead, there should be admission tests, similar to the SAT 1 & 2 & American College Test, that could be used by universities to select students who have the knowledge and aptitude for admission to the relevant programs in each university. Other recommendations included curriculum reform and introducing common subjects in different branches of secondary education, as well as introducing modern approaches to teaching and learning.

On May 9, 2009, a national conference for education reform was held and attended by President Mubarak, who expressed his unlimited support for the proposed reform. However, a few months later the ruling party, the National Democratic Party, which represented the majority in the parliament, refused to endorse the recommendations related to reforming the Thanaweya Amma. Everyone at MOE was deeply disappointed. That was a critical time and spurred Ms. Hala and Dr. Reda to think of alternative strategies and approaches to reform.

THE DREAM TAKES SHAPE

A new dream for change began to take shape at a May 2009 conference in Washington, D.C., attended by Ms. Hala and Dr. Reda. They visited nearby Thomas Jefferson High School for Science and Technology (TJHSST) in Fairfax, Virginia. At the time, *U.S. News and World Report* ranked TJHSST the highest among STEM schools in the United States. In TJHSST, Dr. Reda and Ms. Hala[27] saw the possibility of a new model high school that could fulfill many of the curriculum and teaching reforms called for in Egypt's 2006 National Plan. Upon returning to Cairo, they drafted a concept paper for a model residential Egyptian STEM high school for talented students. A key provision was that students would be exempted from the Thanaweya Amma exams. They presented the proposal to then-minister Dr. Yousry El Gamal, who responded favorably. But he was replaced in January 2010. A year later Dr. Ahmed Gamal El-Din Moussa was appointed minister of education. To make an informed decision about the STEM school proposal, Dr. Moussa held a series of consultations with opinion and education leaders, prominent scientists, and civil society organizations. However, before making a final decision to accept the proposal, he wanted to see for himself a sample of U.S. STEM schools. This is how we came to meet the Egyptian delegation in Philadelphia in August 2011.

Clouds of Uncertainty

As we sat with Dr. Reda in the principal's office at the 6 October STEM School for Boys, the dream seemed clouded with uncertainties. Would the newly appointed Minister of Education, Mr. Gamal El-Araby Ahmad, continue to support the concept of the new model schools? Would he still exempt students from the Thanaweya Amma exams? Would he continue to underwrite the extra costs for a public *boarding* school as well as extra incentive pay for the teachers? Would he allow the 6 October STEM teachers to use a "non-textbook approach" emphasizing inquiry-based labs and projects? If not, the dream would die.

On January 28, 2012, USAID released a $25 million Request for Application for U.S. bidders to propose support for three to five new model residential STEM high schools. World Learning applied with 21PSTEM, the Teaching Institute for Excellence in STEM (TIES), and the Franklin Institute as their technical partners. We would have to wait eight months to find out if we won.

In the meantime, the fledgling 6 October STEM schools' new teachers urgently needed support in a chaotic, ever-changing swirl of external and internal events. Despite the inherent uncertainty of the situation, we saw this as an extraordinary opportunity. The highest levels of the Egyptian Ministry of Education had entrusted us to help them launch a new national high school model. It was a bit surreal. The authors had just finished writing part I of this book about the purpose of education when we were presented with the opportunity to test our thesis.

Dr. Frederic Bertley, Vice President of the Franklin Institute science museum (TFI), took charge of providing emergency teacher professional development on project-based learning and student-centered pedagogy. With USAID support, he flew his teachers from Philadelphia's Science Leadership Academy (SLA) to Cairo to do emergency teacher training.[28] In many ways, the SLA teachers were perfect for the job because the teachers wrote their curriculum using a non-textbook-based approach with a variety of instructional materials.

Ms. Jan Morrison, president of TIES, a national consultancy, had worked with many public school systems to start new STEM schools. She and her consultants developed new school start-up procedures and resource manuals for the Egyptian government. Many of the STEM schools she had helped launch featured engineering-based capstone projects which involves a design challenge to address a real-world problem that requires knowledge from multiple disciplines. Capstones soon became a visible manifestation of how different the Egypt STEM schools would be from the country's traditional high schools.

The role of 21PSTEM as the third organizational member of the technical team was to help the Egyptians develop the new curriculum that included capstones as well as new assessments. However, as we demonstrated in part I, the construction of such a curriculum requires an overarching *purpose* informed by the profound changes that have or are taking place in a country. Thus, it was not enough to establish a new Egyptian model high school as a "STEM high school." The new STEM model had to be *about* something that reflected these profound changes. What then should be the aim of the model STEM schools? Simply importing a U.S. model would not do. It had to be an *Egyptian* model, but to what end?

Addressing Egypt's Grand Challenges

During the technical team's first trip to the 6 October STEM school, author F. Joseph Merlino led a teacher workshop to define the STEM schools' purpose. The teachers were arranged into small groups and two questions were posed to them: (1) What are your aspirations for the future of Egypt, and (2) What kinds of knowledge, abilities, and character do you want your students to acquire by the time they graduate? The teachers wrote their responses on long strips of chart paper. They could not just write "biology." They had to be more specific, e.g., genetics, cells, zoology, botany, etc., and state *why* it was important for the student to learn these subjects. The sentence strips were then collected and pasted onto the classroom walls into one of three categories:

1. Things to develop *within* a student, the *interior*, such as self-awareness and habits of mind;
2. Things regarding *relations with others*, the social and moral; and
3. Specific knowledge and skills that are important for a student to acquire, the *external objects of knowledge.*

The contents within these three dimensions taken together would constitute the STEM schools' purpose. The entries filled two walls of the classroom. The teachers scanned the walls looking for the one big idea that would encapsulate the 6 October STEM school's purpose. Once found, it could help us organize the curriculum and other educative goals around this purpose.

Finally, we saw what we were looking for. It read, *"Equip students to address Egypt's Grandest Challenges."* One cannot go to Egypt without noticing these challenges. The bright green farmland beside the Nile is threatened by a rising tide of ocean water from global warming. There is an abundance of sunlight but little solar energy production. The population is increasing—from 1960 to 2010, Egypt's population tripled from 27 million to 83 million,[29] while fresh water remained limited. Traffic congestion is everywhere while light rail transportation is underdeveloped. Thus, when we asked the 6 October STEM School teachers to list their nominees for Egypt's grand challenges, their choices were readily apparent to all:

- Address the effects of climate change
- Improve the use of arid areas
- Improve sources of clean water
- Improve the use of alternative energies
- Reduce pollution
- Recycle and retain garbage for recycling (now sent to Japan and China)
- Improve urban congestion

- Deal with the exponential population growth
- Increase the industrial base for Egypt
- Increase opportunities for Egyptians to stay and work in Egypt
- Work to eradicate public health issues/disease

The teachers then selected two or three of the most salient entries from the other two dimensions. The result was eight education goals along three dimensions. Together these eight goals, with the Grand Challenges being the lead goal, constituted the 6 October STEM School's core purpose.

External Knowledge
- Equipping students to address the scientific, mathematical, and social dimensions of Egypt's *grandest challenges as a country*.
- Learning the content and ways of knowing that display scientific, mathematical, and technological literacy and subject-matter proficiency.

Interior Abilities/Sensibilities
- Having self-motivation, self–direction, and a hunger for continued learning.
- The ability to think independently, creatively, and analytically.
- The ability to question, collaborate, and communicate at a high level.

Social/Moral
- To be socially responsible leaders.
- Able to apply their understanding to advance creativity, innovation, and invention with a real-world vision with a consciousness and an eye toward a more contemporary Egypt.
- Be admitted to and successful in a university course of studies and then be employable in the Egyptian labor market as well as the world labor market.

All eight goals are interrelated. One cannot address Egypt's grand challenges without having scientific, mathematical, and technological literacy and subject-matter proficiency. Addressing novel and difficult problems requires the ability to think independently, creatively, and analytically. Yet collaboration is necessary to solve big problems, so good interpersonal and social skills are essential. None of these learning goals matter if one does not grow up to be a morally responsible person. The idea of preparing students to address Egypt's Grandest Challenges, challenges that affect every Egyptian, was readily approved by the Ministry.

Once the Egyptian model STEM school settled on a particular purpose, the entire curriculum and school operations would have to be designed to contribute to that purpose—all the courses, projects, labs, capstones, field trips, internships, extracurricular activities, relationships with peers, teachers and mentors, and residential life. The importance of a clear educative purpose to a school, where all facets of the school activities and programs serve that purpose, cannot be overstated. From our experience working in hundreds of schools and school districts, and as documented in the educational research literature, we often found programmatic incoherence and misalignment that hindered student learning.[30] A clearly defined purpose, relevant to the times, that would provide a rationale for curricular choices was necessary for programmatic coherence and alignment. Dr. Reda and the minister ensured that all the components of the Egyptian STEM school model would embrace the school's purpose as defined by these eight education goals.

Curriculum Design Principles

How does one go about actually developing a curriculum from scratch once a model high school's purpose and its interrelated subcomponent education goals are defined? We started by first proposing a set of "design principles" to the minister of education. A design principle is an engineering term that reflects the needs of the client together with the constraints on those needs. The leading design principle was *equipping students to address Egypt's grand challenges.* We felt if we could find a way to meet this goal, the other seven education goals would follow.

A second design principle was to consider *a student's entire school experience* to be the curriculum. In this way, administrators, teachers, staff, students, and parents would have a clear sense of what the school was about—its identity—thereby creating a distinctive culture. A third design principle was semester-long capstone projects. A fourth design principle was that the subjects needed to be integrated or harmonized with each other as much as possible using the Grand Challenges as the organizing basis. One cannot understand the harmful effects of pollution on the human body, for instance, without studying *both* biology and chemistry. We had to design the curriculum so students would study the different STEM subjects in a coordinated way.

School Design Principles

On a parallel track, the Ministry had adopted school design principles that were extremely complementary to and supportive of the new curriculum and assessment system.

- Establishing residential accommodations to be able to draw talented students from all over Egypt;
- Exempting students from the Thanaweya Amma exams;
- Establishing an alternative pathway to university admissions;
- Scheduling mathematics, mechanics, geology, chemistry, physics, and biology to be taught every week (but not every day). To address any Grand

Challenge requires students to learn relevant mathematics, geology, chemistry, physics, and biology content close enough in time for students to see their interrelationships;
- Allocating equal time for arts and humanities courses as the STEM courses;
- Counting the capstone projects for the tenth- and eleventh-grade students for *60 percent* of a student's final semester grade in tenth and eleventh grade;
- Installing digital fabrication and science labs;
- Using a non-textbook-based approach;
- Providing laptops for every student;
- Using the internet and multiple text resources; and
- Allowing students to interact with university professors and business.

During the same trip in early January 2012, Jan Morrison from TIES led the 6 October STEM school teachers to create their first semester-long capstone project. Morrison challenged the teachers to think of a capstone project that related to their country's most vexing scientific issue. The teachers eagerly embraced the task. They articulated a grand challenge of reconciling the paradox of scarcity amid abundance: How can Egypt's abundant solar energy be more efficiently harnessed to alleviate the scarcity of affordable electricity? There are no textbooks for these types of capstones. Teachers must use a non-textbook-based approach. To do so requires extensive teacher training. Thus, in early March 2012, Dr. Frederic Bertley and his team of SLA teachers conducted a weeklong workshop with the 6 October STEM school teachers to develop the Egyptian solar energy capstone lesson plans. Included in the workshop was a portfolio with a detailed scope of work, benchmarks, curriculum examples, pedagogical constructs, and rubrics. The goal was to develop one capstone per semester (two per grade level per year).

As we were scrambling in the spring of 2012 to support the 6 October STEM school, we learned that the ministry scheduled a second STEM school to open in the fall of 2012—the Maadi STEM School for Girls. Given the short-term nature of our contract, the Ministry decided that the same grand challenges and the same design principles of the 6 October STEM school be the template for *all* the other model STEM schools.

THE BIG PROJECT

In August 2012, USAID notified World Learning that it, along with its three technical partners, had won a $25 million grant to implement the STEM school model plan. We had no time to waste. The existing October 6 STEM school teachers needed emergency professional development as they entered their second year of teaching and a new cohort of hired teachers urgently needed training as well. The new Maadi STEM School needed everything: teacher and principal training, labs, new school start-up procedures, and accommodations for the girls.

In October 2012, yet again, a new and equally supportive minister of education took the helm and issued a decree (#382) on setting forth the criteria for the selection of the STEM students and teachers from all over Egypt. The decree also codified as law the STEM curriculum and school design principles. That same month, World Learning convened a large meeting of the entire Egyptian and U.S. project team in Philadelphia to plan the next steps. On the curriculum side, a plan was developed that would involve scores of Egyptian professors, teachers, and ministry officials who had expertise in science, math, and engineering content. The cooperation of the Ministry and university professors was critically important. In this regard, Dr. Reda's and Ms. Hala's diplomatic skills were indispensable.

THE GRAND CHALLENGES DESIGN STUDIO

In January 2013, sixty Egyptian participants including Ministry of Education officials, university professors, and STEM high school teachers participated in a special three-day workshop known as a design studio. Their task was to develop the curriculum based on the design principles as codified by the minister. The U.S. side of the project team had meticulously practiced how we would proceed. That said, we wondered how the plan would be received by people who had never before worked together or with us. We were working in a different culture with participants who spoke a foreign language and had different educational traditions. Exactly what would a "purpose-driven" grand challenges curriculum look like?

Our project team's goal was to collect data from the Egyptian participants that would provide insight into questions about how to construct an integrated curriculum based on Egypt's eleven grand challenges. The Egyptians' expertise and imagination were needed. Most importantly, the project team needed them to embrace the vision of the STEM schools and believe that they could contribute to designing a totally new concept of what the curriculum could be.

The participants were arranged in a variety of small multi-disciplinary groups. Each was given a page that was formatted like the cover of a prestigious international news magazine, but otherwise blank. They were invited to dream about their aspirations for a new Egypt. They had to create a headline for what they would like the cover story to be in ten years. This exercise served to excite and engage the participants to push their imaginations of what *could be* above the ceiling of the present reality.

The project team next introduced the grand challenges and asked participants to think about the relationships between each grand challenge and depict these relations on a big piece of chart paper. Not surprisingly, it turned out that each participant had their own scheme. Three things became quite clear from this exercise: (1) All of the grand challenges were interconnected; (2) there was no one grand challenge that if solved all the others would follow; and (3) there was no obvious starting point. This exercise had the benefit of dislodging *linear* thinking among the participants and moving them toward *systems* thinking. The grand challenges are interrelated systems much like an ecosystem or the human body. Cause and effect are not always linear; rather, they are often *circular,* involving either positive or negative feedback loops—virtuous or vicious cycles. Figure 14.1 shows what one teacher drew.

This kind of systems thinking suggested that a student acquiring knowledge of the separate disciplines (math, biology, chemistry, etc.,) is a necessary but not sufficient condition if they are to address the grand challenges. Nonetheless, the project curriculum specialists had to ensure the new curriculum had adequate depth in each of the five disciplines. This task brought us to the second day of the design studio.

That day we put the Egyptians in small groups according to their discipline, i.e., a biology table, chemistry table, and so on. We then asked each group to examine all the grand challenges and consider the content and skills from their disciplines that a student should know. But they had to be specific. In response to the grand challenge of public health, for example, the members of the biology table could not just say "cells." They had to specify *what it was* about cells that related to public health—and *why*. This last step

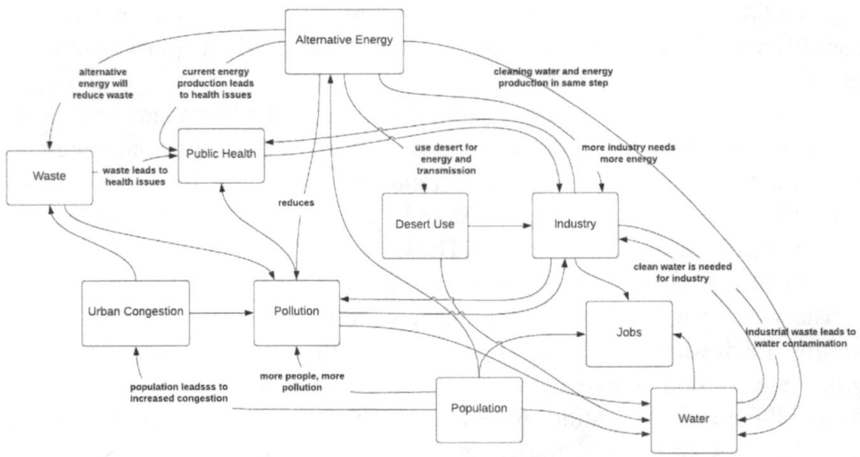

Figure 14.2 A Teacher's Rendition of Connections between the Grand Challenges.
Source: 21PSTEM.

was important as it forced participants to think outside their usual pathways and teaching habits. The U.S. facilitators asked the Egyptian participants to examine how different content in their field applied to real and urgent problems. The facilitators pressed them to make their cases as to why it was important for the STEM students to study this and not that about biology, for example. A recorder was at each table to document each participant's contribution, organize their results, and then reflect the results to the group for validation.

On the third and final day, the sixty Egyptians were arranged into *multi*-disciplinary groups around eight tables. Each table included a math, biology, chemistry, physics, geology, and engineering person. They brought along the discipline-based worksheets they had created the day before. The facilitators then asked each table to take a "deep dive" and discuss the *inter*-disciplinary connections involved with the grand challenges. Each table's task was to look for connections between the subjects. Strong natural linkages between the sciences, including mathematics, quickly emerged. To understand certain concepts in earth or biological science, for example, students had to understand certain atomic and molecular structures and processes in chemistry. Likewise, for students to understand certain concepts in chemistry or physics, they needed to know certain mathematics concepts and acquire computational skills. Time did not permit every interdisciplinary group to discuss every grand challenge. Instead, we asked each table to focus on just a few of the grand challenges.

By mixing disciplines at each table, the hope was that the participants would recognize common characteristics of learning in addition to scientific and mathematical content. Not only did they do that, but they also identified *additional* subject-matter knowledge needed to address the grand challenges including education, communications, language, history, culture, economics, governmental policy, resources, infrastructure, technology, and ethics. As a result, the Egyptian participants quickly embraced the vision of an integrated curriculum without losing their disciplinary identity. As they engaged in animated discussions, the scope and complexity of the grand challenges emerged.

Our team of U.S. facilitators helped the Egyptian groups focus on what students would need to know and be able to do to prepare them to solve the grand challenges. The participants engaged in lively conversations with people with whom they seldom worked, focusing on issues they found both intellectually stimulating and highly relevant. We collected many pages of chart paper full of notes and data. Each page was marked with colors denoting their relationships to various grand challenges. There was palpable excitement in the room as they felt they were laying the foundation for the future of Egypt. Everything about the work was revolutionary.

By the end of the three days, the grand challenge design studio had exceeded expectations. Each disciplinary group had the opportunity to advocate for the inclusion of their respective discipline's content and skills to address the grand challenges. At the same time, other seeds were planted. The design studio's structure made it readily apparent to even the most hardened disciplinary professor that the preparation of students to solve the grand challenges could not be achieved through their discipline alone or through a traditional instructional approach where each subject is taught isolated from the others. Perhaps most importantly, it brought university faculty and high school teachers to work together, each playing a different but equally important role.

But how do you design a new curriculum from this data?

NOTES

1. Jonas Salk, from the 1977 Acceptance Address "Are We Being Good Ancestors?" given upon his receipt of the Jawaharlal Nehru Award for International Understanding; used with permission of the Jonas Salk Legacy Foundation. According to the site, "About," 2023, https://www.salk.edu/about/history-of-salk/jonas-salk/. "Contrary to the era's prevailing scientific opinion, Salk believed his vaccine, composed of 'killed' polio virus, could immunize without risk of infecting the patient. Salk administered the vaccine to volunteers who had not had polio, including himself, his lab scientist, his wife, and their children. All developed anti-polio antibodies and experienced no negative reactions to the vaccine. In 1954, national testing began on one million children, ages six to nine, who became known as the Polio Pioneers. On April 12, 1955, the results were announced: the vaccine was safe and effective."

2. The name commemorates Egypt's Armed Forces Day, a public holiday that observes the starting date of the 1973 Arab-Israeli War.

3. It was a policy of USAID that none of the U.S. teams drive in Cairo.

4. Central Agency for Public Mobilization and Statistics, "Egypt in Figures: Population Estimates by Sex and Age," May 2010, accessed February 14, 2023, https://www.capmas.gov.eg/Pages/Publications.aspx?page_id=5104&Year=23602.

5. Ghada Barsoum, "No Jobs and Bad Jobs: Defusing Egypt's Demographic Youth Bulge Requires Job Creation—and a Safety Net," *Cairo Review* 10 (2013): 160, https://www.thecairoreview.com/wp-content/uploads/2014/12/CR10_Barsoum.pdf.

6. Ghada Barsoum, "Arab Youth: The Challenges of Education, Employment and Civic Participation," *OIDA International Journal of Sustainable Development* 5 (2012): 39–54.

7. United Nations Development Programme and the Institute of National Planning, Egypt, "Human Development Report: Youth in Egypt," January 1, 2010, 151, https://planipolis.iiep.unesco.org/sites/default/files/ressources/egypt_hdr_2010_en.pdf.

8. World Economic Forum, "The Human Capital Report 2013," accessed February 14, 2023, 3, https://www3.weforum.org/docs/WEF_HumanCapitalReport _2013.pdf.

9. Eric A. Hanushek and Ludger Woessmann, "The High Cost of Low Educational Performance: The Long-Run Economic Impact of Improving PISA Outcomes," OECD, 2010, 6, http://www.oecd.org/pisa/44417824.pdf.

10. World Economic Forum, "The Global Competitiveness Report 2009-2010," 137, https://www3.weforum.org/docs/WEF_GlobalCompetitivenessReport_2009 -10.pdf.

11. "Ahmed Zewai: Interview," The Nobel Prize, December 1999, para. 15, https://www.nobelprize.org/prizes/chemistry/1999/zewail/interview/.

12. Barsoum, "No Jobs."

13. World Bank, "Report No. 42796863-EG: Arab Republic of Egypt: Improving Quality, Equality, and Efficiency in the Education Sector: Fostering a Competent Generation of Youth," June 29, 2007, 10, https://documents1.worldbank.org/ curated/en/ 151468021861883/pdf/428630ESW0P08910gray0cover01PUBLIC1.pdf. (Report used data from TIMSS 2003, https://timss.bc.edu/timss2003i/intl_reports .html.)

14. Egypt Ministry of Education, "National Strategic Plan for Pre-University Education Reform in Egypt 2007, Annex 2, Figure 9," https://planipolis.iiep.unesco .org/en/2007/national-strategic-plan-pre-university-education-reform-egypt-200708 -201112-includes.

15. TIMSS 2007 International Mathematics Report: Findings from IEA's Trends in International Mathematics and Science Study at the Fourth and Eighth Grades, 35, https://timss.bc.edu/TIMSS2007/PDF/T07_M_IR_Chapter1.pdf.

16. Egypt Ministry of Education, "The Strategic Plan of Pre-University Education 2014-2030," 2014, 42, https://planipolis.iiep.unesco.org/sites/default/files/ressources/ egypt_strategic_plan_pre-university_education_2014-2030_eng_0.pdf.

17. Partnership for 21st Century Skills, "Framework for 21st Century Learning," 2009, http://www.p21.org.

18. Central Agency for Public Mobilization and Statistics, "Egypt in Figures," 97, https://censusinfo.capmas.gov.eg/Metadata-en-v4.2/index.php/catalog/215/download/309.

19. Taken in June or August.

20. Arab Republic of Egypt Ministry of Education, "National Strategic Plan," 49.

21. Arab Republic of Egypt Ministry of Education, "National Strategic Plan," 83.

22. Arab Republic of Egypt Ministry of Education, "National Strategic Plan for Pre-University Education Reform in Egypt," 2007, https://planipolis.iiep.unesco.org/ sites/default/files/ressources/egyptstrategicplanpre-universityeducation.pdf.

23. Arab Republic of Egypt Ministry of Education, "National Strategic Plan," 44.

24. Arab Republic of Egypt Ministry of Education, "National Strategic Plan," 75.

25. Arab Republic of Egypt Ministry of Education, "National Strategic Plan," 97.

26. Arab Republic of Egypt Ministry of Education, "National Strategic Plan," 45.

27. In Egypt it is common to address and refer to people by their title and first name.

28. USAID uses the term "training" rather than "professional development."

29. Egypt's population in 1960 was 26.63 million. In 2010 it had risen to 82.76 million. By 2020 it was 102.3 million.

30. National Institute of Standards and Technology, "Baldrige Performance Excellence Program," 2019, https://www.nist.gov/baldrige.

Chapter 15

The Design of the Grand Challenges Curriculum

Co-authored with Reda Abou Serie and Hala El-Serafy

EMERGING THEMES

Noted Stanford Professor Elliot Eisner once explained that, "the educational ends we embrace are shaped by our values and our values are shaped, in part, by what we believe we can accomplish and by what we are able to imagine."[1] As described in chapter 14, the Egyptian science, technology, engineering, and math (STEM) project was conceived as a dream of possibilities; however, moving from the dream to reality was a daunting task. The reams of data collected from the January 2013 design studio held in Cairo needed to be analyzed and a new curriculum constructed. Although the U.S. team would have preferred to engage the Egyptian teachers and professors in the actual curriculum design, due to circumstances beyond anyone's control in Egypt at the time we were unable to do that. The 21PSTEM curriculum development team led by author Deborah Pomeroy was charged with this urgent task. A new curriculum had to be ready by the start of the next school year in September 2013.

Deborah prepared for the initial analysis of the chart paper data from the design studio by blocking out the names of each particular science group on each piece of the many reams of chart paper. As she studied the data, to her surprise, she realized that in many cases, she couldn't tell which subject area was which, except for mathematics. She began to realize that she was seeing commonalities from one science discipline to another. Next, she looked for any emerging themes by using different-colored sticky notes and clustering similar entries across the chart papers of all the groups. From the work of most of the disciplinary groups, she was able to see similar themes emerging, again with the exception of mathematics. Occasionally the group recorder had expressly written the word that would be the theme, such as energy, but more often than not the recorders had written sentences or phrases that captured the concepts underlying the theme. The power of the emerging themes was so great she couldn't ignore them.

With tentative themes identified, she took the rolls of chart papers to the 21PSTEM office and invited the rest of the team of experienced subject-matter specialists to see if they could duplicate her analysis. They agreed that it wasn't so much that they saw these actual words in the data as they saw the *ideas* behind the words that started to take shape: energy, equilibrium, systems, data analysis, and so forth. Likewise, mathematicians could imagine how their subject could be organized in a way to support the sciences.

The team wondered if they could come up with six semester themes which might become the glue that could hold together the entire school curriculum including the humanities, arts, and activities. If so, might there be a natural progression or sequence that could work across the disciplines? They settled on the themes and the order in which they would be taught for the six semesters of the Egyptian model STEM schools as shown in table 15.1.

The themes offered a way to organize the subject matter of the science disciplines to maximize the potential for interdisciplinary linkages and integration. The U.S. curriculum team believed that the science and math content could take the form of traditional courses *if* their respective content inside each course was organized around these themes to support and reinforce each other. Mathematics concepts could be organized to support learning in each of the sciences for each semester without loss of coherence. In almost every case, concepts and skills could be linked to one or more grand challenges. Other disciplines were encouraged to focus on the same themes such as "Energy, Force, and Power" in physical education, economics, civics, poetry, music, and so forth. The grand challenges with the strongest links to each semester would become the focus of the capstone challenges.

Table 15.1   The Themes for Each Semester of the Egyptian STEM High School Curriculum

	YEAR 1	
Semester 1		Semester 2
Matter, Form, and Function		*Energy, Force, and Power*
	YEAR 2	
Semester 1		Semester 2
Change, Equilibrium, and Cycles		*Systems and Feedback*
	YEAR 3	
Semester 1		Semester 2
Communication, Sensing, Information, Informatics		*Theories, Models, and Data*

Source: 21PSTEM.

21PSTEM's team designed the Egyptian STEM high school curriculum to include the four sciences and mathematics *every semester*, but not every day. Unlike the United States, which has a layer cake approach to the science disciplines (a different one each year), many countries, including Egypt, teach the different math and science subjects every semester in what is termed a "spiral curriculum." In such a system, a subject like biology is taught over four years, advancing from simple concepts to more complex ones. What a traditional spiral curriculum usually lacks, however, is an overarching purpose, such as addressing the grand challenges. Therefore, the subjects can remain separated from each other in disciplinary silos as there is no organizing principle by which to integrate them.

BIG IDEAS, UNITS, AND LEARNING OUTCOMES

Once the semester themes were identified the project curriculum team asked: (1) What is the one "big idea" of each course that relates to the semester's theme, and (2) How does understanding this big idea enable students to address one or more grand challenges? Once answered, the next daunting task was to arrange every subject's big ideas so that they were meaningfully linked to the big ideas of the other subjects.[2] Each subject's big ideas then had to be *vertically* aligned over the six semesters so that they progressed from simpler big ideas to more complex ones. All the big ideas were arranged into a master matrix across all subjects and grades to ensure their alignment and growth of conceptual depth and complexity. The big ideas in each course were then broken into units and the units were broken down into key concepts and skills. From these concepts and skills, two to four *learning outcomes* within each unit needed to be written for each subject.

At this point, we were able to once again engage the Egyptian teachers and curriculum specialists to work on a small number of learning outcomes for each unit. The first step was to develop a common operational definition of a "learning outcome." The team struggled to reach a consensus, but we were able to settle on this:

A learning outcome is a statement of student learning that is performance-based, authentic, complex, with a high cognitive demand usually covering at least a week's worth of instruction.

The U.S. project team then worked with the Egyptians to write about 260 learning outcomes for the five STEM disciplines. The Egyptians also wrote learning outcomes for the arts and humanities and all other electives—over 600 in all. Once the learning outcomes were written, the capstones, daily lessons, and assessments could be aligned and knit together. Each course would generally have between four and eight learning outcomes per semester that all fit within the units.

After the learning outcomes were developed for all the math and science courses over six semesters, the project curriculum specialists connected each learning outcome to other related learning outcomes. For example, a chemistry learning outcome about molecular bonding in year 1, first semester, might connect with a biology learning outcome about protein synthesis in year 2, second semester. We developed a database to track these connections and make a visual display. Figure 15.1 is a simplified display of the *biology* learning outcomes in twelfth grade that are traced back to the earlier related *chemistry* learning outcomes.

Perhaps the most intriguing aspect of the curriculum, at least from a science educator's point of view, was structuring mathematical ideas and practices to support the science courses and capstone projects rather than being an isolated subject. With mathematics structured in this new, reimagined way, teachers could help students more powerfully model complex real-world problems. This applied approach allows students to see the value of mathematics in ways not afforded in a traditional mathematics classroom. This meant reconfiguring traditional courses in algebra, trigonometry, geometry, calculus, mechanics,[3] probability, and statistics to align with each semester's science theme while at the same time preserving conceptual coherence mathematically. Being able to show these connections visually helped ease math teacher concerns about "Where is math?"

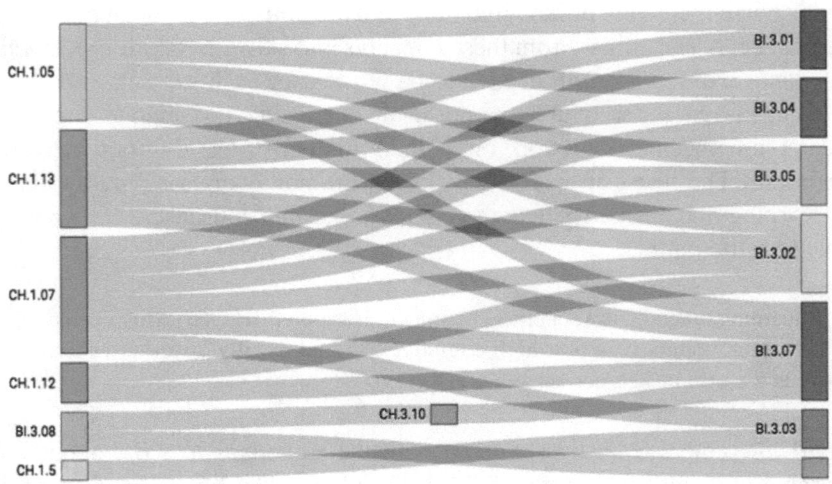

Figure 15.1   Interconnected Learning Outcomes in Chemistry (CH) and Year Three-First Semester Biology (BI). *Source*: 21PSTEM.

Teaching Materials

The Egyptian STEM schools are English-language schools. This decision was made by the Egyptian Ministry of Education who felt that the ability to read, write, and speak English is very advantageous for any Egyptian wanting to further their education abroad, pursue more advanced careers, or obtain high positions in government.[4] Hence, the math, sciences, and capstone courses are taught in English and make use of English-based learning resource materials. These materials included sections of textbooks and online resources.

The project team made use of exemplary materials developed in the United States with funding from the National Science Foundation and other national nonprofit groups that use real-world scenarios to teach their subject. These materials were included more as instructional resources rather than as textbooks for the new integrated curriculum. In some cases, teachers found that whole units and chapters in these selected texts and resources could be mapped directly to the Egyptian semesters' thematic design.[5]

Math and Science Standards

The Egyptian Ministry of Education required that the curriculum meet internationally recognized standards of excellence. Accordingly, teams of Egyptian curriculum specialists worked with the authors to cross-map each learning outcome in the STEM subjects of the Egyptian curriculum to the U.S. standards and the grand challenges. Fortunately, concurrent with 21PSTEM's curriculum work in Egypt, in April 2013, the National Research Council published the *Next Generation Science Standards: For States, By States* (NGSS).[6] The NGSS provides a structure for the integration of otherwise isolated disciplines into a coherent whole, the true meaning of STEM. It provides a way out from what was and is the current structure of the vast majority of curriculum to what can be next. However, the missing element of the NGSS was the idea of *purpose*. And, as a set of standards, it is not a curriculum ready for implementation. In developing the curriculum, much of the NGSS language informed the development of the Egyptian grand challenges curriculum's big ideas, units, and learning outcomes. The scheme we used is illustrated in figure 15.2.

Note that the standards and textbooks in figure 15.2 are off to the side. What drove the curriculum was its purpose. The NGSS and the Common Core Math standards were the guide rails. The NGSS's section on "science practices," for example, describes the expected progressions of children's ability to ask questions; use scientific models; plan and carry out investigations; analyze and interpret data; apply mathematics; construct explanations

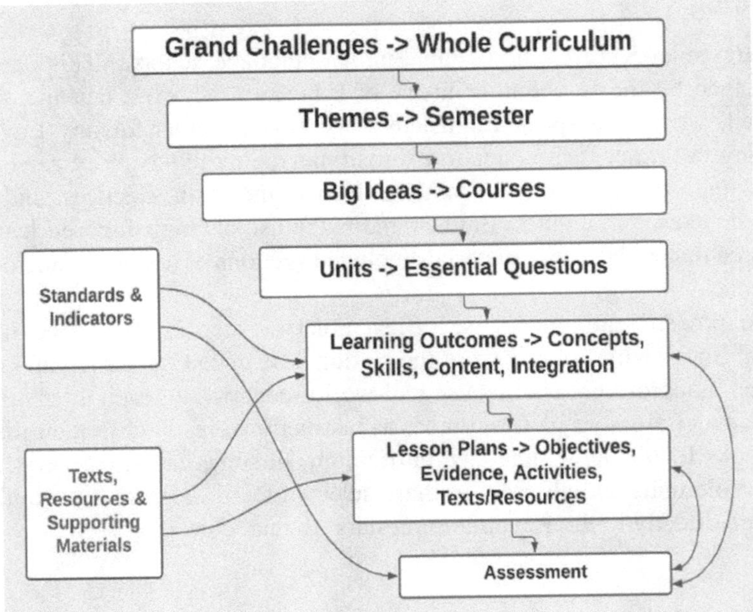

Figure 15.2 Components of the Egyptian-Integrated STEM Curriculum. *Source*: 21PSTEM.

(for science); design solutions (for engineering); engage in argument from evidence; and obtain, evaluate, and communicate information.[7]

The U.S. project team's scope of work included two deliberate limitations. First, the team did not develop daily or weekly lesson plans. It was important for Egyptian teachers to develop these to gain a sense of ownership of what they were about to teach. Instead, extensive ongoing professional development on how to write lesson plans was provided. In addition, the project's IT team developed a Google script curriculum software application so that teachers could see the entire curriculum online and manage their daily lesson plans.

The second limitation was that the project team did not develop curriculum materials for the other subjects taught in the schools, such as Arabic. This task was also left up to the teachers of these subjects. To serve the purpose of STEM schooling in Egypt, students had to integrate the humanities, arts, and behavioral and social sciences into a fuller understanding of the grand challenges. The Egyptians concurred that many of the challenges that face humanity now more than ever require social, political, and economic solutions that must be informed deeply by knowledge of the underlying science and engineering.

THE ASSESSMENTS

The Egyptian Ministry of Education and Technical Education (MOETE) uses a mix of measures and indicators to evaluate their STEM students. In other words, the Egyptians fit the assessments to the curriculum and the purposes of their new STEM school model, and not the schools' purposes and curriculum to the assessments.[8] These new assessment approaches took the place of the Thanaweya Amma exams. We helped design a suite of different types of assessments.

Tests of Concepts

In chapter 13, we argued that it is important for teachers to assess students' naïve concepts or misconceptions prior to instruction to plan meaningful learning experiences. Assessments of lingering misconceptions can be a powerful tool in evaluating the effectiveness of the instruction. Undercovering these misconceptions is the work of disciplinary-based education researchers.[9] One of the earliest physics concept tests developed is called the Force Concept Inventory. Concept inventory tests were later developed for other physics concepts[10] and other disciplines such as chemistry, geology, astronomy, biology, and mathematics.[11] The construction of these tests is based on cognitive interviews with students to uncover their often-surprising erroneous ideas. These misconceptions are then used as "distractors" along with the correct answers in a multiple-choice test. Including these distractors is key to developing a good test of concepts.

The Egypt STEM School Project (ESSP) project team used these concept inventories and their slightly modified versions in Egypt in three ways. First, early in the project, these concept tests were given to the 6 October and Maadi STEM high school students to get a baseline of scores. The student scores on these concept inventories demonstrated to Ministry of Education officials, principals, and teachers that even their best entering tenth-grade STEM high school students scored only between 25 and 50 percent correct. Second, the ministry gave these tests of concepts to prospective STEM high school *teachers* as one of the criteria for being hired. The Ministry reasoned that new teachers should score at least *above* the average score of their STEM high school students. Many teacher applicants were filtered out as a result.[12] Third, tests of concepts were used as part of the students' culminating assessments for graduation. If the Egyptian STEM schools were teaching for conceptual change, then one could expect to see some improvement in student scores by the time they graduated. Moreover, if students had the correct conceptual understanding of a subject, they would be more likely to be successful studying more complex college-level material.

Capstone Courses

As described above, a prominent feature of the model Egyptian STEM schools is their five capstone courses. Students are given a "design challenge" around one or more of the Egyptian Grand Challenges along with certain information for identifying a problem and then designing and testing a solution or partial solution. The capstone challenges are sufficiently complex to require the integration of concepts and skills across different disciplines. Different teams of four to five students work on a project related to the design challenge.

Teaching Institute for Excellence in STEM (TIES) brought U.S. consultants to Egypt with substantial experience in designing capstone courses and structuring them around the *engineering design process* (EDP), a key concept of capstones. The EDP is a multi-step process that is repeated in a cycle until the desired end is achieved in much the same way an English teacher might critique a student's writing as the student does multiple drafts of an essay. Capstones require a very different kind of assessment and grading scheme than other courses. Early failure in the capstone courses is *expected* and *necessary* to arrive at viable solutions. Success depends on repeated failures, reflections on those failures, revised ideas and prototype designs. In the end, it's the *process* to reach a final product that counts. Since a critical feature of the Egyptian capstone courses is the relationship between different disciplines to reach a practical solution to a complex problem, it makes little sense to give students separate subject-matter tests for a capstone course when students are already taking tests in their subject-matter courses.

The biggest question for the Egyptians was how to assess individual students' work if Capstones were done in teams of students. Based on the recommendation of the project's technical team, the MOETE decided that a student's final capstone grade would have two components: an individual component weighing 40 percent and a group contribution component weighing 60 percent. The individual component consists of a series of questions administered every two weeks during the capstone session and answered in students' personal journals. The questions are developed by the Ministry. To maintain objectivity, students' journal entries are evaluated by capstone teachers from other schools. The group contribution component consists of twelve separate elements that culminate in the final capstone project. At the semester's end, the student teams exhibit their work and are evaluated as a group through formal poster presentations and demonstrations of their models or prototypes to panels of university, research, and industry experts.

Exams Based on Learning Outcomes

In tenth and eleventh grade,[13] the remaining 40 percent of a student's semester grade is determined by tests on the learning outcomes for each semester-long course. Each course has about seven to nine learning outcomes that span one to two weeks' worth of instruction. For each learning outcome, students as rated as "high performing" "proficient," or "not yet proficient." The ratings are judged by the teacher using various rubrics that are indicators of proficiency. For many students, this was their first experience with rubrics. Students told project observers they found the rubrics very valuable in helping them understand what was expected and how to strengthen the quality of their work. Table 15.2 shows a rubric used in the first-year chemistry laboratory.

If a student or group is "not yet proficient" on a particular learning outcome, the teacher can provide the student with opportunities to learn from their mistakes and improve. The student can later be reassessed to demonstrate if they have reached proficiency. This process is akin to a coach guiding a player to develop a skill or technique to reach a certain level of performance.

Table 15.2 Rubric Used for Chemistry Laboratory

Skills/Procedures	Proficient	Not Yet Proficient	Not Proficient
Determining Mass	Zeros the balance	Does not zero balance	Does not zero balance
	Uses proper container or paper for massing chemicals	Uses paper or container with a much greater mass than the sample	Puts powdered or chunks of chemicals directly on pan
	Gets tare if using a container or weighing paper	Does not use available tare function on digital balance	Does not get tare if needed
	Gets total mass if not using tare or net mass if using tare	Does not differentiate total from net mass	Does not differentiate total from net mass
	Correctly calculates net mass if needed	Calculation is incorrect	Does not differentiate total from net mass
	Records mass correctly to the correct degree of precision	Leaves off significant zero/s to show precision	Records data with incorrect precision
	Records correct units	Records data with incorrect units	Records data with no units

Source: Deborah Pomeroy.

The Ministry of Education then created common semester mid-term exams and final exams that are supposed to be based on these learning outcomes. Theoretically, a course's learning outcomes serve as the common reference point tying the teachers' continuous classroom assessments to the Ministry's mid-terms and final exams.

Practical Exams

In addition to proficiency in learning outcomes, journals and presentations on capstones, and written exams, the Ministry specialists agreed with the project team on the value of practical exams for the laboratory sciences. These structured laboratory exercises, proctored by external evaluators, require students to perform all requisite procedures in a challenging laboratory investigation. These exams elevated the importance of laboratory work in the curriculum.

University Readiness Test

One of the more difficult challenges the ministry had to overcome with the STEM schools was parental and students' concerns about the criteria for admission to Egyptian universities. If not the Thanaweya Amma exams, what sort of graduation measures would take their place? How would STEM students' college admissions to Egyptian universities be decided for highly sought-after majors? And what would be an acceptable international measure for the STEM school students if they sought admission to universities abroad?

Early in the project, the minister of education decreed a set of graduation measures.[14] To ensure students would be competitive abroad, the Ministry mandated the use of an internationally benchmarked "university readiness test" (URT). The American College Test granted the ESSP project permission to use their practice exam as a stop-gap measure. Later, Management Systems International (MSI), an ESSP partner, developed an Egyptian version of a URT modeled after the ACT exam. This URT was used along with other graduation documents including a test of concepts for each subject, a capstone project, practical lab skill demonstrations, a research presentation, and attendance and participation measures to create a composite student rank.

INDICATORS OF SUCCESS

Everything discussed thus far comes down to this question: In what ways are these admittedly bright Egyptian STEM high school students any different from what they would have been if they simply attended a regular Egyptian public high school? After all, if there is no real difference, what is the point of these schools? How can you tell if there is a true difference?

Many things of value can be quantified, counted, and predicted: the trajectory of a rocket, the expected return on a financial investment, and the quantity and cost of building materials. But there are other things of value that one cannot so easily quantify and measure. For values, such as affection and charm, one discerns *indicators*, signs that point to these qualities. People observe situations, evaluate responses, and reflect on their experiences. No single indicator may be sufficient, but taken together and cross-referenced with each other an impression emerges enough to form a judgment. If one can include metrics along with indicators, so much the better. Yet educational research is replete with randomized control educational studies using only quantitative measures, such as math and reading achievement test scores. This is a problem, as we discussed in chapter 11. The policymakers in Egypt instead made their decisions to initiate and continue their support of the STEM school model using a variety of indicators along with metrics.

When the 6 October and Maadi Egyptian STEM schools opened, the impact on the students was readily apparent. The new entering tenth-grade students[15] and their parents found the STEM schools very different from what they expected in regular high schools. Gone were the Thanaweya Amma exams for which students had been preparing since elementary school. And gone also were the comforts of home. Perhaps the most intellectually challenging, exciting, and emotionally jarring for the young scholars was the different way of learning, e.g., the capstones projects, group work, and the digital fabrication lab all in service to the purpose of the school: to equip them to address Egypt's grandest challenges. It was a call to their youthful idealism to pursue something more than their narrow academic self-interest.

By the second year of attendance in these new schools, Ministry officials and United States Agency for International Development (USAID)-Egypt program officers were already noticing personal transformations in the students from a preoccupation with "me" to "we," from academic competition with peers to cooperation with them, and from thinking only of *their* problems to thinking of Egypt's big challenges. When the STEM students presented their capstone projects to Egyptian university professors they were astonished at the students' technical sophistication. Dr. Nancy Songer, Dean of Education at the University of Utah, said this about the Egyptian STEM students after witnessing their capstone presentations:

They [the STEM students] were able to give complex explanations of *why* they had designed their particular prototype as they did; how it was a solution that was meeting a need for their local community. And even explained very complex kinds of scientific concepts that in America I have seen the quality to be more like a master's thesis than a high school student.

Dr. Kim Dean, an educational psychologist at Arcadia University, concurred:

One of the most impressive aspects of observing the curriculum at the purpose-driven STEM schools was seeing the way that students learned to think across disciplines. They had the opportunity to move through complexity across the three years in the program. I was blown away when I got to see the visual demonstration of this curriculum. How the foundational physics, the foundational mechanics, the foundational cell biology, and all of those different sciences, they found the commonalities and then built from there across the curriculum in ways that really built the capacity of students to approach any situation.

Dr. Stamatis Vokos, theoretical physicist at Cal Poly, likewise remarked:

These students were able to not only express sophisticated content ideas, but also were able to connect them coherently to other ideas. I know that this work is very hard. It is very complex. It involves many, many moving pieces and there are some moments where one wonders about if all the effort and all the emotional investment and the financial investment is worth it. But when one speaks to the students, who are in many ways the ultimate goal of our all of our educational efforts, one is completely convinced that it is well worth it.

International Science and Mathematics Competitions

Another indication of the success of the Egyptian STEM high school model is the overrepresentation of Egyptian STEM students in international math and science competitions. International recognition of excellence is highly prized in Egypt. Few Egyptian high school students, however, had won international science and mathematics competitions. This began to change with the establishment of the Egyptian STEM schools.

The largest global high school competition is the annual International Science and Engineering Fair (ISEF).[16] ISEF annually convenes about 1,700 finalists from the United States and over sixty other countries, regions, and territories. Applicants first compete at local science fairs. Then they are selected to compete at the national level in their respective countries. The winners at the national level are deemed finalists to compete at the international level. ISEF has two broad award categories: Grand, in which there are twenty-one categories; and Special, which are sponsored by various entities. In the 2022 ISEF competition, about $8 million in prize money was awarded.

Before the introduction of the Egyptian STEM schools, only two Egyptian student projects had won ISEF awards, both in the Special awards category.

Thus, it came as a pleasant surprise—a shock, really—that at the 2014 ISEF Grand Awards competition three Maadi STEM school girls captured *third* place in their category for their project, the highest for Egypt at the time. The following year, another Maadi STEM school girl, seventeen-year-old Yasmine Yehia Moustafa, took *first* place in the 2015 ISEF Earth and Environmental Sciences category. Her engineering project was a way to turn rice into biodiesel fuel to purify water and produce electricity.[17] The national Egyptian media celebrated Yasmine's accomplishment.[18] A month after ISEF she was invited to sit at Egypt President Sisi's table during Iftar, the evening meal eaten after sunset during the holy month of Ramadan. Yasmine was then invited to deliver the keynote to the Qatar Foundation school's graduating class.[19] The ministry later distributed a booklet on her life to all schools in Egypt to encourage girls to pursue science.[20] That same year, two other Maadi girls won fourth place in their category for their project entitled "Revolutionary Desalination System."[21] It was a breakthrough for Egypt. Since 2014, Egypt has won nearly thirty ISEF awards, twenty of which have come from its STEM high schools. At the same time, the Egyptian STEM students began to win other international awards. For example, the boys at the 6 October STEM School amassed national and international awards competing in nineteen different national and international competitions, including ISEF.[22]

College Acceptance and Scholarships to U.S. and European Universities

When the 6 October STEM School for Boys opened in September 2011, the parents and students were taking a notable risk. No one knew for certain how acceptance decisions to Egyptian universities for these students would be made. What was certain was that these students would mostly likely have scored very high on the traditional Thanaweya Amma exams, thus ensuring themselves a prime spot on the Egyptian university admissions list. To address these understandable parental and student concerns, the Ministry of Education negotiated an agreement with the Supreme Council of Universities to carve out a quota for STEM school graduates. The anticipated number of STEM graduates accounted for only a small fraction of the hundreds of thousands of traditional public school graduates. Within this quota, the STEM school students would compete with each other for the top spots in Egyptian universities rather than with students from Egypt's regular high schools. The ranking would be according to the new mixed-measures twelfth-grade assessments. This arrangement seemed to reduce some of their anxiety. Concerns were further reduced as the STEM school graduates began to receive acceptance letters from and scholarships to prized U.S., European, and Middle

Eastern colleges and universities such as MIT, Stanford, Bryn Mawr, Penn, and Princeton, to name a few.[23]

Student Voices

Perhaps the most important indicator of the value of these new Egyptian "Grand Challenges" STEM high schools are the voices of the students *after* they have graduated from them. The authors interviewed a group of Egyptian STEM School graduates who were attending colleges and universities in the United States. All talked about their schools' supportive peer and school culture which has resulted in tight-knit friendships and group camaraderie. All were articulate, poised, and grateful. Here are a few excerpts from their interviews.

Sara, a Maadi STEM student graduate, was at the time a Ph.D. candidate in computational biology at the Rochester Institute of Technology:

> When I was a second-year student in [STEM] high school my team and I started this project. It was called a vacuum evaporator for water purification. It was a project to help with the grand challenge that Egypt is facing right now with water, and that's how it all started. And here I am, I came here and four years later graduated. Now I'm getting my Ph.D. in computational biology. It sounds crazy when I talked about the [Maadi STEM] school. A lot of people might say that I'm exaggerating, but I'm really, really not. The school, kind of just, it opens your mind, makes you feel like you can do whatever you want. You can go wherever you want, study whatever you want, be whatever you want.

Maria, a graduate of the Ismailia STEM school, was a first-year student at Swarthmore College at the time of our interview. She described how she learned teamwork through her capstone courses:

> When I first came to Ismailia STEM school, I was like, 'Oh, I'm gonna work with four or five other girls and we have to divide the work among us. . . . And then the teachers and the principals and everyone in the school were so supportive to help us understand who we are to be better, to be able to work in a team environment. The grand challenges let me see the world in a different perspective because it empowered me to be like a citizen in my country, not just a person living my life. Now I'm a citizen and I know how to contribute to the issues I do care about.

Ahmed, a graduate of the 6 October STEM school, was a Ph.D. mechanical and aerospace engineering student at Princeton University. He spoke about doing research as part of a multi-disciplinary approach to problem-solving that he learned at the 6 October STEM school:

> Everyone knows Egypt has an overpopulation problem, a traffic jam problem or pollution problem, but you never really understand how severe a thing is until you actually look at it and do some research. [Without that] you wouldn't really understand the magnitude of the issue. Doing projects that require [the study of the grand challenges] just opens your mind instead of being really passive; just knowing that these things exist and you can't do anything about them, to understanding a bit more about the challenges and maybe there *is* something that you can do.

Menna, a graduate of the Maadi STEM school, graduated from Bryn Mawr College, in computer science and is now employed by Microsoft in Seattle. She described a situation that was very characteristic of situations when students needed something the schools couldn't provide. When she needed to learn a certain type of coding for a project she was doing, she reached out to Makerspace in Cairo and found an engineer who helped her and then ended up volunteering to teach a whole group of girls at Maadi: "There's like some kind of community and connections between people, even the people who come and help us in high school," she said.

Andrew, 6 October STEM school graduate and first-year student at Swarthmore College, described what the STEM school meant to him:

> I remember there were sessions at night led by upperclassmen teaching us what is a capstone and how to write a poster, academic writing, and they would revise everything we do. I remember one time I texted one who was a senior . . . at 2:00 AM . . . because . . . the submission was the following day. And he was like, "Yeah you can, you can come to my dorm," at 2:00 AM! I didn't believe it. I took my laptop; I went to his door. He basically was waking up doing this [rubbing his eyes] and putting on his glasses. And [he] took my laptop. . . . Fifteen minutes later my abstract was totally different! And this is something I'm really grateful for and I don't think you're gonna find it anywhere else except in a boarding school that has residents. A lot of situations like that happened, and when I grew up I became in this position where a freshman would ask me to revise a lot of stuff, help him with his college applications, and I would . . . likely do it because of what I received before.

These stories do not prove the added value of the Egyptian STEM high school model, as would a randomized control trial. But they are an indication. When you hear story after story along with other previously mentioned external indicators and metrics, a picture emerges about the significance and possibilities of these Egyptian model schools for the future of education, not only in Egypt but everywhere.

If the Ministry of Education and USAID had waited until obtaining the results of a randomized control trial, the project would likely have never started. Could research with comparable Egyptian non-STEM students be conducted? Surely. But when the majority of Egyptian ISEF national finalists are from the STEM schools year after year, at what point does such research become academic? When you look at experimental education research, what is almost completely absent are the voices of students, and how *they* see the purpose and value, or lack thereof, of their school experience.[24]

A legitimate question concerns whether any one or two particular features of these Egyptian schools were the main factors of their success. If so, these features could be extracted and applied to other schools to quickly improve them. Perhaps. This is an empirical question that will have to await external researchers. But we offer this word of caution. Beware of reductionism. Just as a human being cannot be reduced to any one organ but instead it is the totality of all parts working in harmony, we believe the success of the STEM schools is due to the totality of its parts working together.

By September 2017, through collaboration between USAID and the Ministry of Education, eleven STEM schools were established in eleven Egyptian governorates. In the same month, the governments of the United States and Egypt signed a bilateral assistance agreement worth nearly $100 million.[25] This assistance agreement provided U.S. technical support to expand the STEM school model to twenty-seven governorates and to develop a completely new STEM teacher preparation program.[26] This revolutionary new program is the subject of our next chapter.

NOTES

1. Elliot Eisner (editor), *Learning and Teaching the Ways of Knowing: The Eighty-fourth Yearbook of the National Society for the Study of Education. Part II* (Chicago: National Society for the Study of Education, 1985), xiii.

2. All elements of the curriculum utilized the principles of backward design as described in Grant Wiggins and Jay McTighe, *Understanding by Design* (Alexandria, VA: ASCD, 2001).

3. In Egypt, mechanics is considered a branch of mathematics and is taught from a theoretical application of physical laws and principles as opposed to the conceptual way emerging out of hands-on investigations that it is generally taught in the United States.

4. French and German are also taught in the STEM schools.

5. The Science Education for Public Understanding Program (SEPUP) is an example, developed by the University of California Berkeley's Lawrence Hall of Science with NSF funding. NSF Award Abstract # 925292906 Science Education for Public Understanding Program (SEPUP): Issues-Oriented Science for Secondary Schools 1992 https://www.nsf.gov/awardsearch/showAward?AWD_ID= 52906

6. National Research Council, *Next Generation Science Standards: For States, by States. Volume 2: Appendices* (Washington, DC: The National Academies Press, 2013).

7. NGSS, vol. 2, p. 48.

8. Some educators have argued that the way to bring about reform is to first change the assessment since what is tested is what tends to become valued. While there is merit in this view, we maintain that purpose should come first and assessments should be about what are the most valued aspects of that purpose. This is the Egypt model.

9. National Research Council, *Discipline-Based Education Research: Understanding and Improving Learning in Undergraduate Science and Engineering* (Washington, DC: The National Academies Press, 2012).

10. See also https://www.physport.org/assessments/

11. J. I. Smith and K. Tanner, "The Problem of Revealing How Students Think: Concept Inventories and Beyond," *CBE Life Sciences Education* 9, no. 1 (2010 Spring): 1–5. https://doi.org/10.1187/cbe.09-12-0094. PMID: 20194800; PMCID: PMC2830154.

12. We used both and Arabic and English version of the FCI. However, since the subjects were supposed to be taught in English, the teachers should have been at least on equal footing with the students in terms of the English language proficiency.

13. There is one capstone in Grade 12 that counts 20 percent toward the final grade.

14. Office of the Minister of Education, Arab Republic of Egypt. Ministerial Decree No (238), dated on July 3, 2012, Concerning High School Graduation Examination Certificate STEM Schools of Science and Technology.

15. The high schools like others in Egypt were a senior high configuration: grades 10, 11 and 12.

16. https://www.societyforscience.org/press-release/2022-regeneron-isef-top -winners/.

17. EAEV049I Rice Straw Power YasmineYehya Moustafa, 17, Maadi STEM School for Girls, Zahraa Elmaadi, Egypt.

18. Almost all of the media attention was in Arabic.

19. https://www.qf.org.qa/education.

20. Louise Hegazzi, *Yasmine Moustafa: Young Scientist, Rising Star* (Heinemann, 2020), https://www.google.com/books/edition/Yasmine_Moustafa/ttkUywEACAAJ ?hl=en.

21. ENEV039T Revolutionary Desalination System Asmaa Atef Sabsouba, 16, Maadi STEM School for Girls, Maadi, Egypt Noha Shokry Abouqara, 17, Maadi STEM School for Girls, Maadi, Egypt.

22. 6 Oct STEM school website.

23. See for example 6 October list of college acceptances, https://www.stemegypt .net/alumni.

24. Alison Cook-Sather, "Sound, Presence, and Power: 'Student Voice" in Educational Research and Reform," *Curriculum Inquiry* 36 (2006): 359–390.

25. "USAID: United States Commits to Over $100 million in Bilateral Assistance for Egypt," September 27, 2017, https://www.usaid.gov/egypt/press-releases/sep-27 -2017-united-states-commits-over-100-million-bilateral.

26. F. Joseph Merlino, Project Director, with Reda Abouserie and Hala Elserafy in Cairo, https://www.usaid.gov/egypt/basic-education.

Chapter 16

Higher Education and the Teacher Preparation Cycle— Grappling with Tradition

Co-authored with Reda Abou Serie
and Hala El-Serafy

The musical *Fiddler on the Roof* starts with a monologue by Tevya in which he explains that in his little village "every one of us is a fiddler on the roof. Trying to scratch out a pleasant, simple tune without breaking his neck. It isn't easy,"[1] Tevya explains. "And how do we keep our balance?" he asks. "That I can tell you in one word . . . tradition!" This is a story of what happens to a community when the world around them changes, disrupting their traditions, their delicate balance, and their sense of purpose and place in the world. *Fiddler*, told in pre-Russian Revolutionary times, is an allegory, pitting tradition against circumstances that require new ways of thinking. In this chapter, we explore the hold of traditions and ways to address them without losing balance.

THE NEED FOR NEW STEM TEACHER EDUCATION PROGRAMS

In this chapter, we discuss why changes in higher education, especially in teacher preparation programs, are both necessary and daunting if schools are going to be repurposed for a new era, and how Egypt is making these changes. The new grand challenges (STEM) high schools require teachers with very different skills and aptitudes. The project team had to provide many weeks of professional development several times a year to help traditionally prepared Egyptian teachers make the transition to teach in these new schools. It became clear that without changes in the curriculum and pedagogy in Egyptian university teacher preparation programs to provide highly skilled, qualified teachers and school leaders, these schools would not be sustainable.

Additionally, without changes in *other* university STEM programs, STEM school graduates would likely experience frustration as they find themselves thrown back into traditional university classrooms.

The urgency for equipping teachers to teach in these new STEM schools became even greater when, based on the early results from the first round of STEM schools as discussed in the previous chapter, Egyptian President Sisi set a goal of establishing model STEM high schools in each of Egypt's twenty-seven Egyptian governorates. While validating the merits of the STEM school model, this goal created more demand for teachers with both a deep knowledge of their disciplines and the ability to teach the integrated STEM curriculum using inquiry and experiential, project-based teaching methods. Moreover, since these STEM schools are to be models for eventual change across Egyptian education, many new teachers would have to be prepared differently. Further exacerbating the demand for well-trained STEM teachers is competition from private schools and other Middle Eastern countries.

A year after the first USAID STEM high school project ended in 2017, USAID awarded a seven-year, $24.2 million contract to 21PSTEM to lead a U.S.-Egyptian team to implement the STEM Teacher Education and School Strengthening Activity (STESSA) project. STESSA had two components. One was to support the establishment of a model STEM high school in each of Egypt's twenty-seven governorates and train teachers in Egypt's 11,000 middle schools in science inquiry and research activities. The second component involved replacing the traditional math and science teacher preparation programs in five very large Egyptian public universities with a new model aligned to the design features of the model STEM high schools.

The U.S. project team consisted[2] of 21PSTEM's home and field offices and its ten partners: Arcadia University, Cal Poly, CSU Fresno, Drexel University, Temple University, Virginia Tech, Center of Science and Industry, Fab Foundation, Teaching Institute for Excellence in STEM, and World Education.

The participating Egyptian universities were Ain Shams, Assuit, Mansoura, Minya, and Zagazig. The university president's cabinet and the deans of education, science, and engineering at each university were deeply involved. The Egyptian governmental authorities that made STESSA possible were the Ministry of Higher Education and Scientific Research, the Supreme Council of Universities (SCU), and the Education Sector Committee (ESC).

ENGAGING UNIVERSITIES

To change university courses and teaching methods, the project team uses three interacting approaches: top-down, middle-out, and bottom-up. All three approaches must work together. Additionally, the team drew upon two theories of change. The first theory of change was that change happens across social, personal, and professional networks. The Egyptian field office drew on their well-developed university, professional, and ministerial networks to facilitate cooperation among and between the Egyptian universities. The project team then arranged U.S. faculty consultants to interact early with their Egyptian faculty counterparts. The second theory of change utilized the principles of conceptual change as described in chapter 13. People must first confront the reality that many traditions are no longer relevant in this new era.

From the Top Down

New programs and courses within Egyptian public universities must undergo multiple levels of approval. The highest level is the SCU. Within the SCU are "Sector Committees" comprised of deans representing their respective discipline-based schools or colleges. For example, the deans of the Faculties of Education[3] of the public universities comprise the "Education Sector Committee" or "ESC." This is the body that makes policy recommendations to the SCU and provides initial approval of the bylaws[4] as they pertain to the Faculties of Education. To implement change, the project team first had to secure approval from the ESC for the selection of the five participating universities. Our field office led by Dr. Reda was critical in negotiating this approval process. Then, the Egyptian deans of education, science, and engineering from each of the five universities needed to be persuaded to join the STESSA project. The agents of persuasion at this level were the STEM high school students themselves. Early in the STESSA project the project team arranged for the Egyptian deans and professors to meet the STEM high students and quiz them on their capstone presentations. To their amazement, the STEM students' responses were like those of PhD candidates. The STEM high school students provided the opening to reconsider the current state of teaching and learning.

The project team then went to each participating Egyptian university to further brief them on the STESSA project. Student team presentations from the STEM schools in their own governorates greatly impressed the university professors. They were the "wow" factor —the first step in the change process. The project team further briefed the Egyptian deans and professors on the STEM school curriculum by including them in active learning demonstrations that revealed surprisingly common subject-matter misconceptions and piqued their curiosity and engagement. Later, in April 2019, a year after the initial STESSA award, the project team arranged a study tour of Philadelphia area universities for the Egyptian deans. The tour served to build a professional network among the deans and solidify their commitment to the STESSA project.

THE NEW TEACHER PREPARATION PROGRAM

In Egypt, a typical secondary mathematics teacher education program can require a student to take up to fifty math and mechanics courses averaging six to seven technical courses per semester over four years in addition to education courses. These technical courses are comprised of theoretical and laboratory components, but there is a minimum amount of application to real problems outside their classrooms and laboratories. In contrast, the purpose of the new STEM teacher preparation program was to produce teachers who could equip their STEM high school students to address Egypt's grand challenges. This kind of teacher preparation program required a very different mindset on the part of the professors.

In January 2020, the project team convened a design studio with Egyptian deans and professors to answer two fundamental questions: *What kind of teacher candidates should the universities produce so they could teach in the STEM schools* and *What should be the features of a new STEM teacher preparation program?* The goal was to identify the desirable and needed qualities for teachers in the STEM schools. It was agreed that teachers should have the same kind of learning experience in their undergraduate training as they would be expected to implement in the STEM schools. The Egyptians agreed to the following design features of new teacher preparation program:

- Courses taught in English;
- Use of technology in teaching and the classroom;
- Capstone projects;
- Transdisciplinary courses;
- Integrated curriculum inspired by the grand challenges;
- Modern pedagogy (i.e., student-centered, project-based learning, active learning);
- Conceptually oriented;
- Inquiry driven; and
- Use of multiple assessments.

U.S. faculty teams were then tasked to design a completely new teacher preparation program based on the above design features. The design teams came up with a unique STEM teacher education program with five different concentrations: math, biology, chemistry, earth science, and physics. The new curriculum framework consisted of eight strands:

1. Six transdisciplinary courses would focus on the STEM concepts embedded in Egypt's grand challenges. These courses would replace the ten traditional introductory math and science courses. An example

of a transdisciplinary course is *Food and Nutrition in Egypt.* In this course, students research cultivation, distribution, preparation, processing, and access to food and explore topics such as human nutrition and metabolism, biology of ecosystems, and pest control. They study math and science content through the lenses of cross-cutting concepts (e.g., scale and systems). Students also engage in STEM practices (questioning, argumentation from evidence, modeling, quantitative analysis, communication of data, and relationships) and studying the nature, history, and philosophy of science.

2. Ten disciplinary courses, one example of which is the biology course: *Application of Basic Genetics in Public Health.* In this course, students use the lens of public health to study the structure and function of genetic information (DNA molecules), investigate the structure and function of proteins, and examine the causes and spread of specific diseases.

3. Seven data science and technology courses such as *Information Communication Technology,* in which students learn to use a variety of software and web tools in various STEM fields for learning, instruction, data presentation, and visualization.

4. Eight practicum and field work courses that give students opportunities to conduct scaffolded observation of STEM Schools in action.

5. Eight English courses that involve practicing STEM language and routines (co-craft questions and problems) while exploring the role of teachers as STEM language teachers.

6. Eight capstone courses in which students carry out a semester-long transdisciplinary project utilizing the engineering design process.

7. Eight education courses.

8. Other required courses.[5]

In total, 140 new undergraduate courses and new forty graduate "diploma" courses[6] had to be developed.

Once the courses were identified, they had to be designed from the ground up because there was scant precedent for these types of courses. Critical to this process was bringing together U.S. and Egyptian professors from the sciences, mathematics, engineering, and education into collaborative groups. This proved to be enriching for all participants.

The most difficult courses to design were the six transdisciplinary courses. All the professors, U.S. and Egyptian, were in unfamiliar territory as they worked together to find ways that their disciplines could contribute to the big ideas of these transdisciplinary courses. Undeterred, the Egyptian professors wanted to do something different. They embraced the challenge of rethinking how to teach their disciplines both in terms of structuring the content and altering their instructional methods.

From the Middle-Out and the Cycle of Tradition

The new STEM teacher preparation program incorporated all the design principals of the STEM schools. This required both U.S. and Egyptian faculty become intimately familiar with these principles, with the grand challenges concept, and with a totally reorganized curriculum. They formed deep partnerships as they learned together. The U.S. faculty worked collaboratively with their Egyptian counterparts to design the new courses and adopt new modes of teaching. The new project-based courses and new pedagogical strategies were designed to change the whole Egyptian teacher preparation experience for both the university students and the professors.

But change is not easy. To appreciate the hold of traditional lecture-based teaching in higher education, we need to first look at the cycle of tradition. Whether in Egypt or in the United States, the basics of the cycle are the same. Traditional modes of teaching that require rote learning favors students who can successfully memorize the subject matter. These students graduate and some enroll in university teacher programs. When they graduate and in turn become teachers, they teach using traditional methods, begetting yet another group of like-minded students and so on as shown in figure 16.1.

Teachers in such classrooms generally use highly prescribed and structured curricula with a long list of topics and facts crammed into them. Students who learn best through active learning experiences and interactions often struggle in such learning environments. But even students who succeed in memorizing facts are afforded little to no opportunity to explore and develop deeper conceptual knowledge, much less apply their knowledge to real-world problems. Traditionally taught students tend to lack experience with open investigations and problem-solving. As a result, they tend to maintain erroneous concepts within a subject. Moreover, their natural curiosity to want to learn more is stifled because the focus has been on memorization for the critical end-of-course exams.

How did the project team break this cycle of tradition? In Egypt, as in the United States, most teachers are educated in public universities. While there are some differences in the traditional teacher preparation programs from university to university, there is a self-reinforcing consistency of practice or cycle of tradition. It was only after a critical number of STEM high schools had been successfully established by the Egyptian Ministry of Education that it became apparent that major changes in teacher preparation at the university level would be necessary. New teachers trained in integrated,

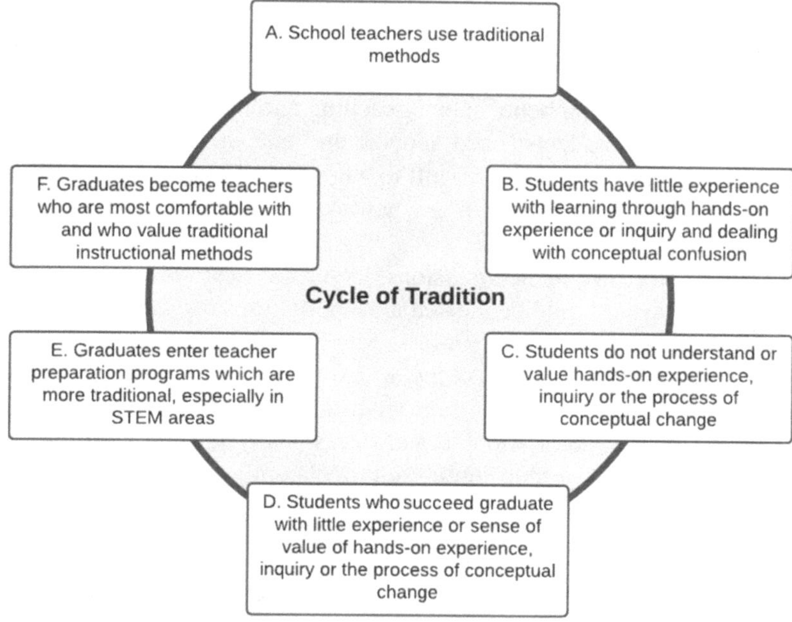

Figure 16.1 The Cycle of Traditional Teacher-Centered Methods. *Source*: Deborah Pomeroy.

student-centered approaches would both strengthen the STEM schools and ultimately support more general reform in K-12 schools.

THE HEART OF TRANSFORMATION

Professors are at the heart of university transformation, because if they do not change their classroom practice, nothing will change. To interrupt the cycle of tradition, the project team needed to disrupt traditional professors' ideas of what constitutes effective teaching. It was important for university professors to actually see and talk with students from the STEM schools. What we were talking about was not theory; it was real. While having students present their capstones to the professors proved to be especially effective in opening their minds to the possibilities of new ways of teaching, the professors needed to relearn how to teach!

The Egyptian professors, impressed by the STEM students, were willing to change, but simply did not know how. In our previous work with U.S. professors in many colleges and universities, we found that when given the opportunity to learn experientially through inquiry, professors often express a sense of *eureka*—a realization that a student-centered approach results in more effective teaching and learning. It may take many cycles of practice, failure, analysis, and refining for professors or teachers to master new techniques and leave behind their more comfortable modes which had been built on more traditional beliefs about teaching and learning. Professors, like teachers and even students, need support and encouragement among their mentors and peers as they slowly shift to a new paradigm of instruction. This is not easy as with the learning of any new skill or art, the learner is prone to make mistakes.

In professional development sessions, the project team stressed that initial failures or mistakes should be viewed as opportunities for further learning. It is an unrealistic expectation for professors to shift from one mode of teaching to another without stumbling. As the authority figures, however, professors are not accustomed to exposing themselves to the possibility of failure. The irony is that if they don't stumble and occasionally fail, they probably are not really moving out of their more traditional comfort zones. Here is where social, personal, and professional networking become especially valuable. In our work in higher education in the United States, we witnessed the value of professors working together in "communities of practice" (CoPs) within and across their disciplines and within and across different levels of schooling such as high school and college.

To begin to develop support networks, the project team included about fifty U.S. science, engineering, and education professors who are strong believers and practitioners of the pedagogies needed for the STEM schools and who were excited about the STESSA project. They also had experience working with colleagues in other disciplines. These U.S. professors worked both in person and virtually with their counterparts from the five Egyptian universities. Working in two languages, along with restrictions due to the COVID-19 pandemic, complicated the task of helping the Egyptian professors' transform their approach to curriculum and pedagogy. Nonetheless, partnering with U.S. professors on this high-profile project provided the Egyptian professors with motivation to persevere.

Leaving the Comfort Zone

Major change, like conceptual change described in chapter 13, is messy. To help faculty reevaluate their teaching practices and curricula, the project team drew on the work of disciplinary education researchers such as David Hestenes and Ibrahim Abou Halloun, two physics professors from Arizona State University. In the 1980s, Hestenes and Halloun were perplexed as to why their students were failing exams even though they had expertly taught them the physics material. In response, they had three choices: blame the students, ignore the failures, or become curious and explore the causes of student failures. They chose the latter. To explore the prevalence and durability of student misconceptions that seemed to be at the root of the problem, they developed a novel test of Newtonian concepts they called the "Force Concept Inventory" or FCI, mentioned in chapter 15. Hestenes and Halloun gave their students a pre-test using the FCI at the beginning of the semester. Then, after a semester of traditional instruction in physics, they retested their students using the same FCI. To their surprise, they found that many of their undergraduate students still retained many of their naïve ideas about force and motion. They explained that "students held firm to mistaken beliefs even when confronted with phenomena [in demonstrations] that contradicted those beliefs."[7] These findings stimulated similar explorations among other physics professors who made use of the FCI and shared their findings. This resulted in rethinking how physics is taught—breaking with tradition.

Eric Mazur,[8] a noted Harvard professor of physics, described his turning point in teaching after reading an article by Halloun and Hestenes and trying out the FCI on his own students:

> The students did well on textbook-style problems. They had a bag of tricks, formulas to apply. But that was solving problems by rote. They *floundered* on the simple word problems, which demanded a real understanding of the concepts behind the formulas. That was a very discouraging moment. Was I not such a good teacher after all? Maybe I have dumb students in my class. There's something wrong with the test—it's a trick test! How hard it is to accept that the blame lies with yourself. I tried to explain one of the FCI questions to the class, but the students remained bewildered. Then I did something I had never done in my teaching career. I said, "Why don't you discuss it with each other?" Immediately, the lecture hall was abuzz as 150 students started talking to each other in one-on-one conversations about the puzzling question. It was complete chaos. But within three minutes, they had figured it out. That was very surprising to me—I had just spent *10 minutes* trying to explain this. But the class said, "OK. We've got it, let's move on."[9]

Mazur chose to enter the messy area of conceptual change to rethink what it means to teach and what it means to learn. He figured out how to transform his large lecture classes into learning experiences in which his students confronted their common misconceptions in physics with each other. As a result of this process, his students emerged with robust new concepts as opposed to transitory memorized rules and formulae. Recalling our first theory of action that change happens across social networks, Mazur came to embrace the pedagogical technique of teacher-guided, peer-to-peer learning for his students.

It must also be noted that Mazur himself attempted to change his teaching practice only after he too found like-minded physics peers who had already done so. Halloun, Hestenes, Mazur, and others became the nucleus of scholars of discipline-based education research in physics and eventually other subjects. Today there is a large community of physicists and professors from other disciplines engaged in reforming their teaching practices. Our goal was to share these kinds of insights and transformations with the Egyptian professors to facilitate their entry into such communities. Accompanying these new courses were extensive professional development and networking activities to support professors' use of an active learning, student-centered teaching approach, the kind exemplified by Professor Mazur.

One needs to remember that professors, especially in disciplines such as science and mathematics, have learned mostly in the traditional paradigm of education. A massive 2018 observational study of over 2,000 university classes taught by more than 500 STEM faculty members across twenty-five institutions found that 55 percent of STEM classroom interactions consisted mostly of lecturing. Less than 20 percent of classrooms were student-centered and included interactive group work and discussions.[10]

The project team understood that simply telling professors about new methods, as in any conceptual change, would not work. And, while seeing the effect of these methods on high school students is important, it is not enough. More importantly, traditional professors must have opportunities to experience these methods themselves as learners to use them effectively. Once the professors see the value of such methods, they will be more likely to use them with their students who likewise will be more motivated to use them when they become teachers. This is the breaking of the traditional cycle.

Employing student-centered, active learning strategies that are new to professors is not always easy or smooth. Early attempts with new strategies are often fraught with stumbling blocks or even failures as with novices in any pursuit. Trying something new and making oneself vulnerable to failure can be terrifying, especially when professional reputations are at stake. This is where a CoP can be especially helpful, reinforcing the importance of social and professional networks which are at the heart of institutional transformation.

STRUCTURES OF TRADITION

Based on our previous work in U.S. colleges and universities, the authors have observed four areas of tradition which constrain the transformation of university STEM education programs in general and teacher preparation programs in particular. These areas are professional isolation, reward structures, traditional assessment systems, and traditional classroom facilities,

1. *A Tradition of Isolation*: Professors tend to be isolated from each other and are likewise isolated from other disciplines. This aspect of higher education culture creates silos of knowledge. Professors' lives are mostly centered around their own offices, laboratories, and classrooms with a minimal amount of collegial interaction. Creating transdisciplinary, integrated courses requires professors to work with one another at a level of sharing and trust that is generally unheard of in higher education. To move from a tradition of isolation to one of collaboration across various networks can be unsettling. When professors from different disciplines wrestle with the rearrangement of content, materials, activities, or pedagogy, however, it becomes easier when it can be facilitated by an outside party. They are all learning a new process of collaboration. It can only work, though, if they all buy into the premise that the product will be so much richer because of their shared work.

   A major factor enabling the development of any transdisciplinary program would be to ensure that professors both within and across the different faculties would have the opportunity, incentive, and time to collaborate. This must become the new norm. In the Egypt project, the required buy-in by the respective deans and their already over-burdened faculties was significant.

   Another aspect of isolation is that professors in science and mathematics rarely have had training in student-centered teaching methods and rarely interact with professors in education. For the most part, they replicate the kind of pedagogy they experienced as students. Our experience is that many professors of math and science do not value the field of education as a topic of scholarly inquiry. Professors achieved their status within the traditional constructs of their disciplines. Changes in their pedagogical practices to a more student-centered approach runs counter to the very teaching traditions that brought them success.

2. *Traditional Reward Structures*: Typically, promotion and tenure policies reward professors' research and publishing over improvements in teaching and student learning. One rarely finds colleges or universities that provide incentives for peer-to-peer collaborations, especially in curriculum and pedagogy. Such collaborations with professors in other disciplines, especially those in the faculties of education or those with expertise in the classroom, are rarely considered to be substantive contributions to their departments and disciplines and hence do not count very much toward promotion. And yet, these are the very requirements for a successful interdisciplinary curriculum in a STEM teacher preparation program.

3. *Traditions of Assessment*: Traditionally, math and science assessments of student learning tend to consist predominantly of mid-term and end-of-course exams. Many students complain that professors' expectations are a mystery to them. Student presentations and projects are generally not the norm in undergraduate education. There is little use of more open-ended student learning experiences such as projects, presentations, and portfolios. Grading scales or letter grades are favored over the use of detailed rubrics which describe the elements of successful completion of open-ended learning activities.

4. *Traditional Classrooms*: Fixed seating in rows and aisles, all facing forward toward the professor, becomes a barrier to interactive student-student engagement. Sitting in groups, on the other hand, naturally invites dialogue and discussion. Additionally, until recently, there was little use of online instructional materials since access to high-speed broadband was not available for all students and professors.

Overcoming Constraints from Traditions

With funding from USAID, the STESSA project team worked with the Egyptian university deans to help develop strategies and provide resources to overcome these traditional constraints. The deans gave their Egyptian faculty members time away from their classrooms to travel to Cairo to participate in many days of course development and planning for implementation. Egyptian education professors were paired with Egyptian disciplinary faculty for many of the new courses. Participating professors were equipped with SMART classrooms that included laptops, high-speed internet, and flexible seating arrangements for group activity. Teaching materials and lab equipment were also procured for the new courses. Faculty peers from the United States assisted hundreds of Egyptian professors to develop course-specific lesson plans, teaching strategies, and different forms of student assessments. Professional learning communities were established for each course and discipline. Each university provided an internal staff person to help coordinate faculty participation and facilitate communication with the project. The deans meet every two weeks with the Egyptian-based project team to resolve implementation issues.

From the Bottom Up—Sustaining Change

The third component of achieving long-term, sustainable transformation of STEM teacher preparation lies with the students themselves at the university level. The project team has heard many Egyptian undergraduate STEM students describe their feelings about the new program in the same way as the

STEM high school students. It is exactly these kinds of students who can help break the cycle of tradition and create a new tradition of meaningful teaching and learning as illustrated in figure 16.2. It starts with new high schools producing graduates whose abilities would provide enough evidence to convince universities, from the highest levels of administration to professors, that they need to change. The top-down mandates of policy change coupled with the mid-level thrust of working with professors on curriculum and pedagogy were essential components to the change process.

Breaking the traditional cycle ultimately depends on the high school graduates who would in turn become educators sustaining the change from the bottom up. Only then would the cycle be disrupted to such a degree that a new cycle with new traditions could replace it. This is exemplified in Ramadan, a graduate of the 6 October STEM school whom we introduced in the previous chapter. The profound impact of his STEM school experience led him to Harvard's Graduate School of Education where he hopes to return to Egypt to work in education policy.

Additionally, while not a part of our program design, observers found that the STEM students themselves have been putting their social networking into action—sharing frustrations, strategies, and successes as they navigate their post-high school experiences. Many STEM high school graduates have reported that they have done just this in their Egyptian university engineering programs. These "STEMers," as they call themselves, support

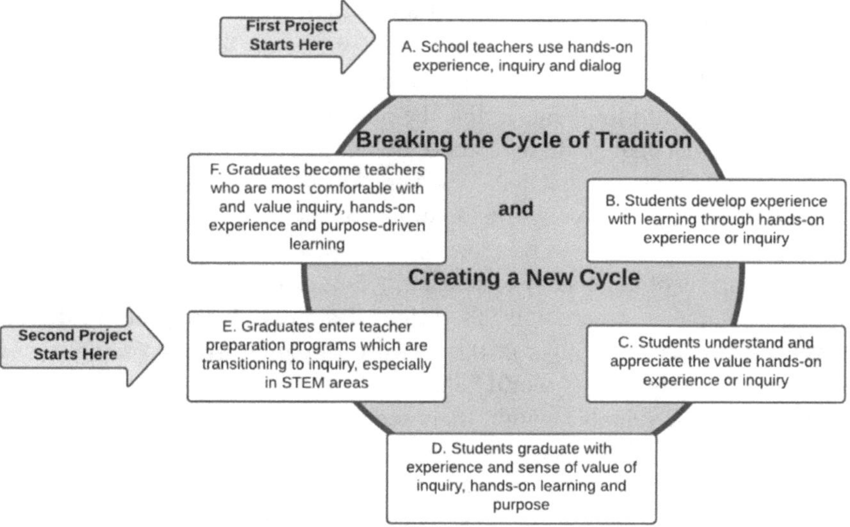

Figure 16.2   Our Long-Range Theory of Change to Break the Cycle of Tradition. *Source:* Deborah Pomeroy and F. Joseph Merlino.

each other, thus demonstrating the third aspect of transformation: *from the bottom up!*

Figure 16.2 shows that a purpose-driven curriculum can be developed to create meaning and value for teachers and students. Non-traditional students are excited to learn in ways that make sense to them, and they begin to explore and develop creative potential and feel valued. Students more comfortable with traditional methods are at first uncomfortable but soon enjoy new experiences as learners as they discover new talents and abilities. Fewer students struggle as learners in such classrooms and students begin to recognize that there are many ways their learning can be expressed and appreciated. Students have developed skills and dispositions to be creative problem solvers and have a purpose in life beyond success in the classroom. University faculty and administrators see the effect student-centered learning on STEM high school students and in turn feel pressure from these graduates in their university classes to change their teaching methods. Universities redesign teacher preparation programs and curricula for inquiry and hands-on learning. Finally, there is a demand from schools that are looking for teachers with inquiry learning expertise. A side benefit is that newly prepared teachers who go into more traditional schools will have the tools and dispositions for initiating change from within.

Leaving and Keeping Traditions

At the very end of *Fiddler*, the villagers load up their carts with their belongings, preparing to leave their beloved home of Anatevka because the world around them has changed so much that they can no longer maintain their lives as they had. Tevye beckons to the metaphorical fiddler up on the roof to come down and join them. In this, he nods to the value of traditions even if they, too, must change. Likewise, we do not just toss out traditions without considering their enduring value. New paradigms, however, enable us to look at our traditions with new eyes and help us understand which are still worth keeping and which need to be modified or replaced. This also holds true in Kuhn's analysis of the history of science: "Though the world does not change with the change of a paradigm, the scientist afterward works in a different world."[11] The scientist looks at the world differently, as if crossing over a bridge and leaving the old world behind.

Traditions are valuable within their societal contexts; they help maintain collective balance. As we described in Part I, as the historical contexts of our country changed, so did the educational traditions. The argument of our book is that the new era that is upon us demands that we examine our traditions and modes of education to determine which are still valuable and which must be modified.

WHERE DO WE GO FROM HERE?

In this book, we have laid out a history of the relationship between profound changes in American society and profound changes in the purposes of education. We have tried to present the case for the need to repurpose education for a new era. The work in Egypt shows how it can be done. As we have told our Egyptian story to friends and colleagues, we have been asked whether this kind of purpose-driven change can be done elsewhere, particularly in the United States. In the final two chapters, we address this question.

NOTES

1. Sheldon Harnack, *Fiddler on the Roof*, 1964.
2. The Trump administration terminated nearly all USAID projects in 2025.
3. Egyptian Faculties of Education are equivalent to U.S. Colleges or School of Education.
4. By-laws are the legal form use for program and course approval.
5. The program also included eleven courses that are mandated by the universities as part of their core.
6. The STEM diploma is a one-year, post-graduate program for teachers and principals.
7. I.A. Halloun and D. Hestenes, "Common Sense Concepts about Motion," *American Journal of Physics* (1985): 1056–1065, p. 1059.
8. Mazur, *Peer Instruction: A Users' Manual* (Englewood Cliffs, NJ: Prentice Hall, 1997).
9. Craig Lamber, "Twilight of the Lecture," *Harvard Magazine*, March–April 2012.
10. M. Stains et al., "Anatomy of STEM teaching in North American Universities," *Science* 359 (2018): 1468–1470.
11. Kuhn, Thomas S. The Structure of Scientific Revolutions. (Chicago: University of Chicago Press) p. 121.

Repurposing Education Beyond the Egyptian Experience

Why are you crying? "Because you give us hope." —Maja from Bosnia and Herzegovina

As fate would have it, as we were working with the Egyptian Grand Challenges STEM schools, we were contacted by two other organizations to help them fundamentally repurpose education. One was a large international children's organization working on a United States Agency for International Development (USAID) grant in the Balkans and the other was a seaport museum in Philadelphia. Along with the Egyptian example, they provide two other illustrations of how education can be repurposed for a new era. We end this chapter by outlining how it can be done at scale in the United States.

THE BOSNIA AND HERZEGOVINA "KBE" ARCHETYPE

In 2017–2018, as the authors were providing teachers with professional development in eleven new grand challenges STEM high schools in Egypt, we received a call from Save the Children (STC) asking if we could help them in Bosnia and Herzegovina (BiH). STC was directing a USAID-funded project to develop a new model K-13 curriculum and train hundreds of teachers in student-centered instructional methods as we described in chapter 13.[1] Consistent with our thesis that new purposes of education emerge from profound social changes, the BiH ENABLE project was initiated in the post-conflict aftermath of the breakup of Yugoslavia in the early 1990s. The dismemberment of Yugoslavia resulted in three and one-half years of a horrific genocidal inter-ethnic/religious war. The new political arrangement that brought peace, the Dayton Accords, is quite complex in its geographical distribution of authority. According to the European Committee of the Regions:

> Bosnia and Herzegovina (BiH) consists of two entities: the Republika Srpska and the Federation of Bosnia and Herzegovina (FBiH) and the Brcko District. The FBiH consists of ten federal units, the Cantons, which have their own Constitution, Parliament, Government, and judicial powers. In total, there are eleven constitutions, governments, and legislators in the FBiH (10 cantonal and one Entity). Cantons operate under the laws of FBiH as a whole. Moreover, they are further divided into seventy-nine municipalities and cities, which constitute the local self-government units. They hold both executive and legislative powers. The Republika Srpska is a unique and indivisible constitutional and legal entity comprising one level of local self-government with 57 municipalities.[2]

Given these tenuous political arrangements, the overriding consensus of BiH authorities for the future of their newly created country is internal peace and prosperity. However, when we were contacted by STC, pessimism among young people was pervasive. According to a youth survey, trust in public institutions was reported as low, mired in perceived corruption, while unemployment has been as high as 60 percent.[3] Many young people sought to leave the country for security and employment opportunities in Europe and elsewhere.

Against this difficult post-conflict environment, the USAID-supported BiH ENABLE project facilitated the development of a new purpose of education built around the idea of preparing students to work in a "knowledge-based economy," or KBE. This new purpose is in service to the aspirational vision of *internal peace and prosperity* across bitterly divided geographic boundaries. Knowledge, information, communications, and science technologies are infused in many modern economic sectors from agriculture to transportation to tourism in ways that transcend geographic boundaries. The premise is that the new KBE curriculum would equip young people to work collaboratively in KBE sectors independent of ethnic/religious boundaries, thus encouraging internal peace and prosperity by helping to build ties across boundaries. This was the intent.

The BiH ENABLE leader, Fatima Smajlovie, was responsible for the strategy of education change over a period of six years. Our team worked with her project team whch included professors from the universities of Sarajevo, Banja Luka, and Mostar, and the Brcko District to conceptualize a new K-13 curriculum based on ten KBE economic sectors. We used the same process in Bosnia as we did in Egypt to guide a team of BiH university professors to develop the KBE curriculum. They first described the KBE STEM/science, technology, engineering, arts, and mathematics (STEAM) content for each of the ten economic sectors, then extracted the big ideas and wrote the learning outcomes for each grade band. Finally, they adjusted the sequence of the learning outcomes and hands-on projects for each subject to allow for maximum alignment and integration. The 21PSTEM IT team developed a special web-based curriculum tool for the new BiH curriculum and made it accessible in four languages.

Since the USAID-funded project ended in 2019, twelve project schools have integrated STEAM learning within 10 percent of the curriculum. The Sarajevo Canton included STEAM in its reformed new curriculum, and it started with the STEAM education of 800 teachers. Significantly, from a political perspective, some 1,400 teachers from Republika Srpska participated in four days of training in the new curriculum.

THE CITY AS CLASSROOM: THE GREATER PHILADELPHIA STEAM INITIATIVE

The rollout of the Egyptian STEM curriculum version 1.0 in September 2013 proved that it was possible to successfully design an integrated curriculum derived from a clearly stated core purpose for a high school, in this case, one based on Egypt's eleven grand challenges. This was accomplished amid the chaos of two revolutions and six different Egyptian ministers of education.

The U.S. team wondered if it were possible to replicate the same curriculum design process in the United States. As it would turn out, we would have the chance to test this possibility. It would not be a residential high school for the best and the brightest, but for all students where the classroom would include many of Philadelphia's scientific, arts and culture, and historical assets as part of the curriculum. For the sake of brevity, we called this endeavor the City as Classroom model and the Greater Philadelphia STEAM Initiative.

The STEAM initiative was led by the president of the Philadelphia Independence Seaport Museum; vice president of External Relations of the Greater Philadelphia Cultural Alliance (GPCA), representing over 400 arts and cultural, historical, and science education nonprofit organizations; vice president of the University City Science Center (UCSC); and author F. Joseph Merlino. The Independence Seaport Museum convened a meeting with twenty informal education directors from arts, culture, and science nonprofit organizations where the author presented our work in Egypt. The School District of Philadelphia's directors of curriculum and external partnerships also attended.

The concept of extending our STEM work to include the arts with the cultural and scientific assets of the city as part of a formal curriculum was received with great enthusiasm. Using the resources of the Independence Seaport Museum, students could also learn the importance of the watershed geography of the Delaware River Basin and the key biological and chemical concepts involved in ensuring their families can drink clean water free of harmful contaminants. Arts representatives were enthused about the chance to integrate the arts into a purpose-driven STEAM curriculum. Cultural and historical societies were eager to help students gain insight into themselves and others by understanding the city's unique historical and cultural significance.

The Barra Foundation, a Philadelphia area charity, awarded a $150,000 grant to 21PSTEM to convene a series of design studios in furtherance of the idea. On November 6, 2015, we brought together a group of 122 individuals representing seventy Philadelphia area arts and cultural organizations, government agencies, school districts, universities, and nonprofit education research groups to rethink urban high school education for a new era.

In this inaugural meeting, we asked the participants to discuss two questions and try to come to a consensus:

1. What are your aspirations for the way of life you would like to see for the Philadelphia region in the next ten years?
2. What does it mean to be an educated person at the end of high school?

Although we briefed the participants on our Egyptian experience, we were careful not to bias them toward producing a "grand challenges of Philadelphia" aspirational vision. We began this process without any preconceptions as to the outcome. Facilitators at each table led the discussions, and participants were arranged to maximize the diversity of the types of organizations. The meeting lasted two and a half hours. We distributed paper questionnaires to each participant and collected their handwritten answers at the end of the session. We later transcribed, typed, de-identified, and synthesized the questionnaires to discover common themes.

After the inaugural session, from mid-January to early February 2016, we conducted six successive small group follow-up sessions with subsets of the November 2015 participants as well as new participants. The goal was to examine and summarize the larger group's responses to the two aspirational questions. Members of our 21PSTEM staff then composed a draft aspirational statement of the future and a new purpose of education. During subsequent design studios, the discussion data was reviewed along with the draft statements for a new purpose of education for the Philadelphia region. The participants were asked to elaborate upon the meaning of the terms in the education aim's statement. Each of the six design studios was conducted over two and a half hours. Here is the result of the process.

ASPIRATIONAL STATEMENT FOR
GREATER PHILADELPHIA BY 2026

We see a region that is diverse in many dimensions, yet united. It is a region with a vibrant economic and cultural life that offers equitable opportunities for all. Its people are engaged in collaborative civic, economic, and cultural efforts to maintain a high quality of life.

We see a region with a thriving economy that supports meaningful employment, sustainability, and a green infrastructure. It is a region that brings forth prosperity with policies that promote equitability of resources for everyone.

We see the Greater Philadelphia region as world-class, a place whose people revere the finer moments in their history while possessing a critical understanding of it, yet who, at the same time, look forward toward a better future. It is a region with a culture of innovation that inspires and draws professionals from all over the world, a hub for STEAM education and careers. It is a place where people work together to achieve a sustainable future from the individual to the global levels.[4]

Once a shared aspiration for Philadelphia's future was reached, the desired attributes of high school graduates came next. Here is what the group defined as their new purpose of education for a new era:

A NEW PURPOSE OF EDUCATION FOR
PHILADELPHIA AREA HIGH SCHOOL STUDENTS

For high school graduates to discover their sense of place in a diverse[5] and united community; who are connected to the regional culture and the economy; who can navigate the world around them and understand levels of complexity within their immediate community and beyond; who possess a sense of purpose and resilience; who can learn both independently and collaboratively with the capacity to think critically, solve problems, adapt, thrive, and create a sustainable life and world; and who act responsibly and respectfully toward themselves and others.[6]

Still, any new purpose of education must have direct curricular and school organizational implications; otherwise, it is only a new label on the same old can of beans. To tease out these implications, we needed to elaborate on keywords in the statement of purpose to guide the selection and emphasis of specific disciplinary and interdisciplinary content. Here is a sample of how we unpacked the meaning of two keywords, *diversity* and *unity,* from the City as Classroom statement of purpose:

Diversity—for students to discover their sense of place in a diverse and united community. We take the concept of diversity in its widest sense as encompassing the universe of differences. The natural world, including living things, manifests a multitudinous variety. Humans speak more than 6,900 languages. We display a wide diversity of physical attributes, genetic make-ups, health, and medical statuses. People live in different locations and housing types and possess different socioeconomic and marital statuses, levels of education, income, and types of employment. People have diverse modes of self-expression, personalities, habits, and dispositions. They have different types of dress, lifestyles, and talents of all kinds. People have different modes and degrees of consciousness, cognitive abilities, and ways of knowing. They have diverse points of view, opinions, ideologies, interpersonal relations, lives, and work experiences. People also have the unique ability to *create* differences through symbols and representations of thought and expression. The arts and humanities provide an almost limitless display of such human-made diversities, virtual worlds that themselves possess a kind of reality as art imitates life and life imitates art. Extending beyond the person, the meaning of diversity encompasses family types, ethnicities, neighborhoods, religious communities, social organizations, and associations of all types. There are diversities of cultures, norms, and values; traditions, such as foods and clothing; group histories and forms of group recreation and entertainment. All these kinds of human diversities situate a person within a given community.

There are also great diversities among businesses and institutions. Different types of industries make up an economy and various jobs and careers within them. A multitude of different types of businesses offer a wide assortment of services and products that require various skills. In a community, there is a diversity of institutions from educational to medical to arts and cultural. There is a diversity of legal and governmental institutions and functions. Within each type of institutional category, there is still yet more diversity. When students understand these kinds of diversities, they can see multiple access points for entry into or impact on these institutions. These institutions are not monoliths.

Furthermore, the concept of diversity is foundational in the natural as well as social sciences. The natural world is understood through the study of different domains of science such as biology and chemistry, but there are still finer subdivisions such as biochemistry, biophysics, molecular biology, radiation biology, etc. It is valuable for students to understand not only the particularity of the world about us but also to understand its great unifying principles.

United—to discover their sense of place in a diverse and united community. While the physical world possesses an almost infinite number of apparent differences from the microscopic to the galactic, it is not random.

Behind these diverse appearances is an underlying natural order that is knowable. Many of the regularities can be quantified in mathematical terms. There is structure and pattern. Simplicity can be found. Three letters, for example, $E = MC^2$, symbolize the unity of mass and energy in the universe.

Likewise, in the world of living things, we have grand unifying ideas, such as evolution in biology. All things living consist of intricate levels of organization within themselves where parts are combined and connected into a whole, which in turn become a part among others to form still larger wholes. Thus, we find molecules forming cells, forming tissues, forming organs to form a living thing, with features and functions distinct from non-living things. In turn, all living things are united through complex relationships as part of local ecosystems which together form our biosphere—the ecosystem of the globe integrating all living beings and their relationships. Of all living things, human beings have the unique power to intentionally create new unities and relationships, to compose sounds and sights, technologies and processes into tangible processes and things. These created realities fold back on us to change our present lived reality and those of generations to follow. It has been said that with the advent of human beings, the universe became conscious of itself.[7]

A curriculum designed to help students study the world around them through these lenses of diversity and unity would help them discover their sense of place in the community. Other key terms in The City as Classroom statement of purpose included students being connected to the *regional culture* and *economy*, students being able to *navigate* the world around them and understand the levels of its *complexity*, and students understanding how to create a *sustainable* life.

In the City as Classroom archetype, we set forth certain design principles for how to develop a new curriculum. The curriculum would have to be: (1) suitable for all students, not only the very talented; (2) designed so that the abundant assets of the city's business, medical, and scientific centers, together with its many informal education arts, cultural, historical, and scientific education organizations could be part and parcel of the formal curriculum; and (3) sustainable and scalable for potential use by many Philadelphia area high schools. To date, the Barra Foundation grant to implement the City as Classroom remains a dream, awaiting sponsorship from a larger private funder or a governmental education authority.

The Egyptian, Bosnia and Herzegovinan, and Philadelphia initiatives represent three different purposes of education derived from their unique cultural contexts. Nevertheless, they all share the element of strong social and moral elements to their purpose. This is what justifies them being public schools and not private ones—they serve a public purpose.

THE SOCIAL AND MORAL DIMENSION OF PURPOSE—PUBLIC VERSUS PRIVATE SCHOOLS

A key element in repurposing education for a new era is the inclusion of a moral and social dimension. It is not enough that public schools serve only students' individual interests. The public supports public schools. They do so because they have a stake in student outcomes whether or not they have children in school. At a minimum, those stakes impact the health, safety, and well-being of others. The public has an interest in seeing that children do not grow up to be "ungovernable animals," as Benjamin Rush[8] would say, that they follow the rules of the road, that they do not drive drunk crashing head-on into oncoming traffic, that they do not shoot up the place, and that they are socialized to respect the rights and liberties of others. Some might argue that ensuring such outcomes is the job of parents/guardians, places of worship, and the criminal justice system. All true. But what happens when parents are absent, abusive, or ungovernable themselves? What happens when young people do not respect the rights of others, harbor intolerant ideologies that infringe on the freedoms of others, or are too swayed by social media peers for their own good? Are there enough police to control the mayhem of street mobs without falling into martial law or a Stalinist-like police state?[9]

To be sure, public schools cannot substitute for the internal self-regulating mechanisms of family and faith. Their role is not to provide mental health services or take the place of the law, courts, and police. Nonetheless, at the most basic level, public schools are a critical institution that, together with other governing systems, can keep the lid on the pot. At a more advanced level, public schools in a democracy can help instill the duty and responsibility in young people for democracy's preservation, as Thomas Jefferson implored. Indeed, all the public education archetypes described in part I, including specialty public schools, have a social and moral dimension to them.

Private schools, such as religious schools and elite college preparatory schools, may well produce upright, civil, and patriotic students with strong and nuanced moral and social sensibilities. But private schools serve the interests of those who attend and pay tuition; their purpose is defined by these private interests. The public has no say in private schools' mission, curriculum, personnel, or operations. To be sure, private schools *can* serve an indirect public purpose as privately paid alternatives to unsafe, incompetent, or corruptly administered public schools. Indeed, a strong argument for private schools and homeschooling is that they serve as alternatives to unsafe and poorly run public schools. Yet the parents most in need of private school alternatives for their children are often the least able to afford them. But private schools and homeschooling can also be oriented toward achieving different types of goals, as defined by students and parents, which are not necessarily as highly valued by the public at large. For example, private, sports-oriented schools serve the professional athletic aspirations of their students.[10]

PUBLICLY FUNDED PRIVATE SCHOOL CHOICE

In an influential 1955 essay, Milton Friedman, a Nobel laureate in economics known for his staunch advocacy for a private, free-market enterprise system, argued that taxpayers ought to subsidize student tuition payments for private, for-profit, or nonprofit schools. The government[11] would issue school vouchers to parents or guardians to purchase K-12 education for their children. Friedman justified taxpayer funding for parental choice to attend private schools because "a stable and democratic society is impossible without widespread acceptance of some common set of values and without a minimum degree of literacy and knowledge on the part of most citizens."[12] The state would be responsible for setting minimum requirements for citizenship, but otherwise parents could choose whatever school they wished. Paradoxically, Friedman acknowledged his scheme could further divide the country along racial, ethnic, religious, class, and ideological grounds rather than uniting around core values needed to maintain a democracy. In an update to Friedman's thesis, Moe and Chubb in their 1990 book, *Politics, Markets, and America's Schools,* again argued for a private-enterprise approach to public education:

> A basic property of markets that operates on the population of schools as a whole: natural selection schools that fail to satisfy a sufficiently large clientele will go out of business. . . . Of the schools that survive, those that do a better job of satisfying customers will be more likely to prosper and proliferate.[13]

The privatization of public schools, whether through vouchers or some other market-based mechanism, may be intuitively appealing, especially to the libertarian- and conservative-minded who believe in minimal government. And then there are those who are distrustful of anything in the social and economic sphere run by any level of government, many expressing fears of "socialism" and "Marxism." This free-market theory of schools also resonates with those in the business sector who regularly operate in a competitive market environment where uncertainty and failure are ever-present risks. Why should schools not be subject to the same market dynamics? The latest political framing of the privatization approach to public schools is to cast it in the form of parental rights and choice. What politician wants to oppose parents? Yet there are three flaws with a private-enterprise approach to public education.

First, the theory that privatizing public education in the form of taxpayer-funded vouchers or public charters would spur innovation and efficiency in *regular* public schools has not proven to be the case. Instead, the private-enterprise approach has led to vitriolic arguments where public school advocates on one side accuse charter schools of taking money away from regular public schools. Free-market advocates on the other side accuse public school advocates of protecting an entrenched school bureaucracy allegedly controlled by and for teacher unions at the expense of greater educational opportunity for students, especially for disadvantaged students. The free-market theory has not brought unity to public education. It has brought division.

The second problem with the free-market theory of public education is the question of its moral and social dimension.[14] Not everything comes down to a transactional market exchange. We do not want doctors, police officers, first responders, or religious leaders to think of us as "customers," and neither do we want teachers to perceive us that way. Professionals and those in positions of trust have a duty of care to others. We do not mean to imply that public charter school founders or CEOs are driven only by profit motives. Many may genuinely want a better learning environment for their students. Nonetheless, the privatization of public schools in the form of vouchers or charters carries with it all the potential excesses of the profit-driven competitive marketplace: false and misleading advertising, bait and switch tactics, executive overcompensation and underpayment of workers, lack of financial transparency, and the selective recruitment of students and reporting of their outcomes.

The third, and perhaps the most critical, problem with the privatization of public schooling is the lack of *public* consensus as to its purpose. Instead, it is left up to the customer. But there are *many* customers to satisfy in any particular school. If parents decide the curriculum, who decides between conflicting parental demands? In a private system, the choice of curriculum thus defaults to the founders or current leaders of the school. The curriculum is whatever attracts enough customers.

In sum, the promise of school privatization, whether through vouchers for private schools or public charter schools, cannot lead to a broad public consensus as to what *should* be the new purpose of education for this new era. Without common purposes, there cannot be a unified community. Rather than unifying the country, privatization is more likely to result in cultural and (mis)informational fragmentation much like the manner in which cable news and social media algorithms slice the audience into encapsulated silos. Moreover, what common measures and indicators can be used to evaluate student outcomes? So, where does this leave us?

RECONSIDERING THE NATION AT RISK ARCHETYPE

As we discussed earlier, U.S. public schools currently operate within the Nation at Risk archetype: the purpose of education being to elevate the academic rigor of traditional core subjects for all students so that there is a sufficiently competent workforce enabling U.S. businesses to compete in the global marketplace. Rigor has been defined by state-level academic standards for each discipline. We are *not* advocating for lower standards or lower expectations for students, or that accountability should be lessened. We are not saying we should do away with math. We *are* saying that the Nation at Risk archetype has lost its relevance for twenty-first-century realities and that new purposes for public education must be considered.

To reach a new consensus about the purpose of education, there must be a restlessness, a sense that the time has come for a change. Our thesis is that new purposes of education can only emerge after a period of societal change when it is apparent that the old ways do not bring hope to a new generation. We believe that the United States is now at such an inflection point. As we described in part III, the Illusions of Educational Reform, the Nation at Risk archetype is ill-suited for the realities and challenges of this new era. What may have been the educational aim some forty years ago is no longer suitable for our current generation growing up saturated in social media where democracy worldwide is under attack and divisiveness abounds. It is time to either revisit and renew previous purposes, such as the Jeffersonian archetype of Education for Democracy, or envision a new and different purpose for education.

ASPIRATIONAL CONVERSATIONS AT SCALE

Reaching a consensus about a new purpose of education for a new era requires first having a conversation about our shared aspirations for our children, our community, and our country. Whether in Egypt, Bosnia and Herzegovina, or Philadelphia, the process of defining future aspirations and the resultant purpose of education was the same. The subsequent development of the curriculum and assessment approaches all take their direction from their respective purposes. When carried out faithfully, this process can produce schools that reflect the aspirations of their communities, be they affluent suburbs, struggling urban areas, or isolated rural communities. This process must also reflect the needs and aspirations of their students, from those highly talented and motivated to those who are barely surviving and feeling undervalued. The content of the curriculum follows the purpose of education.

     Chapter 17

What would it look like to formulate a new purpose of education? How should we arrive at this new purpose? Who would do it? How would final decisions be made and what would be the implications for the choice of curriculum? As we saw throughout our country's 400-year history, conversations about finding a new purpose of education relevant to a new era have started in different ways. In some cases, local communities took the lead; in other cases, it was state, regional, or national non-governmental organizations or federal policymakers. However the conversation begins, it must ultimately engage local communities.

There is a legitimate question as to whether it is practical to initiate grassroots conversations about a community's future aspirations in this new era, reconsider the purpose of education, and remodel local district curriculum based on this new purpose. There are 13,349 public school districts in the United States. That is a lot of conversations to organize and conduct. How representative would the participants of the community be? What if hundreds or thousands of people in a school district wanted to participate in aspirational conversations about their future? What about the cost? And would there be 13,349 different aspirational visions? How could that be unifying? How likely is it that a consensus could even be reached within a single district, let alone thousands of them? The logistics of implementing these community conversations are too detailed to discuss here, but we believe it can be done. Involving local school board members is important but it is not a substitute for a broad-based community conversation that tries to develop a shared understanding and consensus about the future.

The outcomes of these local aspirational meetings may be surprising. People may discover that their neighbors are not as polarized about their aspirations for their future as the social media, cable news networks, or polling outfits might lead them to believe. We believe that if these conversations are well moderated and respectful and the discussions kept close to the lived experience of those in a community rather than being about national or theoretical issues, there could emerge a high degree of consensus among the participants. We would expect some variations from community to community, of course, but there could be a small set of different types of future aspirations depending on the region and the composition of the community—not 13,000 different types. For example, participants from Hazleton, Pennsylvania, a former coal mining town with an influx of Dominican immigrants from New York City, might share similar aspirations with those in former coal towns in West Virginia. Both might be surprised to learn how similar their future aspirations are to those of a low-income Black community in North Philadelphia. Indeed, their aspirations for the future of our society might be similar to those of affluent suburban White communities.

This process can begin locally with just a few districts in a state as a test case rather than the entire country all at once. We think this process would be manageable since about 70 percent of school districts have fewer than 2,500 students. Moreover, it may not be necessary for every person in the community to participate in extended discussions so long as a consensus is reached with a broadly representative group who can serve as informal neighborhood spokespersons about the process.

A few cautions exist in arranging these aspirational conversations. The organizers must have the full support and endorsement of the school and governmental authorities. States determine subject-matter standards, statewide assessments, and high school graduation requirements. These requirements have a dampening effect on people's imaginations to rethink what is possible educationally. It would be helpful to temporarily waive these requirements at the beginning of the repurposing process. Otherwise, without this official commitment to the process, participants in these community conversations will rightly perceive the process as only an academic exercise. There is no benefit to raising people's hopes and then letting them down. Moreover, these authorities must be prepared to act upon the community's consensus about their future aspirations, a restated purpose of education, and the recommended revisions to the district's curriculum, instruction, assessments, extracurricular activities, and relations with informal education entities.

The organizers must mobilize local stakeholders to ensure representation from community groups and interests. The process must be carefully crafted with trained moderators to ensure everyone's voice is heard and not drowned out by a few overbearing ones. Anonymous data from the sessions must be recorded and collected. The entire process must be transparent as repeat sessions will be necessary after the initial group session data is analyzed. We recommend first conducting several small group sessions as rehearsals to gather experience before launching conversations community-wide.

THE TASK OF REPURPOSING EDUCATION

The task of repurposing education so that it is more relevant to the future aspirations of a community and more engaging to its students is not Herculean. It depends on the existing assets of the community, its cultural capacity, and will to adapt. In the United States, an extensive education improvement infrastructure already exists. Decades of reform work have been carried out by tens of thousands of people in terms of education research, teacher preparation, teacher and leadership professional development, standards, curricula, assessments, and so on. What is missing is a more up-to-date purpose that reframes the whole educational enterprise to engage children's and adolescents' interests, dreams, and moral and social relations in a way that is more relevant to our times and their future.

Once new purposes are articulated, a new curriculum can be framed that maps directly to the purpose and is cross-mapped to nationally articulated standards. Redesigned and authentic assessments follow accordingly.[15] Indicators of progress can be built into the system at all levels so that the process of design and implementation can be assessed and reworked as necessary to achieve the aspirational vision. Indicators of desired student outcomes that span elementary and secondary schooling as well as college and career can also be included. Short elective test preparation courses can be offered for certain external testing requirements, such as students who are applying to colleges/universities that still require Scholastic Assessment Test/American College Test exam scores.

While we have been talking about STEM, it is important to note that the arts and humanities are among the most critical components of a repurposing of education. An education system that is devoid of a commitment to creativity; meaningful communication; and moral, ethical, and civic accountability is doomed to failure. To this end, there is power in professional and personal networks if activated around a shared purpose. Business and industry can be called upon as partners at any level from mentoring, field trips, internships, scholarships, or basic funding. Colleges and universities can and must be engaged as valuable resources. Nascent, grassroots engagement can eventually produce powerful allies in sustaining the efforts. Community groups can provide valuable human, economic, and material resources that further, and more meaningfully, root the schools in the community and ensure their growth and sustainability.

We believe economies of scale can be achieved as communities share similar aspirations and purposes. For example, it may be possible for national organizations such as the Council of Chief State School Officers [16] to convene conferences for state education chiefs to showcase exemplary models or repurpose schools in their respective states.

We challenge parents, educators, and policymakers to think in terms of comprehensive systemic change that is built on the principles we have laid out in this chapter. Furthermore, any system must be responsive to feedback—not instantaneous knee-jerk responses, but to the feedback of slowly evolving institutions and challenges of the times.

In figure 17.1, we show our conception of how the evolving nature of society and the contexts within which that society is situated shape the purpose of schooling. The purpose shapes the curriculum and all design aspects of schools, which in turn impact society indirectly through its graduates and those of the universities.

If the purpose is not responsive to the external and internal contexts through such an evolutionary process, the cycle is broken and there is no

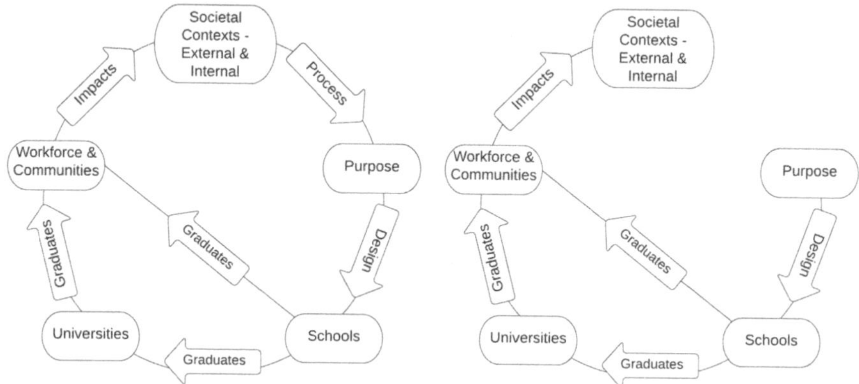

Figure 17.1   How the Purpose of Schooling Shapes How Schools Work and Impacts Society. *Source*: Deborah Pomeroy.

mechanism for addressing evolving contexts and societal needs through schooling. The purpose becomes untethered and increasingly irrelevant to the societal contexts. School is reduced to habit without meaning. That is where we believe we are at this time.

We realize that many questions remain. In our final chapter, we will attempt to address some of the more pressing ones.

NOTES

1. USAID/Save the Children, "Enhancing and Advancing Basic Learning and Education in Bosnia and Herzegovina, ENABLE BIH," November 15, 2018, https://pdf.usaid.gov/pdf_docs/PA00X2BX.pdf.

2. European Committee of the Regions, "Bosnia and Herzegovina," accessed February 21, 2023, https://portal.cor.europa.eu/divisionpowers/Pages/Bosnia-Herzegovina.aspx.

3. US Agency for International Development, "National Youth Survey in Bosnia and Herzegovina," February 1, 2023. https://www.usaid.gov/bosnia-and-herzegovina/reports/national-youth-survey-BIH-2022.

4. The 21st Century Partnership for STEM Education. "The City as Classroom: A New Vision of Public Urban High Schools For the Twenty-first Century The Greater Philadelphia STEAM Initiative: Phase 1 Report," June 2017, 32.

5. Terms that are in bold type need to be unpacked to draw out the implications for the curriculum that would be needed to achieve this purpose.

6. Id. P32.

7. Roger Penrose, Stuart Hameroff, and Subhash Kak, eds., *Consciousness and the Universe: Quantum Physics, Evolution, Brain & Mind* (Cambridge, MA: Cosmology Science Publishers, 2017).

8. As discussed in "The Benjamin Rush Archetype" section in chapter 2.

9. Tom Balmforth, "Life in Stalin's Gulags," *The Atlantic*, March 4, 2013.

10. "Home," IMG Boarding School, updated 2023, https://www.imgacademy.com /boarding-school.

11. Friedman did not specify whether "government" meant federal, state, county, or municipal government.

12. Milton Friedman, "The Role of Government in Education," in *Economics and the Public Interest,* Robert A. Solo, ed. (New York: Vail-Ballou Press, 1955), 124–144.

13. John E. Chubb and Terry M. Moe, *Politics, Markets, and America's Schools* (Washington, DC: Brookings Institution Press, 1990), 32–33.

14. Friedman calls the social and moral benefits to others from a person being educated "the neighborhood effect."

15. By "authentic" we mean that, in as much as possible, the assessment requires the students to perform real-world tasks.

16. The Council of Chief State School Officers is a nonprofit organization composed of chief state school officers in each U.S. state, the District of Columbia, the Department of Defense Education Activity, the Bureau of Indian Education, and five U.S. extra-state jurisdictions. See https://ccsso.org/.

Chapter 18

The New Urgency

Where there is no vision, the people perish.

—Proverbs 29:18[1]

If we are to raise and educate children for this new era, it is urgent to provide a positive vision for their future. What kind of country do we want them to live in? What are our common challenges to be addressed? We cannot repurpose education without first articulating our collective aspirations. We provided three examples of how to do this from our work in Egypt, Bosnia and Herzegovina, and Philadelphia. But what does repurposing look like in the United States writ large? What should be our collective aspiration? Martha Craven Nussbaum, a philosopher and current Ernst Freund Distinguished Service Professor of Law and Ethics at the University of Chicago, had this to say on the matter:

> The goal of democracies that want to remain stable cannot and should not
> be simply economic growth. . . . Thirsty for national profit, nations, and their
> systems of education, are heedlessly discarding skills that are needed to keep
> democracies alive. If this trend continues, nations all over the world will soon
> be producing generations of useful machines, rather than complete citizens who
> can think for themselves, criticize tradition, and understand the significance of
> another person's sufferings and achievements.[2]

People may have other views. Regardless, our conclusion after more than thirty years of working on education reform projects is this: If you want to make major improvements in education in the United States, your state, or community, first define the aspirations for the kind of society you want to live in for the future, then define the purpose of education in the context of those future aspirations in a way that powerfully engages students' interests, dreams, and moral and social relations.

In this final chapter, we address some of the anxieties, concerns, misunderstandings, and misrepresentations that will likely arise if we try to repurpose education for a new era. Perhaps the most anxiety-producing concern is the urgency of change itself.

THE ORDEAL OF CHANGE

Eric Hoffer, a self-educated San Francisco longshoreman, philosopher, farm worker, and Presidential Medal of Freedom awardee,[3] described in his book, *The Ordeal of Change*,[4] how the human species is often terrified of any kind of change. Born in 1902, Hoffer recounts his Depression-era days as a migrant farm worker where just the thought of changing from picking peas to picking green beans as he moved from place to place filled him with anxiety. How much more so for changes in our future aspirations and repurposing education! It is one of the great paradoxes of schooling that what looks so rigid, regular, and routine from the outside, with bus schedules, bells, class periods, and the sturdy structures of bricks and mortar, contains an invisible sea of constant change on the inside. Everything about education involves almost daily changes for parents, students, teachers, and administrators as well as new students, substitute teachers, new learning units, and different tests, to name only a few. Students are growing and changing physically, emotionally, and cognitively. This is one reason why teaching thirty students in a class, five classes a day is so taxing on teachers and why managing hundreds of students and scores of teachers in a school is so demanding of principals. The idea of making such fundamental changes as to the purpose of education must seem nearly impossible by comparison. We suggest, however, that changes involving repurposing education for a new era are not so overwhelming as might first appear. Actually, as we have seen in Egypt, an integrated and coherent curriculum that is more relevant and engaging for today's students will likely result in greater student motivation to learn and more satisfying student–teacher relationships.

We have purposely avoided using the phrase "education crisis." In our view, we are not in an education crisis; rather, we are in a time of urgency. The advanced computing and communication tools of this new era have greatly enlarged the shadows of extreme wealth inequality, nativism, White Christian supremacy, and anti-science. Malevolent actors both at home and abroad can spread misinformation and rumors far faster than truth can correct it. In a study of Twitter users, for example, researchers found it took the truth about six times longer to reach 1,500 people as falsehoods and that "false political news traveled deeper and more broadly, reached more people, and was more viral than any other category of false information."[5] The four shadows listed above get their energy from falsehoods. Any aspirational vision for our future must forthrightly address these shadows.

HYPER-PLURALISM AND THE "FIXING" OF EDUCATION

The subject of education is filled with code words and symbolism for these shadows. As a consequence, nothing quite stirs the blood as talking about education controversies: school segregation and desegregation, bilingualism, sex and gender education, prayer in schools, school funding, racism, and so on. Everyone seems to have an opinion. As surely as a lit match burns through straw, a cacophony of claims and counterclaims flares up whenever the subject of education arises. Some will say college is too expensive and we need more vocational education, others call for greater classroom discipline, and still others believe we need to ban certain books. We have witnessed many such sessions, whether at school board meetings or among teachers. They tend not to be productive. It is human nature to take every opportunity to air grievances, vent frustrations, or stir up trouble. For this reason, one should be wary of speeches that begin with what is wrong with education and how to fix it. Instead, education reform needs to begin with first principles—the framing of our aspirations for our country, our community, and our children's future within them.

These aspirational conversations are necessary because the thirteen archetypical purposes of education discussed in part I are still relevant for our time, yet none are entirely sufficient for it. Repurposing and reprioritization are needed. We should not despair over this task. There has scarcely been a time in our 400-year history when our educational system was not considered to be troubled. Given the enormous changes that have occurred over the span of even a generation, let alone a lifetime, education policymakers never quite reach the goals they have set for students before disruptive economic, social, and technological changes occur again. The education children need and desire at the present moment is not what was designed years, if not decades, prior. As a result, education always seems to be in a constant state of turmoil because it is always, to some degree, out of synchronization with what was planned in the past.

The responses to this perpetual turmoil have been rituals of education reform proposals and policy initiatives every few years. Often these new initiatives are introduced with great fanfare, as if they were the latest and greatest innovation. It is remarkable how most "new" programs have been tried previously. If we are to move forward with improving education, there is a higher urgency to come to some degree of aspirational consensus as to what kind of society and people we want to be for this new era. It is not necessary that the whole country agree on a single purpose of education, but that school curricula should be guided by the aspirational context of the community and state within which they operate.

NAVIGATING CURRENT SCHOOL STRUCTURES

Assuming we settle on an aspirational vision and have agreed upon a revised purpose of education that has been well-defined and elaborated upon, how do we navigate the current school structures? Here are some of the questions that are likely to arise and how we would answer them.

Our school already has a mission, vision, and values statement. What more do we need?

A statement of purpose has three elements that determine how to coherently organize a curriculum and connect many subjects and activities to it. It provides the rationale to teach this and not that. It prioritizes values, not just lists them. The purpose should imbue a school in a way that gives it an identity to form its culture. A student should be able to tell a stranger what it means to be a student at the school, something of what the school means to them, and how it has affected them. If mission, vision, and values statements do all these things, so much the better. If not, it is just rhetoric.

Can one of the archetypical purposes described in part I be used for this new era?

Yes, but they would need to be updated and revised to reflect the realities and community aspirations of this new era. For example, the Jeffersonian archetype of Education for Democracy was conceived when Blacks, Asians, Hispanics, Indians, women, and others were legally disenfranchised from voting. Thus, in today's context, Education for Democracy would need to be extended and elaborated upon as the organizing principle of a curriculum to include much more content. It involves much more than simply adding a civics class.

Can there be more than one purpose of education?

Yes. But there must be a *leading* purpose that best reflects the realities of this new era and the aspirations of the community. This lead purpose serves to direct the overall thrust of the curriculum and the identity of the school. Other purposes can be organized in relation to it. By way of analogy, consider a wedding celebration. While feeding guests is part of the celebration, it is not the *leading* purpose, otherwise it would be a restaurant.

How would you combine two or more purposes of education?

You don't combine them, you *connect* them. The leading purpose is how other purposes are connected. For example, suppose the leading purpose is education for democracy. One of the core ideas is the rule of law: including the rationale and process of creating laws and regulations, the various means of their enforcement, and how acts of corruption impact the well-being of citizens. So, if a school offers career and technical education programs, this aspect of democracy could be connected via the study of various public safety codes, their rationale, formulations, and enforcement mechanisms.

Will repurposing education mean the core academic subjects—math, science, social studies, and English—will no longer be taught?

No. Different aspects of these academic subjects may be emphasized more or less and contextualized to reflect the new purpose. Also, topics from other subjects may be rearranged and reordered to harmonize with each other. For example, the biochemistry of viruses and the mathematics of their transmission could be harmonized as part of a curriculum on pandemics and public health. The key is to have a reason for studying something that can be linked to the ultimate purpose of the school.

What about academic standards—do we do away with them?

No. State standards describe content to be covered in different academic subjects by grade bands (elementary, middle, and high school). They are usually developed by a panel of content experts in the field. But the reason to study a particular subject such as certain histories, for example, is a question of values that are set within a larger purpose. This larger purpose is above standards, but it does not do away with them. A state's academic standards determine the content of the curriculum but typically include much more content than can be reasonably taught. Therefore, choices must be made about what to teach, what to emphasize, and what to test.

Does a repurposing of education mean core academic courses will be "dumbed down"?

No. The current content of the core academic courses should instead be enhanced by making connections to other subjects. One of the great problems with current siloed subjects is that students often forget what they were taught. Research shows that when material is meaningful to students and connected to other subjects, students have greater retention of what they learned over time. Sterilized, siloed subject matter devoid of context and meaning learned only for the next test is soon forgotten.

What if parents disagree about the new purpose of education for a new era?

Repurposing education for a new era depends on both the existing and emerging realities of this era and the community's aspirations for the shape and character of its collective future. The process of agreement begins there and needs to represent all aspects of the public who have an interest in publicly funded education. This includes parents, of course, but it also includes others who have a stake in how new generations of young people are raised and educated. The ideal is to build a consensus as much as possible around common aspirations. Not all may agree, but not all agree now. At least start the conversation. Repurposing the curriculum follows.

What happens to traditional subjects like algebra? Do we have to get rid of it?

No. Algebra will still be taught but it will be in service to the purpose of the school and in the context of phenomena and problems rather than being taught disconnected from other subjects. Also, other math concepts may be introduced, such as applied statistics and probability, game theory and risk assessment, architectural and construction geometry,[6] and social network analysis. The same would be true with other traditional core subjects.

How do we improve low math scores in our districts, especially among students of color and other student subpopulations that are chronically below grade level?

One of the biggest and most persistent misconceptions is that teaching to the test by drilling students on meaningless math problems will somehow lead to better state math scores. The other misconception is that spending time to develop students' understanding of key math concepts using interesting and playful exercises that connect to other subjects is a waste of time. In reality, improved performance on state-mandated tests is a by-product of students who are well motivated to take them and who have a grasp of the underlying concepts of the test questions. Once students attain such understanding, orienting them to the type of questions on the test can be productive.

How do you handle politically divisive topics like critical race theory?

Critical race theory is an examination of how racial discrimination has been built into some U.S. laws and institutional policies. It is a legal and academic framework taught in law schools and graduate school programs. Legalized racial discrimination and unequal treatment is part of U.S. history. For example, in the chapter on White Supremacy and the Doctrine of Discovery, we provided two such examples from the U.S. Supreme Court (Chief Justices John Marshall and Roger Taney). The question as to how the histories of people with different racial, ethnic, religious, national, and gender identities are to be treated in the curriculum is a legitimate question. History is deep and wide. Choices must be made about what to teach because not every aspect of every group or person can be taught. Whether and when it is appropriate to teach students about the Doctrine of Discovery, or the Indian Removal Act,[7] both examples of White Christian Supremacist legal structures depend on the purpose of education. If the purpose is to mythologize the history of America, these legal structures of supremacist terror and oppression would not likely be taught. There is a great political advantage in promoting such mythologies. In Woodrow Wilson's book *The New Freedom*, for example, he continued to perpetrate America's origin myth:

> Columbus did not find, as he had expected, the civilization of Cathay; he found an empty continent. In that part of the world, upon that new-found half of the globe, mankind, late in its history was thus afforded an opportunity to set up a new civilization; here it was strangely privileged to make a new human experiment.[8]

Alternatively, if the purpose of history is to dispel popular myths and portray events and people as accurately as possible from multiple perspectives, then a more honest, complete history should be taught, that is, the continent was not empty but filled with millions of Indigenous inhabitants who had lived on the continent for some 16,000 years; Spain and the U.S. government waged war against Indigenous peoples in the Americas for over 300 years; and so on.

Teaching about certain aspects of American history can be uncomfortable for children. Can't some myths about America be preserved?

As with any purpose of education, what is taught must be age appropriate. Children already come to school with lots of myths, misconceptions, and magical thinking. There is no need to add to them. The Santa Claus myth has its place and time. But how and when these myths are dispelled is a developmental process that the K-12 curriculum scope and sequence should reflect. Some of the more disturbing topics of our history and current events should be deferred until children are more mature so that difficult and complex subjects will not be treated simplistically. Many young people come to school already fearful of the news they hear and people's hateful rhetoric. Some are already traumatized by events in their home life, or by accidents, fights on the street, or active shooter drills in their classrooms. Too many have experienced the trauma of actual shootings, as guns are the leading cause of death among school children and teens.[9] Teachers, too, are caught up in these traumatic events and the threats of more shootings in the future. We must see these issues in proportion to how they are affecting children's and their teachers' lives. But we should expect learning to be uncomfortable and difficult at times. Upending cherished bigotries and myths can be disconcerting, but that is the natural process of becoming educated.

Will my child be less likely to be admitted to a good college or university?

No. Selective college admissions criteria involve many factors and are determined by each college or university. A more relevant purpose of K-12 education that is market relevant should provide more motivation for students to pursue and succeed in higher education.

The United States already has science, technology, engineering, and mathematics (STEM) and science, technology, engineering, arts, and mathematics (STEAM) schools. What is the difference in the need to repurpose education?

This is a misconception. Neither STEM nor STEAM are themselves purposes of education in the sense that we have been using the notion of purpose. Rather, they are acronyms to denote a desired goal of having an integrated approach to multiple subjects. But to what end? Rather, one first needs a clearly stated purpose to serve as the organizing principle by which subjects can be integrated. Simply saying a school is a STEM or STEAM school begs the question as to its ultimate purpose.

THE NATION AT RISK LEGACY

The claim will likely be made that moving away from the Nation at Risk archetype by a repurposing of education for the new era will result in more risk to our nation and greater youth unemployment. A great deal has been invested in trying to achieve the Nation at Risk goals and academic, governmental, and corporate interests are continuing along this track, however obsolete. Therefore, in this concluding chapter, we need to address this potential claim directly.

The *Nation at Risk* report suffered from two faulty premises. The first was that the risk to the nation was and still is economic. The second was that raising the level of educational attainment would be sufficient for global competitiveness and employment.

Wealth as Well-Being

The first faulty premise of the *Nation at Risk* report was its narrow focus on our global economic competitiveness as *the* national risk rather than our national well-being. In the ledger of life, there are two opposing columns. On the positive side are all those things that add value to a person, family, and community. On the other side are all the ills that rob people and societies of life: disease, crime, incarceration, addictions, abusive relationships, theft, preventable accidents, and so on. These negative elements can be assigned an economic cost, but their impact cannot be reduced to it. Losing a child to a fatal opioid overdose, for example, exacts an immeasurable personal cost on a parent.

Thus, there is a definition of wealth that includes personal, familial, and community well-being along with material prosperity. Food, water, housing, medical services, and security are foundational to well-being. Without these, energies are focused on meeting the barest needs of survival and are not available for higher levels of thriving, including the civic participation that a robust democracy relies upon.[10] This is why one of the risks to our nation is the almost unbreachable chasm between the extremely rich and the bottom half of our society. To this risk, we add the other three risks to well-being: the shadows of nativism, supremacism, and anti-science. On the negative side is whatever interferes with the development and fulfillment of individuals' sense of self-worth, creativity, career, family, accomplishments, and all other aspects of life that build community and national well-being. It is the kind of wealth that sustains and enhances the capabilities and/or quality of life for everyone. It allows us to meet our personal challenges as well as national challenges without compromising our economic status. The kind of wealth that refers to well-being is what allows democracies to flourish.

Education can play an important role in adding to the positive side of the ledger and minimizing the negative side. What the *Nation at Risk* report missed was all the other risks to our national life that a repurposed education system could address.

Market-Relevant Knowledge

The second faulty premise of the *Nation at Risk* report was that higher educational attainment in the core academic subjects would increase U.S. global competitiveness and by implication lead to a greater pool of skilled workers with more employment for them. But the causal lines from one to the other were never clearly drawn. As we discussed in part III, there is a tenuous connection between higher education and better jobs. The United States is not alone. All over the world, developing and developed countries are facing the problem of the educated unemployed or underemployed. In a survey of 114 countries, 28 percent of workers (298 million) were over-educated. In total, 935 million workers have jobs that don't match their educational level.[11]

It could be argued that the alignment of education and workforce development could be made tighter, that there is no need to abandon the Nation at Risk archetype as a purpose of education. We agree that the alignment could and should be tighter. The issue is whether the forty-year-old Nation at Risk archetype should remain *the* prime purpose or whether a newer repurpose of education for a new era is called for. We have tried to make the case for the latter. It is a question of priority. Dethroning college and career success from the top priority in education does not mean it has no place. It is not a case of either-or, but both-and. In any event, a closer alignment between content courses and workforce development can happen. How is this to be done?

The short answer is to design curriculum so that it is more market-relevant. What we mean is that subject matter content has aspects to it that can be situated in economic life, thereby providing students insight into the inner workings of various business sectors and the occupations associated with them. This is a task for a team of curriculum developers that includes business and industry people. We will provide a brief illustration of how it can be done. Suppose as part of our new purpose of education we want to equip students to better manage risk to themselves and others. Since many young people tend to think they are bulletproof, lectures of this sort are likely to fall on deaf ears. They are more interested in making money. Instead, a teacher presents this conundrum to them. *What business is one of the largest in the world worth $5.5 trillion in sales,*[12] *but you can't see, touch, taste, hear, or smell it and you cannot buy it in any department store, but you can buy it in any city, state, or country?* After lively guessing and some hints, they finally say, "insurance"! The teacher explains that the entire insurance industry is based on a simple mathematical concept known as "expected value" (the probability of something happening times the cost or benefit of it happening). Now they are likely to be more interested in learning about risk management. This is what we mean by "market-relevant knowledge" that can easily be taught in a math and economics class. A critical piece of market-relevant knowledge involves the "soft skills" of creativity, problem-solving, and adaptability. One annual survey of nearly 1,400 CEOs reported that 77 percent of them had difficulty finding people with the innovation and creativity skills they greatly needed.[13] These skills, essential for the new era, are major components of the purpose- and project-based high schools we helped develop in Egypt and Bosnia and Herzegovina.

SUSTAINING THE VISION, CREATING THE FUTURE

As we have seen in part I of this book, societies are not static; they continuously change, mostly incrementally, but sometimes with major, almost seismic changes. When the proverbial ground has shifted, as we believe it has in this new era, we have to ask how we can be sure that we are building for a still unknowable future and not replicating the past. If we commit to repurposing education for a new era, will it be sustainable in the long run? Should we not also develop a process so that as the ground shifts the institution of education can respond? Just as in our lifetimes in which we have experienced both incremental and seismic shifts, we know that the future will bring more new eras. The process does not stop; if anything, it will accelerate due to our global and technological society and the artificial intelligence that will most likely become part of our technoscape within the next generation.

To repurpose education for a new era, it is neither necessary nor practical to tear down everything and start over. There exists a firm foundation upon which we can build schools for the future. But if the purpose of education is no longer responsive to the external and internal contexts, school is reduced to habit without meaning. That is where we believe we are at this time.

Figure 18.1 examines this cycle of change in greater depth to help the reader understand sustainability. When we talk of a sustainable yet responsive system, we are thinking of the entire complex within which K-12 schools, universities, businesses, services, arts, and culture are situated and interact. We

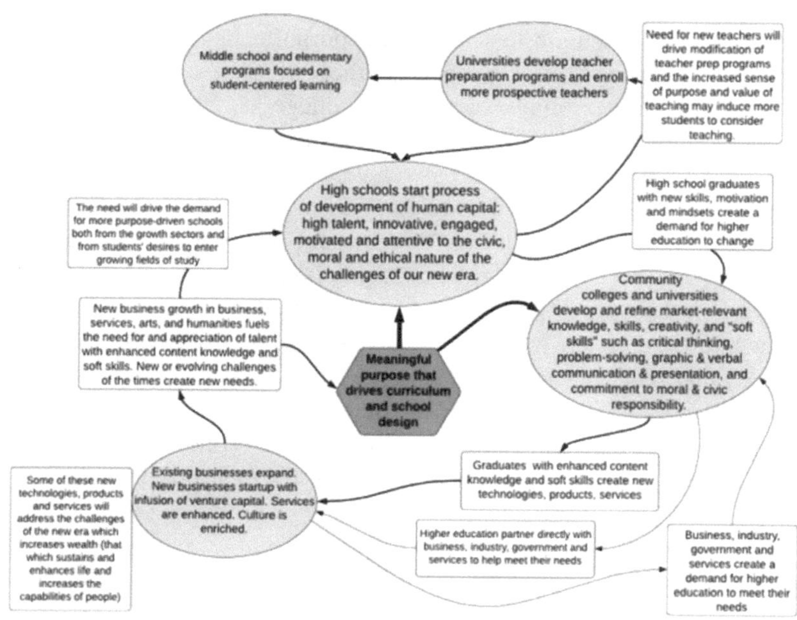

Figure 18.1 A Sustainable Cycle of Change. *Source*: Deborah Pomeroy and F. Joseph Merlino.

believe that true sustainability—the kind that generates energy and enhances the well-being and wealth of all members of the community, be it local, state, national, or global—can only be achieved when the purpose of schooling is relevant to the needs of the community and its institutions while at the same time being meaningful to the students. We see education as an economic enabler by embedding market-relevant realities into academic subjects so that students can gain insight into their possible place in our economic life and thus prepare them to make more informed career and life choices.

One can see that coordination, networking, and feedback are critical to ensure alignment of the main system components. In considering the systemic nature of such change it is apparent that school repurposing for this new era cannot happen overnight, but it is urgent we begin. We are not talking about the traditional curriculum evaluation process that many schools/districts undergo every five or ten years. Such mid-course assessments and adjustments are necessary, but here we are talking of a bigger process.

One can appreciate that for the cycle to be complete and sustaining, it might take as much as twenty years, especially when considering the magnitude and pace of changes in educational institutions. As we have seen in Egypt, however, significant and noteworthy change in high schools is now driving changes in higher education and partnerships with businesses. Elementary, middle, and general education high schools in Egypt are beginning to feel the impact of the STEM schools. The process of repurposing schools and designing a curriculum to support new purposes has moved from theory to practice. We know it can happen when the will is there.

In the United States, many community colleges already have strong ties to businesses and the health and service industries. Some undergraduate and professional graduate programs in universities have internships in these same sectors for students. Hubs for research and development in many sectors connect universities, industry, and even government. Those networks are ripe for inclusion in the process of repurposing schools. Sadly, the arts and humanities have languished with the drive toward technology, but they need to be brought into the process for the insights, talents, creativity, thoughtfulness, reflection, and balance they provide. With appropriate training, many high school graduates will go into the workforce directly where they, too, will contribute to the wealth and well-being generation. Without their work, their human capital, the wheels of our communities would grind to a halt.

AN INVITATION

In the previous chapter, we focused on the task of articulating and deconstructing the purpose of schooling. In this chapter, we have laid out how it can be done and some of the rhetorical and logistical obstacles in doing so. In closing, we invite you to momentarily set aside your past assumptions and personal experiences of schooling to think about your vision for repurposing education for a new era. How do you think we can bring our schools more authentically into the fabric of our communities with a meaningful purpose for our students that does not create ceilings of low expectation? What do you think is the purpose of schooling that will engage our youth in light of the world they see around them? How we as families, communities, and a nation answer these questions will determine our trajectories in the new era in which we find ourselves. To be done well will take time. But there is an urgency to start the process now for the sake of our children and the future of our society as a free people.

NOTES

1. King James Version.

2. Martha C. Nussbaum, *Not for Profit: Why Democracy Needs the Humanities* (Princeton University Press, 2010), 2, 53.

3. Martin Weil, "Eric Hoffer, Author and Philosopher, Dies," *Washington Post*, May 22, 1983 https://www.washingtonpost.com/archive/local/1983/05/22/eric-hoffer -author-and-philosopher-dies/c9e26596-8791-478c-b8e1-558458fbe941/.

4. Eric Hoffer, *The Ordeal of Change Harper & Row*, 1963.

5. Soroush Vosoughi et al., "The Spread of True and False News Online," *Science* 359, no. 6380 (March 9, 2018): 1146–1151, https://doi.org/10.1126/science .aap9559

6. William Blackwell, *Geometry in Architecture* (Key Curriculum Press, 1984).

7. Indian Treaties and the Removal Act of 1830. US State Department Office of the Historian https://history.state.gov/milestones/1830-1860/indian-treaties

8. Woodrow Wilson, *The New Freedom* (Doubleday Page and Co., 1913), 277–278, https://www.google.com/books/edition/The_New_Freedom/MW8SAAAAIAAJ ?hl=en.

9. Matt McGough, Krutika Amin, Nirmita Panchal, and Cynthia Cox, "Child and Teen Firearm Mortality in the U.S. and Peer Countries Kaiser Family Foundation (KFF)," July 8, 2022, https://www.kff.org/global-health-policy/issue-brief/child-and -teen-firearm-mortality-in-the-u-s-and-peer-countries/#:~:text=Firearms%20recently %20became%20the%20number,those%20caused%20by%20other%20injuries.

10. Abraham H. Maslow, *Toward a Psychology of Being* (Simon and Schuster, 2013 [first published 1968]). ISBN 978-1-62793-274-5.

11. Rosina Gammarano, International Labor Organization, Department of Statistics. February 2020, https://ilostat.ilo.org/258-million-workers-in-the-world-are-over -educated-for-their-jobs/.

12. McKinsey.

13. PriceWaterhouseCoopers International, "20th CEO Survey," 2017, https:// www.pwc.com/gx/en/ceo-survey/2017/deep-dives/ceo-survey-global-talent.pdf.

Bibliography

2023 SAT Suite of Assessments Downloadable Full-Length Practice Tests. (n.d.). College Board. https://satsuite.collegeboard.org/digital/digital-practice-preparation /practice-tests/linear.

A Short History of American Labor. Adapted from AFL-CIO American Federationist, Vol. 88, No. 3, March 1981. https://oac.cdlib.org/ark:/28722/bk0003z4v2t/ ?brand=oac4.

Aarons, Dakari I. "Backers Say Chicago Project Not 'Radical.'" *Education Week,* October 9, 2008.

About – NCSSS. (n.d.). https://www.ncsss.org/about/.

About Us - American Association of Christian Schools. (2023, August 3). American Association of Christian Schools. https://www.aacs.org/about-us/.

About Us. (n.d.). MicroSociety - Helping Kids Create Their Own Worlds Inside School. https://www.microsociety.org/about-us/.

About. (2023, October 19). North Carolina School of Science and Mathematics. https://www.ncssm.edu/about.

Achieve. "Contributors." Last modified 2021. https://www.achieve.org/contributors.

Adams, David Wallace. *Education for Extinction American Indians and the Boarding School Experience, 1875-1928.* Lawrence, KS: University Press of Kansas, 1995.

Adams, Frank D. "Sir William Dawson." *The Journal of Geology* 7, no. 8 (November–December 1899): 727–36.

Adelman, Clifford. "Answers in the Tool Box: Academic Intensity, Attendance Patterns, and Bachelor's Degree Attainment." U.S. Department of Education, June, 1999. https://eric.ed.gov/?id=ED431363.

Adelman, Clifford. "The Toolbox Revisited: Paths to Degree Completion from High School Through College." U.S. Department of Education, 2006.

ADP Network. (2017, January 11). Achieve. http://www.achieve.org/adp-network.

Allen, John L. "From Cabot to Cartier: The Early Exploration of Eastern North America, 1497–1543." *Annals of the Association of American Geographers* 82, no. 3 (September 1992): 500–21.

American College Health Association. American College Health Association-National College Health Assessment II: Reference Group Executive Summary Spring 2019. Silver Spring, MD: American College Health Association, 2019. https://www.acha.org/documents/ncha/NCHA-II_SPRING_2019_US_REFERENCE_GROUP_EXECUTIVE_SUMMARY.pdf.

American Federation of Labor | The Online Books Page. (n.d.). https://onlinebooks.library.upenn.edu/webbin/book/lookupname?key=American%20Federation%20of%20Labor.

American Protestant Association. Address of the Board of Managers (1843), 14, 18. https://babel.hathitrust.org/cgi/pt?id=umn.31951001508384m&view=1up&seq=5.

Amuzegar, Jahangir. *The Dynamics of the Iranian Revolution: The Pahlavi's Triumph and Tragedy.* New York, NY: SUNY Press, 1991.

Annenberg Foundation. "The Annenberg Challenge." https://annenberg.org/initiatives/the-annenberg-challenge/.

"An Open Letter to United States Secretary of Education." November 1999. http://www.mathematicallycorrect.com/riley.htm.

"An Original Bill to Reauthorize the Elementary and Secondary Education Act of 1965 to Ensure that Every Child Achieves." Public Law 114–95, December 2015. https://www.congress.gov/bill/114th-congress/senate-bill/1177/text.

AP Data and Research – AP Central | College Board. (n.d.). https://apcentral.collegeboard.org/about-ap/ap-data-research.

Arab Republic of Egypt Ministry of Education. "National Strategic Plan for Pre-University Education Reform in Egypt." 2007.

Archives and Special Collections | City University of New York (CUNY) Research | CUNY Academic Works (n.d.). https://academicworks.cuny.edu/ny_arch/.

Aristotle, *Politics. Book VIII. Part II.* 350 B.C. The Internet Classics Archive. Accessed November 17, 2023. http://classics.mit.edu/Aristotle/politics.8.eight.html.

Arizona State University. "Social Justice and Human Rights, MA." Accessed May 2, 2023, https://newcollege.asu.edu/social-justice-and-human-rights-ma.

Asimov, Nanette. "UC Settles Student Lawsuit, Agrees Not to Use SAT, ACT Scores in Admissions." *San Francisco Chronical,* May 14, 2021. https://www.sfchronicle.com/local/article/UC-settles-student-lawsuit-agrees-not-to-use-16178677.php.

Auchmuty, Richard T. "The Need of Trade Schools." *The Century* (November 1886): 83–92. https://www.unz.com/print/Century-1886nov-00083.

Auritt, Elizabeth S. "Harvard Accepts Record Low of 5.9 Percent to the Class of 2016." *The Harvard Crimson*, March 29, 2012.

Avrich, Paul. *The Modern School Movement: Anarchism and Education in the United States.* Princeton, NJ: Princeton University Press, 2014.

Bailey, Sir Edward B. "James Hutton, Founder of Modern Geology (1726–1797)." In Conference Proceedings of the Royal Society of Edinburgh, Section B.: Biology 63, no. 4 (January 1949), 357–68.

Baldwin, James. "A Talk to Teachers." *The Saturday Review*, December 21, 1963.

Balmforth, Tom. "Life in Stalin's Gulags." *The Atlantic*, March 4, 2013.

Barber, William H., Liz Theoharis, Timothy B. Tyson, and Cornel West. "What Courage to Change History Looks Like." *The New York Times*, June 19, 2020. https://www.nytimes.com/2020/06/19/opinion/floyd-protests-race-america.html.

Barnard, Henry, Ed. "Biography of Ezekiel Cheever with Notes on The Early Free of Grammar Schools of New England." *The American Journal of Education* 1 London: Trubner & Co (1856): 297–314. Google books.

Barsoum, Ghada. "No Jobs and Bad Jobs: Defusing Egypt's Demographic Youth Bulge Requires Job Creation—and a Safety Net." *Cairo Review* 10 (2013): 160. https://www.thecairoreview.com/wp-content/uploads/2014/12/CR10_Barsoum.pdf.

Barsoum, Ghada. "Arab Youth: The Challenges of Education, Employment and Civic Participation." *OIDA International Journal of Sustainable Development* 5 (2012): 39–54.

Baylies, Francis, and Samuel Gardner Drake. *An Historical Memoir of the Colony of New Plymouth: From the Flight of the Pilgrims into Holland in the Year 1608, to the Union of that Colony with Massachusetts in 1692.* Boston, MA: Wiggin & Lunt, 1866.

Beckenstein, Myron. "Maine's Lost Colony: Archeologists Uncover an Early American Settlement that History Forgot." *Smithsonian Magazine*, February 2004.

Beier, Grischa, Silke Niehoff, and Mandy Hoffmann. "Industry 4.0: A Step Towards achieving the SDGs? A Critical Literature Review." *Discover Sustainability* 2, no. 22 (April 2021). doi:10.1007/s43621-021-00030-1.

Bennett, Charles A. *History of Manual and Industrial Education 1870-1917.* Peoria: The Manual Arts Press, 1937. https://ia800206.us.archive.org/31/items/historyofmanuali00bennrich/historyofmanuali00bennrich.pdf.

Berdnychenko, Yuliia and Olha Petrykovets. "Evolution of World and Domestic Production of Internal Combustion Engines." *History of Science and Technology* 9, no. 2 (2019): 139–46. doi:10.32703/2415-7422-2019-9-2(15)-139-146.

Berkman, Michael B., J. S. Pacheco and E. Plutzer. "Evolution and Creationism in America's Classrooms: A National Portrait." *PLOS Biology* 6, no. 5 (May 20, 2008). doi:10.1371/journal.pbio.0060124.

Bernstein, Barton J. "Sacrifices and Decisions: Lewis L. Strauss." *The Public Historian* 8, no. 2 (April 1986): 105–120. doi:10.2307/3377436.

Best 389 Colleges 2024. (n.d.). https://www.princetonreview.com/college-rankings/best-colleges.

Bhagavad Gita, Chapter 11, Verse 32 –The Song of God. (n.d.). Edited by Swami Mukundananda. https://www.holy-bhagavad-gita.org.

Blackmer, Alan R., Henry Wilkinson Bragdon, McGeorge Bundy, E. Harris Harbison, Charles Seymour, Jr. and Wendell H. Taylor. *General Education in School and College: A Committee Report by Members of* the *Faculties of Andover, Exeter, Lawrenceville, Harvard, Princeton, and Yale.* Cambridge, MA: Harvard University Press, 1952.

Blackwell, William. *Geometry in Architecture.* Oakland, CA: Key Curriculum Press, 1984.

Blum, Lawrence P. "Research News and Communications." *The Journal of Educational Research* 45, no. 1 (1951): 67–74. doi:10.1080/00220671.1951.1088 1921.

Board of Governors of the Federal Reserve System. "Distribution of Household Wealth in the U.S. Since 1989." https://www.federalreserve.gov/releases/z1/dataviz/dfa/distribute/table/#quarter:133;series:Net%20worth;demographic:networth;population:all;units:shares.

Boston Latin School. (n.d.). http://www.bls.org.

Bourguignon, Francois and Christian Morrisson. "Inequality Among World Citizens: 1820- 1992." *The American Economic Review* 92, no. 4 (2002): 727–44. doi:10.1257/000282802603444443.

Bowden, Mark. "The Desert One Debacle." *The Atlantic,* May 2006.

Brainard, John G. "Genesis of the ENIAC." *Technology and Culture* 17, no. 3 (July 1976): 482–88.

Bransford, J. D. eds. *How People Learn: Brain, Mind, Experience, and School.* Washington, DC: National Academy Press, 2000. doi:10.17226/9853.

Breakstone, Joel, Mark Smith, Sam Wineburg, Amie Rapaport, Jill Carle, Marshall Garland and Anna Saavedra. "Students' Civic Online Reasoning: A National Portrait." *Education Researcher* 50, no. 8 (2019): 505–15.

Breig, James. https://www.colonialwilliamsburg.org.

Brenan, Megan. "40% of Americans Believe in Creationism." *Gallup,* July 26, 2019. https://news.gallup.com/poll/261680/americans-believe-creationism.aspx.

Broton, Katharine M., and Clare L. Cady. *Food Insecurity on Campus Action and Intervention.* Baltimore, MD: Johns Hopkins University Press, 2020.

Brown, Sarah Kropp. (2021, September 30). *Are Evangelicals Anti-Science?* National Association of Evangelicals. https://www.nae.org/evangelicals-anti-science/.

Bryk, Anthony S., Valerie E. Lee and Peter B. Holland. *Catholic Schools and the Common Good.* Cambridge: Harvard University Press, 1993.

Building a World-Class Education Ecosystem in Qatar. (n.d.). Qatar Foundation. https://www.qf.org.qa/education.

Burtt, Edwin Arthur. *The Metaphysical Foundations of Modern Physical Science.* New York: Taylor & Francis, 2014.

Bush, George H. W. "The State of the Union." January 31, 1990. http://webarchive.loc.gov/congressional-record/20160311160455/.

Cady, L. F. "Elementary Classical Instruction." *The American Journal of Education* 12, (1862): 562–70. Accessed November 18, 2023. https://archive.org/details/sim_american-journal-of-education-1855_1862-12_12_4/page/560/mode/2up?view=theater.

Cai, Jinfa and F. Joseph Merlino. "Metaphors: A Powerful Means for Assessing Students' Mathematical Dispositions." In 73rd Yearbook: Motivation and Disposition: Pathways to Learning Mathematics, edited by Daniel J. Brahier and William R. Speer, pp. 147–56. Reston, VA: National Council of Teachers of Mathematics, 2011.

California Department of Education. "Mathematics Framework." Modified July 14, 2022. https://www.cde.ca.gov/ci/ma/cf/.

California School Boards Association. "The School Board Role in Creating the Conditions for Student Achievement." May 2017. https://www.csba.org/GovernanceAndPolicyResources#gsc.tab=0.

Callender, Guy Stevens. *Selections from The Economic History of the United States 1765-1860.*

California: Ginn and Co., 1909, pp. 271–344.

Camera, Lauren. "Lawsuit Against University of California System Challenges SAT, ACT Admissions Requirement." *U.S. News and World Report*, December 10, 2019.

Campus Compact. "Deepening the Roots of Civic Engagement: 2011 Annual Membership Survey - Executive Summary". *Higher Education*, 2011, p. 152. https://digitalcommons.unomaha.edu/slcehighered/152.

Causey, J., A. Pevitz, M. Ryu, A. Scheetz and Shapiro, D. Completing College: National and State Report on Six-Year Completion Rates for Fall 2015 Beginning Cohort, ebook. National Student Clearinghouse Research Center, 2022. https://nscresearchcenter.org/wp-content/uploads/Completions_Report_2021.pdf.

Cavanagh, Sean. "New Algebra 2 Test Suggests States Face High Hurdles." *Education Week,* August 27, 2008. http://www.edweek.org/ew/articles/2008/08/27/01achieve.h28.html.

Center for Education Statistics. "Summary of Expenditures for Public Elementary and Secondary Education and Other Related Programs, by Purpose: Selected Years, 1919-20 through 2017-18." Accessed November 21, 2023. https://nces.ed.gov/programs/digest/d20/tables/dt20_236.10.asp.

Centers for Disease Control and Prevention. "COVID-19 Science Update." Last modified December 18, 2021. https://www.cdc.gov/library/covid19/scienceupdates.html?Sort=Date%3A%3Adesc.

Central Agency for Public Mobilization and Statistics. "Egypt in Figures: Population Estimates by Sex and Age." Accessed February 14, 2023. https://www.capmas.gov.eg/Pages/Publications.aspx?page_id=5104&Year=23602.

Central Intelligence Agency. "USSR-Iran Boundary, 1951." Declassified report 4/17/2000. https://www.cia.gov/readingroom/docs/CIA-RDP79-00976A000200010003-4.pdf.

Chambers, John Whiteclay. *The Tyranny of Change: America in the Progressive Era, 1890- 1920,* 3rd edition. Newark: Rutgers University Press, 2000.

Chancel, Lucas, Thomas Piketty, Emmanuel Saez and Gabriel Zucman. "World Inequality Report 2022." World Inequality Lab. https://wir2022.wid.world/.

Charles Koch & Family. (n.d.). Forbes. https://www.forbes.com/profile/charles-koch/?sh=7163e7ed57d7.

Chen, Xianglei and Matthew Soldner. "STEM Attrition: College Students' Paths Into and Out of STEM Fields (NCES 2014-001)." Institute of Education Sciences, U.S. Department of Education, November 2013. http://nces.ed.gov/pubs2014/2014001rev.pdf.

Cherlet, Michael, Charles Hutchinson, James Reynolds, Joachim Hill, Stefan Sommer and Graham Von Maltitz, eds. "World Atlas of Desertification." Publication Office of the European Union, 2018. http://wad.jrc.ec.europa.eu.

Chubb, John E. and Terry M. Moe. *Politics, Markets, and America's Schools.* Washington, DC: Brookings Institution Press, 1990.

Clinedinst, Melissa. "2019 State of College Admission." National Association for College Admission Counseling. ebook (2019). https://nacacnet.org/wp-content/uploads/2022/10/soca2019_all.pdf.

Coalition of Essential Schools. "Common Principles: From 9 to 10." http://essentialschools.org/common-principles-from-9-to-10.

Coate, Douglas and James VanderHoff. "Public School Spending and Student Achievement: The Case of New Jersey." *Cato Journal* 19, no. 1 (1999): 85–99.

Cocks, Edmund. *Early History of the Public School System in Bucks County*, Doylestown Meeting, May 7, 1938." The Bucks County Historical Society Papers Reads Before the Society and Other Historical Papers, Volume VIII, 21. https://archive.org/stream/buckscountyhisto08buck/buckscountyhisto08buck_djvu.txt.

Cohen, Sol. "The Industrial Education Movement 1906-1917." *American Quarterly* 20, no. 1 (Spring 1968): 95–110.

Cole, David. "Classical Education." *The American Journal of Education* 1 (1856): 71–2, 77.

Collection: Cigar Makers' International Union of America records | Archival Collections. (n.d.). https://archives.lib.umd.edu/repositories/2/resources/1659.

College Board. "Inside the Test." Accessed May 28, 2023. https://collegereadiness.collegeboard.org/sat/inside-the-test.

Columbus, Christopher. *Epistola Christofori Colom* (Letters of Christopher Columbus), Rome. Stephan Plannck, Rare Book and Special Collections Division, Library of Congress), https://www.loc.gov/exhibits/exploring-the-early-americas/columbus-and-the-taino.html..

"Common Core State Standards." Common Core State Standards Initiative. Modified 2023. http://www.corestandards.org/.

Comptroller General of the United States. "Report to Congress: Issues Related to U. S. Military Sales and Assistance to Iran." October 21, 1974. https://www.gao.gov/assets/120/111930.pdf.

Conley, David T. *College and Career Ready: Helping All Students Succeed Beyond High School.* Indianapolis: Jossey-Bass, 2011.

Contributors. (2018, April 9). Achieve https://www.achieve.org/contributors.

Cook, Benjamin I., J. E. Smerdon, E.R. Cook, A.P. Williams, K.J. Anchukaitis, J. S. Mankin, K. Allen, L. Andreu-Hayles, T. R. Ault, S. Belmecheri and S. Coats. "Megadroughts in the Common Era and the Anthropocene." *Nature Revisions Earth & Environment* 3 (2022): 741–57. doi: 10.1038/s43017-022-00329-1.

Cook-Sather, Alison. "Sound, Presence, and Power: 'Student Voice' in Educational Research and Reform." *Curriculum Inquiry* 36 (2006): 359–90.

Coram, Robert. *Political Inquiries, to Which Is Added a Plan For the Establishment of Schools Throughout the United States.* Wilmington, DE: Andrews and Brynberg, 1791.

Cotton, John. "The Powring Out of the Seven Vials: Or An exposition, of the 16. Chapter of the Revelation, with an Application of it to Our Times" (1642).

Accessed November 17, 2023. https://quod.lib.umich.edu/e/eebo2/A80630.0001 .001?view=toc.

Council on Competitiveness. "Innovate America: National Innovation Initiative Summit and Report." 2005, 7. https://competeorg.wpengine.com/wp-content/uploads/ ncf-reports/nii-innovate-america-2005.pdf.

Crawford, Evan. "How Nonpartisan Ballot Design Conceals Partisanship: A Survey Experiment of School Board Members in Two States." *Political Research Quarterly* 71, no. 1 (March 2018): 143–56.

Cress, Joseph. "Army to Disinter Remains of Six Carlisle Indian School Students in June." *The Sentinel,* March 3, 2022. https://cumberlink.com/news/local/history/.

Critical Explorers (n.d.). https://criticalexplorers.org/.

Cultural Principles and Education Framework Cultivate Strong Hawaiian Identity in KS Learners. (January 9, 2017). Kamehameha Schools. https://www.ksbe.edu/article/cultural-principles-and-education-framework-cultivate-a-strong-hawaiian-ide.

Cuthbertson, Ken. *The Halifax Explosion: Canada's Worst Disaster.* Toronto, ON: Patrick Crean Editions, 2017.

Daniels, John D. "The Indian Population of North America in 1492." *The William and Mary Quarterly* 49, no. 2 (April 1992): 298–320.

Darwin, Charles. *The Descent of Man, and Selection in Relation to Sex.* London: John Murray, 1871.

Darwin, Charles. *On the Origin of Species by Means of Natural Selection, or the Preservation of Favoured Races in the Struggle for Life.* London: John Murray, 1859.

Davie, H. (2018, October 19). Soviet Casualties - Factors, Effects and Outcomes — History of Military Logistics. https://www.hgwdavie.com/blog/2018/10/6/soviet -casualties.

Davis, Kristina and Gary Robbins. "University of San Diego, Local Families Caught Up in College Admissions Scandal." *San Diego Union-Tribune*, March 12, 2019.

Dawson, Scott. *The Lost Colony and Hatteras Island.* Cheltenham, Gloucestershire: The History Press, 2020.

de Riencourt, Amaury. *The American Empire.* Dial Press, 1968.

Dervarics, Chuck and Eileen O'Brien. *Eight Characteristics of an Effective School Board.* Center for Public Education, 2019. https://www.nsba.org/-/media/NSBA /File/cpe-eight-characteristics-of-effective-school-boards-report-december-2019 .pdf.

Des Moines Register. "Tornado Archive: A History of Twisters: Tornadoes in Iowa since 1950 as of 2023." Accessed May 8, 2023. https://datacentral.desmoinesregister.com/tornado- archive.

Dewey, John. *Experience and Education.* New York: Macmillan Company, 1938.

DiAngelo, Robin. "White Fragility." *International Journal of Critical Pedagogy* 3, no. 3 (2011): 54–70.

Dion-Schwarz, Cynthia, David Manheim and Patrick B. Johnston. *Terrorist Use of Cryptocurrencies: Technical and Organizational Barriers and Future Threats.* Santa Monica, CA: RAND Corporation, 2019.

Dixon-Román, Ezekiel J., Howard T. Everson and John J. McArdle. "Race, Poverty and SAT Scores: Modeling the Influences of Family Income on Black and White High School Students' SAT Performance." *Teachers College Record* 115, no. 4, (2013): 1–33. https://www.cs.jhu.edu/~misha/DIReadingSeminar/Papers/Dixon-Roman13.pdf.

Douglass, Frederick. "Speech on the Dred Scott Decision." ebook (1857). http://www.libraryweb.org/~digitized/books/Two_Speeches_by_Frederick_Douglass.pdf.

Douglass, Paul H. *American Apprenticeship and Industrial Education.* New York: Columbia University, 1921.

Doyle, Don H. *The Cause of All Nations: An International History of the American Civil War.* New York: Basic Books, 2015.

Dragoset, Lisa, Jaime Thomas, Mariesa Herrmann, John Deke, Susanne James-Burdumy, Cheryl Graczewski, Andrea Boyle, Rachel Upton, Courtney Tanenbaum and Jessica Giffin. "School Improvement Grants: Implementation and Effectiveness: Executive Summary (NCEE 2017-4012)." Institute of Education Sciences, U.S. Department of Education, January, 2017. https://files.eric.ed.gov/fulltext/ED572213.pdf.

Duarte, Vanessa and Soumodip Sarkar. "A Cinderella Story: The Early Evolution of the American Tractor Industry." CEFAGE-UE Working Papers 2009/16. https://ideas.repec.org/p/cfe/wpcefa/2009_16.html.

Dubin, Michael J. *United States Presidential Elections, 1788–1860: The Official Results by County and State.* Jefferson, NC: McFarland Publishing, 2002.

Duckworth, Eleanor R. *The Having of Wonderful Ideas and Other Essays on Teaching and Learning.* 2nd edition. New York: Teachers College Press, 1996.

Dulles, John Foster. "The Strategy of Massive Retaliation." Speech before the Council on Foreign Relations, ebook, 1954. http://msthorarinson.weebly.com/uploads/4/1/4/5/41452777/dulles_address.pdf.

Dunlop, Richard, Olive Jocelyn and Douglas Denham. *English Apprenticeship and Child Labor.* New York: Macmillan, 1912. Accessed November 17, 2023. https://quod.lib.umich.edu/g/genpub/AGC2692.0001.001?rgn=main;view=fulltext.

Dvorkin, Maximiliano A. "Jobs Involving Routine Tasks Aren't Growing." Federal Reserve Bank of St. Louis, January 4, 2016. https://www.stlouisfed.org/on-the-economy/2016/january/jobs-involving-routine-tasks-arent-growing.

Dweck, Carol. *Mindset: Changing the Way You Think to Fulfil Your Potential.* Boston, MA: Little, Brown, 2017.

Dyck, Joshua J. and John Cluverius. "Survey of American Adults." Center for Public Opinion, University of Massachusetts-Lowell, 2020. https://www.uml.edu/docs/2020-Nat-Survey-RJ- Topline_tcm18-330167.pdf.

Education Law Center (n.d.). https://edlawcenter.org/litigation/abbott-v-burke/abbott- history.html.

Education Sciences Reform Act of 2002, Pub. L. No. 107-279. Section 102 18 B iv. https://www.congress.gov/107/plaws/publ279/PLAW-107publ279.pdf.

Edwards, Jonathan. "Sinners in the Hands of an Angry God" (1741), section 3. http://www.jonathan-edwards.org/Sinners.pdf.

Egypt Ministry of Education. "National Strategic Plan for Pre-University Education Reform in Egypt 2007, Annex 2, Figure 9." https://planipolis.iiep.unesco.org/en/2007/national-strategic-plan-pre-university-education-reform-egypt-200708-201112-includes.

Egypt Ministry of Education. "The Strategic Plan of Pre-University Education 2014-2030." 2014. https://planipolis.iiep.unesco.org/sites/default/files/ressources/egypt_strategic_plan_pre-university_education_2014-2030_eng_0.pdf.

Eisner, Elliot (editor). *Learning and Teaching the Ways of Knowing: The Eighty-fourth Yearbook of the National Society for the Study of Education, Part II*. Chicago, IL: National Society for the Study of Education, 1985, p. xiii.

Ellen Bara Stolzenberg, M. K. Eagan, H. B. Zimmerman, J. Berdan Lozano, N. M. Cesar-Davis, M. C. Aragon and C. Rios-Aguilar. *Undergraduate Teaching Faculty: The HERI Faculty Survey 2016–2017*, ebook. Los Angeles: Higher Education Research Institute at UCLA, 2019. https://heri.ucla.edu/monographs/HERI-FAC2017-monograph.pdf.

Ellman, Michael and S. Maksudov. "Soviet Deaths in the Great Patriotic War: A Note". *Europe-Asia Studies* 46, no. 4 (1994): 671–80.

Ennis, Sharon R., Merarys Rios-Vargas and Nora G. Albert. "The Hispanic Population: 2010." U.S. Census Bureau, May 2011. https://www.census.gov/content/dam/Census/library/publications/2011/dec/c2010br-04.pdf.

Erisman, Jan Willem, Mark A. Sutton, James Galloway, Zbigniew Klimont and Wilfried Winiwarter. "How a Century of Ammonia Synthesis Changed the World." *Nature Geoscience* 1 (2008): 636–9. doi:10.1038/ngeo325.

European Committee of the Regions. "Bosnia and Herzegovina." Accessed November 21, 2023. https://portal.cor.europa.eu/divisionpowers/Pages/Bosnia-Herzegovina.aspx.

Ewert, Stephanie. "U.S. Population Trends: 2000 to 2060." U.S. Census, October 15, 2015. https://pdf4pro.com/view/u-s-population-trends-2000-to-2060-5f9c6e.html.

Ewert, Ulf Christian. "Exploration of Markets at Distant Shores: Knowledge, Investment and Governance in 15th Century Portuguese Trade with West Africa." Presented at the 10th European Historical Economics Society Conference, London September 6–7, 2013. London: https://ehes.org/conferences/ehes2013/ehes2013.html.

Explore the Full WSJ/THE 2022 College Rankings List. September 22, 2021. WSJ. https://www.wsj.com/articles/college-rankings-list-2022-11632246093.

Facebook users by country 2023 | Statista. (2023, August 29). Statista. https://www.statista.com/statistics/268136/top-15-countries-based-on-number-of-facebook-users/.

Federal Reserve Bank of St. Louis. "Real Median Household Income in the United States." Accessed November 21, 2023. https://fred.stlouisfed.org/series/MEHOINUSA672N.

Federal Reserve Bank of St. Louis. "Student Loans Owned and Securitized." Accessed November 21, 2023. https://fred.stlouisfed.org/series/SLOAS.

Federal Reserve of New York. "The Labor Market for Recent College Graduates." Accessed November 21, 2023. https://www.newyorkfed.org/research/college-labor-market/index#/underemployment.

Feldman, Deborah L, Antony T. Smith, and Barbara Waxman. *Why We Drop Out: Understanding and Disrupting Student Pathways to Leaving School.* New York: Teachers College Press, 2017.

Festinger, Leon. *A Theory of Cognitive Dissonance.* Stanford, CA: Stanford University Press, 1962.

Fitzpatrick, Anne C. "Teller's Technical Nemesis: The American Hydrogen Bomb and Its Development within a Technological Infrastructure." *Society for Philosophy and Technology Quarterly* 3, no. 3 (Spring 1998): 119–23.

Fitzpatrick, Erika. "Innovation America: A Final Report." The National Governors Association. (July 2007). 1. http://eric.ed.gov/?q=Innovation+America&id=ED504101.

Flaherty, Colleen. "What Employers Want: AAC&U Survey of Employers Shows Liberal Arts Skills are Valued and Sought Out in the Workplace But Raises Questions About Student Preparation." *Inside Higher Education* (April 6, 2021). https://www.insidehighered.com/news/2021/04/06/aacu-survey-finds-employers-want-candidates-liberal-arts-skills-cite-preparedness.

Fleming, Susannah, M. Thompson, R. Stevens, C. Heneghan, A. Plüddemann, I. Maconochie, L. Tarassenko and D. Mant. "Normal Ranges of Heart Rate and Respiratory Rate in Children from Birth to 18 Years of Age: A Systematic Review of Observational Studies." *Lancet* 19, no. 377 (March 19, 2011): 1011–18. https://www.thelancet.com/journals/lancet/issue/vol377no9770/PIIS0140-6736(11)X6012-9.

Fortenbaugh, Robert. *The Nine Capitals of the United States.* York: Maple Press, 1948.

Founders Online: To James Madison from Thomas Jefferson, 20 December 1787. (n.d.). https://founders.archives.gov/documents/Madison/01-10-02-0210.

Fourth Annual Message | The American Presidency Project, December 4, 1832. http://www.presidency.ucsb.edu/ws/index.php?pid=29474#ixzz1KxreOKkS.

Fox, George. *Journal,* Vol. 2, 8th and Bicentenary Edition. London: Friends' Tract Association, 1891. http://www.qhpress.org/quakerpages/qwhp/dec1660.htm.

Fox, George. *Some Principles of the Elect People of God Who in Scorn are called Quakers.* London, 1661. http://www.qhpress.org/texts/gfprinc.html#s19.

Framework for 21st Century Learning (2009). Partnership for 21st Century Skills. http://www.p21.org.

Franklin, Benjamin. *Autobiography of Benjamin Franklin.* New York: Henry Holt & Company, 1916; originally published in 1791. https://www.gutenberg.org/files/20203/20203-h/20203-h.htm#III.

Franklin, Benjamin. *Proposals Relating to the Education of Youth in Pensilvania.* 1749. https://archives.upenn.edu/digitized-resources/docs-pubs/franklin-proposals/.

Freire, Paolo. *Pedagogy of the Oppressed.* New York: Bloomsbury, 1970/2000.

Friedman, Norman L. "Nativism." *Phylon* 28, no. 4 (1967): 408–15.

"From Benjamin Franklin to Peter Collinson, May 9, 1753." *Founders Online.* National Archives. https://founders.archives.gov/documents/Franklin/01-04-02 -0173.

Galinec, Darko, Darko Možnik and Boris Guberina. "Cybersecurity and Cyber Defence: National Level Strategic Approach". *Automatika* 58, no. 3 (2017): 273– 86. doi:10.1080/00051144.2017.1407022.

Gammarano, R. (2022, August 23). 258 Million Workers in the World are Over-Educated for Their Jobs. ILOSTAT. https://ilostat.ilo.org/258-million-workers-in -the-world-are-over-educated-for-their-jobs/.

Gasbarro, N. (2018, August 6). Massacre of the Connestoga Indians, 1763 (2). *Lykens Valley: History & Genealogy.* https://www.lykensvalley.org/massacre-of-the-con-nestoga-indians-1763-2/.

Gateway Academy in Florida. (n.d.). https://christianmilitaryschool.org/.

General Assembly. "An Act to Amend the Act Concerning Slaves, Free Negroes and Mulattoes (April 7, 1831)." *Encyclopedia Virginia.* December 20, 2020. https:// encyclopediavirginia.org/entries/an-act-to-amend-the-act-concerning-slaves-free -negroes-and-mulattoes-april-7-1831/.

George Washington's Mount Vernon. "Naturalization Acts of 1790 and 1795." https://www.mountvernon.org/education/primary-source-collections/primary -source-collections/article/naturalization-acts-of-1790-and-1795/.

Gibson, Campbell. *Population of the 100 Largest Cities and Other Urban Places In The United States: 1790 to 1990.* (2022, March 24). Census.gov https://www.cen-sus.gov/library/working-papers/1998/demo/POP-twps0027.html.

Gibson, Campbell and Kay Jung. "Historical Census Statistics on Population Totals By Race, 1790 to 1990, and By Hispanic Origin, 1790 to 1990, For The United States, Regions, Divisions, and States." https://www.census.gov/content/dam/Cen-sus/library/working-papers/2002/demo/POP-twps0056.pdf.

Gillingham, John. "The Beginnings of English Imperialism." *Journal of Historical Sociology* 5, no. 4 (1992): 392–409. doi:10.1111/j.1467-6443.1992.tb00033.x.

Ginsburg, Herbert P., and Sylvia Opper. *Piaget's Theory of Intellectual Development,* 3rd edition. Englewood Cliffs, NJ: Prentice Hall, 1987.

Glenn, William J. "School Finance Adequacy Litigation and Student Achievement: A Longitudinal Analysis." *Journal of Education Finance* 34, no. 3 (2009): 247–66.

"*Global Social Media Statistics*" (October 2022). Datareportal. https://datareportal .com/social-media-users.

Goals 2000: Educate America Act. Pub. L. No. 103–227, § 102, 108 Stat. 130.

Goe, Laura and Leslie M. Stickler. "Teacher Quality and Student Achievement: Mak-ing the Most of Recent Research." *TQ Research and Policy Brief*, 2007. https://eric .ed.gov/?id=ED520769.

Goodrich, Charles A. A History of the United States (1852), as quoted in "Mas-sachusetts Bay Colony: A Brief History. (n.d.). Celebrate Boston. http://www .celebrateboston.com/history/massachusetts.htm.

Gorman, Amanda. "New Day's Lyric." Instagram, December 29, 2021. https://www .instagram.com/reel/CYEpCgxBTAf/.

Greeley, Horace, Leon Case, Edward Rowland, John B. Gough, Philip Ripley, F. B. Perkins, L. B. Lyman, Albert Brisbane and Rev. E. E. Hall. *The Great Industries of the United States: Being an Historical Summary of the Origin, Growth, and perfection of the chief industrial arts of this country.* Hartford: J.B. Burr & Hyde, 1872.

Grubb, W. N. "Multiple Resources, Multiple Outcomes: Testing the "Improved" School Finance with NELS88." *American Educational Research Journal* 45, no. 1 (2008): 104–44.

Guterres, António. "The Future of Education is Here." United Nations, August 4, 2020. https://www.un.org/en/coronavirus/future-education-here.

Hacker, J. David. "A Census-based Count of the Civil War Dead." *Civil War History* 57, no. 4 (2011): 307–48.

Hague, Dyson. "The Doctrinal Value of the First Chapters of Genesis." In *The Fundamentals: A Testimony to the Truth*, Volume 8. Chicago, IL: Testimony Publishing, 1910, p. 74.

Haliczer, Josef. "The Population of Europe, 1720, 1820, 1930. A Paper Read at the International Congress of Geography at Warsaw, August 193." *Geography* 19, no. 4 (1934).

Hall, David. *The Legacy of John Calvin: His Influence in the Modern World.* Phillipsburg, NJ: P&R Publishing, 2008.

Halliburton, Jr., R. "Arkansas' Anti-Evolution Referendum." In Conference Proceedings of the Oklahoma Academy of Science, 1964, pp. 159–166.

Halloun, I. A. and Hestenes, D. "Common Sense Concepts about Motion." *American Journal of Physics* 53, no. 11 (1985): 1956–1065.

Hamilton, Alexander. "Speech at the Federal Convention, June 18, 1787." In *The Works of Alexander Hamilton*, Vol. 1, edited by Henry Cabot Lodge. New York: Putnam, 1904. https://oll.libertyfund.org/title/lodge-the-works-of-alexander-hamilton-federal-edition-vol-1#Hamilton_0249-01_1098.

Hampton University. "History." Accessed April 29, 2023. https://home.hamptonu.edu/about/history/.

Hanushek, Eric A. and Ludger Woessmann, The High Cost of Low Educational Performance: The Long-Run Economic Impact of Improving PISA Outcomes, ebook. OECD, 2010, p. 6. http://www.oecd.org/pisa/44417824.pdf.

Hanushek, Eric A. and Ludger Woessmann. "The Role of Cognitive Skills in Economic Development," *Journal of Economic Literature* 46, no. 3 (2008): 607–668.

Harley, Lewis R. "The School System of Pennsylvania: An Historical Review." *Education* 20, no. 7 (March 1900): 389–395. Google books

Harris, Elise. "Do Aliens Exist? Pope Francis Tackles This (and Other Things) in New Interview," *Catholic News Agency*, Oct 15, 2015. https://www.catholicnewsagency.com/news/32820/do-aliens-exist-pope-francis-tackles-this-and-other-things-in-new-interview.

Harris, Gordon. "Historic Ipswich: The Great Dying 1616-1619, 'By God's Visitation, a Wonderful Plague.'" Accessed November 17, 2023. https://historicipswich.net/2023/11/17/the-great-dying.

Harvard's The Private Universe. (n.d.). https://www.learner.org/series/a-private- universe/1-a-private-universe/).

Hawai'I State Department of Education. "Hawaiian Studies." http://www.hawaiipublicschools.org/TeachingAndLearning/StudentLearning/HawaiianEducation/Pages/HSP.aspx.

Hawkins, David, Edith C. Truslow and Ralph Carlisle Smith. *Manhattan District History Project Y: The Los Alamos Project*, Los Alamos Scientific Laboratory of the University of California. OSTI: Los Alamos, December 1, 1961. https://www.osti.gov/opennet/manhattan-project-history/publications/LANLMDHProjectYPart1.pdf.

Heath, Dwight B. Ed. *Mourt's Relation: A Journal of the Pilgrims at Plymouth*. Bedford, MA: Applewood Books, originally published in 1622.

Hegazzi, Louise. Yasmine Moustafa: Young Scientist, Rising Star. Heinemann, 2020. https://www.google.com/books/edition/Yasmine_Moustafa/ttkUywEACAAJ?hl=en.

Hening, William Waller. Ed. *The Statutes at Large; Being a Collection of All the Laws of Virginia from the First Session of the Legislature, in the Year 1619*. New York: R. & W. & G. Bartow, 1823, p. 88.

Henry, Joseph. "Philosophy of Education." *The American Journal of Education*, Ed. Henry Barnard, 1856, Vol. 1, p. 43. https://openlibrary.org/books/OL7081980M/The_American_journal_of_education.

High school scientists win nearly $8M at Regeneron International Science and Engineering Fair - Society for Science. (2023, March 3). Society for Science. https://www.societyforscience.org/press-release/2022-regeneron-isef-top-winners/.

Hirschman, Charles and Elizabeth Mogford. "Immigration and the American Industrial Revolution from 1880 to 1920." *Social Science Research* 38, no. 4 (December 2009): 897–920. doi:10.1016/j.ssresearch.2009.04.001.

History and Mission. (n.d.). Harvard Divinity School (HDS). https://hds.harvard.edu/about/history-and-mission.

History of Computing in the Twentieth Century. United Kingdom: Elsevier Science, 1980, pp. 525–539.

History. (n.d.). The Geological Society. http://www.geolsoc.org.uk/en/About/History.

Hoffer, Eric. *The Ordeal of Change*. New York: Harper & Row, 1963.

Hofstadter, Richard. *Anti-Intellectualism in American Life*. New York: Alfred A. Knopf, 1963.

Hossler, Don. "The Problem with College Rankings." *About Campus*, 5, no. 1 (2000): 20–24. doi:10.1177/108648220000500105.

Howard, Jacqueline and Veronica Stracqualursi. "Fauci Warns of 'Anti-Science Bias' Being a Problem in US." CNN Politics, June 18, 2020. https://www.cnn.com/2020/06/18/politics/anthony-fauci-coronavirus-anti-science-bias/index.html.

Humphries, Jane. "Child Labor: Lessons from the Historical Experience of Today's Industrial Economies." *The World Bank Economic Review* 17, no. 2 (2003): 175–196.

Huntington, John. "The Kennedy Speech that Stoked the Rise of the Christian Right," *Politico*, March 8, 2020. https://www.politico.com/news/magazine/2020/03/08/the-kennedy-speech-that-stoked-the-rise-of-the-christian-right-123369.

Hutton, James. "Theory of the Earth; or an Investigation of the Laws Observable in the Composition, Dissolution, and Restoration of Land upon the Globe." *Transactions of the Royal Society of Edinburgh*, vol. I, Part II (1788): 209–304.

Ikenberry, G. John. *Reasons of State: Oil Politics and the Capacities of American Government.* Ithaca, NY: Cornell University Press, 1988.

Immigration and Refugee Board of Canada. "Iran: Information on SAVAK." Accessed October 14, 2020. https://www.refworld.org/docid/3ae6aaa724.html.

Impact of Historical Trauma. (n.d.). The National Native American Boarding School Healing Coalition. https://boardingschoolhealing.org/education/impact-of-historical-trauma/.

"Indian Treaties and the Removal Act of 1830." Office of the Historian. U.S. Department of State. https://history.state.gov/milestones/1830-1860/indian-treaties.

Inside the Test. (n.d.). College Board. https://collegereadiness.collegeboard.org/sat/inside-the-test.

Intel ISEF 2015 Grand Award Winners - Society for Science. Society for Science, May 14, 2015. https://www.societyforscience.org/press-release/intel-isef-2015-grand-award-winners/.

International, Price Waterhouse Coopers. "20th CEO Survey," ebook. PWC, 2017. https://www.pwc.com/gx/en/ceo-survey/2017/deep-dives/ceo-survey-global-talent.pdf.

"International Typographical Union, Local 2 (Philadelphia, Pa.) Records 1850-1967," Historical Society of Pennsylvania .https://www.portal.hsp.org/finding-aids/international-typographical-union%2C-local-2-%28philadelphia%2C-pa.%29.-record%2C-1850-1967-%28collection-2076%29.

Iowa Association of School Boards. *Leadership for Student Learning: The School Board's Role in Creating School Districts Where All Students Succeed.* Des Moines: Iowa Association of School Boards, 2016, p. 6. https://www.ia-sb.org/docs/default-source/iasb-general/books-pubs/leadershipforstudentlearningbookupdatedd82bca6a-de70-4321-aa3c-0df32d0fbe97.pdf?sfvrsn=703da278_3.

Irwin, Véronique, Josue De La Rosa, Ke Wang, Sarah Hein, Jijun Zhang, Riley Burr, Ashley Roberts, A. Barmer, F. Bullock Mann, R. Dilig and S. Parker. "Report on the Condition of Education 2022 (NCES 2022-144)." U.S. Department of Education, 2022. https://nces.ed.gov/pubsearch/pubsinfo.asp?pubid=2022144.

Irwin. Véronique, Ke Wang, Jiashan Cui and Alexandra Thompson. "Report on Indicators of School Crime and Safety: 2021." Institute of Education Sciences, June 2022. https://nces.ed.gov/pubs2022/2022092.pdf.

Jacobsen, Annie. *Operation Paperclip: The Secret Intelligence Program that Brought Nazi Scientists to America.* New York, NY: Little, Brown & Company, 2014.

Jacoby, Daniel. "The Transformation of Industrial Apprenticeship in the United States." *The Journal of Economic History* 51, no. 4 (December 1991): 887–910.

Janina Z. Klawe. "Bartholomew Dias and the Voyage of Christopher Columbus." *Organon* 24 (1988): 129–37.

Jefferson, Thomas. "A Bill for the More General Diffusion of Knowledge." June 18, 1779. https://founders.archives.gov/documents/Jefferson/01-02-02-0132-0004-0079.

Jefferson, Thomas. "Notes on the State of Virginia, Queries 14 and 19." 1784. https://press-pubs.uchicago.edu/founders/documents/v1ch18s16.html.

Jennings, Francis. *The Invasion of America.* Chapel Hill, NC: University of North Carolina Press, 1975.

"John Cabot." National Archives. https://www.nationalarchives.gov.uk/education/resources/significant-people-collection/john- cabot/.

Johnson, Caleb. Mayflower History, "Letter of Edward Winslow, 11 December 1621," http://mayflowerhistory.com/letter-winslow-1621.

Johnston, Robert C. "Hornbeck Quits as Power Shifts in Philadelphia." *Education Week*, June 14, 2000.

Johnstone, Gerry, and Daniel W. Van Ness, eds. *Handbook of Restorative Justice.* London: Taylor & Francis, 2013.

Joint Statement on Rights and Freedoms of Students. (2022, January 25). AAUP. https://www.aaup.org/report/joint-statement-rights-and-freedoms-students#:~:text=As%20citizens%2C%20students%20should%20enjoy,by%20virtue%20of%20this%20membership.

Jones, Alice Hanson. *Wealth of a Nation to Be: American Colonies on the Eve of the Revolution.* New York: Columbia University Press, 1980.

Jones, Beau Fly. "James Baldwin, The Struggle for Identity." *The British Journal of Sociology* 17, no. 2 (June 1966): 107–21.

Jorgensen, Timothy J. *Strange Glow: The Story of Radiation.* Princeton, NJ: Princeton University Press, 2016.

Jung, Carl G. *Collected Works of C.G. Jung, Volume 13: Alchemical Studies.* United Kingdom: Princeton University Press, 1953.

K-12 MathMatters. "Open Letter on K-12 Mathematics." Accessed May 28, 2023. https://sites.google.com/view/k12mathmatters/home.

Kaestle, Carl F. *Pillars of the Republic: Common Schools and American Society 1780-1860.* New York: Hill and Wang, 1983.

Kamehameha Schools. "Cultural Principles and Education Framework Cultivate Strong Hawaiian Identity in KS Learners." Accessed November 21, 2023. https://www.ksbe.edu/article/cultural-principles-and-education-framework-cultivate-a-strong-hawaiian-ide/.

Kashatus, William C. *A Virtuous Education: Penn's Vision for Philadelphia Schools.* Wallingford, PA: Pendle Hill Publications, 1997.

Kaufman, Stuart Bruce. "Birth of a Federation: Mr. Gompers Endeavors Not to Build a Bubble," *Monthly Labor Review* (November 1981): 25. https://www.bls.gov/opub/mlr/1981/11/art4full.pdf.

Kennedy, John F. "Special Message to Congress on Urgent National Needs." May 25, 1961, JFK Library. https://www.jfklibrary.org/asset-viewer/archives/JFKWHA/1961/JFKWHA-032/JFKWHA-032.

Kerr, William Jasper. "Some Land Grant Problems." In Conference Proceedings of the Twenty-Four Annual Convention of the Association of American Agricultural Colleges and Experiment Stations. Washington, D.C. November 16–18, 1910, p. 51.

Kerr, William Jasper. *The Spirit of the Land-Grant Institutions.* Portland: Association of Land-Grant Colleges and Universities, 1931, p. 10.

Klein, Alyson. "Remember When K-12 Education Got a $100 Billion Windfall from Washington?" *Education Week*, February 18, 2019. https://www.edweek.org /policy-politics/remember-when-k-12-education-got-a-100-billion-windfall-from -washington/2019/02.

Klepp, Susan E. *The Swift Progress of Population: A Documentary and Bibliographic Study of Philadelphia Growth 1642-1859*. Philadelphia: American Philosophical Society, 1991.

Kliesen, Kevin L. "The 2001 Recession: How Was It Different and What Developments May Have Caused It?" Federal Reserve Bank of St. Louis, 2003. https://files .stlouisfed.org/files/htdocs/publications/review/03/09/Kliesen.pdf.

Klopfenstein, Kristen and M. Kathleen Thomas. "The Link between Advanced Placement Experience and Early College Success." *Southern Economic Journal* 75, no. 3 (January 2009): 873–91.

Koch, Charles. "The Business Community: Resisting Regulation." *Libertarian Review* (August 1978): 30–35.

Kotkin, Joel. "The Changing Demographics of America." *Smithsonian Magazine,* August 2010. https://www.smithsonianmag.com/travel/the-changing-demograph-ics-of-america-538284/.

Kristensen, Hans M. and Matt Korda. "Nuclear Arsenals of the World." *Federation of American Scientists Nuclear Notebook*. https://thebulletin.org/nuclear-notebook/ #post-heading.

Kuh, George D., Jillian L. Kinzie, Jennifer A. Buckley, Brian K. Bridges and John C. Hayek. What Matters to Student Success: A Review of the Literature. National Postsecondary Education Cooperative, 2006. https://nces.ed.gov/npec/pdf/kuh _team_report.pdf.

Kujovich, Mary Yeager. "The Refrigerator Car and the Growth of the American Dressed Beef Industry." *Business History Review* 44, no. 4 (1970): 460–82. doi:10.2307/3112669.

LaFranco, Rob and Chase Peterson-Withorn. "The Forbes 400 2022." *Forbes Media*, 2023. https://www.forbes.com/forbes-400/.

Lamber, Craig. "Twilight of the Lecture." *Harvard Magazine*, March-April 2012. https://www.harvardmagazine.com/2012/02/twilight-of-the-lecture.

Lee, John Hancock. *The Origin and Progress of the American Party in Politics; Embracing a Complete History of the Philadelphia Riots in May and July, 1844, with a Full Description of the Great American Procession of July Fourth, and a Refutation of the Arguments Founded on the Charges of Religious Proscription and Secret Combinations*. Philadelphia: Elliot & Gihon, 1855. https://archive.org/ details/originprogressof00leejuoft.

Lemon, James T. and Gary Nash. "The Distribution of Wealth in Eighteen-Century America: A Century of Change in Chester County Pennsylvania 1693-1802." *Journal of Social History*. 2, no. 1 (1968): 1–24. doi:10.1353/jsh/2.1.1.

Levesque, Karen, Jennifer Laird, Elisabeth Hensley, Susan P. Choy, Emily Forrest Cataldi and Lisa Hudson. "Career and Technical Education in the United States: 1990 to 2005" (NCES 2008-035). National Center for Education Statistics, U.S. Department of Education. https://nces.ed.gov/pubs2008/2008035.pdf.

Library of Congress. "Exploring the Early Americas." Accessed April 12, 2021. https://www.loc.gov/exhibits/exploring-the-early-americas/columbus-and-the -taino.html.

Lichten, William. "Whither Advanced Placement?" *Education Policy Analysis Archives* 8, no. 29 (June 24, 2000). doi:10.14507/epaa.v8n29.2000.

Lima, Christina. "Facebook Under Fire: A Whistleblower's Power: Key Takeaways from the Facebook Papers." *The Washington Post*, October 21, 2021.

Lindahl, Amy. "Facing Cancer: Social Justice in Biology Class." *Rethinking Schools* (Summer 2012). https://rethinkingschools.org/articles/facing-cancer-social-justice -in-biology-class/.

Lindsay, Drew. "The Success Factory." *Washingtonian Magazine,* October 2009.

Locke, John. "Two Treatises of Government." In *The Works of John Locke*, Vol. V. London: McMaster University Archive of the History of Economic Thought, 1823. https://www.yorku.ca/comninel/courses/3025pdf/Locke.pdf.

Lockwood, Lewis C. *Mary S. Peake: The Colored Teacher at Fortress Monroe.* Boston, MA: American Tract Society, 1862.

Logsdon, John M. "R-7," Encyclopedia Britannica, May 17, 2015. https://www.britannica.com/technology/R-7.

London, V. C. O. (2020, December 7). "A Declaration of the State of the Colonie and Affaires in Virginia" (July 22, 1620) - Encyclopedia Virginia. Encyclopedia Virginia. https://encyclopediavirginia.org/entries/a-declaration-of-the-state-of-the -colonie-and-affaires-in-virginia-july-22-1620/.

Losses by Month - Ships hit by U-boats - German and Austrian U-boats of World War One - Kaiserliche Marine - uboat.net. (n.d.). https://www.uboat.net/wwi/ships_hit/ losses_year.html?date=1917-11.

Lutchen, Kenneth R. "Years of Anti-Science sentiment has Left America in a Terrifying Predicament." *Business Insider*, September 17, 2020. https://www.businessinsider.com/american-anti-science-sentiment-comes-back-hurt-us-wildfires -pandemic-2020-9.

Lybyer, Albert Howe. "The Ottoman Turks and the Routes of Oriental Trade." *The English Historical Review* 30, no. 120 (October 1915): 577–88.

Lynch, John. *The Spanish American Revolutions, 1808-1826,* 2nd edition. Woodstock, VT: W. W. Norton & Company, 1986.

Ma, Debin. "The Great Silk Exchange: How the World was Connected and Developed." In *Pacific Centuries; Pacific and Pacific Rim History Since the 16th Century*, edited by D. Flynn, Lionel Frost, and A.J.H. Latham. New York: Routledge Press, 1998.

Machiavelli, Niccolo. *The Prince.* London: Penguin Books, 1961, written in 1513.

Maland, Charles. "Dr. Strangelove (1964): Nightmare Comedy and the Ideology of Liberal Consensus," *American Quarterly* 31, no. 5 (Winter 1979): 697–717.

Mandell, Melissa. "The Kensington Riots of 1844." Historical Society of Pennsylvania. http://www.philaplace.org/story/316/.

Manross, William W. *A History of the American Episcopal Church.* Milwaukee: Morehouse Publishing, 1935.

Marani, Marco, Gabriel G. Katul, William K. Pan, and Anthony J. Parolari. "Intensity and Frequency of Extreme Novel Epidemics." *Proceedings of the National Academy of Sciences* 118, no. 35 (August 23, 2021). doi:10.1073/pnas.2105482118.

Marr, J. S. and J. T. Cathey. "New Hypothesis for Cause of Epidemic Among Native Americans, New England, 1616-1619." *Emerging Infectious Diseases* 16, no. 2 (2010): 281–86.

Marzano, Robert J., Barbara B. Gaddy and Ceri Dean. *What Works in Classroom Instruction.* Aurora, CA: Mid-continent Research for Education and Learning, 2000. https://www.researchgate.net/publication/265663591_What_Works_In _Classroom_Instruction.

Marzano, Robert J., Debra Pickering and Jane E. Pollock, *Classroom Instruction that Works: Research-Based Strategies for Increasing Student Achievement,* 1st edition. Alexandria, VA: Association for Supervision and Curriculum Development, 2005.

Maslow, Abraham, H. (1968, January 1). *Toward a Psychology of Being.* Princeton, NJ : Van Nostrand. ISBN 978-1-62793-274-5.

Massachusetts Commission on Industrial and Technical Education. *Report of the Commission on Industrial and Technical Education Submitted to the Senate and House of Representations, Massachusetts.* New York: Teachers College, Columbia University, 1906. https://babel.hathitrust.org/cgi/pt?id=coo1.ark:/13960/ t8w95r05k&view=1up&seq=7.

Mathematics Framework. (2023). California Department of Education. https://www .cde.ca.gov/ci/ma/cf/.

Mather, Cotton. *Diary of Cotton Mather, 1681-1724.* Boston, MA: Massachusetts Historical Society, 1911. https://ia800202.us.archive.org/11/items/cu31924092202500 /cu31924092202500.pdf.

Mayer, Jacob. "Evolution Tops State Board of Education Debate Topics." *Amarillo Global News*, October 17, 2012. https://www.amarillo.com/story/news/local/2012 /10/18/evolution-tops-debate- topics/13110954007/.

Mayer, Jane. *Dark Money: The Hidden History of the Billionaires Behind the Rise of the Radical Right.* New York: Doubleday, 2016.

Mazarr, Michael J., Abigail Casey, Alyssa Demus, Scott W. Harold, Luke J. Matthews, Nathan Beauchamp-Mustafaga and James Sladden. *Hostile Social Manipulation: Present Realities and Emerging Trends.* Santa Monica, CA: RAND Corporation, 2019.

Mazur, Eric. *Peer Instruction: A Users' Manual.* Englewood Cliffs, NJ: Prentice Hall, 1997.

McCaffrey, L. J. *The Irish Catholic Diaspora in America.* Washington, DC: Catholic University of America Press, 1997.

McCoy, Roger M. *On the Edge: Mapping North America's Coasts.* Oxford: Oxford University Press, 2012.

McDonough, Patricia M. "Democratized College Knowledge for Whom?" *Research in Higher Education* 39, no. 5 (October 1998): 513–37.

McGough, Matt, Krutika Amin, Nirmita Panchal and Cynthia Cox. "Child and Teen Firearm Mortality in the U.S. and Peer Countries." Kaiser Family Foundation.

July 8, 2022. https://www.kff.org/mental-health/issue-brief/child-and-teen-firearm -mortality-in-the-u-s-and-peer-countries/.

Meriam, Lewis. *The Problem of Indian Administration.* Baltimore, MD: Johns Hopkins Press, 1928.

Merlino, F. Joseph, J. Y. Baker, and R. Seltzer. "Are Educational Expenditures Associated with 11th Grade Student Achievement in Pennsylvania School Districts?" The 21st Century Partnership for STEM Education (November 2010).

Mervis, Jeffrey. "Packard Heir Signs Up for National 'Math Wars.'" *Science* 287, no. 5455 (February 11, 2000): 956–59.

Mielke, Brad and Kelly McCarthy. "8 Schools in the Washington, DC, Area Announce Plan to Eliminate AP Program." *ABC News*, June 20, 2018. https://abcnews.go.com /US/schools-washington-dc-area-announce-plan-eliminate-ap/story?id=56027089.

Minnesota Department of Education. "83.3 Percent of Minnesota's Class of 2021 Graduated in Four Years." https://content.govdelivery.com/accounts/MNMDE/ bulletins/311010e.

Modern Immigration Wave Brings 59 Million to U.S., Driving Population Growth and Change Through 2065, September 28, 2015. Pew Research Center. https:// www.pewresearch.org/hispanic/2015/09/28/chapter-2-immigrations-impact-on -past-and-future-u-s-population-change/.

Moehlman, Conrad Henry. *School and Church: The American Way, A Historical Approach to the Problem of Religious Instruction in Public Education.* New York: Harper & Brothers, 1944.

Moeller, Julia, Marc A. Brackett, Zorana Ivcevic and Arielle E. West. "High School Students' Feelings: Discoveries From a Large National Survey and an Experience Sampling Study." *Learning and Instruction* 66 (April 2020). doi:10.1016/j. learninstruc.2019.101301.

Mokyr, Joel. "The Second Industrial Revolution 1870-1914." ebook. Chicago, August 1998. https://faculty.wcas.northwestern.edu/jmokyr/castronovo.pdf.

Mora, Camila, Tristan McKenzie, Isabella M. Gaw, Jacqueline M. Dean, Hannah von Hammersteir, Tabatha A. Knudson, Renee O. Setter, C. Z. Smith, K. M. Webster, J. A. Patz and E. C.Franklin. "Over Half of Known Human Pathogenic Diseases Can Be Aggravated by Climate Change." *Nature Climate Change* 12 (2022): 869–75. doi:10.1038/s41558-022-01426-1.

Morris, Henry M. *Scientific Creationism.* San Diego: C.L.P. Publishers, 1974, p. 12.

Morrison, Henry C. "Vocational Training and Industrial Education." *Educational Review* 36 (October 1908): 242.

Morse, Robert and Eric Brooks. "How U.S. News Calculated the 2022 Best Colleges Rankings." *US News and World Report,* September 12, 2021. https://www.usnews .com/education/best-colleges/articles/how-us-news-calculated-the-rankings.

Moussa, Adnan and Susan Bickerstaff. *Creating Accelerated Pathways for Student Success in Mathematics.* ebook. New York: Columbia. University, Community College Research Center, Teachers College, October 2019. https://www.lumi-nafoundation.org/wp-content/uploads/2019/11/accelerated-pathways-student-success-mathematics.pdf.

Mullis, I. V. S., M. O. Martin, P, Foy, D. L. Kelly and B. Fishbein. TIMSS 2019 International Results in Mathematics and Science. Retrieved from Boston College, TIMSS & PIRLS International Study, 2020. Center. https://timssandpirls.bc.edu/timss2019/international-results/.

Myre, G. (2012, November 10). Gas Lines Evoke Memories Of Oil Crises In The 1970s. NPR. https://www.npr.org/sections/pictureshow/2012/11/10/164792293/gas-lines-evoke-memories-oil-crises-in-the-1970s.

National Academies of Sciences, Engineering, and Medicine. *How People Learn II: Learners, Contexts, and Cultures.* Washington, DC: The National Academies Press, 2018.

National Academy of Sciences, National Academy of Engineering, and Institute of Medicine. *Rising Above the Gathering Storm: Energizing and Employing America for a Brighter Economic Future.* Washington, DC: The National Academies Press, 2007. doi:10.17226/11463.

National Archives. "Alien and Sedition Acts (1798)."

National Association for College Admission Counseling. "Counseling Trends Survey, 2018- 19." https://files.eric.ed.gov/fulltext/ED608316.pdf.

National Association of Manufacturers. *Industrial Education. Report of the Committee on Industrial Education, H. E. Miles, Chairman, at the Twenty-First Annual Convention of the National Association of Manufacturers, New York City, May 15, 1916. Library of Congress.* https://www.loc.gov/item/e16000576/.

National Center for Education Statistics Blog Editor. "New International Data Show Large and Widening Gaps Between High-and Low-Performing U.S. 4th- and 8th-Graders in Mathematics and Science." February 10, 2021. https://nces.ed.gov/blogs/nces/post/new-international-data-show-large-and-widening-gaps-between-high-and-low-performing-u-s-4th-and-8th-graders-in-mathematics-and-science.

National Center for Education Statistics. "120 Years of American Education: A Statistical Portrait." 77. https://nces.ed.gov/pubs93/93442.pdf.

National Center for Education Statistics. "Undergraduate Enrollment."

National Center for Education Statistics. "Average Undergraduate Tuition, Fees, Room, and Board Rates Charged for Full-time Students in Degree-granting Postsecondary Institutions, By Level and Control of Institution: Selected Years, 1963-64 through 2020-21." Table 330.10. https://nces.ed.gov/programs/digest/d21/tables/dt21_330.10.asp.

National Center for Education Statistics. "Characteristics of Children's Families." Figure 5. 2022. https://nces.ed.gov/programs/coe/indicator/cce/family-characteristics.

National Center for Education Statistics. "Characteristics of Postsecondary Faculty 2022." Accessed December 1, 2022. https://nces.ed.gov/programs/coe/indicator/csc.

National Center for Education Statistics. "Characteristics of Private Schools in the United States: Results From the 2007–08 Private School Universe Survey." March 2009. http://nces.ed.gov/pubs2009/2009313.pdf.

National Center for Education Statistics. "Digest of Education Statistics, 2010: Table 5." (NCES 2011-015). 2011. https://nces.ed.gov/programs/digest/d10/tables/dt10_005.asp.

National Center for Education Statistics. "Digest of Education Statistics, Table 105.50." https://nces.ed.gov/programs/digest/d21/tables/dt21_105.50.asp.

National Center for Education Statistics. "Enrollment in Public Elementary and Secondary Schools, by Region, State, and Jurisdiction: Selected Years, Fall 1990 Through Fall 2023, Table 203.20." https://nces.ed.gov/programs/digest/d13/tables/dt13_203.20.asp.

National Center for Education Statistics. "The Classification of Instructional Programs 2020." https://nces.ed.gov/ipeds/cipcode/browse.aspx?y=56.

National Center for Education Statistics. "Winter 2020–21 Student Financial Aid Component" and "Fall 2020 Institutional Characteristics Component." Digest of Education Statistics 2021, Table 330.40. https://nces.ed.gov/programs/coe/indicator/cua/undergrad-costs#fn4.

National Center for Education Statistics. "Table 225.40: Percentage of Public and Private High School Graduates Taking Selected Mathematics and Science Courses in High School, by Selected Student and School Characteristics: Selected Years, 1990 through 2009." https://nces.ed.gov/programs/digest/d19/tables/dt19_225.40.asp?current=yes.

National Center for Science and Engineering Statistics (NCSES). "National Survey of College Graduates: 2021." NSF 23-306. 2022. https://ncses.nsf.gov/pubs/nsf23306/.

National Commission on Excellence in Education. "A Nation at Risk." April 1983. https://archive.org/details/nationatrisk0000unse/page/24/mode/2up?view=theater.

National Consortium of Secondary STEM Schools. "About." Last updated 2023. https://www.ncsss.org/about/.

National Education Association Research Land Grant University "Brief No. 1: Land Grant Institutions: An Overview" (2022). https://www.nea.org/sites/default/files/2022-03/Land%20Grant%20Institutions%20-%20An%20Overview.pdf.

National Governors Association. "Postsecondary Education." https://www.nga.org/bestpractices/post-secondary-education/.

National Institute of Standards and Technology. "Baldrige Performance Excellence Program." 2019. https://www.nist.gov/baldrige.

National Research Council 2013. *Next Generation Science Standards: For States, By States. Volume 2: Appendices.* Washington, DC: The National Academies Press.

National Research Council, *America's Lab Report: Investigations in High School Science.* Washington, DC: The National Academies Press, 2006.

National Research Council. *Discipline-Based Education Research: Understanding and Improving Learning in Undergraduate Science and Engineering.* Washington, DC: The National Academies Press, 2012. doi:10.17226/13362.

National Research Council. *Discipline-Based Education Research: Understanding and Improving Learning in Undergraduate Science and Engineering.* Washington, DC: The National Academies Press, 2012. doi:10.17226/13362.

National Research Council. *Early Childhood Development and Learning: New Knowledge for Policy.* Washington, DC: The National Academies Press, 2001. doi:10.17226/10067.

National Research Council. *Everybody Counts: A Report to the Nation on the Future of Mathematics Education.* Washington, DC: The National Academies Press, 1989. doi:10.17226/1199.

National Research Council. *How People Learn II: Learners, Contexts and Cultures.* Washington, DC: National Academies Press, 2019.

National Research Council. *How People Learn: Brain, Mind, Experience and School.* Washington, DC: National Academies Press, 1999.

National Research Council. *How People Learn: History, Mathematics and Science in the Classroom.* Washington, DC: National Academies Press, 2005.

National Research Council. *Learning and Understanding: Improving Advanced Study of Mathematics and Science in U.S. High Schools.* Washington, DC: The National Academies Press, 2002. doi:10.17226/10129.

National Research Council. *National Science Education Standards.* Washington, DC: National Academy Press, 1996.

National Science Foundation. "National Science Foundation Awards." https://www.nsf.gov/awardsearch/download.jsp.

National Science Foundation. "Advancing Informal STEM Learning (AISL)." August 17, 2022. https://www.nsf.gov/funding/pgm_summ.jsp?pims_id=504793.

"National Science Foundation." Performance.gov, last updated January 7, 2021, https://trumpadministration.archives.performance.gov/NSF/#:~:text=The%20National%20Scienc e%20Foundation%20(NSF,people%20to%20create%20knowledge%20that).

National Science Foundation. *The First Annual Report of the National Science Foundation, 1950–1951.* Washington, DC: U.S. Government Printing Office. https://www.nsf.gov/about/history/ann_report_first.pdf.

National Science Teaching Association. "Position Statement: Science Teacher Preparation." https://www.nsta.org/nstas-official-positions/science-teacher-preparation.

National Society for the Promotion of Industrial Education. "Bulletin 1: Proceedings of the Organization Meetings." 1907. https://www.google.com/books/edition/_/5I44AQAAMAAJ?hl=en&gbpv=0.

National Writing Project. "Home." Last modified 2023. https://www.nwp.org/.

"Naturalization Acts of 1790 and 1795." (n.d.). George Washington's Mount Vernon. https://www.mountvernon.org/education/primary-source-collections/primary-source-collections/article/naturalization-acts-of-1790-and-1795/.

Nehm, Ross H. and Leah Reilly. "Biology Majors' Knowledge and Misconceptions of Natural Selection." *BioScience* 57, no. 3 (March 2007): 263–272. doi:10.1641/B570311.

Neville B. Smith. "A Tribute to the Visionaries Prime Movers and Pioneers of Vocational Education, 1892-1917." *Journal of Vocation and Technical Education* (Fall 1999).

Newton, Isaac. *Mathematical Principles of Natural Philosophy* (usually called the *Principia*), 1687.

Next Generation Science Standards Lead States (NGSS). *Next Generation Science Standards: For States, By States,* Vol. 2. Washington, DC: The National Academies Press, 2013. doi:10.17226/18290.

Noah Webster MicroSociety Magnet School, Hartford Public Schools, Hartford, Connecticut. (n.d.). https://www.nwmms.org/.

Norris, Robert S. and Hans M. Kristensen. "Global nuclear weapons inventories, 1945– 2010." *Bulletin of the Atomic Scientists* 66, no. 4 (July/August 2010): 77–83.

NSF Award Search: Award # 9252906 - Science Education for Public Understanding Program (SEPUP): Issues-Oriented Science for Secondary Schools. (n.d.). https://www.nsf.gov/awardsearch/showAward?AWD_ID=9252906.

Nussbaum, Martha C. *Not for Profit: Why Democracy Needs the Humanities.* Princeton, NJ University Press, 2010.

Oates, Sarah. "The Easy Weaponization of Social Media: Why Profit has Trumped Security for U.S. companies." *Digital War* 1 (2020): 117–22. doi:10.1057/s42984-020-00012-z.

Oberrlo. "Facebook Ad Revenue." Accessed November 21, 2023. https://www.oberlo.com/statistics/facebook-ad-revenue.

Office of the Governor. "Memorandum to the Members of the California Assembly." October 12, 2019. https://www.gov.ca.gov/wp-content/uploads/2019/10/AB-751-Veto-Message.pdf.

Office of the Minister of Education, Arab Republic of Egypt. Ministerial Decree No (238), dated on 3/7/ 2012 Concerning High School Graduation Examination Certificate STEM Schools of Science and Technology.

Old Deluder Satan Act of 1647. (n.d.). https://www.mass.gov/doc/old-deluder-satan-law/download.

Olson, Keith W. "The G. I. Bill and Higher Education: Success and Surprise." *American Quarterly* 25, no. 5 (December 1973): 596–610. doi:10.2307/2711698.

OMG Center for Collaborative Learning. "College Access and Success in Philadelphia Part II: College Enrollment Activity." October 29, 2010. https://search.issuelab.org/resource/college-access-and-success-in-philadelphia-part-ii-college-enrollment-activity.html.

"Open Letter on K-12 Mathematics." K-12 MathMatters, para. 2, 3 and 7. Accessed May 28, 2023. https://sites.google.com/view/k12mathmatters/home.

Organisation for Economic Co-Operation and Development (OECD). "The High Cost of Low Educational Performance, 2010. doi:10.1787/9789264077485-en.

Organisation for Economic Co-Operation and Development (OECD). PISA 2018 Results (Volume I): What Students Know and Can Do (2019), 85. doi:10.1787/5f07c754-en.

Our Mission. (2022, November 5). Netter Center for Community Partnerships. http://www.nettercenter.upenn.edu/about-center/our-mission.

Padhi, Asutosh, Gaurav Batra and Nick Santhanam. *The Titanium Economy: How Industrial Technology Can Create a Better, Faster, Stronger America.* New York: Public Affairs, 2022.

Page, Brian and Richard Walker. "From Settlement to Fordism: The Agro-Industrial Revolution in the American Midwest." *Economic Geography* 67, no. 4 (October 1991): 281–315. doi:10.2307/143975.

Parker, Kim, Rich Morin and Juliana Menasce Horowitz. "Looking to the Future, Public Sees an America in Decline on Many Fronts Majorities." Pew Research

Center, March 21, 2019. https://www.pewresearch.org/social-trends/2019/03/21/public-sees-an-america-in-decline-on-many-fronts/.

Parton, James. *Life of Andrew Jackson.* New York: Mason Bros, 1860.

Pauls, Elizabeth Prine. "Native American." *Encyclopedia Britannica.* Accessed November 21, 2023. https://www.britannica.com/topic/Native-American.

Payne, Charles M. *So Much Reform, So Little Change.* Cambridge, MA: Harvard University Press, 2017.

Peevely, Gary L. and John R. Ray. "Does Equalization Litigation Effect a Narrowing of the Gap of Value Added Achievement Outcomes Among School Districts?" *Journal of Education Finance* 26, no. 3 (2001): 319–32.

Penn, William, Jr. "Preface to the Frame of Government." May 5 1682. https://avalon.law.yale.edu/17th_century/pa04.asp.

Pennsylvania Constitution 1838 "ARTICLE III Section I. The 1790.

Pennsylvania Department of Education Division of Data Quality. "Cohort Graduation Rates 4-year 2021-22." https://www.education.pa.gov/DataAndReporting/Cohort-GradRate/Pages/default.aspx.

Pennsylvania Historical and Museum Commission. Chester County History. http://www.phmc.state.pa.us/bah/dam/rg/di/IncorporationDatesForMunicipalities/pdfs/chester.pdf?catid=15.

Penrose, Roger, Stuart Hameroff and Subhash Kak, ed. *Consciousness and the Universe: Quantum Physics, Evolution, Brain & Mind.* Cambridge, MA: Cosmology Science Publishers, 2017.

People. (n.d.). Metanexus Institute. https://metanexus.net/people/.

Performance.gov. "National Science Foundation." Last updated January 7, 2021. https://trumpadministration.archives.performance.gov/NSF/#:~:text=The%20National%20Science%20Foundation%20(NSF,people%20to%20create%20knowledge%20that.

Perkins Career and Technical Education Improvement Act of 2006, Pub. L. No. 109-270, 120 Stat.

Peterson-Withorn, C. (2022, September 27). *The 2022 Forbes 400 List Of Richest Americans: Facts And Figures. Forbes. https://www.forbes.com/sites/chasewithorn/2022/09/27/the-2022-forbes-400-list-of-richest-americans-facts-and-figures/?sh=49db984e18e4.*

Phillips, Kevin. *Wealth and Democracy: A Political History of the Rich and Poor.* New York: Broadway Books, 2002.

Physport.org. https://www.physport.org/assessments/. PhysPort Assessments. (n.d.). PhysPort. https://www.physport.org/assessments/.

Plutzer, Eric and Michael B. Berkman. "Defeating Creationism in the Courtroom, But Not in the Classroom." *Science* 331, no. 6016 (January 28, 2011): 404–5. https://www.science.org/doi/10.1126/science.1198902.

Plutzer, Eric, Glenn Branch and Ann Reid. "Teaching Evolution in U.S. Public Schools: A Continuing Challenge." *Evolution: Education and Outreach* 13, no. 14 (June 9, 2020). https://evolution-outreach.biomedcentral.com/articles/10.1186/s12052-020-00126-8.

Polkinghorne, John C. *Quantum Physics and Theology: An Unexpected Kinship*. New Haven: Yale University Press, 2007.

Powell, J. W., Charles C. Royce and Cyrus Thomas. "1899—Eighteenth Annual Report of the Bureau of American Ethnology—1896-97, Part 2." https://digitalcommons.csumb.edu/hornbeck_ind_1/2/.

President Andrew Jackson Second Annual Message to Congress. (December 6, 1830). https://millercenter.org/the-presidency/presidential-speeches/december-6-1830-second-annual-message-congress.

President of the Royal Geographical Society. "Fourth Centenary of the Voyage of John Cabot, 1497." *The Geographical Journal* 9, no. 6 (June 1897): 604–15.

Price, D. A. (2023, October 25). Jamestown Colony | History, Foundation, Settlement, Map, & Facts. Encyclopedia Britannica. https://www.britannica.com/place/Jamestown-Colony.

"Privileges and Prerogatives Granted By Their Catholic Majesties to Christopher Columbus: 1492." *The Avalon Project*. Lillian Goldman Law Library, Yale Law School. https://avalon.law.yale.edu/15th_century/colum.asp.

Purvis, Thomas L. "The European Ancestry of the United States Population 1790: A Symposium." *The William and Mary Quarterly* 41, no. 1 (January 1984): 85–101.

Quantitative Reasoning for College Graduates: A Complement to the Standards | Mathematical Association of America. (n.d.). https://maa.org/programs/faculty-and-departments/curriculum-department-guidelines-recommendations/quantitative-literacy/quantitative-reasoning-college-graduates.

Randal, Jonathan C. "SAVAK Jails Stark Reminder Of Shah's Rule." *Washington Post*, December 13, 1979. https://www.washingtonpost.com/archive/politics/1979/12/13/savak-jails-stark-reminder-of-shahs-rule/b2b37be2-356a-43e2-ba68-dd474e9023b0/.

Reagan, Ronald."Address Accepting the Presidential Nomination at the Republican National Convention in Detroit, July 17, 1980." The American Presidency Project, 1980. https://www.presidency.ucsb.edu/documents/address-accepting-the-presidential-nomination-the-republican-national-convention-detroit.

Rebell, Michael A. "Professional Rigor, Public Engagement and Judicial Review: A Proposal for Enhancing the Validity of Education Adequacy Studies." Teachers College Record 109, no. 6 (2007): 1303–1373.

Register, D. M. (n.d.). Des Moines Tornado Archive. Des Moines Register. https://datacentral.desmoinesregister.com/tornado-archive.

Reinsel, David, John Gantz and John Rydning. The Digitization of the World from Edge to Core, ebook (International Data Corporation White Paper, November 2018). https://www.seagate.com/files/www-content/our-story/trends/files/idc-seagate-dataage-whitepaper.pdf.

Religious Landscape Study: Adults in Texas, 2014. Pew Research Center. https://www.pewresearch.org/religion/religious-landscape-study/state/texas/.

"Requirement: Pronouncement to be Read by Spanish Conquerors to Defeated Indians, 1510." National Humanities Center. http://nationalhumanitiescenter.org/pds/amerbegin/contact/text7/requirement.pdf.

Restrepo-Echavarria, Paulina, and Maria A. Arias. "Tigers, Tiger Cubs and Economic Growth." Federal Reserve Bank of St. Louis, May 25, 2017. https://www.stlouisfed .org/on-the-economy/2017/may/tigers-tiger-cubs-economic-growth.

Richard Henry Pratt. "The Advantages of Mingling Indians with Whites." In Proceedings of the National Conference of Charities and Correction, edited by Isabel C. Barrows Boston, MA: Press of Geo. H. Ellis, 1892, pp. 45–59. https://www.google .com/books/edition/Proceedings_of_the_National_Conference_o/XE00AAAA-MAAJ?hl=en&gbpv=0.

Richter, Daniel K. and James H. Merrell, eds. *Beyond the Covenant Chain—The Iroquois and Their Neighbors, 1600–1800*. University Park, PA: Penn State University Press, 2003.

Riddle, Travis and Stacey Sinclair. "Racial Disparities in School-Based Disciplinary Actions Are Associated with County-Level Rates of Racial Bias." In Conference Proceedings of the National Academy of Sciences 116, no. 17 (April 2019), pp. 8255–8260. doi:10.1073/pnas.1808307116.

Ritter, Gary W. and Sherri C. Lauver. "School Finance Reform in New Jersey: A Piecemeal Approach to a Systemic Problem.*" Journal of Education Finance* 28, no. 4 (2003): 575–98.

Rizga, Kristina. "The Alaska Native Teacher Upending the Legacy of Colonial Education." *The Atlantic*, April 4, 2020. https://www.theatlantic.com/education/archive/2020/04/teaching-native-culture-in-alaskas-classrooms/609292/.

Roberts, Alasdair. *America's First Great Depression: Economic Crisis and Political Disorder After the Panic of 1837*. Ithaca, NY: Cornell University Press, 2012.

Roberts, Michael. "Genesis and Geology Unearthed." *The Churchman* 112, no. 3 (October 1998): 225–55.

Roediger, Henry. Retrieval Practice Enhances Long-Term Retention of Science Learning, (n.d). The 21st Century Center for Research and Development in Cognitive Science and Instruction. http://cogscied.org/henry-roediger/.

Roosevelt, Franklin D. Letter to Vannevar Bush.(November 17, 1944). National Science Foundation. https://www.nsf.gov/about/history/nsf50/vbush1945_roosevelt _letter.jsp.

Roosevelt, Theodore. "The Man Who Works with His Hands." Address at the Semi-Centennial Celebration of Michigan State Agricultural College. May 31, 1907, pp. 239–240. https://archive.lib.msu.edu/DMC/Sesqui/pdf/sesqui.pdf.

Rossiter, W. S. "A Century of Population Growth: From the First to the Twelfth Census of the United States: 1790-1900." U.S. Census, 1909. https://www2.census .gov/library/publications/decennial/1900/century-of-growth/1790-1900-century-of -growth-part-1.pdf.

Rothschild, Eric. "Four Decades of the Advanced Placement Program." *The History Teacher* 32, no. 2 (February 1999): 175–206.

Rothstein, Richard. *Class and Schools: Using Social, Economic, and Educational Reform to Close the Black-White Achievement Gap*. New York: Teacher College Press, 2004.

Rowe, Mary Budd. *Wait-Time and Rewards as Instructional Variables, Their Influence in Language, Logic, and Fate Control*. Paper presented at National

Association for Research in Science Teaching. Chicago, 1972. https://files.eric.ed
.gov/fulltext/ED061103.pdf.

Rowe, Mary Budd. "Wait Time: Slowing Down May Be a Way of Speeding Up."
American Educator 11 (Spring 1987): 38–43, p. 47.

Rush, Benjamin. A Plan for the Establishment of Public Schools and the Diffusion
of Knowledge in Pennsylvania; to Which Are Added, Thoughts upon the Mode of
Education, Proper in a Republic, 1786. https://quod.lib.umich.edu/e/evans/N15652
.0001.001?rgn=main;view=fulltext.

Russell, Robert John, Nancy Murphy and Arthur R. Peacocke, Eds. *Chaos and Complexity: Scientific Perspectives on Divine Action.* Vatican City State: The Vatican
Observatory Publications, 1996.

Salk, Jonas. "Are We Being Good Ancestors?" *World Affairs: The Journal of International Issues* 1, no. 2 (1992): 16–18. http://www.jstor.org/stable/45064193.

Sarason, Seymour B. *The Predictable Failure of Education Reform.* San Francisco:
Jossey- Bass, 1990.

Sarkar, V. D. S. (2009). *A Cinderella Story: The Early Evolution of the American
Tractor Industry.* ideas.repec.org. https://ideas.repec.org/p/cfe/wpcefa/2009_16
.html.

Schaeffer, Katherine. "10 Facts About Today's College Graduates." Pew Research
Center, Key facts about U.S. college graduates | Pew Research Center. (2022,
April 12). Pew Research Center. https://www.pewresearch.org/short-reads/2022
/04/12/10-facts-about-todays-college-graduates/.

Schoenfeld, Alan H. "The Math Wars." *Education Policy* 18, no. 1 (January 2004).
doi:10.1177/0895904803260042.

Scholarship of Teaching & Learning (SOTL) | Academic Technology. (n.d.). https://
at.humboldt.edu/content/scholarship-teaching-learning-sotl.

Serafino, Nina, Curt Tarnoff and Dick K. Nanto. "Report to Congress: U.S. Occupation Assistance: Iraq, Germany and Japan Compared." March 23, 2006. https://sgp
.fas.org/crs/natsec/RL33331.pdf.

Seybolt, Robert Francis. *The Public Schools of Colonial Boston.* Cambridge, MA:
Harvard University Press, 1935.

Sheldon Harnick on Fiddler on the Roof (n.d.). PBS.org. https://www.pbs.org/video/
sheldon-harnick-on-fiddler-on-the-roof-w48r4h/.

Silverberg, Marsha, Elizabeth Warner, Michael Fong and David Goodwin. "National
Assessment of Vocational Education: Final Report to Congress." June 2004. U.S.
Department of Education. https://files.eric.ed.gov/fulltext/ED483149.pdf.

Silverman, David J. "Guns, Empires and Indians." *Aeon,* October 13, 2016. https://
aeon.co/essays/how-did-the-introduction-of-guns-change-native-america.

Singer, Susan R., Natalie R. Nielsen, and Heidi A. Schweingruber, eds. *Discipline-
Based Educational Research: Understanding and Improving Learning in Undergraduate Science and Engineering.* Washington, DC: National Academies Press,
2012. https://www.nap.edu/catalog/13362/discipline-based-education-research
-understanding-and-improving-learning-in-undergraduate.

Smil, Vaclav. *Creating the 20th Century: Technical Innovations of 1867-1914 and
their Lasting Impact.* Oxford: Oxford University Press, 2005.

Smil, Vaclav. *Enriching the Earth: Fritz Haber, Carl Bosch and the Transformation of World Food Production.* Cambridge: MIT Press, 2001.

Smith, J. I. and K. Tanner. "The Problem of Revealing How Students Think: Concept Inventories and Beyond. *CBE Life Science Education* Spring 9, no. 1 (2010): 1–54. doi: 10.1187/cbe.09-12-0094.

Smith, Mitch. "Social Justice Revival." *Inside Higher Education* (January 31, 2012). http://www.insidehighered.com/news/2012/01/31/colleges-embrace-social-justice -curriculum.

Soroush, Vosoughi, Deb Roy EB and Sinan Aral. "The Spread of True and False News Online." *Science* 359, no. 6380 (2018): 1146–1151. https://www.science.org /doi/10.1126/science.aap9559.

Southern Regional Education Board. "65 Years Helping States Improve Education." 2013. https://www.sreb.org/sites/main/files/file-attachments/13e04_65_years.pdf ?1458835252.

Sports Academy. (n.d.). IMG Academy. https://www.imgacademy.com.

Stains, M., M. K. Barker, S. V. Chasteen, R. Cole, S. E. DeChenne-Peters, M. K. Eagen Jr., J. M. Esson, J. K. Knight, F. A. Laski and M. Levis-Fitzgerald. "Anatomy of STEM Teaching in North American Universities." *Science* 359 (2018): 1468–1470. https://www.science.org/doi/10.1126/science.aap8892.

Stark, Rodney and Roger Finke. "American Religion in 1776: A Statistical Portrait." *Sociological Analysis* 49, no. 1 (Spring 1988): 39–51.

STEM Ecosystems. "Why Cultivate STEM Learning Ecosystems?" https://stemeco-systems.org/what-are-stem-ecosystems/.

Stolzenberg, Ellen Bara, Melissa C. Aragon, Edgar Romo, Victoria Couch, Destiny McLennan, M. Kevin Eagan and Nathaniel Kang. *The American Freshman: National Norms Fall 2019*, ebook. Los Angeles: Higher Education Research Institute at UCLA, 2020. https://heri.ucla.edu/monographs/HERI-FAC2017-monograph.pdf.

Strauss, Lewis L. "Freedom's Need for the Trained Man: Remarks to Sixth Thomas Alva Edison Foundation Institute, November 24, 1955." In Conference Hearings Before the Joint Committee on Atomic Energy, Congress of the United States. Washington, DC: U.S. Government Printing Office, 1956, p. 40.

Streichler, Stuart A. "Justice Curtis Dissent in the Dred Scott Case: An Interpretative Study." *Hastings Constitutional Law Quarterly* 24, no. 2 (Winter 1997). https:// repository.uclawsf.edu/hastings_constitutional_law_quaterly/vol24/iss2/5.

Stuart, Alexander H. H. "Report of the Secretary of the Interior." (First Session of the Thirty-Second Congress. Washington, DC: Boyd Hamilton, 1852, p. 502. https://www.govinfo.gov/content/pkg/SERIALSET-00612_00_00/pdf/SERIAL-SET-00612_00_00.pdf.

Sweet, William V., Benjamin D. Hamlington, Robert E. Kopp, Christopher P. Weaver, Patrick L. Barnard, David Bekaert and William Brooks. "Global and Regional Sea Level Rise Scenarios for the United States: Updated Mean Projections and Extreme Water Level Probabilities Along U.S. Coastlines." National Oceanic and Atmospheric Administration. February 2022. https://oceanservice .noaa.gov/hazards/sealevelrise/sealevelrise-tech-report-sections.html.

T. T. (2011, May 27). *TEDxDU Temple Grandin -- Different kinds of minds.* You-Tube. https://www.youtube.com/watch?v=aF4sP-uC-yI.

Taalbi, Josef. "Origins and Pathways of Innovation in the Third Industrial Revolution." *Industrial and Corporate Change* 28, no. 5 (October 2019): 1125–48.

Tashman, Brian. "Texas Textbook Reviewer Sheds Light on Creationist Efforts to Undercut Science Education." *Right Wing Watch,* September 12, 2013. https://www.rightwingwatch.org/post/texas-textbook-reviewer-sheds-light-on-creationist-efforts-to-undercut-science-education/.

Task Force on Higher Education and the School. "The Need for Quality: A Report to the Southern Regional Education Board by its Task Force on Higher Education and the School." June 1981. https://files.eric.ed.gov/fulltext/ED205133.pdf.

Taylor, Kate. "Lori Loughlin and Mossimo Giannulli Get Prison in College Admissions Case." *The New York Times,* August 21, 2020. https://www.nytimes.com/2020/08/21/us/lori-loughlin-mossimo-giannulli-sentencing.html.

"Textile Industry meets Demand of Booming US Population." Textile World, October 1, 2005, https://www.textileworld.com/textile-world/textile-news/2005/10/textile-industry-meets-demand-of-booming-us-population/.

The 21st Century Partnership for STEM Education, Cambridge High School Report Summary, ebook. Wayne, PA: 21st Century Partnership for STEM Education, 2009. https://www.21pstem.org/_files/ugd/bf6da2_99b345b0a34e4f40bc287a0d03617c72.pdf.

The 21st Century Partnership for STEM Education. "The City as Classroom: A New Vision of Public Urban High Schools For the Twenty-first Century The Greater Philadelphia STEAM Initiative: Phase 1," June 2017. https://www.21pstem.org/publications.

The Annenberg Challenge. (n.d.). Annenberg Foundation. https://annenberg.org/initiatives/the-annenberg-challenge/.

The Annenberg Foundation. "Research Perspectives on School Reform: Lessons from the Annenberg Challenge" (2003). "The Annenberg Challenge: Lessons and Reflections on Public School Reform" (2002); "The Arts and School Reform: Lessons and Possibilities from the Annenberg Challenge Arts Projects" (2003).

"The Bay of Pigs." John F. Kennedy Presidential Library and Museum. https://www.jfklibrary.org/learn/about-jfk/jfk-in-history/the-bay-of-pigs.

The Best STEM High Schools in America. (n.d.). https://www.usnews.com/education/best-high-schools/national-rankings/stem.

The Committee on the Objectives of a General Education in a Free Society, General Education in a Free Society: Report of the Harvard Committee, ebook. Cambridge: Harvard University Press, 1950, p. viii. https://ia902606.us.archive.org/34/items/generaleducation032440mbp/generaleducation032440mbp.pdf.

"The Constitution of the United States." National Archives. https://www.archives.gov/founding-docs/constitution-transcript.

"The Cuban Missile Crisis, October 1962." *Office of the Historian.* U.S. Department of State. https://history.state.gov/milestones/1961-1968/cuban-missile-crisis.

The Largest Bomb Ever Dropped. Military.com. https://www.military.com/video/nuclear-bombs/nuclear-weapons/the-largest-bomb-ever-dropped

/13186593315001#:~:text=Sorry%20for%20the%20black%20part,powerful %20nuclearweapon%20ever%20detonated.

The Last Helicopter: Evacuating Saigon. (2016, March 25). Newsweek. https://www .newsweek.com/last-helicopter-evacuating-saigon-321254.

The Manufacturing Institute. "The Future Skill Needs in Manufacturing: A Deep Dive." October 2022. https://www.themanufacturinginstitute.org/wp-content/ uploads/2022/10/NAM_Rockwell-PTC-Study.pdf.

The National Native American Boarding School Healing Coalition. Minneapolis, MN: https://boardingschoolhealing.org/education/impact-of-historical-trauma/.

The Need for Quality: A Report to the Southern Regional Education Board by its Task Force on Higher Education and the School, 1981. https://files.eric.ed.gov/ fulltext/ED205133.pdf.

The Nuclear Testing Tally (2022, August). Arms Control Association. https://www .armscontrol.org/factsheets/nucleartesttally.

The Organisation for Economic Co-operation and Development (OECD). PISA 2018 Results: Combined Executive Summaries Volumes 1, II & III (2019) (n.d.) https:// www.oecd.org/pisa/publications/pisa-2018-results.htm.

The Project Gutenberg E-text of State of the Union Addresses, by Theodore Roosevelt. (1906). https://www.gutenberg.org/files/5032/5032-h/5032-h.htm.

The Racist "Great Replacement" Conspiracy Theory Explained. (2022, May 17). Southern Poverty Law Center. https://www.splcenter.org/hatewatch/2022/05/17/ racist-great-replacement-conspiracy-theory-explained.

The Specialized High Schools Student Handbook 2011-2012 (2011). New York City Department of Education Office of Assessment and the Division of Portfolio Planning. https://testprepshsat.com/wp-content/uploads/2014/05/SHSAT_2011_HandbookFinal.pdf.

Thomas Edison Center at Menlo Park. (n.d.). https://www.menloparkmuseum.org/ history.

Thornton, Russell. "Population History of Native North Americans." In *Population History of North America,* edited by Michael R. Haines and Richard H. Steckel. New York: Cambridge University Press, 2000.

TIMSS 2007. International Mathematics Report: Findings from IEA's Trends in International Mathematics and Science Study at the Fourth and Eighth Grades, ebook (2007), p. 35. https://timss.bc.edu/TIMSS2007/PDF/T07_M_IR_Chapter1 .pdf.

"TIMSSVIDEO." TIMSSVIDEO, n.d. http://www.timssvideo.com/.

"Tornado Archive: A History of Twisters: Tornadoes in Iowa since 1950 as of 2023." Des Moines Register. Accessed May 8, 2023. https://datacentral.desmoinesregister .com/tornado-archive.

Transforming America's Scientific and Technological Infrastructure, Recommendations for Urgent Action, (January 2006). Project Kaleidoscope https://www.pkallsc .org/resources/report-on-reports-ii/.

Treaty of Tordesillas. (n.d.). UNESCO. https://en.unesco.org/memoryoftheworld/ registry/613.

Truesdell, Leon E. *"Farm Population: 1880 to 1950."* U.S. Census Technical Paper #3 (1960).

Trytten, Merriam Hartwick. *Student Deferment in Selective Service: A Vital Factor in National Security.* Minneapolis, MN: University of Minnesota Press, 1952. https://archive.org/details/studentdeferment0000tryt/page/54/mode/1up?view=theater.

U.S. Agency for International Development. "United States Commits to Over $100 million in Bilateral Assistance for Egypt." September 27, 2017. https://eg.usembassy.gov/united-states-commits-100-million-bilateral-assistance-egypt/.

U.S. Agency for International Development/Save the Children. "Enhancing and Advancing Basic Learning and Education in Bosnia and Herzegovina, ENABLE BIH." November 15, 2018. https://pdf.usaid.gov/pdf_docs/PA00X2BX.pdf.

U.S. Attorney's Office, District of Massachusetts. "Arrests Made in Nationwide College Admissions Scam: Alleged Exam Cheating & Athletic Recruitment Scheme." March 12, 2019. https://www.justice.gov/usao-ma/pr/arrests-made-nationwide-college-admissions-scam-alleged-exam-cheating-athletic.

U.S. Bureau of Labor Statistics. "Employment Projections, Table 1.7." https://www.bls.gov/emp/.

U.S. Census Bureau. "Table VII: Population of Each State and Territory." https://www2.census.gov/library/publications/decennial/1870/population/1870a-34.pdf.

U.S. Census Bureau. "2017 National Population Projections Tables: Alternative Scenarios." Accessed May 13, 2023. https://www.census.gov/data/tables/2017/demo/popproj/2017-alternative-summary-tables.html.

U.S. Census Bureau. "Quick Facts: Fairfax County, Virginia." https://www.census.gov/quickfacts/fairfaxcountyvirginia.

U.S. Census Bureau. "Real Median Family Income in the United States." Updated September 13, 2022. https://fred.stlouisfed.org/series/MEFAINUSA672N, October 13, 2020.

U.S. Census Bureau. "Series A 210-263: Land Area of the United States, by States and Territories: 1790 to 1970." *Historical Statistics of the United States: Colonial Times to 1970.* 2003, p. 38. https://www2.census.gov/prod2/statcomp/documents/CT1970p1-02.pdf.

U.S. Census Bureau. "Series A 6-8: Annual Population Estimates for the United States: 1790 to1970." *Historical Statistics of the United States: Colonial Times to 1970.* 2003, p. 8. https://www2.census.gov/prod2/statcomp/documents/CT1970p1-02.pdf.

U.S. Census Bureau. "Series C 120-137: Immigrants, by Major Occupation Group: 1820 to 1970." *Historical Statistics of the United States: Colonial Times to 1970.* 2003, p. 110. https://www2.census.gov/library/publications/1975/compendia/hist_stats_colonial-1970/hist_stats_colonial-1970p1-chC.pdf.

U.S. Census Bureau. "Series C 89-119: Immigrants, by Country: 1820 to 1970," Historical Statistics of the United States: Colonial Times to 1970. 2003, p. 105.

U.S. Census Bureau. "Series H 433-441: School Enrollment Rates Per 100 Population, by Sex and Race: 1850 to 1970," *Historical Statistics of the United States: Colonial Times to 1970. 203,* pp. 369–370. https://www2.census.gov/library/

publications/1975/compendia/hist_stats_colonial-1970/hist_stats_colonial-1970p1
-chH.pdf.

U.S. Census Bureau. "Series H 520-530: Public Elementary and Secondary Day
Schools— Attendance and Instructional Staff: 1870 to 1970." *Historical Statistics
of the United States: Colonial Times to 1970. 2003*, p. 375. https://www2.cen-
sus.gov/library/publications/1975/compendia/hist_stats_colonial-1970/hist_stats
_colonial-1970p1-chH.pdf.

U.S. Census Bureau. "Series H 545-571: "Public Secondary Day Schools—Percent of
Pupils Enrolled in Specified Subject: 1890 to 1965." *Historical Statistics of the United
States Colonial Times to 1970*. 2003. https://www2.census.gov/library/publications
/1975/compendia/hist_stats_colonial-1970/hist_stats_colonial-1970p1-chH.pdf.

U.S. Census Bureau. "Series H 598-601: High School Graduates, by Sex: 1870 to
1970," Historical Statistics of the United States: Colonial Times to 1970. 2003,
p. 379. https://www2.census.gov/library/publications/1975/compendia/hist_stats
_colonial-1970/hist_stats_colonial-1970p1-chH.pdf.

U.S. Census Bureau. "Series K 184-191: Farm Machinery and Equipment: 1910 to
1970." *Historical Statistics of the United States: Colonial Times to 1970*. 2003,
p. 469. https://www2.census.gov/library/publications/1975/compendia/hist_stats
_colonial-1970/hist_stats_colonial-1970p1-chK.pdf.

U.S. Census Bureau. "Series K 445-485: Manhours Per Unit and Yield Per Unit of
Production of Selected Crops and Livestock to Produce Specific -1970." *Historical Statistics of the United States: Colonial Times to 1970. 2003*, p. 500. https://
www2.census.gov/library/publications/1975/compendia/hist_stats_colonial-1970/
hist_stats_colonial-1970p1-chK.pdf.

U.S. Census Bureau. "Series K 550-563: Hay, Cotton, Cottonseed, Shorn Wool, and
Tobacco—Acreage, Production, and Price: 1790 to 1970." *Historical Statistics of
the United States: Colonial Times to 1970*. Census Bureau, 2003, p. 518. https://
www2.census.gov/library/publications/1975/compendia/hist_stats_colonial-1970/
hist_stats_colonial-1970p1-chK.pdf.

U.S. Census Bureau. "Series P 231-300: Physical Output of Selected Manufactured
Commodities: 1860 to 1970." *Historical Statistics of the United States: Colonial
Times to 1970*. 2003, p. 690. https://www2.census.gov/library/publications/1975/
compendia/hist_stats_colonial-1970/hist_stats_colonial-1970p2-chP.pdf.

U.S. Census Bureau. "Series Q 321-328: Railroad Mileage and Equipment: 1830 to
1890." *Historical Statistics of the United States: Colonial Times to 1970. 2003*,
p. 731. https://www2.census.gov/library/publications/1975/compendia/hist_stats
_colonial-1970/hist_stats_colonial-1970p2-chP.pdf.

U.S. Census Bureau. "Series Y 79-83: Electoral and Popular Vote Cast for President,
by Political Party 1789-1968." *Historical Statistics of the United States: Colonial
Times to 1970. 2003*, pp. 1073–1074. https://www2.census.gov/library/publica-
tions/1975/compendia/hist_stats_colonial-1970/hist_stats_colonial-1970p2-chY
.pdf.

U.S. Census Bureau. *A Century of Population Growth: From the First Census of the
United States to the Twelfth, 1790–1900*. Baltimore, MD: Genealogical Publishing
Company, 1969.

U.S. Census Bureau. *Bicentennial Edition: Historical Statistics of the United States, Colonial Times to 1970.* Washington, DC: Bureau of the Census, 1975.

U.S. Census. "Statistics of the United States Slave Population of the United States. 1850, p. 82. Accessed November 21, 2023. https://www2.census.gov/library/publications/decennial/1850/1850c/1850c-04.pdf.

U.S. Congress. House. "National Defense Education Act of 1958." https://history.house.gov/HouseRecord/Detail/15032436195.

U.S. Congress. Senate. "Final Report of the Select Committee to Study Governmental Operations with Respect to Intelligence Activities." 1976. https://archive.org/details/ChurchCommittee/Church%20Committee%20Book%20I%20-%20Foreign%20and%20Military%20Intelligence/.

U.S. Constitution, art. 1, sec. 2.

U.S. Constitution, art. 1, sec. 3.

U.S. Constitution, art. 1, sec. 4.

U.S. Department of Defense, Office of the Undersecretary for Policy. "Department of Defense Climate Risk Analysis: Report Submitted to National Security Council." 2021. https://media.defense.gov/2021/Oct/21/2002877353/-1/-1/0/DOD-CLIMATE-RISK-ANALYSIS-FINAL.PDF.

U.S. Department of Education Highly Qualified Teacher (HQT) requirements by state, ebook. Washington, DC: U.S Department of Education, 2006. https://sites.ed.gov/idea/files/HQT_10-5-06.pdf.

U.S. Department of Education Math and Science Education Expert Panel. "Exemplary and Promising Mathematics Programs." 1999. https://eric.ed.gov/?q=Exemplary+and+Promising+Mathematics+Programs&id=ED434033.

Richard Riley. "An Open Letter to United States Secretary of Education." November 1999. http://www.mathematicallycorrect.com/riley.htm.

U.S. Department of Education, Institute of Education Science. "What Works Clearinghouse." Accessed November 21, 2023. https://ies.ed.gov/ncee/wwc/.

U.S. Department of Education. "A History of the Individuals with Disabilities Education Act." Accessed May 11, 2023. https://sites.ed.gov/idea/IDEA-History.

U.S. Department of Education. "Every Student Succeeds Act, Assessments under Title I, Part A & Title I, Part B: Summary of Final Regulations." https://www2.ed.gov/policy/elsec/leg/essa/essaassessmentfactsheet1207.pdf.

U.S. Department of Labor. "Skills and Tasks for Jobs: A SCANS Report for America 2000." 1991. https://eric.ed.gov/?id=ED350414.

U.S. Department of State. "The Great Seal of the United States." https://usa.usembassy.de/etexts/gov/great_seal.pdf.

U.S. Energy Information Administration. "Oil and Petroleum Products Explained." Modified November 2, 2022. https://www.eia.gov/energyexplained/oil-and-petroleum-products/imports-and-exports.php.

U.S. News Best Colleges. U.S. News and World Report, 2022. https://www.usnews.com/best-colleges.

U.S. Parents' College Funding Worries Are Top Money Concern. October 9, 2023. Gallup.com. https://news.gallup.com/poll/182537/parents-college-funding-worries-top-money-concern.aspx.

U.S. Patent and Trademark Office. "U.S. Patent Activity Calendar Years 1790 to the Present." https://www.uspto.gov/web/offices/ac/ido/oeip/taf/h_counts.htm.

Ubelaker, Douglas H. "Patterns of Demographic Change in the Americas." *Human Biology* 64, no. 3 (June 1992): 361–79.

Uenuma, Francine. "20 Years Later, the Y2K Bug Seems Like a Joke—Because Those Behind the Scenes Took It Seriously." *Time Magazine,* December 30, 2019.

United Kingdom. Office for National Statistics. "UK Population Estimates 1851 to 2014." July 6, 2015. https://www.ons.gov.uk/peoplepopulationandcommunity/populationandmigration/populationestimates/adhocs/004356ukpopulationestimates1851to2014.

United Nations Development Programme and the Institute of National Planning, Egypt. "Human Development Report: Youth in Egypt." January 1, 2010, 151. https://planipolis.iiep.unesco.org/sites/default/files/ressources/egypt_hdr_2010_en.pdf.

United Nations. "UN Report: Nature's Dangerous Decline 'Unprecedented'; Species Extinction Rates 'Accelerating'." 2019. https://www.un.org/sustainabledevelopment/blog/2019/05/nature-decline-unprecedented-report/.

United States Commission on National Aid to Vocational Education. Report of the Commission on National Aid to Vocational Education Together with the Hearings Held On the Subject, Made Pursuant to the Provisions of Public Resolution No. 16, Sixty-third Congress." Washington: Government Printing Office, 1914.

United States Department of Homeland Security. "Yearbook of Immigration Statistics 2022, Table 1." https://www.dhs.gov/immigration-statistics/yearbook/2022.

United States Department of Transportation, Bureau of Transportation Statistics. "Table 1-23: World Motor Vehicle Production, Selected Countries." https://www.bts.gov/archive/publications/national_transportation_statistics/table_01_23.

United States Environmental Protection Agency. "Summary of the Atomic Energy Act." Last modified March 21, 2022. https://www.epa.gov/laws-regulations/summary-atomic-energy-act.

United States Naturalization Act of 1795 (1 Stat. 414, enacted January 29, 1795), para. 4.

United States Office of the Attorney General. "Partnership Among Federal, State, Local, Tribal, and Territorial Law Enforcement to Address Threats Against School Administrators, Board Members, Teachers and Staff." October 4, 2021. https://www.justice.gov/ag/page/file/1438986/download?utm_medium=email&utm_source=govdelivery.

United States Senate Committee on Armed Services: "Hearings Before the United States Senate Committee on Armed Services: The Preparedness Investigating Subcommittee Inquiry into Satellite and Missile Programs November 25, 25, 27, December 13,14, and 17, 1957, January 10, 13, 15, 16, 17, 20, 21 and 23, 1958." https://babel.hathitrust.org/cgi/pt?id=uc1.b5107082&view=page&format=plaintext&seq=46&q1=TellerNovember%2025.

United States Senate Committee on Commerce, Science and Transportation. "Statement of Frances Haugen." October 4, 2021. https://www.commerce.senate.gov/services/files/FC8A558E-824E-4914-BEDB-3A7B1190BD49.

Ure, Andrew. *A New System of Geology in which The Great of the Earth and Animated Nature are Reconciled at Once with Modern Science and Sacred History.* London: Longman, Rees, et al., 1829.

Ussher, James. "The Annals of the World: The Origin of Time, and Continued to the Beginning of the Emperor Vespasian's Reign and the Total Destruction and Abolition of the Temple and Commonwealth of the Jews." London: Printed by E. Tyler, for F. Crook, and G. Bedell, 1658.

Van der Spiegel, Jan. ENIAC-on-a-Chip. University of Pennsylvania. Last updated December 27, 2012. https://www.seas.upenn.edu/~jan/pictures/eniacpictures/ EniacChipPackaged.jpg.

Velez, Erin Dunlop, Terry Lew, Erin Thomsen, Katie Johnson, Jennifer Wine and Jennifer Cooney. "Baccalaureate and Beyond (B&B:16/17): A First Look at the Employment and Educational Experiences of College Graduates, 1 Year Later." (NCES 2019- 106)." National Center for Education Statistics. https://nces.ed.gov/ pubs2019/2019241.pdf.

Verrastro, F. A. And G. Caruso. The Arab Oil Embargo—40 Years Later, May 10, 2016. https://www.csis.org/analysis/arab-oil-embargo%E2%80%9440-years-later.

Vi, P. A. *Inter Caetera - Papal Encyclicals. Papal Encyclicals,* April 28, 2017. https://www.papalencyclicals.net/category/alex06.

Vinovskis, Maris A. "The Road to Charlottesville: The 1989 Education Summit, National Education Goals Panel." September 1999. https://govinfo.library.unt.edu /negp/reports/negp30.pdf.

Wages, Michele. *The Achievement Gap: A Poverty Crisis, Not an Education Crisis.* Rowman and Littlefield, 2018.

Walker, Nick. "The Disaster that Reshaped a City." *Canadian Geographic,* December 6, 2017.

Warner, Sam Bass. *The Private City: Philadelphia in Three Periods of its Growth.* Philadelphia: University of Pennsylvania Press, 1968.

Watch Operation Varsity Blues: The College Admissions Scandal | Netflix Official Site. (n.d.). https://www.netflix.com/title/81130691.

Watson, Bruce and Richard Konicek. "Teaching for Conceptual Change: Confronting Children's Experience." *Phi Delta Kappan* 71, no. 9 (May 1990): 680–85.

Watson, Robert J. *History of the Office of the Secretary of Defense Volume IV: Into the Missile Age, 1956-1960.* Washington, DC: Government Printing Office, 1997.

Wead, Charles K. "Aims and Methods of the Teaching of Physics." *Circulars of Information,* no. 7 (1884): 672.

WebbAlign About Dok Explained. (n.d.). https://www.webbalign.org/about/dok -explained

Wei, Cindy. "Connections." *NCSSSMST Journal* 12, no. 2 (Spring 2007): 12–13.

Weil, Martin. "Eric Hoffer, Author and Philosopher, Dies." *Washington Post,* May 22, 1983. https://www.washingtonpost.com/archive/local/1983/05/22/eric-hoffer -author-and-philosopher-dies/c9e26596-8791-478c-b8e1-558458fbe941/.

Weinberg, Meyer. *A Chance to Learn: A History of Race and Education in the United States.* Cambridge: Cambridge University Press, 1977.

Wellerstein, Alex. "Counting the Dead at Hiroshima and Nagasaki." *Bulletin of Atomic Scientists* (August 4, 2020). https://thebulletin.org/2020/08/counting-the -dead-at-hiroshima-and-nagasaki/.

White, William. *Economic History of Tractors in the United States – EH.net.* (n.d.). https://eh.net/encyclopedia/economic-history-of-tractors-in-the-united-states/.

WHO WE ARE | fourgirls. (n.d.). Fourgirls. https://www.fourgirlsforfamilies.org.

Why Cultivate STEM Learning Ecosystems? STEM Ecosystems. https://stemecosys-tems.org/what-are-stem-ecosystems/.

Why STEM Needs Girls. (2016, March 10). Council on Foreign Relations. https://www.cfr.org/blog/why-stem-needs-girls.

Wickersham, James Pyle. *A History of Education in Pennsylvania.* Lancaster: Inquirer Publishing, 1886.

Wickersham, James Pyle. "The Fight for Free Schools in Pennsylvania." *Historic Pennsylvania Leaflet* no. 6 (1891). Pennsylvania Historical and Museum Commis-sion. https://archive.org/details/FightForFreeSchoolsInPennsylvania/mode/2up.

Wiencek, Henry. *An Imperfect God: George Washington, His Slaves, and the Cre-ation of America.* New York: Farrar, Straus, and Giroux, 2003.

Wiggins, Grant and Jay McTighe. *Understanding by Design.* Alexandria, VA: ASCD, 2001.

William Penn Charter School. "About Us." Accessed November 21, 2023. https://www.penncharter.com/about-us/quaker-education.

Williamson, Jeffrey and Peter H. Lindert. "Long-Term Trends in American Wealth Inequality." In *Modeling the Distribution and Intergenerational Transmission of Wealth*, edited by James D. Smith. Chicago: University of Chicago Press, 1980.

Wilson, Woodrow. *The New Freedom.* New York and Garden City: Doubleday, Page and Co. 1913. https://archive.org/details/newfreedomacall01halegoog/.

Winthrop, John. "A Modell of Christian Charity (1630)." In *A History of the U.S. Political System: Ideas, Interests and Institutions,* edited by Richard A. Harris and Daniel Tichenor, p. 135. Santa Barbara, CA: ABC-CLIO, 2009.

Wolff, Edward N. and Maury Gittleman. "Inheritances and the Distribution of Wealth or Whatever Happened to the Great Inheritance Boom?" *The Journal of Economic Inequality* 12 (2014): 439–68.

Wong. Alia. "The Schools That Tried—But Failed—to Make Native Americans Obsolete." *The Atlantic*, March 5, 2019. https://www.theatlantic.com/education /archive/2019/03/failed-assimilation-native-american-boarding-schools/584017/.

World Bank. "GDP (current US$): Germany, Japan, United States." https://data .worldbank.org/indicator/NY.GDP.MKTP.CD?locations=DE-JP-US.

World Bank. "Youth Unemployment Rate for Bosnia and Herzegovina." SLUEM1524ZSBIH. Retrieved from FRED, Federal Reserve Bank of St. Louis October 9, 2023. https://fred.stlouisfed.org/series/SLUEM1524ZSBIH.

World Bank. "Report No. 42863-EG: Arab Republic of Egypt: Improving Quality, Equality, and Efficiency in the Education Sector: Fostering a Competent Gen-eration of Youth." June 29, 2007. https://documents1.worldbank.org/curated/en /796151468021861883/pdf/428630ESW0P08910gray0cover01PUBLIC1.pdf.

World Economic Forum. "The Global Competitiveness Report 2009-2010." https://www3.weforum.org/docs/WEF_GlobalCompetitivenessReport_2009-10.pdf.

World Economic Forum. "The Human Capital Report 2013." Accessed February 14, 2023. https://www3.weforum.org/docs/WEF_HumanCapitalReport_2013.pdf.

World Intellectual Property Organization. "Historical Data Sets prior to 1980." https://www.wipo.int/ipstats/en/#resources.

World Meteorological Organization. "State of the Climate in Latin America and the Caribbean 2020." WMO-No. 1272, 2021. https://library.wmo.int/doc_num.php?explnum_id=10876.

Wright Brothers National Memorial (U.S. National Park Service) n. d. https://www.nps.gov/wrbr/index.htm.

Wright, Carroll D. "The Work of the National Society for the Promotion of Industrial Education." *Annals of American Academy of Political and Social Science* 33, no. 1 (1909): 12.

Xvi, Pope Gregory, Mirari Vos: On Liberalism and Religious Indifferentism, August 15, 1832. Kansas City: Angelus Press, 1998.

Young, Filson. *Christopher Columbus and the New World of His Discovery*, vol. 2. Philadelphia, PA: Lippincott, 1906.

Zahai, Avihu. "Theocracy in Massachusetts: The Puritan Universe of Sacred Imagination." *Studies in the Literary Imagination* 27, no. 1 (March 1, 1994). https://openscholar.huji.ac.il/sites/default/files/avihuzakai/files/theocracy_in_massachusetts.pdf.

Zawail, Ahmed. "The Nobel Prize in Chemistry 1999." Interview by Sture Forsen and David Dishart. December 1999. *Nobel Prize Outreach* AB 2023. Sun. 12 Nov 2023. https://www.nobelprize.org/prizes/chemistry/1999/zewail/interview/.

Zinn, Howard. *The People's History of the United States*. New York: Harper Collins, 2010.

Index

About the Authors

F. Joseph Merlino is president of *The 21st Century Partnership for STEM Education* (21PSTEM), a nonprofit research and action organization founded in 2007. Over the past thirty years, Merlino has directed numerous federally funded education, math, and science reform projects involving thousands of teachers, hundreds of schools, and dozens of colleges and universities throughout the United States. Internationally, he has co-directed large-scale reform projects for the Egyptian Ministries of Education and Higher Education and helped lead reform efforts in Bosnia and Herzegovina and in Turkey for UNESCO's International Bureau of Education.

Dr. Deborah Pomeroy is an associate professor emerita of science education at Arcadia University. She started her career in research at the Lawrence Livermore National Laboratory and the University of Alaska's Institute of Arctic Biology. Shifting her career into science education, she taught high school science for nineteen years in Fairbanks, AK, during which time she received the Presidential Award for Excellence in Science Teaching. Following her high school teaching career, she earned her doctorate at the Harvard Graduate School for Education. She then taught science education at Arcadia University for fourteen years where she was also involved in multiple education reform projects K-16. Later, in Egypt, she helped to lead a massive project to develop a new integrated STEM high school curriculum for the Ministry of Education funded by the U.S. Agency for International Development.